BIBLICAL FOUNDATIONS FOR SMALL GROUP MINISTRY

An Integrative Approach

Gareth Weldon Icenogle

INTERVARSITY PRESS
DOWNERS GROVE, ILLINOIS 60515

InterVarsity Press® is the book-publishing division of InterVarsity Christian Fellowship®, a student movement active on campus at hundreds of universities, colleges and schools of nursing in the United States of America, and a member movement of the International Fellowship of Evangelical Students. For information about local and regional activities, write Public Relations Dept., InterVarsity Christian Fellowship, 6400 Schroeder Rd., P.O. Box 7895, Madison, WI 53707-7895.

All Scripture quotations, unless otherwise indicated, are taken from the HOLY BIBLE, NEW INTERNATIONAL VERSION®. NIV®. Copyright © 1973, 1978, 1984 by International Bible Society. Used by permission of Zondervan Publishing House. All rights reserved.

Permission requested from SCM, London, for use of material in James Dunn, Jesus and the Spirit.

In the Name of Jesus by Henri M. Nouwen. Copyright © 1989 by Henri M. Nouwen; reprinted by permission of The Crossroad Publishing Company.

Permission requested from HarperCollins, San Francisco, for use of material in Paul Hanson, The People Called.

ISBN 0-8308-1771-9

Printed in the United States of America ∞

Library of Congress Cataloging-in-Publication Data

Icenogle, Gareth Weldon, 1949-
   Biblical foundations for small group ministry/Gareth Weldon
Icenogle.
     p.   cm.
   Includes bibliographical references (p.   ).
   ISBN 0-8308-1771-9
   1. Church group work. 2. Small groups in the Bible. I. Title.
  BV652.2.I34   1993
253'.7—dc20   93-32390
                                                  CIP

17   16   15   14   13   12   11   10   9   8   7   6   5   4
07   06   05   04   03   02   01   00   99

I dedicate this book to the small group
who help form my practice of ministry:
My wife, Vida, who has been my faith partner in many small groups
through twenty-one years of marriage.
My kids, Tamara and Tonya, who continually challenge
my group behavior, but love me no matter what.

Introduction

Part One
Old Testament Foundations for Small Group Ministry

Part Two
Jesus' Small Groups: Gospel Foundations for Small Group Ministry

Part Three
The Church as Multiple Groups: Apostolic Foundations
for Small Group Ministry

Conclusion

Introduction

WHY DO WE NEED
BIBLICAL FOUNDATIONS FOR
SMALL GROUP MINISTRY?

I've just come from a small group gathering where real life was being shared, lived, prayed and planned, and where both emotions and intellect were challenged. It is a typical Christian small group. The reason we gather is to experience life together, expecting Jesus Christ to be present and participate. We gathered in the home of a group member. We met for two hours. One couple was traveling on vacation and not able to be present. We prayed for their safety and rest. One spouse was not there. She was studying for exams. We prayed for her health, endurance and clarity of mind. One man just found out he may lose his job of twenty years. We prayed for him to experience God's purpose and vocation. Another couple revealed that they were having some of the best years of their lives. We thanked God for the grace of their lives together. A woman described her frustration because her new business was so slow in getting started. We prayed for her to have patience and perseverance. As we told our stories, shared our pain, assessed our common humanity, dreamed, hoped, held hands, and gave each other hugs of greeting and goodby, we thanked God for the freedom and opportunity to gather as friends in face-to-face relationships, to speak the truth, to demonstrate love and to share faith in Christ. Nothing spectacular happened. But heaven was clearer. God was closer. And Jesus was more real. Thank you, Lord, for a small group of real people who love me.

We live during a unique period in history when large bureaucratic institutions are downsizing and integrating intentional face-to-face circles of empowerment and ownership. Top-down control systems are giving way to participative and decentralized democratic networks often called *quality circles*. We have come through a significant period of history—the industrial revolution—where hierarchy and power pyramids seemed necessary to gain productivity through established chains of command. The major themes of business and the institutional church have been "management" and "control." We are now emerging out of this darker and more controlled world where our organizations, including the church, were functionally structured so that each member knew his or her place and did a specific job.

We are beginning to catch a glimpse of an emerging new world, "a new paradigm," where power is shared and work is accomplished through partnerships and networks of colleagues and coworkers. The key words of this new world are "leadership" and "empowerment." People are becoming just as, if not more, important as productivity. We have discovered that persons honored as feeling and thinking members of a group are more productive and creative. Small group, hands-on, human connections and communications are the order of business, education, government and the church. We are moving quickly into an age of small group empowerment. We have moved from the pyramid to the circle, from power down to power around, from bureaucracy to organic structures that enable a group to serve one another as well as the world.

While many say this interest in and need for small group process is part of a "paradigm shift" of human culture, Christians can look deep into our faith roots and discover small groups are not new. Small groups are reflective of the very nature of God and humanity. They are both a demand of creation and a need of human culture. In this shifting period we are returning to our human and faith origins in search of community.

We appear to be at a catalytic junction in human history when the small group demand of the culture and the creation mandate for humanity to flourish in small groups seem to be converging in all arenas of life. We may be entering a "golden age" of small group life and action. This book is about how God launches, sustains and completes humanity through the mutual ministry of small group community.

In this book "community" should be understood as the movement between persons to experience "common" life. Bonhoeffer called this "life together." God said, "The two shall be one flesh." Community is about the interpersonal connections between two or more beings. God exists in community. Community implies that persons with differences come together for a common life. God also exists as different persons with a common, intimate and interconnected life. God created human beings to be unique, separate and different, but also to have a common life. Community is the process of individual persons coming together into unity (*com* + *unity*). God is separate and very different from humanity, but Scripture teaches us God's great creation desire is to be in community with humanity. The search for community is a very important reason for the existence of the Bible. Community is the reason for creation. Community is the purpose for Jesus Christ, the Son of God, being born, living among us, dying and being raised from the dead.

Community, then, is the common life between God and humanity, and small groups are the most visible and frequent form of this community.

The Basis of This Book

This is not a "how-to" book. This is a "why" book. For several years the subject of small groups has become more popular in psychological and behavioral writing. The church of the 1990s is pursuing many kinds, styles and formats for small groups ministry: Bible study, recovery, mission, evangelism, support, house church, ministry team, sharing, prayer and so forth. Some churches worldwide have gathered huge numbers of members by making the small group the core focus of their ministry strategy (like the meta-church model).

While the Christian world is increasingly bullish on small groups, the Christian small group movement has experienced very little theological depth. Small groups still tend to be a program or technique of ministry rather than a call to return to the roots of the very nature of what God created humanity to be. Most of the current small group activity in the church is not organic but technical and curricular. Churches do groups because they work. Deeper theological explora- tion is long past due in a church charging off into small group platoons without a declaration of war or a battle plan.

This is not a completely bad situation. God's initiative in ministry always seems to precede theological reflection about the nature of the ministry. The modern small group initiative in the church was launched over fifty years ago. Only now, in the 1990s, are we beginning the reflection and fine-tuning of what the Spirit has been doing in the church through small groups. The theological tuning and rooting of small group ministry is the purpose of this book.

While many books have been written on the psychology and practice of small groups and on the programmatic life of Christian small groups, few works have attempted to articulate the biblical and theological foundations for small group ministry and to integrate this material with parallel knowledge in spirituality, ecclesiology, psychology, sociology and anthropology. Bits and pieces of biblical and theological material may be found as introductory material in several small group books. Also, many books have been written on the general themes of Christian community and the nature of human community, but few books focus Christian community into the small group framework.

This book is more than an attempt to add small group concerns to the general theme of Christian community. It is an exploration of Christian community in the very nature and character of God. The general thesis is that God has set in motion from the beginning certain divine and human realities that are uniquely "imaged" and "reflected" where two or more persons come together in the presence of God.

In geometry, the triangle is the radical anticipation of the circle. The circle could be seen as the complete geometric image reflective of God's intention for human community. Three (the triangle) form a community from the beginning: God, man and woman. The original small group in the Garden of Eden may be a reflection of the divine small group Christians have historically called the Trinity. The Trinity of God beckons to the trinity of humanity, and Jesus Christ is the pivotal person in both triangular (circular) paradigms of community. The triangle, as the microcosm and smallest group of divine and human community, expands into a circle as more and more persons are added to the community. It could be said that heaven may be the great perfect circle of the people of God gathered in the presence of the transcendent circle of Father, Son and Spirit.

Admittedly, little biblical material specifically addresses the modern behavioral concept and practice of small groups. However, the Bible is full of comment, observation, reflection and admonition about the need for good human relationships where God is an integral presence. Scripture was written out of, to and for human community. Humanity naturally gravitates to grouping, and Scripture naturally points to the need for healthy human groups, large and small. The small group is the rudimentary and simple version of the more complex human community called forth by God.

This book, as it deals with selected biblical texts, is written, first of all, to be an *inductive* exercise into the nature of human community. The intent of the inductive process is to allow the subject or text observed to speak for itself, to create its own agenda for the observer, reader and listener. In exploring the topic of small groups we discover that they have a behavioral life of their own. The scientific study of small groups is also an inductive discipline. In this work these two inductive disciplines, biblical study and small group behavioral study, are brought together. They are then correlated with work in other disciplines. The product is an attempt at the integration of multiple disciplines based upon foundational biblical material.

The biblical material sets the agenda for the exploration into small group life. While many relevant scriptural texts could be examined in this study, the ones selected carry a somewhat more obvious relationship to the general theme of small group community. If we affirm the underlying value that all Scripture is God-breathed and that God is the Creator of all community, then Scripture must have something to contribute to the connection between theology and small group gatherings of men and women.

Historically, the inductive exploration of biblical texts has been an important agenda for the Christian small group. Throughout church history, small groups of saints have met together to explore what the Bible has to say to them. The texts included here have been examined and discussed in various small group contexts among Christian leaders, pastors and laity, supplying a good portion of the material for theological reflection and ministry. The next step could have been to produce this book through a small group process, but the pragmatism of limited time prevented such a discipline.

An Integrative Approach

While the biblical texts form the inductive foundation upon which this study is done, there is continual dialogue with the insights of other disciplines: theological, philosophical, psychological, sociological and educational. As such, this book takes an integrative approach to the biblical and theological, with an ultimate eye on the real practice of ministry. As a theology of small group ministry, it is written for pastors, parachurch leaders, lay leaders, consultants, teachers and seminary professors to inspire and help God's people to practice intentional small group ministry.

The content of this book attempts to cover a wide spectrum of biblical and experiential themes related to small group ministry. But as in all ministry and theology books, God is the subject, not small groups. Small groups are the vehicle for humanity to carry out God's will in everyday life. No matter how much "rugged individualism" one might have, the individualist will eventually find herself or himself in a small group working through the issues and opportunities of life.

This book is laid out according to three major biblical sections—before, during, and after Jesus' life on earth. Jesus is the pivotal person for the church and for human redemption. Jesus lived and worked in the community of a mobile small group, interrelating with many other various sized groups. The chapters focus on the biblical material as it tends to relate to major small group concerns: origins, covenants, leadership, communication, structures, ministry, models and so forth. The general themes of the book emerge like a classic creedal statement: God, creation, sin, covenant, Christ, Spirit, church, eternal life.

The general thesis of this book is that the small group is a generic form of human community that is transcultural, transgenerational and even transcendent. The call to human gathering in groups is a God-created (ontological) and God-directed (teleological) ministry, birthed out of the very nature and purpose of God's being. God as Being exists in community. Humanity as the imaged beings of God were created in community and are called to live and mature in community. The natural and simple demonstration of God's communal image for humanity is the gathering of a small group.

There are several popular definitions of a small group, but for this book a

*3
activities* →

simple definition is all that is needed: the small group is a face-to-face gathering of a few (three to twenty) persons to be, to share and to act for the betterment of one another and the wider good of others.

The biblical history of the people of God is as a *covenant* community. Covenant is the intentionality and responsibility of being together in relationship. We know from Scripture that the movement of covenant is out of the very nature of God. God refuses to let go of the ones who continue to run away from God and from one another. God calls us back into face-to-face relationship and into face-to-face gatherings. The very freedom for us to come together is based upon God's covenant with us. This real covenant community most often takes the form of a small group gathering. Humanity accomplishes much of its life in small group gatherings. The people of God have affected human history through small group gatherings and networks of many small groups together.

Jesus changed human history through the process of forming an intentional small group of twelve persons. The various small groups around Jesus—consisting of women, men, young, old, Jew and Gentile—give a clear signal as to how God desires humanity to move into our salvation future. The human future like the human past is worked out through various sized gatherings of groups, but mostly through small groups (large groups generally are gatherings of many small groups).

During New Testament times, the people of God continued to meet together in small home groups called *ecclesia* (gatherings or churches). These small groups define the nature and purpose of the larger church, that is, multiple gatherings of small groups of people around the person of Jesus Christ, in the presence of the Spirit, in humble openness and vulnerability to God as loving Father-Parent. The coming together of individuals from diverse racial, cultural, sexual and familial histories is the call of God to be the church, the ecclesia. The small group is the primary arena and vehicle for Christian ministry in a hostile world. The hunger for reconciliation of persons with God and with one another moves the Christian small group to become a space for welcoming, worship, confession, forgiveness, service and hope.

Small groups have a theological and historical role and purpose. All human endeavor works to fulfillment and completion through small group experience. The sociological, psychological and formational sciences thrive in the analysis and enablement of face-to-face relationships where two, three or more persons come together for a common purpose and life. The gathering for pursuit of common purpose and life together is affirmed in the New Testament. This gathering for common life is called *koinōnia*.

Biblical and theological foundations are of little value unless real people in real places come to know and love Jesus in his relationship with "Abba" God as the Way of Life, and that is "life together." These are biblical and theological foundations for small group ministry. While it is not the purpose of this book to look more expansively into the strategic ministry implications of these foundations, such is the implied hope and intent. It may be appropriate to anticipate a sequel to this work entitled *Systems and Structures for Small Group Ministry.* The possibility of such a future work now exists in the category of eschatological hope. For, in the Last Day, when all things are accomplished by God, if there are small group gatherings in heaven (and I'm convinced there are), my theological suspicion will be vindicated: that is, that the ministry of small groups is an *eternal* ministry. But first, in anticipation that small groups are, in fact, a significant part of God's great redemptive plan, let our theological reflection start with biblical beginnings.

Part One
OLD TESTAMENT FOUNDATIONS FOR SMALL GROUP MINISTRY

1
SMALL GROUP ORIGINS

Then God said, "Let us make humankind in our image, according to our likeness, and let them have dominion over the fish of the sea, and over the birds of the air, and over the cattle, and over all the wild animals of the earth, and over every creeping thing that creeps upon the earth." So God created humankind in his image, in the image of God he created them; male and female he created them. God blessed them, and God said to them, "Be fruitful and multiply, and fill the earth and subdue it." (Gen 1:26-28 NRSV)

Sylvia was a well-educated and successful lawyer who had agreed to be part of a small group experiment. She was looking for a place to build deeper relationships with other people. A competitive trial lawyer, she had come to realize that the marketplace was a desert for building close friendships, particularly among her often combative peers and colleagues. She had been studying New Age patterns of living and had met in a few salon groups for meditation and getting in balance with the cycles of nature. This new group was made up of several men and women who were Christians. At the first meeting the group discussed setting aside some time for verbal prayer.

Sylvia reacted immediately. "Definitely not! If I have to pray out loud in this group, there's no way I'm staying. Let's get this straight from the beginning. I don't pray. I don't even think there's a personal God out there anyway. I'm more comfortable with the idea of quiet meditation to get in touch with my own presence in the universe."

Another member of the group responded carefully, "Would you mind if we prayed? We would not expect you to pray out loud. You can meditate silently while we pray."

Sylvia relaxed and said, "OK, I guess I can handle that."

For several weeks the group met, shared life together and prayed. While Sylvia entered into the dialogue, personal sharing and study, she would not enter into the prayer. Then, about the sixth week, Sylvia interrupted the meeting with an unusual request. "Would you all mind if I prayed for this group? During the past several weeks, I've come to trust that you all are sincere and honest about your belief that there is a God out there who listens. I'd like to see if God will listen to me."

From that meeting on, Sylvia entered into the dialogue of prayer with the group. She soon affirmed her faith in Jesus Christ with the comment, "I didn't think prayer had a purpose. I didn't think there was a God who would listen. But this group showed me a new and personal way to get in touch with God. When I saw and heard this group pray, I could feel something special. I began to understand this was God speaking to me. I was beginning to feel the love of Christ. This small group community convinced me to have faith in a God who is alive and interested in me personally."

Sylvia discovered God in community. Sylvia also discovered God as community.

God's Call to Small Group Community

The Bible begins with the word *bet*. The first letter of the Hebrew Bible is the second letter of the Hebrew alphabet. When prefixed to the beginning of a word, bet is a simple preposition usually meaning "in" as in "In the Beginning." But bet not only means "in." It also represents the plural, the conjunctive, the number "two"—the human species starts as two. . . . One is nothing. Two is everything. One is not even a number. Two is the beginning of all numbers. . . . Plurals are basic to all that God creates. . . . Unitariness was the first thing God didn't like.[1]

T. S. Eliot said, "There is no life that is not in community. And no community not lived in praise of God."[2] Scripture begins and ends with God calling humanity into relationship with the divine community and with one another. A survey of salvation history reveals the struggle of God and humanity to be in intimate relationship with one another. This is a warfare for human persons who can be redeemed only as God intercedes in human relationships and activity. God beckons us into the presence of divine and human persons and relationships. This is a battle cry to call humanity away from relational tyranny and anarchy into interdependent stewardship for all real and living things, not only "on earth," but also "in heaven." This Old Testament section is a brief survey of God's struggle to create, re-create and participate in the shalom of human community.

Small groups are microcosms of God's creation community. Wherever two or more persons come together, they become an actual reflection of the image and likeness of God. Small groups are the basic arena for either imaging the redeeming presence of God or projecting destructive human systems. Every small or large gathering of humanity exists in this tension of manifesting an inhuman structure or embodying divinely redemptive relationships. The biblical record calls every small group to consider their source and purpose. This biblical recollection is a calling to remembrance of God's image for human community as it makes an impact on the being and service of small groups.

The Old Testament has no specific theology of small group community. However, there is much reflection on tribal community, marital community, familial community and friendship. Many of the key characters are described as they relate to one, two or more others. For example, the book of Ruth is about three women and a man, all related by family ties, who share in the faith history and ancestry of Jesus. Their interpersonal relationships are not those of a modern small group, but their face-to-face relationships are a classic small group case study, carrying all the ramifications of complex group dynamics. This group story deals with grief, friendship, love, loneliness, journeying, self-sacrifice, sorrow, security needs, values, bitterness, personal faith, unanswered questions, confrontation, money, food, work, grace, reconciliation, thankfulness, providence, risk, courage, redemption and hope. They live life together as a community. This small band of people search together in a harsh world for God's intervention and mercy.

So it was from the beginning; God created men and women to live together in small groups of faith. In these interpersonal groups human beings have discovered that God created us for one another. "It is not good that the man should be alone; I will make him a helper as his partner" (Gen 2:18 NRSV).

God as Small Group

It may be overly dramatic to say that God lives as a *small group*, but the church has historically described God as Trinity, three persons in one. In any case, the creation account presents both divinity and humanity as *communities* of being and action. God is described as existing in divine community, in dialogue with other members of the God-self, an *intra*communicating group who also created humanity to exist in group intracommunication. God created and addressed humanity as community with community, as group with group. The divine community has existed in *inter*community with human community from the beginning. Three areas of dialogue and community are established from the beginning: within (intra) God's group self, within (intra) the human group and between (inter) God's group and the human group.

The human community is created as male and female, a reflection of the image and likeness of God.[3] Male and female together is intrinsic to the address of and receptivity to God. In order to reflect this full community of God rightly, both men and women must be together in human community. Men together in isolation from women, or women together in isolation from men, are not community reflective of divine community. So creation mandates human community as men and women together. Together they are given charge over creation. Together they were created to be in partnership with their Creator who also exists as community.

From another perspective we could say that, from the beginning, God existed in community as *group being* in creative action. From a historically classic trinitarian view of God, the divine group existed as three persons in conversation and mission. The Genesis account does not initiate an immediate trinitarian understanding of God, but does affirm a *community* of God in action through creation. Since this community is reflected in "image" and "likeness" on the human side as male and female together, we can extrapolate that God exists in plural being of at least two persons. Classic theological history understands God to be revealed as three: Father, Son and Holy Spirit. Ray Anderson, in *On Being Human,* clarifies this historical temptation of theology to move too quickly from the plurality of God to a classic trinitarian model. Talking about Genesis 1:26-27, Anderson says:

> It is instructive that the plural pronoun is used with reference both to God and to "man" as created in the image and likeness of God. One must be careful about inferring from the plural pronoun here a trinitarian concept of God as "three persons," but there is at least an intentional correspondence in this text between the intrinsic plurality of human being as constituted male and female and the being of God in whose likeness and image this plurality exists. . . . Quite clearly the *imago* is not totally present in the form of individual humanity but more completely as co-humanity. It is thus quite natural and expected that God himself is also a "we."[4]

The small group is the ideal microcosm in which to explore the simplicity and delicacy of the full God-human community (which includes both male and female) in action. The human community exists foundationally as *small group,* that is, at least one man and one woman in relationship with God. Three persons were together in the Garden "in the cool of the day" (Gen 3:8). The foundational theological community is man, woman and God together. The complete primal human community is man, woman and God together in the midst of all living and earthly things on the "sixth day." The human community is given charge over the substance of the earth and over all living things created from days one to five (Gen 1:1-31). Leonard Sweet has affirmed the intimate connection be-

tween all of creation and the human community: we are "members of an eco-
logical community encompassing the whole of creation. . . . We human beings
require life around us. . . . We cannot do without the living world any more than
we can do without food or sleep. . . . With nothing around us, we die."[5]

The small group is the *base community*[6] in which men and women can meet God
and one another to be, to plan, and to act for the careful nurturing of relationships
with created things. This small group is not only a *being* group for the nurture of
persons but an *acting* group for the benefit of creation. Paul Hanson asserts that
this primeval group is the "homestead" for humanity with God on earth.[7]

Since human community has its origin and center in personal and relational
divinity, it is not determined or controlled by cycles of nature or the rhythms of
creation. Hanson points out that it is a pagan view of human community that
would make it subject to "naturalistic determinism . . . or the forces of nature."[8]
While the human group is interdependent with the things of creation, their
existence and purpose is not controlled by the earth. The human group is accountable to God and responsible for its life together within creation. Because
it is community in God, it is a community of the Spirit. As Karl Barth suggested,
it is community born out of the "Sixth Day" of creation and being beckoned into
the "sabbath community" of God in the "Seventh Day." "The Goal of Creation,
and at the same time the beginning of everything that follows, is the event of
God's Sabbath freedom, Sabbath rest and Sabbath joy, in which [humanity] too
has been summoned to participate."[9]

This is good news for persons or groups who are trapped in biological or
astrological prisons. In a postmodern world now affected more by eastern religions like pantheism or Hinduism, where New Age crystals are thought to have
an effect upon the life of a gathered group, it is very important to know that the
God of creation did not make the success of human community dependent upon
rocks or other natural elements. Entering into human community with God is
a "movement of release" from the determinism of such naturalistic pagan fates.
God is at the center of human community or there is no *human* community. It
may be a collection of animals or zombies, but without God it is not a community
of human beings being called into deeper fellowship with the *Theos* of the universe.[10] Human small groups do not look within themselves or around themselves to nature for their meaning and purpose. Human small groups find their
purpose only in God who leads them to serve one another and nurture creation
with a God-shared knowledge and balance.

The earth-"ruling" responsibility of humanity can be fulfilled only within the
mutuality and interdependence with God and among multiple human beings.[11]This rule or dominion is the stewardship of men and women together in

community. The ability to rule properly is set askew if human community is reduced to only male community or only female community. Karl Barth affirmed male and female community as "covenant partnership" with God and "co-human-ity" with one another. This covenant from Barth's perspective preceded the meaning and purpose of marriage.[12] Small groups must be places for men and women to learn to rule and lead together in the image and likeness of God.[13] Small group leadership and life, in being, relationship and action, like larger forms of human community, is the responsibility of both men and women *together*.

The stewardship of creation is the responsibility of human community.[14] Small groups are base camps for the stewardship of creation. Creation ministry rolls out of the health of human relationships. Unhealthy or "dysfunctional" human community unleashes its destructive forces on creation. The human small group can be an arena for nurturing healthy male and female relationships in the presence of God and having a positive ministry impact on the living and material things of creation. Small groups can be stewardship teams for God's fullness and fulfillment in creation.

 Community and creation are always in tension as interdependent poles of God's purpose. Relationship without mission (purpose or task)[15] is not a complete view of small group life and not a true reflection of the nature of God. God is in relationship to accomplish the completion of creation. Creation is in formation to enable the fulfillment of divine and human community. Leonard Sweet has affirmed this intimate connection and tension between "relational energy" and the "ecology of creation."[16] "Energy and matter" are interrelated. Relationship and work are both forms of community. "We are in symbiotic relationship with the earth." Small groups are called to be work teams (or supportive teams of workers) who build their community while accomplishing a purpose. Too often the church has been concerned with the "souls" of people and not their bodily presence in the midst of creation. Creation is being redeemed by the God who exists in community. God has always called small groups of men and women to care for the creation. "The LORD God took the man and put him in the Garden of Eden to till it and keep it" (Gen 2:15). Too often small groups have a reputation for being caring and supportive of one another but having no positive impact on the way people behave toward creation or the world beyond.

On the other hand, things and tasks can often interfere with the development of intimate community. We live in a very busy world where doing and things can rob us of presence and relationship. Small groups must also be places where the things and jobs of creation are servants to the redemption of community. To gain the whole world but lose one's soul is a continuing tragedy of human community. The human soul is nurtured through face-to-face communication. "We take on our identity only in relation to community."[17] The small group lives out the call of God to become part of the seventh day as they discover ways to rest and enjoy the presence of God and the presence of one another.

■ SMALL GROUP MINISTRY IMPLICATIONS

1. Groups should ensure that their two primary reasons for meeting are for building relationships and accomplishing mission or tasks. Their community together should have an impact on their mission or task. Early in the life of the group a great deal of time should be invested in members getting to know each other. Since there is not always preparation time to do this in advance, mission or task groups should take time out to invest in their relationships while in the midst of their task.

2. Groups too often allow the "things" around them to block the development of their life together. In our high-tech world, a group may allow a grandfather clock to interrupt an intimate moment, be distracted by a glowing television, be unable to hear through a loud stereo, be unnerved by the sudden ring of a telephone, or be disrupted by the need to let out the cat. Some of these interruptions may not be preventable, but many are. The good things of creation can rob us of the presence of one another as well as the presence of God. There is something to be said for the Quaker silence of presence when two or three gather together to listen for God and to hear one another.

3. There are good reasons to have only men or only women in a small group, particularly if group members are wrestling with the freedom to share themselves and the opposite sex is seen as a threat or a stumbling block. However, over the long haul, if men or women only meet with their same sex they will never come to the potential place of seeing or hearing the complete character of God. Small groups are places for us to come to know God in fullness and depth. One-sex groups carry an inherent limitation toward this ultimate discovery.

4. If groups can truly discover God in community, then one thing a small group might consider is reflecting back upon their life together and sharing how God has been discovered or more fully known through the experience of this group. This discussion could also be from the negative side: How has this group inhibited or blocked my relationship with God? But to share such a negative perspective would usually be too confrontational or would degenerate into a passing of judgment or condemnation. Such interaction around the negative needs strong leadership and careful monitoring. Positive sharing of life usually leads to group building. The positive sharing of the group's life together as a reflection of the nature of God could be a powerful formational process.

2

SMALL GROUP PARADOX

The LORD God said, "It is not good for the man to be alone. I will make a helper suitable for him."

Then the LORD God made a woman from the rib he had taken out of the man, and he brought her to the man. The man said, "This is now bone of my bones and flesh of my flesh; she shall be called 'woman' for she was taken out of man."

The man and his wife were both naked, and they felt no shame.

Then the eyes of both of them were opened and they realized they were naked; so they sewed fig leaves together and made coverings for themselves. . . . And they hid from the LORD God among the trees of the garden. (Gen 2:18, 22, 25; 3:7-8)

Today we say that human relationships that are not working are dysfunctional. When small groups get together, the relationships between people are impaired, incomplete, abnormal or broken. Every gathering of humanity comes together with the suspicion that our hopes will not be fully realized, and with the fear that something is deeply wrong with our human relationships. Kenwyn Smith and David Berg call this *group paradox*:

If we go directly to people's experience and ask them what it is like to belong to a particular group, individuals do talk about the exhilaration of work in groups, but their comments are usually focused on the problematic experiences: "It's very frustrating—I have so many things on my mind, but I never seem able to say them." "Sometimes we work well together; at other times it is impossible, because there is so much tension." "Everyone seems so ambivalent about everything—it's overwhelming." "It's so paradoxical—we all

like each other, but we never seem to connect."[1]
All human communities exist in a state of brokenness and ambivalence, caught between the seventh day shalom (peace) of God and the temptation to withdraw into the "darkness" and "chaos" of the first day. The people of God throughout history have called this human state *sin*. Sin is the failure and destruction of human community. Sin is the disability of human beings to connect with each other. Sin is the inability of humanity to enter into community with the God of community. Sin is the poverty of relationship we experience when we try to become intimate with another person. Sin is the brokenness of community between God and humanity. Small groups are trapped in the "paradox" of hunger for intimacy ("it's not good to be alone") and fear of intimacy ("they sewed fig leaves to cover themselves").

The Struggle for Intimacy
We know that "aloneness" is not a good state for humanity.[2] Aloneness is not God's desire for men and women.[3] Loneliness and hiddenness are the result of humanity's misguided desire for independence from and equality with God. Only God can bring humanity into partnership and community. Human attempts to become equal with God (or to become God), and to enter forcibly into intimacy with the Holy, shatter the delicate fiber of community.

But we sense that we are deeply alone. We are cut off. Yet we are hungry to be with others. Our spirits cry out to be known by another, to be loved by another, to be affirmed by another. Small groups are gatherings of individuals who want to be together but fear losing their separateness or independence in one another's presence. Every coming together of two or more becomes a state of paradox and ambivalence. The social psychologist Lillian Rubin calls this "the approach-avoidance dance." She elaborates on how this is reflective of the struggle for intimacy:

> [Intimacy] is an idea that excites our imagination, a word that seems larger than life to most of us. It lures us, beckoning us with a power we're unable to resist. And just because it is so seductive, it frightens us as well—seeming sometimes to be some mysterious force from outside ourselves that, if we let it, could sweep us away.[4]

From Genesis 3 we can see that the brokenness of human community is fragmented in two directions: the man and woman "hide" from one another, and they "hide" from God. Hans Walter Wolff describes the origins of dysfunctionality: "Shame in the form of embarrassment and inhibition only penetrates the duality of man and woman as the result of their mistrust towards God."[5] The tendency of human beings to hide out of shame for our "nakedness" is the destructive force against human community. We hide both our sexuality and spirituality in the presence of another being, whether God or human. While the desire for relationship is strong, the fear of intimacy is also strong. Not only are men and women afraid of God, they are afraid of one another. Human relationships float over the undercurrent of fear and shame of being in the presence of each other. John Bradshaw has also described this shame:

> Toxic shame . . . is an excruciatingly internal experience of unexpected exposure. It is a deep cut felt primarily from the inside. It divides us from ourselves and from others. In toxic shame we disown ourselves. And this disowning demands a cover-up. . . . It loves darkness and secretiveness.[6]

To remove ourselves from the feeling of this sense of inadequacy we often venture into our dark sides for solutions. Paul Hanson affirms that the violence, murder and war in Genesis 3—11 are demonstrations of the dark side of human relationships feeding on brokenness.[7]

While few contemporary small groups degenerate into the darkest behaviors of personal destruction, every group dances around the edges of avoidance, denial, deception, hiding and condemnation. In the gathering there are constant assessments of how much one should reveal. How much can be said before the delicate relationships are endangered? Who can be trusted to maintain the confidentiality of what is being revealed? Has too much already been released to maintain a sense of dignity and distance? When the temperature on the group's shame thermometer starts rising, every member of the small group begins to look for a place to hide. The group as a whole may practice denial, or particular individuals may look for the nearest "leaves and trees" behind which to hide. If someone in the group pushes in too close for a look, the shamed member may attack, shut down and, most often, eventually disappear from the group.

John and his wife, Diane, were new in the community and had just joined a new small group. They were hesitant participants in the group at first. They were careful about who could be trusted. Since both were from dysfunctional families, they were slow to let themselves be known by the group. After several meetings, however, their self-confidence about being in the group blossomed. Unfortunately, other members of the group weren't committing. John and Diane would sometimes be the only persons present with the group leader. The leader could tell the group wasn't coming together, but John and Diane were feeling more and more attached to the leader and to other members who occasionally showed up. Then John lost his job and went into a depression. He stopped coming consistently. Out of desperation, the leader announced that she was aborting the group. Diane was angry and John was furious. The group was the one thing that was going well in their lives and it was suddenly ripped away. The leader was shocked by their passionate reaction. All she could see was that the group had fallen apart. In some ways she felt that John and Diane had driven the other members away. The group ended in disaster. Everyone felt let down and hurt. John and Diane felt the shame and anger of rejection.

Small Group Family Systems

Like John and Diane's group, small groups are gathering places that dramatize human brokenness. The fear and shame of relationship with God and with others of the same sex and the opposite sex can be exposed in the small group where there is no place to hide. Every small group, as well as its individual members, carries its own system of fear and shame. As Keith Miller has so clearly articulated, sin is the original and ultimate reason for addiction and codependency.[8] Small groups, each to their own degree, are family systems of shame before God and humanity. While the small group is called out of its creation origins to reflect the plural image of God, the same group is caught simultaneously in addictive prisons and disabling relational patterns of broken persons, men and women, young and old. Groups can become codependent slaves to the addictive power of a dominating person. Couples' groups can be breeding grounds for sustaining male addictions and female codependency. Small group Bible studies can degenerate under the tyranny of an autocratic fact-teller or opinion-giver or become narcoleptic circles emeshed in the anarchy of mutual clichés and superficialities.

Understanding first of all that sin has dominion within every human group, the small group can then become a place for the healing and restoration of broken individuals, and broken relationships. Every small group is a reenactment of the "hiding behind" garden leaves and trees. Every group will experience the feelings of fear and shame that our nakedness will be seen by God and others. But as continuing paradox, in admitting that these dysfunctions are happening, the small group can establish a confessional base to rebuild into God's redemptive future.

The sick small group or family system can breed generations of sick people, sick relationships and other sick systems. As we discover in reading Genesis 4 and 9, both Adam's and Noah's families displayed immediate fruits of second-generation systems errors. Sick systems breed sick persons. In Genesis 4 the violent case of Cain is intensified through Lamech and the violent cities of Cain. Noah's family group rediscovered the shadows of nakedness and shame haunting them from the Garden, even after God supposedly wiped out all evil people from the face of the earth. Evil lives on in family groups and individuals, even in and among the special people of God. Dysfunctional small groups breed more dysfunctional groups. Dysfunctional group leaders breed more dysfunctional groups.

A broken community can lead to anger, bitterness and, potentially, violence. While one should not avoid the expression of anger in the nurture of human community, the inability of humanity to focus and discipline anger leads to relational and physical destructiveness. In Genesis 4:5-8 we see that God did not condemn Cain for feeling downcast and angry, but attempted to hold him accountable to "master it." It is interesting that this story affirms the ongoing dialogue and interaction with divine community. There is continuing conversation between God and Cain even after Cain kills Abel. God sustains the gracious movement of reconciling community with Cain after the human relationships are severed, even after murder is committed. Cain has to live with the guilt or deal with God personally and directly. Cain's refusal to reconcile with God leads to the destruction of Abel and the establishment of arrogant and violent people group systems. The small group can be that continuing place of confrontation to deal with past abuse or current dysfunction. Or it can be the greenhouse where generations of weedy groups sprout up uncultivated, chaotic and stifling.

The faithful small group must be a place for members to learn to deal with anger through disciplined and healthy dialogue with God and fellow group members. Faithful small groups can hold angry people accountable and provide a carefully defined environment in which they can work constructively to focus anger and initiate peace. Small groups can become spaces for persons to learn the art of reconciliation with God and with fellow human beings.

The Cain and Abel story underscores that the brokenness of human relationships is not just between men and women. If two brothers can be divided, any human grouping can be divided and destroyed. All human groups exist in a state of intergroup and intragroup brokenness. They nurture fear and anger before God and one another. The members of a small group will not only war among themselves but the group will also do battle with other groups. Whether groups are mixed, with men and women together, all men or all women, their life together can be caught up in the frustrations of sinful histories and ambivalent presence. Given longevity of their life together, their warring nature will eventually come to light.

Such intragroup divisiveness has been demonstrated from the beginning in the Garden. In the primeval group with God, Adam and Eve's awareness of and discomfort with their differentiation resulted in their practice of hiding. They were divided four ways. First, each of them ended up in an isolated world, cut off from the other and functioning in very different perspectives and roles. They lost their common world. Second, the community of God is cut off from the community of humanity. Third, the community of men is cut off from the community of women. Finally, the community of men is fragmented in itself (implying similar fragmentation for women). Each person became an isolated subculture to himself or herself. The plurality and oneness of the primeval family system in the Garden gave way to a plurality of isolated and individualistic subcultures of persons. Every small group suffers the divergence of this original brokenness.

Each human small group gathering now exists unto itself as a divergent culture of individual and personal subcultures coexisting in a state of hiddenness and brokenness. The city of Babel (Gen 11:3-9) may be a primeval case study of what happens to a group of people who try to work together, only to discover each individual is cut-off and hidden from every other individual, each developing his or her own subculture, each communicating isolating and fragmented language forms. With dysfunctionality and separation penetrating so deeply into the core of every person, each has a tendency to develop his or her own isolated culture and language. With such disintegration of common symbols and life there is little possibility for group cohesion. Then there is meager basis for common communication or common understanding. Persons are driven away from one another and "scattered over the face of the earth."

The brokenness of every group would continue except that God refuses to leave us alone to self-destruct. God enters into our midst and bids us come out from behind our leaves and trees. C. S. Lewis, in *The Great Divorce*, pictures hell as the great expansion of increasing space between angry people who keep moving farther and farther apart because they cannot stand to be near one another. He pictures Napoleon, for example, as being several hundred light years out. In contrast Lewis pictures heaven as the place where persons move toward the light and toward one another on their journey toward the "horizon."[9] Small groups cannot prosper as gatherings of little napoleonic anarchists trapped in the tyranny of their isolated subcultures of anger and avoidance. Small groups must be spaces of heaven where people move closer to God and one another.

Every small group, as a reflection of the Garden's primeval group, has three interrelated cultural arenas of relationship: the divine community, the human sexual (male and female) community, and the community of individual cultures (race, age, education, status and so forth). Dr. William Pannell of Fuller Theological Seminary has suggested that racism might be a product of sexism, and that ethnically isolated groups might begin more profound actions of reconciliation if the men and women in each ethnic group begin to treat one another with more complete human dignity.[10] Calvin Hernton hints at this in his book *Sex and Racism in America*: "Because of sexism in black progressive circles, and because of racism in white progressive circles (including feminist circles), the sexualization of racism is made all the more impossible to avoid."[11]

The small group circle, in its hiddenness and brokenness, is a complex system of individual and interconnected subcultures and languages where God (the divine community) is in the midst, calling us out from behind our self-determined arrogance to common life, common language, common work and common values.

The Paradox of Countercovenant

The whole earth had one language and the same words. . . . And they said to one another, "Come, let us make bricks, and burn them thoroughly." And they had brick for stone, and bitumen for mortar. Then they said, "Come, let us build ourselves a city, and a tower with its top in the heavens; otherwise, we shall be scattered abroad upon the face of the whole earth." The LORD came down to see the city and the tower, which mortals had built. And the LORD said, "Look, they are one people, and they have all one language; and this is only the beginning of what they will do; nothing that they propose to do will now be impossible for them. Come, let us go down, and confuse their language there, so that they will not understand one another's speech." So the LORD scattered them abroad from there over the face of the earth, and they left off building the city. (Gen 11:1-8 NRSV)

Now the LORD said to Abram, "Go from your country. . . . I will make of you a great nation . . . so that you will be a blessing." (Gen 12:1 NRSV)

The movement from Babel in Genesis 11 to Abram in Genesis 12 is a countercovenant movement. The people of Babel were a kind of covenant people. They were functioning out of their countercovenant humanity. This was the remnants of humanity left after intimacy was shattered in the Garden. People of broken human community build great systems, structures and cities. The first signs of the fruit of broken community came from the alienated Cain. Cain "built a city and named it Enoch after his son Enoch" (Gen 4:17). Ham, the errant son of the broken family of Noah, begat a line of great city and civilization builders, including Nimrod, who built Babel and all the cities of Shinar and Ninevah in Assyria. Other descendants built Egypt and the great Philistine cities (a rather awesome and industrious heritage for the cursed sons of Canaan). When exploring these early Genesis texts we must ask what the connection is between broken human community and the establishment of powerful city-nation states. Why was it that Cain and Ham, the low-faith, nonrelational, insensitive sons of the elect Adam and Noah would turn out to be such powerful and influential men? And why does Abram suddenly appear as the lone family of election out of the midst of the great cities of the Chaldeans?

Genesis 1—11 is about a theology of community in paradox and appears as a countermovement with the establishment of cities and civilizations. Broken humanity builds cities. Covenant humanity builds covenant family communities.

Human sin finds expression in the building of functionally interrelated things. Covenant finds expression in the nurture of relationships, families and groups. Covenant builds community. Broken humanity is cut off (like Cain) from the presence of God. The people of Babel had no covenant experience with God, so they expressed their blurred covenant image in the building of things that showed themselves as gods. Rather than wait for God to come down from heaven to build a covenant with them, they said, "Let us build a tower which reaches heaven." This was humanity's attempt to express covenant from the down side, from earth to heaven. God's expression of full covenant is always from heaven to earth. When humanity enters into a countercovenant movement community is not the result. The countercovenant movement of humanity builds structures, bricks, buildings, functions, hierarchies, pyramids, tyrannies or anarchies, but cannot build community. Community flows out of the very nature and presence of a covenant God, a God who convenes people into healing and intimate relationships.

The realization that humanity's orientation is constantly moving in a countercovenant direction gives us insight about the pseudocommunity possibilities of small group gathering. Humanity without God will convene itself to accomplish great things. Wherever there are multitudes of human beings, if they do not hear the convening voice of God they will attend to their own convening voice and gather together to build something. The gathering instinct in us is powerful. When we say, "Let us build . . . ," our countercovenant industriousness will build great cities, influential governments, high-rise structures, asphalt jungles, "principalities and powers" and pyramidal hierarchies. But we cannot, by ourselves, say, "Let us make community." Only God who exists as a covenantal community of being can create human community, for such community only flourishes in the intimate presence of a God who comes down to walk with humanity in the "cool of the day." Humanity can build only a faint replica of community, a pseudocommunity where God is not present, a community that shatters under the stress of construction, fragmenting and scattering people to the four winds.

Many gatherings of people look like small group community, but the common language of the group is not covenantal. These are countercovenantal groups that say, "Let us make for ourselves . . ." Pseudocommunity does not have a long life, a real life or a sense of God's covenant. Such groups have a "form" of godliness, but deny the power and presence of the convening God. Such groups are demonstrations of the paradox humanity confronts daily as a result of being driven out of the Garden, missing the presence of God and not hearing God's call.

Building Covenant Community

The ongoing reality of Genesis 11 and the city of Babel is why God calls Abram in Genesis 12. The countercovenant language of a common humanity is "Let us build." God's covenantal and conciliatory response is "Let us confuse and scatter," then "I will make you a great nation." Abram is the leader called by God to gather and nurture God's community, a contrasting action to humanity's self-initiative. The human initiative ends in fragmentation. God's initiative ends in eternal covenant community. Every small group has to wrestle with being formed of their own initiative or being formed by the covenantal presence of God who draws them into life together in the very presence of the nature of God's plural being.

The small group paradox is *productivity* together or *life* together. At first the two images may look the same, but over time the healing results are much different. Long-term small group community is not possible except that God has intervened into the lives of group members and group relationships. Groups that continue to gather without the enlivening presence of the covenant God are reduced to activity without relationship (games), meeting without presence (avoidance) or dissonance without recognition (denial). Such groups will typically disband (scatter) rather than tolerate such ambivalence in gathering.

This paradox of productivity or life together was experienced by a mainline church that had a strong history and reputation for mission group activism. They had several small groups working to meet needs in various parts of the city: a homeless shelter, a food center, a center for battered women, a group to help children find foster parents, a group to work with government to meet the needs of the poor, a group to build homes for the poor, and a group to visit in the area jails and prisons. They had a phenomenal small mission group network, growing newer ones each month. However, as they reviewed the quality of life in these mission groups, they discovered that people were generally feeling disconnected from one another and from God. They were out doing wonderful things, but they had little sense of mutual covenant or community. In sensing the vacuum of personal presence this congregation decided to invest in the spiritual disciplines of group prayer, personal storytelling and interpersonal Bible study. They encouraged their mission groups to reflect on the nature of covenant and community and allow God to reform their life together. They continued to do their mission work, but with a new passion to experience the presence of God and to know one another. Their mission groups were transformed. The need and deed groups also became gatherings who experienced the transforming presence of God's love.

The antidote for fragmentation resulting from pseudocommunity can only be the intervention of the God of covenant. The core of small group life must be a personal experience of the God who makes covenants with people. Small groups must be God's groups or they become the fragmented groups of human industry, losing any sense of common life together. Sin is choosing to be outside the presence of God or not choosing to be in the presence of God. Powerful human structures will eventually collapse while delicate gatherings of God's people will grow and thrive. This is the paradox of human depravity and God's grace.

■ SMALL GROUP MINISTRY IMPLICATIONS

1. Expectations are often very high for finding the perfect group. If sin and dysfunctionality are normal assumptions about group life, members may not be so shocked or disabled by the trouble they encounter in being together. These high expectations are particularly true today in the church when people are "consumer-oriented" about ministry. They may not have the patience or desire to work through the brokenness they discover in their relationships. The role of leadership is to prepare small groups with a realistic picture of small group life. A carefully articulated theology of sin, with an equally prepared strategy for experiencing reconciliation, can give a group a realistic launch in its life together. Helping groups experience and work through relational brokenness is the core of the gospel of Jesus Christ.

2. Small groups always have sexual dynamics as well as cultural dynamics. Small group leaders should be given guidance about how to handle sexual brokenness. Sexuality and intimacy are loaded values in our sexually repressed culture. Groups need to be encouraged to name what they feel about the sexual implications of group intimacy. Groups that develop and keep their sexual family secrets eventually will be undone by them. Avoidance or denial is no solution. Unnamed seduction or abuse can haunt a potentially meaningful group. Intimacy that is preoccupied with sexuality is loaded with destructive ammunition. Christian groups need to confront their sexual temptations, ambivalence or harassment.

3. Spirituality and sexuality are closely connected for the serious faith community. Small groups that focus upon nurturing their personal and relational spirituality may discover that sexual feelings are not far below the surface of their spiritual dynamics. Intimacy is a spiritual and a sexual reality. Sin confuses and distorts the spiritual and sexual feelings and behaviors. However, avoidance, denial, repression or legalism do not build the disciplines of human relationships. People in small groups must be given permission and guidance to explore the deeper spirituality and intimacy of their life together. Anticipating the sexual ramifications of such spiritual life together is a good thing to plan. More and more groups are also dealing with the transference of homosexual feelings. The re-

demptive and reconciling work of Christ must inform groups struggling between spiritual hunger and sexual distortion.

4. New groups hardly ever fight. They are not yet in touch with their differences. New groups have not built up negative patterns that wear out their members. People in new groups do not see each other's disability and dysfunctionality. Recognition of the dark sides of group members takes time. In order for the group to reach the precipice of dangerous relational cliffs, they must usually be together for one or two years. Then, when confronted with the potential coming darkness of their life together, they must have the courage to stay together and work through the devastations of sin in their midst. This is tough going for human relationships and small groups. Yet they must hang tough during the painful confrontations of their life together. Too many small groups bail out when they see the chasm coming. Too many fall into the canyon and crash because they weren't looking for the abrupt turns. Long-term small group ministry must help people deal with their personal sin and relational sin. More small groups must have the courage to work through the tough times. At the other side of the dark and deep periods is the promise of more and better journeys together.

5. Many common things will bring people together. The "common things" that bring us together may be parenting, marriage, singleness, illness, Bible study, food, games, recovery, grief, disability and so forth, but these "needs" or "deeds" are not community. It is important to affirm continually that these "common things" are not covenantal community in the character of God. Too many small groups are hooked on the "need" and not on the God who meets us and brings us together in the midst of our need. This is also true of mission and outreach concerns. A small group may be investing in good outreach activity, but still not be meeting the God of covenant, or allowing the God of covenant to help them meet one another.

3

SMALL GROUP COVENANTS

The LORD appeared to Abram, and said to him, "I am God Almighty, walk before me and be blameless. And I will make my covenant between me and you, and will make you exceedingly numerous." Then Abram fell on his face; and God said to him, "As for me, this is my covenant with you: You shall be the ancestor of a multitude of nations. No longer shall your name be Abram, but your name shall be Abraham; for I have made you the ancestor of a multitude of nations. I will make you exceedingly fruitful; and I will make nations of you, and kings shall come from you. I will establish my covenant between me and you, and your offspring after you throughout their generations, for an everlasting covenant, to be God to you and to your offspring after you. And I will give to you, and to your offspring after you, the land where you are now an alien, all the land of Canaan, for a perpetual holding; and I will be their God." God said to Abraham, "As for you, you shall keep my covenant, you and your offspring after you throughout their generations." (Gen 17:1-9 NRSV)

In the Bible *covenant* is relationship defined by God. It is God's nature to be in relationship, and covenant is what God wants the relationship to be. A covenant, then, emerges out of God's very nature. It is God's "unilateral" word and action.[1] Karl Barth said that covenant "is the fellowship which originally existed between God and man, which was then disturbed and jeopardized."[2]

Covenant always implies community, just as community always implies covenant. The coming together of persons finds its origin in the God whose very nature is being together. God calls humanity into relationship by being and declaring covenant. God's invitation to be together is built into the very fiber of creation. Creation is the arena where covenant is constantly active. God is always grouping; he is always bringing things and persons together. There is no coming together without covenant being a reality, and without the reality of divine covenant being.

God creates community with purpose, and redeems community for purpose. The character and purpose of all human groups are founded in God's existence as divine community. God shares divine purpose with human groups. That is, God has brought humanity through history in groups with a purpose. God gives human groups a sense of direction. God gives this sense of direction and purpose to those leaders and groups who are willing to listen and act upon what they hear God saying. God transmits this message of purpose in the lives and relationships of faithful groups.

Making a Covenant

The word *covenant* has its etymology in the word *covene*. Covenant brings two or more persons together. It is a "binding and solemn agreement made by two or more individuals to do or not to do specific things." The gathering of persons into a small group carries the immediate implication of *covenant*. There is no human gathering that does not reflect the foundational covenant of a convening God. God's covenantal personality may be blurred or obscured by human brokenness, but the personality of interactive divine community still haunts, if not beckons to, every human gathering.

By definition then, covenant first of all implies *group*. People are gathered for a reason. Someone or something has brought them together—they have something in common. They may be in the same room just to wait or they may be in an elevator to go up the building. The foundational common ground of a group is their common Creator and their common humanity. Their gathering creates common space and common place. The very fact that they are together implies that the covenant personhood and promise of God have been invoked and the covenant process has already begun. Once the individuals are gathered they are no longer just individuals—they are now a constituted group. Their life together may be short-lived or eternal, but for this moment they are a group. They are together. They must deal with one another. They must decide how to engage and how much to engage. Those who are not convened and gathered are fragmented, disconnected or isolated individuals. The covenant presence of God works to bring order and group life out of this disconnection and fragmentation. "Order precedes and overcomes disorder. When viewed apart from covenant, creation appears as sheer randomness and capriciousness."[3]

Second, covenant implies *family*. As Ray Anderson has said, "Being connected means being human, and being human means being part of a family."[4] Covenant implies the gathered group is potential family, where the group members are interwoven into each other's lives by the creative presence of a "family" God who brings people together to be a covenant community. While the word *group* may carry a certain sound of clinical sterility, the term *family* may suggest more accurately the idea that the gathered group is a reflection of the intimacy God creates through personal presence and voice. Human groups have the freedom to approach and to know one another in the way God approaches and knows us. This may be one of the positive reasons for the church's historical and doctrinal love affair with its theology of the Trinity. The description of God as Father, Son and Holy Spirit has a family sound and feel. Wherever a small group gathers, covenant works to draw that group together as human family no matter what resistance might exist.

Third, covenant implies *small* family group. Every large group gathering probably began as a small group whom God called together and gave the mission to call the larger group gathering. God's covenant with Abraham first includes Sarah and then Lot and continues to include vast numbers of persons throughout history. The small group precipitated the larger gathering of many groups. The covenantal gathering process of Israel by Moses began with God meeting Moses face to face in the burning bush (Ex 3). Moses was not called out of a vacuum. He was identified and called out as a member of a small faithful family group (the Midian tribe) among whom was Jethro, the "priest of Midian." Moses' relationship with Jethro and the Midian community formed him spiritually and prepared him to hear the voice of God while tending sheep. Moses' call came in the midst of his life in the smaller tribal group. Before he attempted to gather all the Hebrew people he clearly heard God's strategy to meet with the smaller group of elders to confirm and enable the calling out of the larger group. God said to Moses, "Go, assemble the elders of Israel" (Ex 3:16-18). In addition to meeting with the elders, he was to go with them to confront the king of Egypt: "You and the elders are to go to the king of Egypt." Even as Moses feared a lack of personal "eloquence," God enabled the smaller group of Aaron and Moses to become a leadership team together (Ex 4—5). Again, most often, larger called gatherings of God emerge out of the covenant mission of smaller called leadership meetings of God.

A recent example of this advance leadership covenant occurred when God brought together a small group of people to establish the National Conferences on Growing the Church Through Small Groups, held in 1987, 1988, 1989 and 1990. The combined vision and passions for small groups of Roberta Hestenes, Lyman Coleman, Richard Peace, Kenneth Haugk, Robert Slocum, Al Jepson, Jolene Anderson and myself brought together four major organizations to host these four events, each with a thousand participants. Out of the vision and call of the small group, the larger group was gathered. Out of the covenantal life of a few, God reestablished a covenant of national ministry with hundreds of congregations and thousands of church leaders.

God is the original "convener" of such human communities. From the beginning the people of God have heard the voice of God in the plural, "Let us make . . ." (Gen 1:26). Since God created human community, the primal covenant for human community has been established to flourish. Covenant is the process of God convening groups and sharing a communal nature and purpose with human groups. God creates these faithful groups through the purpose and process of covenant by calling the group into being around group leaders, by making a covenant with the called group, and by establishing an inner framework around which all healthy human group covenants are built.

God Calls Groups into Being Around Leaders

The LORD had said to Abram, "Leave your country, your people and your father's household and go to the land I will show you. I will make you into a great nation and I will bless you; I will make your name great, and you will be a blessing. . . . and all peoples on earth will be blessed through you." (Gen 12:1-3)

Every faithful gathering of persons in a small group is a response to God's initiative and call. God most often communicates this initiative through a founding leader or a leadership core group. Abram moved because God spoke. Abram's family group moved because Abram spoke. The word of God is heard only in relationship—it is spoken only in community. God *calls* groups of people together through visionary leaders who share the blessing with others. God's communication to human leaders, the Word delivered and received, is often called *election*. The election of Abram is an election of an individual *and* a community. Even before God let Abram know that there was a place for him to go and a job for him to do, God spoke to Abram. God had established a beginning relationship with Abram. God enabled Abram to hear and act upon this personal communication. Thus, when God spoke, Abram heard and acted. So he launched out from Ur with Lot and Sarai and their entire households.

From the beginning Abram was called to be a community *with* God and to become a community *for* the benefit of all people. Abram was called to be the initiating leader of a new, unique and separate family group system, formed by God for the purpose of revealing the divine character as loving and blessing community for an estranged world lost in hiddenness and brokenness. The individual is not called alone to become a new individual to impact the world with

God, but is called to establish a new community. The *lone* Abram became the *loved* Abram. God's covenant community with Abram empowered Abram to become the initiator of a new covenant community. Abram's call was to *lead* a new community to a new place to begin a new ministry of God's visible presence in the world. Abram's family group, Lot, Sarai and their traveling entourage, was out among alien people groups. Abram was in divine and human community from the beginning of God's call.

From this base community of Abram and Sarai the new generations of God's new family groups were to come into existence. Each successive patriarch (leader) after Abram represented a family system that encountered and wrestled with the character of God in community. The patriarchal communities were called to reflect the divine community of God.

The individual group leader and family always bring along their original family system, which God must confront, heal, transform and renew. God's confrontation began when Abram and company left Ur. Due to continual quarreling, Abram and Lot and their families separated (Gen 13:5-9). Abram's group worked to get Lot's group out of trouble in Sodom and Gomorrah. However, Lot's family group sank deeper into brokenness and eventually disappeared from the blessing of salvation history (Gen 13—19). Abram's family struggled through their pain to establish God's new community. Their brokenness was healed as Abram and Sarai learned to trust God's voice and presence. The renewing of their family came when Abram and Sarai became the new group of Abraham and Sarah with Isaac. God created this new community out of divine blessing and graciousness, without the help of human expertise or scheme. Isaac was born to the community in spite of Sarah's age and the impossibility of conception, beyond the group's "Hagarian" scheme to produce the new community of their own ingenuity (Gen 21).

The individual is not called alone to establish new communities of ministry. Rather, God calls individuals together into ministry through ministering groups. Hans Walter Wolff argues that the patriarchs and prophets were godly individuals who called others into community with themselves for the purpose of showing the world an earthly reflection of divine community.[5] The individual leader is called to minister *to* the community, *among* the community, *with* the community and *from* the community. The community, in response, also ministers to the individual leader.

Throughout salvation history, new faith-centered groups emerged by the power of God through divinely authored family group covenants. Isaac and Rebecca succeeded Abraham and Sarah, and God renewed the covenant by making a new covenant with Isaac (Gen 26:23-25). Good covenants tend to birth good covenants. Healthy groups tend to breed healthy groups. Small groups of the faithful tend to coalesce around leaders who are willing to listen to the call of God. These leaders convene and bring new family groups into estranged places and among foreign groups to be the people of God together. God gathers the group together and calls it into ministry; the leader represents God to the called group, and the group represents God to the hostile world.

The ministry of the group is among and for other people with whom the members of the group come in touch. Faithful small groups should have both an *intragroup* and *intergroup* ministry orientation. They are called together to experience the salvation of God among one another and to bring the shalom of God to persons and groups outside themselves. Every covenant group has a call to itself and a call beyond itself. Every covenant group has a call to meet God and a call to help others meet God.

To help stimulate intragroup ministry, a small group leader must have the personal courage to risk the face-to-face vulnerability of encounter even though the rest of the group may sit in fear. The example of the leader letting go of his or her protective shield and venturing into the presence of another beckons the group to consider doing likewise. God initiates this summoning covenant relationship, but the group leader provides the human initiative to respond to God in the covenant, drawing others into the depth of God's personal confrontation and intimacy.

The call of God for a group to move, or the call of God for a leader to move a group, sets the group in motion. God, the leader and the group move on the way together. The covenant is that God is going with them, that God has a place for them to go, and that the group will be transformed together on the way of the journey. God enters covenant partnerships with special leaders to develop special groups. Every faithful small group has such a covenant origin. Every faithful small group has had faithful initiating leaders who heard, received and acted on God's call.

God Makes Covenants with Groups

Hear, O Israel, the decrees and laws I declare in your hearing today. Learn them and be sure to follow them. The LORD our God made a covenant with us at Horeb. It was not with our fathers that the LORD made this covenant, but with us, with all of us who are alive here today. (Deut 5:1-3)

The covenant that God has established with any group of people is not limited to the past or to the few. Abraham, Isaac, Jacob, Joseph and Moses are not the only inheritors of God's covenant. God has made the covenant with every member of the community whom the leader brought together. Their covenant life reaches out to others in the present generation and into future generations. Covenant group life always touches persons beyond its immediate group and beyond its immediate time.

The consistent rehearsal and remembrance of healthy covenant life within a particular group forms the character of that group. Their continual and consistent self-awareness over the days, months and years that God is their convener and empowerer forms their nature and attitude. Each new group has to experience a unique and personal encounter with the God of covenant for them to affirm this covenantal reality of their life together.

Only within the safe boundaries of intragroup community can people venture out from behind the leaves and trees of the Garden as God calls them and enables them to come out. The gathered group discovers that God is on their side. Their gathering creates time, space and place to be a different and special community— a community where brokenness, hurt, woundedness and struggle are confessed, absolution is declared, and repentance is practiced. Only the forgiving group, the group formed in the nature of God and the group in covenant with God, has the power to be transformed and to help transform others beyond itself. God makes covenants with groups so that individuals and relationships will be held accountable to grow and to be better within the group so their life together can have a positive effect on the wider culture and world.

The God-initiated covenant implies specific parameters for community with God and with every human group. The Ten Commandments are a primary example of human covenant life being ordered by faith in a living and loving God. These commandments point to the need for a group to give God and humanity their full dignity in relationship and in community. According to Paul Hanson, the foundation of these commandments is the community's "experience of God entering the concreteness and particularity of human life."[6] The first four commandments affirm the supreme covenantal presence of a jealous God who tolerates nothing interrupting the group's intimate connection with divine community. The remaining six commandments set key guidelines in human relationships that, when the group tends to them, can help to restore the image of God blurred in the Garden (Genesis 3). As Hanson says, this restored image, this shalom of God, can appear only "where the consciousness of the individual and the community" are filled with God.[7] Hanson's use of *shalom* is concomitant with the restoration of the image of God blurred in the fragmentation of community in Genesis 3. The Ten Commandments, when practiced, help the group to participate in God's covenantal life. When ignored, the group degenerates farther into chaos and anarchy, into noncommunity. The Ten Commandments provide an outer order of community that the group can eventually embrace as an inner order as they become more open to sharing the presence and heart of God.

The personal covenant of God is the relationship presupposed behind and below the written commandments. God's love and desire for reconciliation with humanity is the foundational ground upon which the Decalogue is built.[8] Without God's desire for restored relationship with humanity, there is no foundational meaning for the Ten Commandments. The Decalogue has meaning only as it reflects the desire of God for loving relationship with and among human groups. These "commandments" provide concrete ways for the community to relate to God and to one another.

Human small groups come into being through the theological and historical reality of God's covenant. God embraces humanity and empowers humanity to embrace one another. God initiates, liberates and sustains people to meet one another in the group context. Based upon this eternal and historical covenant action of God, every human group can come together in an implied covenant for human relationships, oriented toward shalom and built upon the character and community of God. As Hanson has said, the first three commandments "secure the heart of Israel's faith" in a "compassionate God," releasing the flow of this character through all aspects of community life.[9] The covenant is implied because it is built into the fabric of humanity created in the image and likeness of God. However, until the group recognizes the presence of God and intentionally affirms and practices the implied covenant, the intimate knowledge of God will not govern the group's life. If the group practices or enforces the Ten Commandments without experiencing the real presence of God, they will never experience the covenant life implied behind and beyond the Decalogue. Such a legalistic imposition of rules can rob the group of the heart of covenant life; that is, God's love and personal presence.

Through the adoption of God's covenant a small group sets out, like Israel, on a journey of exodus, conquest and domestication in relationships, leaving disabling values behind and embracing new empowerment values for shalom relationships being drawn into the image of God and the seventh day of creation.

As Hanson has written, "Through the commandments a space was secured, an orbit of 'shalom,' within which God's people could flourish, safe from harm or fear of harm. Within that space they could devote themselves to life's consummate purpose, worship and praise."[10]

The covenant for every God-centered group has its rootedness in the nature of a communal God who desires to rectify and reorder human relationships. The foundational and concrete expression of God's covenant is concisely expressed in the Ten Commandments. The Decalogue is the historical, specific and written *charter* that emerged out of God's personal and intimate covenant relationship with Israel. This foundational group charter sets the ground upon which every faithful group can build a life together.

■ SMALL GROUP MINISTRY IMPLICATIONS

1. Every small group needs a purpose for its existence. Very often this purpose is articulated by the leader who first calls the group together. Every member of the group needs to understand the group's purpose. Often groups with poorly articulated purposes have a difficult time helping their members commit. Sometimes the purpose is in the mind of the leader, but is not clearly presented to the group. The more simply articulated the group purpose, the more likely members will commit themselves for extended periods of time. There are short-term purposes and long-term purposes for small groups. It is tough to keep a long-term group around a short-term purpose.

2. Articulated small group purposes are usually the product of a leader who is trying to give direction to the group. Purposeless groups fail. Leaderless groups also fail. Small groups need direction, purpose and leadership. There can be multiple leaders in a small group, but there cannot be a healthy group without leadership. Leadership gives direction and meaning. Direction and meaning roll out of God's covenant life.

3. Small group covenants grow out of articulated purposes, leadership guidance and shared ownership for group behavior. The covenant gives concrete reality to the purpose. Leaders hold the group accountable to the purpose and the covenant. Small group covenants, often called contracts, are the detailed guidelines that help the group to function together and in a common direction. All small group covenants should understand and reflect the nature of God's covenant with humanity. All small group covenants should find a common foundation in the Ten Commandments. While every small group covenant does not need to name the commandments, the integrity of spiritual and sexual relationships in the group must reflect an innate understanding of the moral implications of the Ten Commandments for human community.

4

THE TEN COMMANDMENTS FOR SMALL GROUPS

These are the commands, decrees and laws the LORD your God directed me to teach you to observe . . . so that you, your children and their children after them may fear the LORD your God as long as you live by keeping all his decrees and commands . . . and so that you may enjoy long life. . . . Be careful to obey so that it may go well with you. . . . Love the LORD your God with all your heart and with all your soul and with all your strength. These commandments that I give you today are to be upon your hearts. Impress them on your children. Talk about them when you sit at home and when you walk along the road, when you lie down and when you get up. (Deut 6:1-3, 5-7)

According to the biblical theologian Paul Hanson, the Ten Commandments are a foundational "charter" for healthy covenant community that "embodies and immortalizes for all ages the essence of the covenant community ideal."[1] We can understand these commandments as "charter" because they establish the foundational parameters around which any group can be formed. Using the Decalogue as a universal model, ten general categories of guidelines can be established for any small group. These "commands and prohibitions were not presented to the community as harsh and onerous impositions, but as loving protections safeguarding this space for fellowship with God. The "ten words" have historical and revelatory importance for all groups. Such was true for Israel as a family system.[2] Each universal "commandment" carries a positive implication and affirmation for life together in a small group. These covenant guidelines also bear quiet judgment upon group relationships that fail to pursue a journey together of wholeness (shalom) into the presence of God.

This ancient charter for human community establishes theological and ethical foundations for every small group to localize and concretize its personal covenant for life together. As Louis Evans Jr. has said, the "foundation of the biblical small group movement" was the group of ten who kept the Law, the *minyan*, which emerged out of the leadership of Moses in proximity to the giving of the covenant Law. These gatherings of ten have carried the Jewish people through thousands of years of prosperity, transition, trouble and oppression. Evans connects this pattern of ancient covenant to the establishment of Christians living in small groups together where Jesus is the covenant presence of God.[3] Every small group covenant should reflect the ethos and substance of the Decalogue in its life together before God and one another. Such group covenants may be verbal or written, stated or implied. But every small group committed to the nurture of community in the presence of God builds upon an *implied* covenant after the manner of God's nature in covenant, and further articulated (orally and scripturally) in the Decalogue. With the Decalogue as a biblical and covenantal paradigm, the further meaning of covenants for small groups can be explored.

The Small Group Has One Lord
You shall have no other gods before me. (Ex 20:3)
Lordship is leadership. Leadership is humanity following God's model and lead. God lives and leads as divine community. God exercises Lordship as community for community. God takes the initiative to establish the group so the group can take the initiative to pattern their life together after the nature and model of God. Human leadership of a group of God's people is always penultimate to the ultimate leadership or lordship of God. The primary leader of any small group is God. All exercise of leadership in the group finds its original identity and purpose in the leadership character of God. God is the one who calls, liberates and reconciles people together to become a group. God as primary leader calls human group leaders to draw other members of the group into group participation and leadership. God as Lord of the group calls members of the group to exercise God-originated character and nature as a reflection of God's image in human creation, that is, "shared ruling dominion" (see Gen 1:26-28). Human societies can be seen in microcosm through the developing life of a small group.

Every call of God into community is a call to bring the members of the community into leadership. The exodus liberation was a liberation into shared leadership for the restoration of the whole of creation. God shares this dominion of creation so humanity may learn to share leadership and become partners in the dominion. Leadership births leadership. Lordship births leadership. Men and women are brought into the shared dominion of group leadership because

God is the divine community who ushers them into shared charge. Men and women together are to lead one another in the character and model of their Creator and Redeemer. The call to serve *one* God is the demand to allow no human or created thing to become god, lord or leader alone. If God is Lord of the group, all group members are participants into the redemption of shared leadership. If God is Lord all group members are called to participate in the group's dominion.

God does usually call an *initiating* leader to bring a group together. But it is destructive if the initiating leader tries to grasp that role of leadership exclusively and permanently. To constrict the role of primary leadership to one created being denies that group leadership ultimately rests in the presence of a covenant God who dwells in the midst of a covenant people. The usurping of this divine leadership role by one person is an act of idolatry, breaking the intention of the covenant. Groups that prolong the reign of one leader negate the ultimate covenant intention of God toward shared dominion and partnership in creation. Group leaders who hold tightly to an exclusive role are treading on Yahweh's turf and live under Yahweh's judgment.

God calls an initiating leader to lead a motley group into a new way and place, into new self-awareness, new relationships, new patterns of communication, and into a new life mission. In the gathered and redeemed group every member has leadership to give. In Exodus 19:5-6 the participation in the covenant and following of the charter creates a new *holy* group of persons who become "a kingdom of priests." Moses is the priest who proclaims the priesthood of all, the leader who proclaims the leadership of all. This proclamation does not guarantee that all members of the group will risk the responsibility and freedom of leadership, but it does clarify God's ultimate intention for creating the group in the first place. The world is hungry to see a whole nation of people who share mutual priesthood and leadership. In microcosm, the world is hungry to see just one small group of people who share mutual priesthood and leadership. This concept of shared leadership was underscored in Exodus 18 when Jethro criticized Moses' leadership style. This iconoclastic and empowering perspective on leadership can be brought into human reality only by the presence of the one God who is ultimate reality and ultimate community. If people can recognize God's lordship in community, they will glimpse God's lordship for community. As Hanson has asserted, "I am Yahweh" is the core reality of divine community. The corollary, "I am Yahweh's," becomes the identity of every member of the community. Yahweh, the Lord, has made us to become Yahweh's people, the members and then leaders of Yahweh, together.[4] God's lordship reigns as among a community of leaders, that is, as shared leadership.

②
The Group Centers All Things in God's Presence

You shall not make for yourself an idol. (Ex 20:4)

Every member of a small group should be seen in light of God's view of that person. God's perspective is the *centering* reality of the group. Group members are invited to see and understand one another through the eyes and mind of God. In order for this transforming perspective to develop as a group ethic, the group must first invest deeply in the presence of God as the foundation for understanding and for defining each person and relationship. Such centering comes about through prayer and listening for the voice of God, through continued intimate relationship with God and intimate knowledge of the historical writings of God's people. In the faithful small group there is a dynamic relationship between the group's immediate experience of God and the historical record of the experience of the people of God. Torah and grace, law and gospel, are in constant flux within the group to keep the *centering* on Yahweh personal and present.[5] The group should live in existential gratitude for what God has done for them while they study and reflect upon what God has done for others in the past. The integrity of group relationships with God and with one another is held in balance through prayer as an immediate experience of God in community. Biblical study is the historical experience of God in community. The process of the group's study and reflection merges the experience of past and present communities of God together as one extending and continuous community.

As the group experiences God as its personal center, the identities and relationships of the members are placed in the context of ultimate meaning. If a group member becomes the center, or if a human system becomes the center, or if some created object becomes the center, the group has been seduced from its primal mooring in the nature of God. Only God is sufficient to give focused identity to a human group. The faithful small group is a community of persons who live from this *center* out. Their journey outward into the risks and fullness of life is meaningful only in light of their journey inward toward God. Their journey inward to meet God is only as complete as their willingness to risk a real outward journey to embrace one another, to embrace creation and to embrace an unredeemed world.

It is important to note that the biblical exposition of the second commandment is connected to the nurture of future generations of family systems: "I the LORD your God am a jealous God, punishing children for the iniquity of parents, to the third and the fourth generation of those who reject me" (Ex 20:5 NRSV). The right locus of purpose and leadership in the original group expands out into the love of thousands: "but showing steadfast love to the thousandth generation of those who love me and keep my commandments" (20:6). The implication of misfocused leadership is idolatry, and leads into the misappropriation of group leadership for multiple generations of groups beyond the immediate family group. The right leadership of the group leads into the blessing of many other groups over many generations.

Family and organizational systems research has affirmed this impact of living in or out of the covenant of the second commandment to be both devastatingly and marvelously true. Anne Wilson Schaef and Diane Fassel, organizational consultants, have observed that the key leader in a group impacts the whole group. "In addictive organizations, an active addict can have tremendous influence, because an addict's behavior draws an excessive amount of attention and is a constant drain on the time and energy of others."[6] Elsewhere they note that "scores of non-recovering addictive and co-dependent employees are inevitably replicating their dysfunctional family system in the workplace. . . . They do what they know best, and that is to operate addictively wherever they are."[7] What is true for organizations is even more true for small groups. Addictive persons who abuse group power are usually the product of an abusive parent or leader from their family or previous formative group. The small group with a controlling leader or member can become like the abused family and has the explosive potential of destroying other family systems and groups, both small and large.

Such a case happened in a mainline church where a litigation lawyer dominated every group in which she found herself. When she wasn't controlling the dialogue, she sat nervously agitated while others were talking until she could break in, often to attack the speaker, point out the poverty of the speaker's thinking, and proceed to give the "correct" perspective. After three consecutive groups over a period of five years were dismantled by her controlling behavior, the fourth group finally confronted her destructive behavior. The confrontation precipitated her walking out in a flurry of anger and bitterness, proclaiming how "unloving" and "intolerant" the group was with an "assertive" woman. But she eventually returned to that same group as a transformed person, admitting that she had discovered she had a problem but could not find the courage to face herself until the group confronted her. The "fourth generation" group in her life was her point of forgiveness and redemption. They had the courage to counter her idolatrous control of God's gathering people.

③ **The Group Articulates God's Nature**

> You shall not make wrongful use of the name of the LORD your God. (Ex 20:7 NRSV)

Conversation in the faithful small group is contoured by the very character of God, that is, by the kind of relationship and conversation that God has with humanity and that humanity is empowered to have with God. Vanity, triviality and superficiality are aberrations of God's nature. God's name permeates *all* language. All group conversation should be reflective of the character and purpose of God, reflective of the name and nature of God. Vain communication is taking God for granted. Being superficial is denying the profundity and simplicity of God's word to us and presence with us. The small group that takes God seriously is the group that takes all communication seriously.

Hanson is right when he bemoans the overuse of the word *God*, a practice he sees as a desacralization. Those who too frequently use such exclamations as "Praise the Lord" or "Thank God" may be practicing a form of religious profanity. As Hanson suggests, an awe of language "is close to an awe of God." Experiencing the unspeakable Presence may be where silence is more appropriate than evocative words.

On the other hand, words are tools for expressing reality. The group needs to develop verbal communication as an act of worship, sustaining divine integrity. This means appropriate exclamations of emotion, but not superficial ones. Scripture is full of ugly and terse terms to describe reality. Verbal integrity in a small group must imply graphic vulnerability and honesty. The Hebrew writings are earthy and descriptive. Too much evangelical language is "nice" but bland. The God-centered group must develop the courage to be descriptively bold and verbally articulate.

The group is called to creative, confessional and redemptive conversation, not to "clichéd" conversation. The Catholic author and counselor John Powell says that this light level of conversation "represents the weakest response to the human dilemma and the lowest level of self-communication. In fact there is no communication here at all, unless by accident."[8] Words are important. The ideas and feelings of persons can be eloquent expressions of their humanity. The careful selection of words to communicate life with God and with one another is reflective of humanity in the image and likeness of God. God has communicated through the Word and law, that is, through communication which is understandable to humanity. God does not waste or abuse communication. God makes every action and word count. In God's community, every action and word can have special and unique meaning.

In the Exodus text, the misappropriation of language about God is connected to the ongoing carrying of human guilt: "for the LORD will not hold anyone guiltless who misuses his name" (Ex 20:7). In the Hebrew language, the name of something reflects its true nature. Small group members must be able to reflect upon and speak openly and seriously of the loving activity of God in the world. There is no other vehicle of communication for the completion of their personal and interpersonal liberation from oppression and guilt. In negating, reducing or obscuring the nature of God, the group invokes the name of God in vain. Triviality and superficiality are acts of hiding from the fullness of life and from the God who loves and redeems all things. Ernst Becker said, "Modern man is drinking and drugging himself out of awareness, or he spends his time shopping, which is the same thing."[9] The pursuit of the trivial and the superficial are human games of avoidance and denial. God cannot be encountered by the small group that works hard at running away from human realities of joy, pain, guilt, and abuse. The teachable and vulnerable group that hungers after God and talks about the mysteries of God will find God in forgiveness, release from guilt, recovery and healing.[10] Carefully framed language which communicates the full range of human experience and imagination allows the group to explore the depth of the nature of God and the height of human yearning to know God. Passivity or passionlessness as a regular group behavior is a clear sign of rejecting the lifegiving vitality of God. Such ambivalence risks little and leaves groups lost in ongoing guilt and random nothingness.

(4)

This Group Meets with God

Remember the sabbath day, and keep it holy. (Ex 20:8 NRSV)

The faithful small group should become the sabbatical space for shalom in relationship with God and with one another. As Hanson has suggested, "Through the commandments a space was secured, an orbit of *shalom*, within which God's people could flourish, safe from harm or fear of harm. Within that space they could devote themselves to life's consummate purpose, worship and praise."[11] The fourth commandment is a call to make prime space and time for intimate relationships. Intimacy between group members pours out of intimacy with God. If the group can invest energy to be in God's presence, the hunger to experience one another's presence is not far behind.

Such space for relational health and wholeness is made possible through the exercise of *intentional* spiritual disciplines. The setting aside of sabbath space was the first and most important spiritual discipline of the people of God. Martin Luther saw the fourth commandment as the practical outworking of the first and second commandments.[12] Without the intentional discipline of sabbath, relationship with God would never emerge as an important regular agenda for the people. The fourth commandment is a strong biblical apology for the pursuit of time management as a group spiritual discipline.

To affirm this strong call to set aside special and protected space to be in the presence of others, Presbyterian pastor Keith Brown has defined a vision for small group ministry which affirms the fourth commandment. As Brown often affirms in the life of this large congregation, "we must intentionally set aside sabbath space for God, for self, for family and friends, and for others farther away."[13]

The practice of sabbath opens the way for exercising other specific spiritual disciplines to bring a group into the presence of God and of one another. The group must agree on the practice of such mutual disciplines that enable them to live in a world which normally suffocates those who would choose to breathe spiritual air. The alienated world tends to snuff out space for God unless it is assertively and specifically set aside. Spiritual disciplines which intentionally call the group into mutual relationship are corollaries to the keeping of sabbath space and time. When a small group schedules its meeting to include specific disciplines of personal sharing, Bible study and prayer, it is working out the practical implications of sabbath and shalom. The gathering of small groups can, in themselves, be courageous acts of sabbath. In the epistle to the Hebrews, meeting together is held up as an important value in "spurring" the community toward love and compassionate action (Heb 10:25). The call to "gather" is declared in the same context as "drawing near" to God and "being cleansed" from guilt. The spiritual discipline of gathering in small groups enables people to experience God and God's good life together.

The small group that devotes regular and prime time to gathering is affirming critical human values. Such a small group gathering becomes a *sacramental* act of making room for God and humanity. In 1 Corinthians 11:17-33, Paul argued that the Lord's Supper creates space for God and for the people of God. According to Paul, discernment of God's presence is coupled with discernment of the people who are present. All are brought together as a body or group to be present with one another.

It is important that a faithful small group finds its center in God, sets aside space and time to experience God's presence, and practices the disciplines of human relationships that continue to affirm God as center. The group discipline of sabbath opens the way for the small group to practice many other group disciplines suggested by the Ten Commandments, such as balanced sexuality, shared time, mutual honor, conflict management, sharing, valuing and leadership.

The Group Is the Family of God

Honor your father and your mother. (Ex 20:12)

The faithful small group can become the new family of God's people wherever it meets together. Sensitivity to the vulnerability, intricacy, and connectivity of each member is its spiritual and human agenda.[14] Each group member needs to be valued as if a member of God's family. God needs to be valued as creator, parent and progenitor of each new family group. Each group member is a group treasure. The group should treat each of its members with honor and dignity because it has been embraced by God as parent with honor and dignity. The group should encourage each member to become full, complete and functional members of its faith family. Age, sexuality, economic status, maturity, success or longevity should not increase or decrease a member's value to the group. The member's value is in the recognition of their God-created humanity. The common humanity of all members immersed in God's redeeming presence makes them members of the divine family.

Such an egalitarian perspective of the importance of every group member emerges out of a deep sense of God's character and compassion for all people. If some members are difficult to love, honor or respect by ordinary cultural standards, the group declares its covenantal identity and sets about the discipline of giving these tough members careful boundaries, special attention and dignity.

Each group member has potential leadership gifts to bring to the group and to take into the world for ministry and mission. The group lives out the vision of a family who share all good things together after the character and nature of God. Each member is honored as brother or sister as the group honors God as Parent (Father and Mother).

The fifth commandment attending commentary suggests that such high valuing of human worth leads to long life in the family group and in the world: "Honor . . . so that you may live long in the land the LORD your God is giving you" (Ex 20:12). Hanson has suggested that the vulnerability of old age makes this commandment especially important. It is a call to protect and care for the weak, to give them value when they cannot be as productive as the young and strong. This should be expanded to include all who are weak or, more completely, all those who have weaknesses. The group becomes the place where persons with weaknesses are loved, supported and granted dignity for their value as God's created and redeemed creatures. The compassionate treatment of weaker members of the small group community is an act of obedience to God's order of creation, sustaining the shalom of creation and leading to longevity of life.[15] When group members are given high esteem as brothers and sisters God's shalom is affirmed. And God's shalom practiced in a family group brings healing, health and longevity. Healthy human relationships provide the nurture and support for human beings to live longer and healthier lives. Healthy relationships empower small groups to sustain life together for longer periods of time. Long-tenured groups have worked through the rough spots of being family together and have come to respect the parenting of God along the way. The giving of

God's honor and dignity to every group member transforms the group into a divine family. They become a small group family full of growing safety, health, trust and stability.

A Korean elder in a large church, who had been a member of a small group for over twenty-five years, told the story of how their intergenerational group struggled for five years before learning to live together as a trusting family. At first, they all had their own agendas and needs which seemed to cause continual tension. But after much honest sharing and resolved conflict they broke through to a sustained life together of mutual care and respect in spite of their diversity of age, stage, ethnicity and denominational history.

The Group Deals with Hostility

You shall not murder. (Ex 20:13)

The sustaining healing trait of a faithful family group is *forgiveness*. Forgiveness is the pivotal act of reconciliation and sustained bonding. In order to carry out the practical implications of sabbath and honor during all stages of group life, the members of the group must continually choose between forgiveness and vengeance, between reconciliation and hostility. If the small group is to sustain friendship it must deal with the human inclination toward vindictive anger.

In Genesis 4:2-26 we see what unresolved anger can do to a group. Cain did not "master" the desire for revenge, and murder was the outcome. The potentiality of the Cain syndrome permeates every human group. Men and women live in a constant temptation to blame another human being for their sense of inadequacy, poverty, rejection or failure. The spiritual discipline of reversing this attitude is key to the success of human groups. Vindication breeds separation and death while forgiveness breeds reconciliation and life. Anger is the pivotal human emotion. Each group member must have a healthy way to deal with anger before the emotion turns to a negative motion of murderous intent.

Dealing with anger is connected to the commitment to sabbath and mutual honor. The opposite of a community where love and mutual protection are held in high esteem is the community where anger is allowed to spoil, hostility run rampant and various forms of violence subvert the sabbath space. When one person within the group is preoccupied and self-absorbed, God and others are shut out, self-awareness is lost, and the group is endangered. When one group member gives in to the temptation to project his or her own failure onto other group members, a self-defeating (suicide) pattern of undisciplined anger drives the individual toward an attitude of war (homicide). The vindictive member turns the group into a battle zone where other members are the enemy. Acts of vengeance become the order of the group, which becomes a community of fear.[16] The angry small group member begins to act as a relational terrorist. This often affects other group members who, under a state of attack, fight back, run away, hide, or die. The war is on and the state of reconciliation is lost. Often this persists until someone is sacrificed. Fear has murderous effects upon the whole group. Persons are cut off, relationships are broken, and the group lives in a state of siege. Conflict resolution skills and the spiritual disciplines of confession, forgiveness and repentance are needed for intervention and restoration of the group's life. If the pivotal human emotion in conflict is anger, small groups must have a way to express anger and guide it into constructive insights, solutions and actions.

As we see in Genesis 4:6-7, God did not call Cain to stop feeling angry, but to discover why he was angry, to rectify the problem, and to master (discipline or direct) the angry feeling. Cain did none of this. The result is usually a sacrificed member of the family. If the group cannot find purpose and direction through anger, the result will often be some form of group death.

The group's suppression or denial of anger or fear (the dark side of anger) is not the solution. Hidden anger undermines the group in a more insidious way. Only the open and vulnerable presentation of fear and anger leads to healthy solutions. One could speculate what could have happened if Cain had admitted his weakness, gone to his brother with his sense of rejection by God and sought the help of the family group member who seemed to understand how to live life in reconciliation with God and humanity.

Such a group discipline of openness is not a natural or normal cultural practice. The norm is more often silent or indirect retribution. The group must choose to cease its orientation toward retribution and practice the spiritual disciplines of confession and forgiveness. This demands acts of leadership and courage on the part of at least one group member to call the rest into the vulnerable practices of confession and reconciliation.

(7)

Healthy Group Sexuality

You shall not commit adultery. (Ex 20:14)

Sexuality and spirituality are intimately connected in the community life of small groups. In Genesis 3:7-8 we recognize that sexual isolation is immediately coupled with spiritual isolation. Man and woman hide from one another even as they together hide from God. Every small group begins with an orientation to hide spiritually and sexually. The twisting and bending of confused sexuality and spirituality makes every small group a potential minefield for sexual misunderstanding and manipulation. Clarification of the group's spiritual agenda and the careful practice of relational disciplines can help a group prayerfully find its way through this wilderness of intimacy.

Men and women who are drawn to be reconciled to God are also being drawn to be reconciled to one another. Wholeness of spirit eventually leads to wholeness of sexuality. But groups quickly discover that this call to wholeness of spirit and sex has many penultimate frailties. The fear of the presence of God is deeply connected to the fear of the presence of another human being, especially of the opposite sex. As James Loder of Princeton Seminary has suggested, relational prayer may be "more intimate than sex."[17] In any case, prayer and sexuality are deeply interconnected. For the group unwilling to deal with both sides of intimacy, the spiritual and sexual, both dimensions of community, will continue to be obscured and blurred, hidden behind closed doors. Sexual avoidance and abuse is an immediate result of spiritual isolation. Intimacy with God paves the way for a small group's sexual health. Only the group which discovers the openness of spiritual restoration will exhibit sexual health.

Other covenant parameters for healthy spiritual community are interconnected to God's call for sexual reconciliation. The honoring of every group member, whether man or woman, young or old, the intentional creation of sabbath space for every member, whether male or female, and the freedom from the need to worship or control the opposite sex (idolatry) find their expression in the seventh commandment.

In Hosea 3 idolatry and adultery are synonymous movements attached to the misuse of leadership and power. Israel was called to give up all visible signs of self-centered power and identity before it could be willing to return to God. The practices of sexual and spiritual abuse are intercepted when God chooses to re-embrace the people, as Hosea chose to love Gomer again. A small group that opens itself to the life of God's Spirit is also opening itself to the righting of interpersonal sexual relationships. The healing of spiritual brokenness is deeply tied to the healing of sexual brokenness. As the group works on its spiritual development, the members must attend to their sexual maturity.

A small group of women had been meeting for five years. They felt they had become very close and were growing spiritually. At a normal and typical meeting, one of the women, married with three children, told the group she had been wrestling with telling the group something very important. She felt since the group had grown so close, they were now able to handle this long-term dilemma. She confessed she was a lesbian. The group was stunned. The impact of her broken sexuality was so great that the group could not bring itself to meet with her. In fear and disillusionment the group disbanded. The group was not as spiritually mature as they had thought. The confrontation with their fragile sexuality and broken trust could not hold the group together.

It is often affirmed that the Old Testament and New Testament perspective on male and female relationships is defined primarily by marriage. Many have implied that there is no other general parameter for men and women to be together in community.[18] From this theological perspective it is also often argued that there is little basis for men and women who are not married to be in heterosexual groups together. This foundational attitude has set the ministry precedent for men and women to be in groups where marriage defines their primary relationships and roles. However, such a bias in small groups often implies discussion of sexuality should be limited to private discussions between husbands and wives and never shared in the larger group. Such a bias tends to cut spirituality off from sexuality and suggest spirituality is a group concern but sexuality is a private-personal domain of the individual or couple.

Groups deal with sexual fear in many ways. Some choose to have only men or only women in groups; others may have men and women in the same group, but only married couples are together. If men and women must be in the same group, some choose to keep the conversation away from deeply emotional or sexual issues. These group tactics may be appropriate as early disciplines for the faith community while men and women are learning to be open and healthier in one another's presence. But if such separation tactics are never shifted and merged into the maturing process of enabling men and women to live in healthy community together, the spirituality of community will continue to be bound and gagged by the fear of group sexuality. Since the Garden, humanity has had a fear of confronting sexuality in a face-to-face context. Unresolved sexual dysfunction will always block the path to deep spiritual community.

Another case in point was a pastor and spouse who were in a small group of couples in which one member from each of two other couples had an affair. This precipitated the divorce and remarriage of both couples and shattered the group. Because of that experience the pastor refused to allow men and women to be in the same group, saying such grouping patterns were too vulnerable to adultery. Rather than deal with the discontinuity between our pursuit of spiritual community and our avoidance of healthy sexual community, we seal the separation of the sexes so we never deal with broken sexuality in face-to-face small groups.

In such a protective environment the fear of adultery will not be replaced by a hope for sexual wholeness. The fear of sexual seduction will not be overcome by a commitment to growing spirituality. This has been one of the historical critiques of monasticism and a parallel fear of undisciplined sexuality. While Protestants have often critiqued the monastic movement (and its occasional sexual abuses), Protestant groups continue to practice their own kinds of heterosexual monasticism: isolation of the sexes, restrictive attitudes about sexual feelings, avoidance of emotional and sexual conversation, or control of roles men and women play in the community. Small groups can become wonderful environments in which careful covenantal commitments, leadership, and sharing can help men and women open themselves to God and to one another to become more complete sexual-spiritual beings.

The healthy small group must begin to move toward the principle behind the seventh commandment: honor and respect persons of the opposite sex, allowing their spiritual and sexual balance to develop as they relate in accountable community. The reality of men and women together in healthy community can reflect more accurately the image of God in *shared dominion* (Gen 1:26-28). However, this process of bringing men and women together into healthy and intimate spiritual community is not an easily achieved goal. Small groups that accomplish such spiritual community are usually carefully guided by healthy and mature leaders into this uncharted (but divinely covenanted) territory. Such well-prepared and disciplined leaders have learned to be whole persons usually because they too have been nurtured in loving communities where faithful spirituality has allowed balanced sexuality to be formed into their attitudes, character and relationships.

Small group leaders need to be especially sensitive to this goal of sexual integrity. Group power and sexual attraction are subtly interrelated. Authoritative group leaders can become inadvertently or intentionally sexually manipulative or seductive. In 1 Samuel 11, King David held the seductive power of position, wealth, good looks and self-awareness that seduced Bathsheba. David's abuse of leadership led to a breaking of the community's covenant of sexual and stewardship ethics. Such inordinate focus of group power in one influential and dysfunctional leader is a breaking of the second commandment, leading to the breaking of the seventh and tenth commandments. When group leaders take upon themselves godlike proportions, idolatry and adultery are not far away. In such situations group members may transfer their sexual attention and act seductively toward the dominant leader. Sexuality and power must be held in loving accountability in the small group community. Unchecked power inevitably leads to sexual abuse. Checking power is a spiritual responsibility of the close small group community.

Such was the case with a pastor who was confronted by a female counselor who was in his small group leadership training group. The female counselor observed that the pastor acted differently toward female members of the group, particularly the more attractive ones, than he did toward male group members. The counselor took the pastor aside and shared her observations with him. He was dumbfounded with her feedback, but during subsequent group meetings became aware that her observations were indeed true. This is an example of the positive effects a male-female leader partnership can have on the development of sexually healthy group leadership.

Equitable Group Time and Space

You shall not steal. (Ex 20:15)

All members of a small group bring into the group their total humanity, both helpful and hurtful (brokenness, pain, personhood, gifts, skills, history, knowledge, experience, dreams and hope). Who they are and what they have can be gifts or detriments for the whole group. But in order to share the goodness of their personal giftedness and story, they must be given *space* and *time* in the group. Therefore group space and time must be managed in such a way as to give all members abundant opportunity to share themselves and to receive the feedback and sharing of all other members. This is a foundational group ethic. Stealing from the time and space of another group member breaks this primal group covenant. Stealing is a reflection of how one really feels about God.[19] The robbing of another group member's space is an attack upon or an ignoring of God's covenantal valuing of each human being.

The management of group time and space is an act of leadership. Someone in the group needs to hold the group accountable to set aside time and space for every member. For newer or less mature groups this must be a strict discipline. For mature groups this attention to equitable time is a learned, and eventually, discerned discipline. New groups need stronger covenantal guidance to learn the discipline. Eventually, such an externally accounted discipline (law) can become an internally nurtured discipline (grace).

Communication consultants have affirmed that relational disciplines, like physical and spiritual disciplines, move from an externally structured awkwardness to an internally guided natural competence.[20] An early time-binding discipline may be, for example, the simple appointment of a time-keeper who holds group members to sharing within specific preset time allotments. The early space-keeping discipline may also suggest the careful prearrangement of a room so that every member has a good place to sit inside an oval or circle where there are no visual blockages between members.

Many church facilities do not have comfortable rooms or chairs for small groups of adults to meet for long periods of time. The traditional American church is structured for the one-hour class or committee meeting. Such simple oversights reveal the insensitivity of the typical congregation to developing intentional and growing relational community. Most American church members have better relational space in their homes. The church facility should be obviously hospitable to the equitable distribution and nurturing of good small group time and space. This is especially true today when the baby boom generation is looking for quality and community in church ministry.

As groups grow in their mutual maturity and skillfulness, many of the initial and overt disciplines can become implied and assumed disciplines. Although an egalitarian awareness may at first mean *equal* time and space, eventually the group's expanded sensitivity may allow every member adequate, appropriate or strategic time and space. The healthy and mature group discerns how much time each member needs at each meeting. Some need more at one meeting than at the next. Strict long-term equity time-keeping may eventually rob some hurting member of special needed and extended ministry. Mature groups allow for such adjustable and flexible covenant life because the Spirit of reconciliation and forgiveness has built within them trust, awareness, patience and tolerance. The early stricter disciplines of equitable time and space need to become more gracious and flexible disciplines of appropriate time and space.

Giving adequate space and time to every member of the small group is an issue of compassion and justice. Justice suggests that every member deserves a place. This is similar to the Old Testament concept of *nahala*, as Hanson has described it: "the land was to be divided equitably among the people." While most Christian small groups are not interested in real estate and land distribution, they must become sensitive to space and time distribution. The intragroup sensitivity to space and time distribution can open and lead into the larger theological issue of global distribution of intergroup wealth. The stewardship practices of small group righteousness could and should be the foundational launching pad for the group's practice of compassion and justice in the wider world.[21]

Compassion suggests that some members have greater needs for time and space at various times. Giving more attention to meet the immediate need of the hurting member is an act of group compassion. Enforcing a time parameter around a dominating group member may also be an act of justice. Some members may try to steal the time or space that belongs to other group members. Only intragroup accountability will keep such a controlling or manipulating member from imposing an anarchical dominance of time and space. Such group covenantal expectations can be sustained under the general covenant parameter of "love your neighbor as yourself" (Lev 19:18). In such a case, love equals the giving of good time and space, and justice is the group's keeping of covenant accountability to hold members accountable who are tempted to steal time and space.

Leadership style and awareness impacts the group's concern for space. An overly autocratic or dominating leader may be stealing time and space from other members of the group. It is the responsibility of leadership to guide the group into God's long term destiny for healthy community, that is, shared ministry and shared space. The group leader who views herself as overlord of the group is not only robbing God of divine space but robbing group members of relational space. As Hanson has suggested, kingship posed a major threat to Israel's notion of community. Kings were notorious for stealing the land that belonged to others (1 Kings 21). *Nahala* belonged to all the people, not just to one dominant leader. Israel's desire for kingship often led to their loss of spacial equity. The tribal (small group) distribution of land held this temptation to abuse space ownership in tension and accountability.[22]

Small Group Honesty and Integrity

You shall not bear false witness against your neighbor. (Ex 20:16 NRSV)

Lying destroys trust. Betraying group confidentiality is an act of lying to the group. A lack of truth, openness and confidentiality keeps a group in a state of turmoil and immaturity, eventually causing the group to fall apart. The Old Testament concept of not giving "false witness" has to do with the keeping of relational integrity, of keeping one's word and speaking the truth. This is so a neighbor is not abused by any lack of truth pervading the group. Lack of truth destroys personhood and relationship. Community only grows in the presence of truth. Small groups develop trust if the truth is spoken and upheld as a foundational group ethic.

A universally important and traditional primary small group commitment is that of keeping group confidentiality. Whatever is shared in the group should not to be shared outside the group without permission.[23] The breaking of confidentiality is a breaking of group trust. This is a breaking of the primal group covenant which affirms that every group member should become a person of truth and integrity and call the group to honesty and accountability.

Small groups are only as strong as their ability to develop mutual trust. Trust flows out of every member's freedom to tell the group the truth about themselves, be accepted in their vulnerability and honesty, and have that delicate truth protected within the group's life together. The freedom for an individual to be honest grows out of the group's discipline to value truth.

The establishment of group trust is a process that is bound by discipline, time and energy. Group trust is maintained delicately.[24] Trust is a major stage of a successful and nurturing group's life.[25] The sharing of the truth sustains the group into the advanced stages as deeper and deeper patterns of intimacy are experienced. The avoidance of truth breaks the growing trust pattern. This can open a dark door to distrust and move the group into a period of unrest until the truth is reestablished through confrontation, confession and forgiveness.

Sustained periods of unrest and avoidance of the truth will cause even the strongest of groups to disintegrate. Disintegration of a small group is the result of trying to live in community without the delicate marriage of truth with intimacy. Truth cannot be shared without intimacy, and intimacy cannot be sustained without truth. Truth, love, and justice must all work together in group life.

10

The Group's Freedom to Serve

You shall not covet your neighbor's . . . (Ex 20:17)

The tenth commandment is about the integration of truth, love and justice. Small groups do not exist just for themselves. The gift of "life together" is a gift of God for the wider world. Dietrich Bonhoeffer raised this concern that a small group community may become isolated. The small group must be open to receive and share with those from the broken world, "even the weak, insignificant and seemingly useless people." It also must "not form itself into a movement, an order, a society, a *collegium pietatis*, but rather understand itself as being a part of the one holy catholic Christian Church, where it shares actively and compassionately in the sufferings, struggles and promise of the whole church."[26] The small group is part of a greater body of people. A healthy community is the launching pad for life to be shared with hungry people outside the group. Hanson has spoken to this overarching theme of balance in biblical community which he calls the "triadic notion": worship, righteousness and compassion. Worship is the just relationship with God, righteousness is the just relationship of persons with one another inside the community, and compassion is the just mission of the community into the world.[27] All grace and goodness that is learned and received inside the group is meant to be shared with persons outside the group. The opposite of this compassionate movement is when groups keep their good life to themselves, or even more demonically, when they meet to take life away from others. The coveting of things that belong to other people (Ex 20:17) is the opposite of a life of compassion, which is the giving away of that which belongs to the group or to the individual. The coveting group robs life from outside groups and persons. The compassionate group gives away its life to outside groups and persons.

The interior work of the small group is the building up and affirmation of its members, gifts and relationships. In recognizing and affirming its gifted members and relationships the group validates the importance of each gifted person and their relationships being made available to the greater world. The group's responsibility is the stewardship of these gifts of being and acting, of personhood and relationship.

As a group develops confidence in mutual ministry among themselves, they are released and empowered to share that ministry outside themselves in the wider world. The redeemed group therefore becomes a family of priests and a community of compassion. Their need to control and "covet" is transformed into the freedom to give, to minister and to serve through acts of compassion. As the delivering God calls the group together, so the group is also redeemed and called into the character of God to become a delivering people.

God brought together a motley group of slaves out of Egypt and made them into a "people," a cohesive group, with God as their common presence and center.[28] God's act of deliverance and their experience of redemption was a constant beacon to the people to become a delivering people. Their freedom was secured to breed freedom for other groups. But the process of becoming free and acting out that freedom is a mandate. It is not a fast and sure reality. The memories, effects and practices of slavery lingered on in Israel's ethos for several thousand years, during which few substantive periods of truly compassionate mission to the rest of the world were unleashed. A group's freedom to act justly in the larger context is always bound by its temptation to deny such abundant life within itself.

The small group is called out to become a new community and a new family in order to move into the world as an inviting, embracing and compassionate group. The power of the love experience with God in the group provides the courage to risk the priestly and loving ventures of mission into a more hostile world.

The tenth commandment's mandate for small groups is that it should not hoard its abundant life together, but turn facing the world with servant attitudes and priestly compassion. As the group learns to be a priestly community, it is beckoned by God to share its priestly wealth with the wider world. Rather than coveting all the good things in life for itself, it shares all its good gifts of God with others. This is a dramatic leap of life for most faithful groups. But in turning outward and giving their life away, the group will discover the fullness of God and covenant life together. Sharing truth and love only comes to its fullness when it is allowed to flow beyond the group reservoir into a thirsty humanity.

A Summary of the Ten Commandments for Small Groups

1. This group may have many leaders, but only one Lord, God ("You shall have no other gods before me," Ex 20:3).

2. This group will discern all persons, relationships and things in recognition and measure of the ever-present Creator God ("You shall not make for yourself an idol in the form of anything in heaven above or on the earth beneath or in the waters below," Ex 20:4).

3. This group will speak of and address God with creativity, sincerity and

passion ("You shall not misuse the name of the LORD your God," Ex 20:7).

4. This group will set aside prime and regular times to meet God in solitude and in community ("Remember the Sabbath day by keeping it holy," Ex 20:8).

5. This group will treat one another with dignity, honor and respect, as members of one family in God ("Honor your father and your mother," Ex 20:12).

6. This group will practice giving and receiving forgiveness in the process of dealing with conflict and anger ("You shall not murder," Ex 20:13).

7. This group will nurture healthy relationships between men and women ("You shall not commit adultery," Ex 20:14).

8. This group will give just time and space for each member to share who they are and what they have ("You shall not steal," Ex 20:15).

9. This group will encourage each member to speak truthfully, in love, confidentiality and integrity, to and about every other group member ("You shall not give false testimony against your neighbor," Ex 20:16).

10. This group will affirm the gifts of each member and every relationship for sharing, in compassionate service, its life together with people outside itself ("You shall not covet your neighbor's house," Ex 20:17).

■ SMALL GROUP MINISTRY IMPLICATIONS

1. To build an initial small group covenant, a particular group may want to take the "Ten Commandments for Small Groups" and discuss how these guidelines might direct their life together. They may choose a few of these upon which to focus over the duration of a specific contractual period. They may wish to take one commandment each week for reflection and discussion before forming a more long-term agreement based upon all ten.

2. Some groups are uneasy with the idea of a written covenant. The group should discuss the pros and cons of such a written contract before deciding to do one. The establishment of covenant is not dependent upon writing it out. The group may wish to form an oral covenant until the time it decides that a written covenant might be more helpful. The important principle here is that the small group should recognize the divine power of "covenant" as a reality of God's life among them. To avoid building and affirming an intentional covenant is for the group to allow its more dominant members to establish a covenant or to allow the submerged or subversive values of the existing culture to determine its covenant by default. Whether the group chooses to recognize it or not, its life together will be formed by some covenantal assumptions, for better or for worse. Groups cannot avoid covenant. Covenant is generic to human gathering.

3. Some groups are comfortable merging into the stated covenant of an initiating leader. This willingness to buy into the leader's stated contract is particularly

true of new groups or immature groups. Such groups are looking to the leader to show them the way of covenant life. This places much responsibility upon the leader to be a person of knowledge, wisdom and integrity. A less-prepared, less-abled or low-integrity leader can lead a group into self-destructive patterns. This is one of the reasons initiating leaders must be carefully chosen, trained and supported for healthy small group ministry. In such powerful leadership roles the covenant is incarnate in the leader. Such was the case with Moses and with Jesus.

4.The specifics of small group covenants are both theological and ethical, philosophical and practical. Too often a group creates a covenant with high ideals, but no practicality. Their doctrine of life together is good but their practice of life together is not integrated. Since we live in a western society which tends to divide belief from action, faith from work, or covenant from "contract," a small group needs to be shown how to integrate their covenant life. Sometimes the opposite is also true; the group may have a very practical contract for how to live together, but they lose or miss the meaning of why covenant life is so important to God. They have a life, but no theology or vision or purpose behind, before, or under their life. They act but have no ground of being. Such groups need to have leaders who are trained in the biblical purpose of human community. Contemporary gnostic patterns which divide the real from the heavenly, must be countered in small covenant communities. To say God is Lord but not give love and speak truth is incongruity. Small groups must be arenas where faith and action are integrated.

5
SMALL GROUP RELATIONSHIPS

Hear, O Israel, the decrees and laws I declare in your hearing today. Learn them and be sure to follow them. The LORD our God made a covenant with us at Horeb. It was not with our fathers that the LORD made this covenant, but with us, with all of us who are alive here today. The LORD spoke to you face to face out of the fire on the mountain. (Deut 5:1-4)

God desires ("face-to-face" relationships with humanity. And God desires to bring people into "face-to-face" relationships with one another. The very nature of God is face-to-face community. The covenant relationship that God has established with specific people is not limited to the past or to the few. Abraham, Isaac, Jacob, Joseph and Moses were not the only inheritors of God's covenant. God seeks personal relationships with every human being and with every human group. God made the covenant "face to face" with every member of the community at Horeb. Moses may have sensed the need to stand in the gap between God and the people, or the people may have desired to put Moses in the way, but God's desire was to meet the whole community, person to person, face to face.

As we read in Exodus 20:18-21, however, the people were so terrified of being in the presence of God that they said to Moses, " 'Speak to us yourself and we will listen. But do not have God speak to us or we will die.' . . . The people remained at a distance, while Moses approached the thick darkness where God was." While the people themselves were not ready to meet God face to face, from God's perspective it was a face-to-face meeting where the people were invited into a community lifestyle of face-to-face relationships.

The Group as Face-to-Face Community

The covenant community is called to be a face-to-face community with God and with other people. It is the community where people can come out from behind the leaves and trees of a new garden because God calls them and enables them to come out. However, God's invitation to come out strikes terror in the hearts of those who are not prepared to do so. As in Israel's case, only a few of the community's leaders may be ready and willing to meet God face to face. But it is the responsibility of community leadership to encourage the community not to be afraid and to model a "coming out" and a "facing" lifestyle.

God is on our side. God has made a covenant of community with all of us to be our God. God desires to meet us face to face, person to person, persons to persons. The role of the spiritual community leader is to invite all the people themselves to meet God face to face and to overcome the intimidation of divine presence.

This call into a face-to-face encounter with God is risky and threatening. As Hanson has noted, the Decalogue was the charter of the covenant community, "an eloquent formulation of the divine imperative stemming from its primal encounter with Yahweh without losing the awesome power inherent in the original experience."[1] The Ten Commandments were an outer boundary within which face-to-face life with God could be established among the people of God. These "rules" of life were not as much articulated to keep people from escaping through outer boundaries as they were to encourage people to draw close to God at the center of the community, and to draw close to one another in healthy and appropriate ways. At the center of the "commandment" community was Horeb, the mountain of God, where they were invited into face-to-face relationship with the God who revealed a loving but frightening face. God showed them a welcoming face, one that lifted up a falling face and smiled on a wondering face.

The face is the expression of the inner self, revealing the true nature of a person. The face reflects the heart and soul of what one thinks, feels and senses. It is the most vulnerable and transparent organ of being. The rest of the body is an expression of what happens through the face. The intimate foci of the face are the eyes, the window to the inner person. The eyes tell the story of a person's life. The face is the fuller expression of the eyes. God made humanity with faces to express the delicacies of the soul. The face of a human being is made in the image and likeness of God, who desires to face humanity. The freedom to enter into face-to-face relationships flows out of the very nature of God, who exists as eternal face-to-face community. God's circle of being is a face-to-face circle of persons who come together as "one face" and "One who faces" others.

Small groups are about face-to-face community. Roberta Hestenes defines a small group as "an intentional, face-to-face gathering of 3 to 12 people."[2] Face-to-face relationships do not occur unintentionally. The freedom to enter into face-to-face relationships is first established by God's intentional and covenantal coming to face humanity. God faced Adam and Eve "in the cool of the day" (Gen 3:8), but they could no longer face God or face one another. God faced Abraham, Isaac and Jacob even before they were able to face God. God "looked [faced] with favor on Abel and his offering, but on Cain and his offering he did not look [face] with favor." Therefore, "Cain was very angry and his face was downcast [turned toward the ground]" (Gen 4:4-5). Cain could not face the disfavorable face of God. Adam and Eve were afraid to face God in their nakedness. Facing God is an awesome encounter, especially if we think God's face is not filled with favor toward us. We would rather hide than deal with God's face of disfavor.

God addressed both Abel and Cain face to face. But the face of God left opposite impressions on each. The face of God saw their inner attitude and character. In facing God they had to face themselves. In facing Abel, Cain had to face God's disfavor. He had to live with God's face-to-face connection and affirmation of Abel and his own lack of freedom to face God. While he could not run away from God's face, Cain could obliterate Abel's reflective and shining face. In the same way, in order to avoid the gaze of God we may strike out to obscure the glowing face of another.

Faces are powerful expressions of intention and intimacy. God's face penetrates our hiding places. Those who dwell in the presence of the face of God can turn and face us with similar intensity and integrity. In Exodus 34:29-35 Moses' face shined with the "glory" of having seen the face of God, but the people could not stand to gaze upon the face of Moses: "When Aaron and all the Israelites saw Moses, his face was radiant, and they were afraid to come near him." He was forced to wear a covering over his head for the people to bear his presence. Living in the presence of God, in face-to-face relationship, intensifies the radiance of relationship and presence. The small group can be a place where we learn to meet God's gaze and share the gaze of God's people.

Small groups are "faceful" communities. Small groups are only faithful as they receive and reflect a face full of God and one another. Within a faithful small group the leader can bring group members to meet God and each other face to face. Like Moses, the small group leader must have the personal faith and courage to risk the face-to-face vulnerability of encounter even though the rest of the group may turn away in fear. A leader who lets go of the personal protective shield and ventures into the presence of another beckons the whole group to consider doing likewise. This summoning covenantal relationship is initiated by God, who comes "down" to us in search of face-to-face encounter. But the group leader, like Moses, provides the human initiative and example to meet the God of covenant, thereby drawing others into the depth of such personal confrontation and intimacy. In the darkness we occasionally face the light of the moon which gives light as it faces and reflects the sun. So the group leader faces God and enlightens the group, inviting them to seek the primary source for more light.

A man was once heard talking with a frustrated member of the church about their pastor. The frustrated member was upset because she had not received a personal visit from the pastor. The man listened quietly and then replied, "Why don't you go to the small group training event which the pastor leads? I was there, and I've personally seen the shine on the pastor's face when we're in the small group together. Go and see the face of a pastor who cares."

The group that cannot embrace the awesome face-to-face encounter with God and face-to-face encounter with one another has no place to go with their shame, pain and guilt. The healthy small group allows space for confrontation with God and the vulnerability of life. The group that shares, faces the veracity of their weakness and guilt, embraces the presence of God and learns to speak of God and one another with care, honor and dignity. The group that comes in touch with the fires of deeper human passions (love, affirmation, faith, hope, despair, loneliness, anger), fully inflamed by the face of God, learns to speak of God and of God's creation in humble, sensitive and open language. Such passionate face-to-face encounters with God and with other persons are often confrontational and confusing, but as we shall see in a brief case study of Job and his small group of friends, face-to-face communications are ultimately confirmational, confessional and consolational. However, face-to-face groups can reflect a dark side, especially if the faces of the group are not facing the full reality of the face of God.

The Confrontational Community of a Small Group

When Job's three friends . . . heard about all the troubles that had come upon him, they set out from their homes and met together by agreement to go and sympathize with him and comfort him. When they saw him from a distance, they could hardly recognize him; they began to weep aloud, and they tore their robes and sprinkled dust on their heads. Then they sat on the ground with him for seven days and seven nights. No one said a word to him, because they saw how great his suffering was. (Job 2:11-13)

[The LORD] said to Eliphaz, . . . "I am angry with you and your two friends, because you have not spoken of me what is right." (Job 42:7)

Gerald Egan, the noted interpersonal specialist, said that small groups have many names, but "whatever the name, the members of the group sit face-to-face and speak to one another." Egan, like many specialists in twentieth-century small group behavior, emphasized the "encounter," "transaction" or "gestalt" of persons with one another in the small group situation:

> If they can forge themselves into a supportive and understanding community—a community in which the members are basically "for" one another and come to see the world through one another's eyes—then they can train themselves to engage in the kinds of behavior that make for interpersonal growth: exploration of one's interpersonal style, a freer and more responsible expression of human emotion, a willingness to challenge others caringly and to be challenged.[3]

Egan also cautioned that "sitting face-to-face in such a small group is usually seductive, intriguing and demanding." Such experiences "can facilitate interpersonal growth or retard it." There is possibility or peril in every face-to-face encounter.

The biblical case of Job gives this type of cautioning perspective on the benefits and detriments of small group encounter and confrontation. In Job's situation the group of three friends provided some important and helpful human community. First, they gathered around Job to be his supportive community and surrogate family in the midst of his personal crisis. The three friends "set out from their homes" to be "with" Job (2:11). This was an act of sensitivity to Job's loss of household and a commitment to become his temporary support group. Second, they provided a base for reflection upon Job's difficult issues of life. Their dialogue was a reflection on the foundational nature of common Hebrew wisdom. They entered together into mutual and shared theological reflection around the question of Job's predicament (chap. 1). Third, they entered into the depths of Job's passion and pain, being aware of the intensity of his feelings (2:12-13). The clear detail of this story points to the importance that the reader recognizes the full existential reality of Job's pain, and the group's willingness to enter into reflection about his suffering. In addition, it should be noted that they "met together by agreement" (2:11). They acted on the primal human covenant and developed a small group contract to be available to Job. Finally, they entered into dialogue with one another to seek a solution to Job's dilemma. The main body of the book of Job as wisdom literature is set in poetic dialogue form. For Hebrew people, wisdom was gained through the serious dialogical reflection of adult people of faith. This dialogical setting reflects a historical practice in the faith community to discover the mysteries of God's work in the world through mutual reflection.[4]

On the other hand, Job's small wisdom group (the play on "small wisdom" is intentional) demonstrates the potential shortcomings of intentional group confrontation and insight. In an attempt to be Job's support community the group modeled the inadequacy of wisdom collected through small group process which is not attentive to seeking the face of God. For example, they consistently rejected Job's theological perspective about the nature and purpose of human suffering. Their dialogue was more often a mockery of Job's insights and feelings than a supportive or confrontational discussion (17:2). Also, their seeming mutuality and encouragement soon turned into group intimidation and a power struggle of the majority to manipulate or dominate the individual.

Small groups can enter into a state of "groupthink," that is, where no pattern of thought is tolerated except the dominant group's narrow and self-protected thought. Sometimes a group tries to force an individual to think the thoughts of the majority if he or she is likely to continue to desire to be a member of the group. If the group refuses to listen to a more expansive and wise perspective of an individual in order to maintain the limited order of their penultimate universe, the group has moved into an inverse form of tyranny and authoritarianism. That is, the group is trying to control the individual. This is in contrast to the more typical pattern of the individual trying to control the group. Johnson and Johnson say this about the groupthink syndrome:

> Perhaps the most destructive form of defensive avoidance in group decision making is groupthink . . . a collective striving for unanimity that overrides group members' motivation to realistically appraise alternative courses of action (and thought) and thereby leads to (1) a deteriorization of mental efficiency, reality testing, and moral judgment and (2) the ignoring of external (eternal) information inconsistent with the favored alternative course of action (thought).[5]

In sociopolitical terms, Job's support group was tempted to slide into a fascist dynamic. The group tried to pressure Job into adopting their narrow interpretation of the reason for Job's predicament. They sought to suppress the individual thought, experience and conscience of Job, while trying to preserve their own more limited perspective of how God interrelates with humanity. The group defended its limited theology of righteousness, suffering and vindication while attacking Job's more expansive skeptical and expansive questioning of their existing theological system. Job, in fact, as affirmed by God ("You have not spoken of me what is right, as my servant Job has," Job 42:8), was finally the righteous group member who refused to allow the group to narrow his field of experience or intimidate his expression of the reality of God.

This is key to understanding the important process of wisdom work in the

Hebrew faith community. For the Hebrew, wisdom was God's gift to the community, not just by group process and not by majority vote, but by revelation through an individual who had a face-to-face relationship with God. This wisdom could be shared in the group and affirmed or critiqued in the ongoing dialogue of the group's experience. As Hanson has noted, Job was the wise and prophetic individual in the midst of the group who "rises up in opposition to a facile orthodoxy that would reduce life in human community to a set of rigid doctrines and rules, to be forced on all life's situations regardless of the cost in human pain and anguish."[6] Such is the result of groups who pay too much attention to the orders of community and not enough attention to the nature of community or the nature of the One who is Community.

Only when the small group is willing to submit its penultimate agendas to the primary reality of God will it enter into the ultimate life agenda. The group will then find itself immersed in constant discovery of the mystery and will of God for its individual members and their life together. To maintain such a confrontational and healthy pattern of life, the small group must not be seduced into adopting the thinking, perspective or will of any majority or minority as sufficient to determine the fullness of group or individual life. God's face must shine most brightly in the midst of a faithful group. The constant temptation to eclipse God's mystery and face must be confronted by faithful group members who refuse to be led into the more narrow and darker corridors of "small" group thinking. The story of Job is a wake-up call for a small group to enter into constant dialogue, prayer and reflection, intentionally ridding itself of the seduction to become a "small" world unto itself. In such a smaller world the limited wisdom of the group (or more dominant members of the group) becomes the only insight, advice and counsel its individual members. It is in this small (and often shrinking) world that the phenomenon of groupthink begins to control thought and purpose.

Bonhoeffer called the group who enters into this kind of narrow band thinking the *mass*. He contrasted the "mass" with the "community" by defining the mass as the "structure called into being by external stimuli which rests upon the parallelism of will of several persons" where "the boundary of the personal disappears, the individual ceases to be a person, and is only a part of the *mass*, drawn along with it and led by it. The mass is a unity which is not supported by the differences of persons."[7] The mass is faceless. Groupthink and mass action are an abuse of God's call for humanity to enter into face-to-face and confrontational community. Only in face-to-face relationship and mutuality is the integrity of the individual balanced with the interdependent life of the whole group. If God freely enters into the face-to-face life of a group, how much more is the group also called to enter into such sharing and face-to-face community!

Job fought against the group's desire to sustain a self-developed life and doctrine. His small group was a microcosm of the larger society and religious culture. The greater community of Israel and of the church have been helped and healed because of Job's willingness to confront such small group intimidation. Job's open, questioning perspective and prayer has helped move the people of God into more liberating, joyous and abundant lives together. If the small group had successfully stifled Job, the historical faith community may have had one less reminder that groups can be consumed by their temptation to embrace a narrowing and idolatrous life together in which God is reduced to a set of formulistic principles instead of transcendent face-to-face encounter.

Because Job was the courageous member of the group, and willing to say "no" to groupthink, the whole group—and the larger faith community—was called into confrontation, confession, repentance and new life together (42:7-11). "This [Job's] honest doubt and courageous faith significantly deepened the primal quality of the Yahwistic notion of community."[8] The face-to-face dialogue between God and Job was the core of the group's confrontation. If Job had not opened himself to be confronted by God, there would have been no confrontation of the group's theological values. Such confrontation demands that the faithful individual or subgroup (prophetic agents) be willing to lay down their lives in sharing the wisdom of God with the whole group.

As Peter Block has cautioned, there is a potential "bureaucratic mentality" in every group where "the lines of authority need to be clear and understood" and where it is implied "that we must submit to [this] authority." This "authority relationship must remain unquestioned, and if a person does not submit to authority, [she] is labelled with the ultimate accusation—disloyalty."[9] In such a group this "disloyal" person may need to take a risky initiative of leadership to perform an "act of courage" in confronting the group's narrow perception and limited sources of authority. Block explains what this "act of courage" is:

The conventional belief is that if we stand up we will be shot. Our choice is to move ahead even in the face of the risk we are taking as an act of courage. It requires courage to communicate understanding. . . . If our primary commitment is to contribute, to be of service [to the world], treat people well, and maintain our integrity, then we are doomed to a course of adventure, uncertainty and risk.[10]

Block goes on to say that he sees three specific "acts of courage" needed to nurture ongoing healthy groups: first, facing the harsh reality of the group's real predicament—to see things as they really are; second, facing our personal contribution to the problem of where the group is now, and third, being authentic in the face (faces) of disapproval—willing to speak the truth.[11] It is important to note Block's use of "face" language in describing the action of courageous group confrontation. Block understands the underlying value of healthy face-to-face relationships. While he does not develop this theme from a theological perspective, his behavioral advice for the business community has sound biblical and theological foundations.

In the conflict, confrontation or cooperation of individual wills—God's with members of the group and members of the group with one another—a small group can open and nurture its identity with God and with one another, thus breaking the pattern and power of group sin. Bonhoeffer said, "Community is community of will, built upon the separateness and difference between persons, constituted by reciprocal acts of will, with its unity in what is willed, and counting among its basic laws the inner conflict of individual wills."[12] In Job's case such was demonstrated by the constant barrage of the three to influence and control the individual conscience of the one. "Whereas the primal relationship of man to man is a giving one, in the state of sin it is purely demanding."[13] Faces of real persons in real groups are obscured by the tendency of group members who can only live in relation to a structure or system and fear the freedom of vulnerability in the face of another being.

In the end it was the persistent face and will of God—not the demand of the three nor the questions of Job—upon Job and the three that led the group through its conflict into a new and more mysterious theological perspective and life together. It was Job's determination to live in the face of and to listen to the will of God that was, as Peter Block would say, the "act of courage" that leads to the transformation of the small group and their entrée into a greater experience of God. Block has argued that organizations (groups) are only as strong as the individuals within them are courageous. Someone must confront (face) the group with the truth. Someone must call the group to face God and one another. Someone must say "no" to limiting institutional (groupthink) or systemic ideas and practices which rob the group of God's face. Someone must call the group to pursue a creative and entrepreneurial freedom of will for the benefit of the whole group.[14]

A small group can be a faceless mass of intimidation or a face-to-face community of mutuality. There will always be the temptation for one part of a group to control another. Only when a small group places itself intentionally into the mutual submission of God's face-to-face presence will they be able to live in the ongoing tension of not yielding to such narrowing demands or controls. This means that group leadership must be aware of the temptation to suppress one another's faces and call the group to pursue God's face. Group leadership must live in a state of openness and repentance, yielding to God the ultimate mystery of biblical, personal and strategic lordship. Just as Bonhoeffer discovered in his growing understanding of the relationship between confession and communion, such a face-to-face mutuality in personal submission is a pattern of group inter-action difficult to maintain. Sin constantly drives the face-to-face group toward seeing the penultimate as ultimate, and works to draw the group into self-iso-lating patterns of a more destitute life.[15] Humanity flourishes as we are willing to live openly in the face of God and the faces of one another.

Five Levels of Interpersonal Sharing

Small groups should be instructed in recognizing different levels of face-to-face communication. There may be several ways to categorize such interpersonal encounters, but below you will find one of the more classic taxonomies of inter-personal communication. Every small group should begin to understand how to listen for deeper levels of sharing and when to recognize superficial avoidance patterns. These five levels are adapted from John Powell's *Why Am I Afraid to Tell You Who I Am?*[16]

Level One: Cliché Conversation. This represents the least willingness to share our-selves with others. In fact there is no intentional communication here at all, but conversation that avoids engagement. It is questions and comments that expect no thoughtful response from the other. It is simply a word of recognition that the other person is present. Such words or phrases are often called clichés.

Level Two: Reporting the Facts. This represents a minimal sharing of ourselves— a sharing of objective knowledge. Raw data is being communicated without per-sonal reflection. It is speaking the quantitative truth without any qualitative perspective.

Level Three: Sharing My Ideas and Opinions. This represents giving more of my individual and unique self. I am the only one with these specific ideas or opinions. No one else can give my opinion unless they first hear it from me. This demands more risk-taking on my part, for the other person has the potential to reject my idea or opinion. Such a rejection could have a negative impact on my sense of security or esteem. Another may pass judgment on my idea or opinion. The group may reject me based upon my idea or opinion. Much human communica-tion ends at this level. This is the deepest level to which much education and business goes.

Level Four: Sharing My Feelings, Values or Emotions. These words represent my more personal self. I am now speaking out of a more hidden part of my being. You are seeing the real me peeking out to see if it is safe to be fully human. You are hearing the feelings, values, attitudes and emotions that form the real face and break through the façade. As I speak I have senses alert to how my words are received. I am looking for others' feelings in response to mine. A level three response to a level four question may be a roadblock or a passing of judgment. I am looking for others to return the sharing of feelings. While some may share my opinions, I am the only one who can have my feelings. Values are the deep stuff behind my feelings. I feel because I value some things more than others.

(5)   *Level Five: Confessional Sharing.* This represents peak communication. These are the experiences and feelings I may not ever share with another. These are only spoken in very safe relationships. This may be the stuff I might not even say to myself. These are the fears or hopes I may only share with God. Here are my deep wounds and crimes of my heart. Here is where my childhood damages are hidden or repressed. Here is the stuff I share only when there is a gracious, compassionate and merciful listener facing me. Here is my most intimate self released only when I am in the face of a loving, forgiving, and compassionate person.

■ SMALL GROUP MINISTRY IMPLICATIONS

1. Face-to-face communication implies that small groups need to be arranged in ovals or circles so that each member may see the face of every other member. Rows prevent members from seeing some of the faces of others in the group. Three or more persons on a couch make it tough for the end persons to talk to each other. This makes communication less than personal. The face reveals the person. Other obstructions that may block the view of faces should be removed: furniture, flowers, lamps and so forth. However, it is better to have a comfortable place for all to sit than to become legalistic about the circle. The goal is to pursue a discipline of face-to-face encounters even if there are occasional times when seeing each person's face is not practical.

2. Seeking the face of God in prayer is obviously not as simple as sitting in an oval or a circle. The group may be led to see God's face in many ways: reading Scripture that describes God, Jesus or the church at work; allowing quiet time for the group to reflect upon the nature of God; calling the group to talk about their personal encounters with God; encouraging the group to fantasize about their vision of heaven. For the faithful group the face of God is seen as their spiritual minds are nourished and as their imaginations are disciplined by such intentional spiritual reflection. Every group must allow abundant time for members to talk about God and their face-to-face encounters with God.

3. It is not easy for a small group to encounter God face to face. The levels of personal and relational resistance are powerful. The group must willingly choose to practice face-to-face disciplines of encounter. Confession is a very important entry into the presence of God's face. Most Protestant Christians are

not prepared to practice interpersonal confession in the small group. However, a helpful leader may guide the group into simple and low-risk confessional patterns, such as asking questions like, "What prevents you from having the freedom of talking to God in this group? As you picture God in your mind, what do you see in the face of God that would cause you to be afraid to approach God?"

4. Another way to help the group think about face-to-face relationships is to have them reflect back upon the meeting they just had and share what they remember seeing in one another's faces at different points in the evening. This could be taken one step further to encourage them to share about how their view of God might affect their facial attitudes and expressions. Another version of this would be to ask the group the question, "How would you describe the face of each member of this group, and what might this tell you about the face of God?" However, such a question tends to lead a group toward a more confrontational meeting. Such questions might best be used in groups that have built higher trust relationships over a sustained period.

5. Much of our bias toward how we picture God's face has been influenced by the faces of persons in our lives who have carried great authority for us, like our parents, teachers, bosses or pastors. It may be helpful for the group to take some time to talk about how these influential persons have impacted their vision of the face of God and how their response to God has been formed by our previous relationships with such powerful people.

6

SMALL GROUP
LEADERSHIP

So all the elders of Israel gathered together and came to Samuel at Ramah. They said to him, "You are old, and your sons do not walk in your ways; now appoint a king to lead us, such as all the other nations have."

But when they said, "Give us a king to lead us," this displeased Samuel; so he prayed to the LORD. And the LORD told him: "Listen to all that the people are saying to you; it is not you they have rejected, but they have rejected me as their king. As they have done from the day I brought them up out of Egypt until this day, forsaking me and serving other gods, so they are doing to you. Now listen to them; but warn them solemnly and let them know what the king who will reign over them will do." (1 Sam 8:4-9)

Every group is tempted to appoint a king or allow a king to emerge. Almost every group has members who are tempted to be king and lord. As has been previously suggested human leadership suffers the possibility of being seduced into an abuse of the first and second commandments. The people of God have always had to deal with a pervasive susceptibility of leaders to be deluded into making godlike decisions and taking godlike actions on behalf of the whole group.

Leadership is not *lordship*. Lordship is the holding and exercising of ultimate authority. The etymology of the English word *lord* is "loaf keeper." The lord of the group is the person or system that provides the primary sources of nourishment for the group. It is that which ultimately feeds and sustains the group. Lordship is therefore given the person or system that holds ultimate authority for the group. The Hebrew word most often translated by the word *lord* is *Jehovah*, which means "self-existent" or "eternal."[1] Jehovah is the Being who exists before all things—the Author of all created things. Every group has to ask itself the question, Who or what is lord of our group? Who or what is the author or creator of our group? The biblical answer to this question for the faithful small group is that God has called us together. We are constituted as a covenant community because the God of covenant has brought us together. This covenantal God is our Lord, who holds ultimate authority for the group. Healthy group leadership defers lordship to God and moves the group toward a wider sharing of leadership and dominion because God is the Lord who shares dominion with the humanity of creation.

The human leadership of a group is always sustained within the greater context of that group's assumptions about its source of ultimate authority and lordship. Many religious small groups refuse to face this primary question and refuse to use "lord" or "god" language as if to distance themselves from the responsibility of dealing with this essential foundation. In the mid-1970s, when the songwriter Bob Dylan was courting Christianity as a way of life, he wrote the song, "You Gotta Serve Somebody." Dylan came to understand that every individual and group serves something or somebody. If the small group does not deal with its presuppositions about its sources of authority and power, it will never deal with an important theological foundation about the subordinate nature of any small group leadership. Healthy group leadership therefore must call the group to attend to their primary authority—their primary covenantal relationship with God.

But long-term groups are often tempted to substitute some form of intermediate and controlling leadership to deal with the chaos and stress of working together in ongoing mutuality and community. Groups tend toward giving specific people more ultimate authority than God may wish them to have. This was the case in Israel during the time of the prophet Samuel. The ambiguity, volatility and relativity of tribal group leadership moved the people to hunger for a primary human "loaf-keeper" or "bread-giver" or "lord." Their demand for a group king led to their rejection of the lordship of God. Larger and more complex groups have greater needs to establish such a primary lord, but every small group also wrestles with this temptation.

The Example of Israel
This movement toward a kingship was a gradual and subtle shift in Israel's expectation of primary leadership. The judges, or tribal leaders, tended to play only temporary roles of pervasive leadership when the people were in crisis. Once the crisis was over, the temporary judge went back to his or her own tribe. This

was a dramatic period of *shared* leadership in Israel's history, especially during times of crisis. This was also a dramatic period of *faith* leadership. The person with the unusual faith emerged to lead the people through the crisis. But the people were not satisfied with this transitional and shared leadership and with God as their king. In Judges 8:22-23, when Gideon refused to play the lordly permanent ruler of Israel, the people tried to pull him into the kingly role: "Rule over us— you, your son and your grandson." They hungered for a human lord, a visible king, a godlike leader. And while the earliest king, Saul, had limited power, the later kings were given more and grabbed more absolute power. God was gradually dislocated from Israel's centerstage of leadership. The king became their god on earth through whom God in heaven led. Power shifted from the tabernacle to the palace.

This historic reduction into the one office of king of shared and dynamic human leadership was not God's desire for humanity. It was one more step away from their Creator's authority and continuing call to shared dominion. This temptation toward human idolatry was somewhat held in check by the ongoing presence of the prophets, who confronted the kings with accountability to the will of God. However, the kings were constantly killing the prophets to eliminate this nagging and irritating bias of God to implement a wider responsibility and sharing of group leadership under the lordship of God.[2]

It is not surprising to see that during the period of shared faith leadership depicted in Judges 4—5 Israel was open to the primary leadership of a woman, Deborah. She invited a man, Barak, to share her leadership. During Deborah's leadership a primary honor for a victory was given to another woman, Jael. Yet as Israel moved away from this period of shared leadership, women in primary and positive leadership roles seemed to be lost until New Testament times. When leadership is in touch with God's creation agenda for humanity, there is a consistent movement toward men and women having mutual dominion in the guidance of groups.

This God-ordained vision of leadership-sharing tends to move a faithful and maturing small group from the parental leading of the few to the communal leading of the many. Such is a clear sign that the rule of God is active in the group. This movement of shared leadership is potentially inclusive of all members, especially of both men and women. The fulfillment of the tenth commandment in the faithful group is giving up the need to own or control another man or woman or group. It is an affirmation of the destiny of that man or woman to share his or her God-given identity and giftedness with the immediate group and with the greater world. It is an encouragement of individuals within the group to share their God-given leadership beyond themselves, both within and beyond the group.

The tribal and prophetic communities of the Old Testament seemed to advocate for and function with such a mutually interdependent group model. Hanson has pointed out that the prophetic and priestly visions (the Deuteronomistic vision) of leadership "accepted the existence of kingship," but "the king, like every Israelite, stood under the sole authority of the Horeb covenant" and was not "allowed to encroach on Yahweh's sole sovereignty." This "limited kingship" allowed for the temporary leadership of a charismatic prophet like Moses, but made "the central confession of Yahwehism" the prophetic balance to such visible human authority.[3]

Dialogue during a crisis in the 1980s film *The Emerald Forest* revealed a primal view of empowering tribal leadership. An American tried to convince an Amazon tribal chief to command his men what to do. The chief's response was, "The day I have to tell these men what to do, they will stop being men, and I will stop being chief."

The prophet Isaiah confirmed this need to experience God as leader "among" the community of people, and not just the primary human leader-king, when he declared, "The virgin will be with child and will give birth to a son, and will call him Immanuel [God with us]" (Is 7:14). Every small group needs to come to the real messianic expectation that God is "with" them together, not just in their primary leader. Leadership is a communal action of humanity which reflects the communal leadership nature of God.

So it was that the prophets lived together in small communities where they could nurture this shared understanding of the Spirit of God given to each of them to lead God's community together (note the frequent references to "the company of the prophets" around Elisha in 2 Kings). Theirs was a paradigm of divine leadership and community in constant juxtaposition to the hierarchical model of kingship and palace. The prophetic group always gathers as the check-and-balance community for accountability and critique of the temptation to move toward institutional bureaucracy and kingly centralized control systems.

Fear of Responsibility

The prophetic group understood that authority and power originates with God and not with the kingly acting leader. Yet many small groups will continue to avoid embracing such mutual development of leadership because the group members fear taking responsibility for their personal or group life. In their book *The Paradoxes of Group Life* Kenwyn Smith and David Berg wrestle with this paradoxical phenomenon of how groups embrace or resist various kinds of authority:

Authority is something that is built or created. . . . In a group, members can authorize an individual. . . . The process of authorization creates the conditions in which the individual contributions can have an influence on the work of the group and the group can be influential in the larger system to which it belongs. In this regard, authority is closely linked to empowerment. One develops power as one empowers others. Taking the power that is available and using it often creates a vacuum, because it is experienced as depriving others of a scarce commodity. As a result, power-taking is resisted. Individuals often refuse to accept or exercise the power that is available to them in a group simply to avoid the accusation of having stolen it from someone else or having gained it at another's expense. Yet, the very avoidance of taking and using the available power makes individuals in a group, and ultimately the group as a whole, feel powerless.[4]

Small groups cannot function in a healthy way without the positive exercise of authority and the shared movement of power between people. Authority is the source, and power is the flow of energy through relationships. Leadership is the willingness to plug into the source and share God's energy of life with others. Since every group member is unique and gifted differently, the power of God flows through each one to the group in diverse ways. Every group member has the opportunity and responsibility to allow the power of God to flow through him or her into the group. Resistance to participation in this mutual empowerment blocks essential leadership and direction to the whole group. The gathering of power into one member or the refusal of other members to participate in the flow of power prevents a group from becoming and doing all that God has gifted them to be and do. Such is the paradox of groups who refuse to share power: while the group is starved for power, there is much power to be shared, but there is a general resistance to exercising power and a gnawing feeling of powerlessness.

The Dark Side of Small Group Leadership

The contrast of dark-side and light-side empowerment as connected to controlling or shared leadership was illustrated dramatically in the movie *The Karate Kid*. The contrast in leadership styles between the coaches of the competing karate students was illustrative of contrasting purposes. Leadership which controls also destroys. Leadership which empowers, nurtures life. In the dark-side case the students destroy not only the competition but also one another. The coach was willing to destroy the whole team to gratify his own hunger for control. On the other hand, the light-side coach taught the karate kid the value of respecting the opponent and respecting life. One group leadership style kills; the other gives life. One style controls; the other empowers.

Because a group has minimal vision of the nature of God or confidence that

God can empower each person for some task of leadership, many small groups fail to develop the healthy and maturing practice of shared leadership. In such limiting group situations the authority and power to lead is carefully cloistered into the hands of the group's chosen leader, who is either unwilling to share the power or is unable to help the group take responsibility for exercising their power. This is why Israel wanted a king. This is why small groups often live with little Napoleons. This is why the people of God often fail to grow beyond relational childishness or adolescence and why many Christians do not develop their spiritual giftedness or set out upon lives of compassionate, risk-taking service.

Dark-side leadership comes in many forms. For instance, "shared" leadership is very different from "rotated" small group leadership. Leadership sharing is an intentional empowerment of group members who are able and willing to take initiative in the group. Rotated leadership is often the passing of leadership responsibility to members whether or not they are able and willing. Sharing leadership evokes the brightest and the best the group has to give. Rotating leadership reduces the group to frequent forays into mediocrity.

There is a dark side to shared leadership. The dark side of shared leadership is anarchy. The word *anarchy* literally means "without a leader." In this state individual liberty is prized more highly than any cooperative form of group government. We read in Judges 21:25, "In those days Israel had no king; everyone did as he saw fit." This could have been good news if God had been at the center of the community, but the inference here in the text is that the people were constantly tempted to be centered in themselves or their tribal leaders. Most were not leaders who treasured face-to-face relationship with God, but many were isolating leaders who called groups only to themselves.

Israel's human solution to their chaotic problem of anarchy was to move toward the establishment of tyranny (one absolute and oppressive leader) in the appointment of a king. Both extremes of leadership are movements away from God as the Lord who empowers the people for shared priesthood and leadership. Tyranny and anarchy are both the result of the broken covenant to "love God and love your neighbor." These are the failures of face-to-face relationships with God and people. Israel's community covenant called for God to be Lord, not the many and not the one. Their love was to be expressed in sharing life and leadership in the presence of a common Lord, as the community confessed and affirmed in Deuteronomy 6. The light side of group leadership is always a reflection of the primary shining of God's face in the midst of the people.

Leadership Styles
Small groups go through various stages of life together during which they need

to experience shifting styles of leadership. Paul Hersey and Ken Blanchard have argued that effective groups in various stages and situations need different styles of leadership. However, their four-style definition of healthy situational leadership does not delve into the darker extremes at both ends of their leadership continuum. It is in these divergent extremes of the leadership-style continuum that groups tend toward anarchy or tyranny.[5]

Anarchy and tyranny are abandonments of healthy patterns for a small group on the way to shalom community. In the American culture where the "rugged individualist" is celebrated, even among Christian groups, these two dark-side styles of leadership tend to haunt the shadows of every gathering. Robert Bellah and others, in their sociological analysis entitled *Habits of the Heart: Individualism and Commitment in American Life*, quote Walt Whitman's poetic articulation of this individualistic pursuit of life:

Afoot and light-hearted I take to the open road,

Healthy, free, the world before me,

The long brown path before me, leading where I choose.[6]

The generic American leadership style tends toward the extreme of this rugged individualism—anarchy. Today, in the American culture we are encouraged and affirmed to "do your own thing," even in many small groups. The very gathering and success of a group may become a prophetic action in such an individualistic culture. However, the anarchist who tries to lead a group will most likely use tyranny as an initial style of leadership, for the rugged individualist does not want to do "the group's thing" or "another's thing." Such an individualist would most likely try to control the group with a "personal" agenda rather than help the group to discover "their" agenda together. This is what makes the way of American individualism such a rough road for a small group to travel.

The leadership dark side of such rugged individualism was at work when a small group of entrepreneurial men decided to form a Bible study group. Each man had his own view of what small group Bible study should be. Each week one of the men would try to lead the Bible study with his own unique style and bias. Each week the group ended in frustration and tension. They could not find one style compatible to all. Each had learned "small group Bible study" in a different school of discipleship. Each was sure his was the best way to do it. Each was suspicious that the others were out of tune with God's will for their group. For many months the group struggled with establishing a mutually acceptable pattern of study, but it was not until one of the group "declared control" that the group settled into one pattern. However, as a result of this "takeover" half of the men in the group left. Some of the rugged individualists could hang in there as long as their personal agenda had some influence. The "self-proclaimed" leader could stay only if his agenda was "enforced." This group moved from one dark-side form of leadership to another, from anarchy to tyranny. But there is a better and more positive pattern for small group leadership.

The primary value of group leadership is that God calls members to share power, leadership and dominion in the group. This kind of leadership and empowerment is a gradual and sustained process. Centralized human control or the absence of common direction can only corrupt the group which is so errantly led.

In *Seven Myths About Small Groups*, Dan Williams dispels the misconceptions of two dark-side leadership patterns. Groups suffer when one leader becomes too demanding, and groups also suffer when no one takes initiative or responsibility to lead. His solution is that every group member needs to take responsibility to lead in the way God has gifted and matured each. One member of the group may take responsibility to "coordinate" the whole group into a pattern of mutually helpful leadership. Williams defines leadership as "exercising one's gift to produce an effect on others." He suggests that a small group develop "progressive leadership," which is having every member "develop in their expressions of leadership during the life span of the group." Williams's view of good group leadership is built upon solid biblical foundations.[7]

Developing the concept of *situational leadership*, Hersey and Blanchard point out that this does not erase the occasional need for a more autocratic leadership style during a crisis or period of group immaturity. Occasionally, a brief period of autocracy may be an appropriate leadership style. But such short-term leadership intervention should always be exercised with the intent of calling the group back to God and into the mutual care of one another. The apostle Paul asserted that the Law could be viewed as an autocratic pedagogical style of God's leadership for humanity which anticipated the coming of Christ to be every group's suffering Servant and their living Law (Gal 3).[8] Leadership by law of a group must blossom into a divine leadership where God is embraced as the loving Lord who leads the group into the shared dominion of their life together.

The Bright Side of Small Group Leadership

Once Joseph had a dream, and when he told it to his brother, they hated him even more. He said to them, "Listen to this dream that I dreamed. There we were, binding sheaves in the field. Suddenly my sheaf rose and stood upright; then your sheaves gathered around it, and bowed down to my sheaf." His brothers said to him, "Are you indeed to reign over us? Are you indeed to have dominion over us?" So they hated him even more because of his dreams and his words.

Joseph could no longer control himself before all those who stood by him, and he cried out, "Send everyone away from me." So no one stayed with him when Joseph made himself known to his brothers. And he wept so loudly that the Egyptians heard it , and the household of Pharaoh heard it. Joseph said to his brothers, "I am Joseph. Is my father still alive?" But his brothers could not answer him, so dismayed were they at his presence. Then Joseph said to his brothers, "Come closer to me." And they came closer. He said, "I am your brother, Joseph, whom you sold into Egypt. And now do not be distressed, or angry with yourselves, because you sold me here; for God sent me before you to preserve life." (Gen 37:5-8; 45:1-5 NRSV)

Leadership is about having a dream; it is about being open to the dream God has given an individual or group. Leadership is about having a strong sense of direction; it is about the desire to help others go in the direction that will be most beneficial for them. It is about enduring the flak from others when they are not happy with this sense of direction. Leadership is about being led by God through tough times and leading others through stressful situations. Leadership is about settling quarrels, helping others to change and being a good model to show others a better way.

Small group leadership is about becoming the whole person God wants each person to be. It is about becoming vulnerable to help others become more open, to help others change for the better, to hold others in the group accountable to improve their lives and lifestyles. Small group leadership is about the freedom to show emotion and share feelings; it is about drawing close to others in the group. Small group leadership is about developing and nurturing the freedom to see, touch and embrace. Small group leadership is about helping the group resolve their conflicts. It is about calling the group back into covenant relationship with God. Small group leadership is about building a stronger sense of family in the midst of broken relationships. It is about giving up control and about giving away resources. Small group leadership is about creating a home for others, empowering others to live their own lives, and equipping them to go away and help others.

As an Old Testament model, Joseph's relationship with his eleven brothers can be viewed as a paradigm for small group leadership and process. In the Genesis narrative, Joseph is introduced as a young leader with a vision among the small group of twelve brothers. The rest of the group staunchly rejected Joseph's vision for their future together. In spite of many adversities and setbacks, Joseph's faithful relationship with God empowered him to experience the vision of leadership that not only led the brothers' group out of famine, but led much of the known world. Joseph demonstrates how positive group leadership can help influence and transform a hostile and dysfunctional small group as well as empower a person to lead others beyond their immediate group. Even though the brother's group tried to reject Joseph's leadership, God empowered Joseph to help the group in spite of themselves.

Good group leaders are God-centered and group-empowering. As we read in Genesis 45, Joseph, of all Israel's leaders, stood out as one who struggled against the seductiveness of abusive masculine power. He refused to allow his natural talents to be used to take advantage of those around him. His faithful choices in relationship with God, even in the midst of a series of negative events, prepared him to regain and lead his family group. He learned to lead without the need to manipulate or control. He led groups with a strong sense of the present and active character of God. Grace, mercy, love and compassion were the result of God's guidance. Joseph allowed his personal desires to be formed by God's presence and character. He used the power given him for the care and growth of people. His personal experience of deliverance moved him to lead Egypt into the compassionate intervention of famine for several other groups of people.

But the key movement in the biblical narrative about Joseph had to do with his relationship with his eleven brothers and the impact this relationship had on the faith of his father, Jacob. Even though Joseph became leader of a great nation, the biblical story begins and ends around the theme of Jacob's faith, and how his small group of twelve sons was led into reconciliation and redemption. Joseph is clearly called by God to lead the whole family group into a deeper faith experience. Not until the family group (the twelve sons) was reconciled and rejoined did Jacob return to Beersheba, the place of his father Isaac's encounter with God (Gen 26:23-25), where he "offered sacrifices to the God of his father Isaac" (Gen 46:1). Joseph is the one who brought the family back together and helped restore his father's faith in God. From the early days of the deception of his father-in-law, Laban (Gen 29:25), Jacob's two wives, Leah and Rachel, had been in competition for Jacob's love (Gen 30:1-24), and their sons had carried on the family feud. This small group and dysfunctional family system was led into wholeness through the faithful model and leadership of Joseph.

The theological meaning of leadership is formed out of the very character of God. We see in Genesis 1 that God's nature is to create humanity to take responsibility for creation and share dominion with men and women. God's ultimate style of leadership is the empowerment and delegation of leadership to humanity. Scripture is the salvation history of God's desire to redeem humanity and give us the power and authority for which we were created. The Spirit of God at work in human groups is an empowering Spirit, a delegating Spirit, and a Spirit for the nurturing of shared and mutual ministry. This Spirit seeks to bring growing leadership to the faithful small group. As Mary, the mother of Jesus, understood in such an intimate way, it is the very nature of God to bring down tyrants from their thrones and empower the humble (to paraphrase Lk 1:52). When God gathers people into groups, there is no Spirit of tyranny or authoritarian control—there is only the Spirit who nurtures mutual leadership and the priestly gifts of all.

Such God-centered leadership, which gives away power and shares dominion, is an outpouring of love. The act of a leader who shares power is an act of love that will be imitated through expanding concentric circles of influence, rippling out from the originating small group. Moses' discovery, at the advice of Jethro, of sharing leadership with a few carefully chosen people (Ex 18) was another step in the continued outpouring of God's love to all nations through the creation of a "nation of priests" (Ex 19:6). Godly acts of sharing power breed wider acts of shared power. Healthy leadership in small groups forges the basis of healthier leadership in larger groups.

Leadership gives vision, direction, guidance, knowledge, wisdom and accountability to a small group. Leadership gathers the isolated and disconnected, and helps them to focus upon the core values of life. Moreover, leadership calls the group into face-to-face relationship with God. Leadership holds the group accountable to its covenantal life. It helps the group remember its faith history and celebrate its life together. Leadership provides a model for the group to imitate as it learns the disciplines of healthy community. Leadership nurtures more leadership. It understands when to intervene and knows when to let go.

During the sixties and seventies in many churches it was fashionable to say, "Small groups don't have leaders but facilitators or coordinators." This was usually argued in reaction to an industrial age pattern of dogmatic, manipulative or task-driven leaders who might grab hold of an unsuspecting group and drive it into the ground. However, by the 1980s, it became increasingly apparent that leaderless groups were going in circles, but there was no leadership to declare the problem or point the way. Many small groups would rather wander than allow someone to take the initiative and give direction. Many facilitated groups were directionless groups. The nondirective approach to psychotherapy had robbed faith groups of direction and discipline. In the nineties it is important that healthy groups have both facilitative and directive leadership.

A leader is responsible to call a small group to practice and experience mutual honor and dignity. The leader calls a group to responsibility for learning the art of giving as much honor to each member as they may give their leader. In giving away power and sharing leadership, the leader affirms God's nature and view of the dignity and giftedness of every member. The directive leader calls the group to live according to God's creative will and purpose. The leader affirms that God wants every person to discover and grow into the role of priest to God, to one another, to others outside of the group and to all of creation. This should be the vision and purpose of any faithful small group leader. Facilitative leadership helps the group build its relational intracommunity, but directive leadership gives the group a sense of vision, mission, purpose and destiny.

■ SMALL GROUP MINISTRY IMPLICATIONS

1. Every small group needs leadership. The concept of "leaderless groups" is not valid. This does not mean that groups need only one dominant leader. This means that a good group needs good leadership, whether from one or from all. A vast heresy at large in the church today suggests that groups do not need leaders. This attitude came about as an apologetic response to authoritarian pastoral and lay leadership. The pendulum swing to no group leadership at all has been an overreaction to the problem. Thousands of Christian small groups were begun in the 1950s, 1960s, 1970s and 1980s without a clear concept of leadership. As a consequence, many continuing groups have no sense of direction. Many people have dropped out of such groups because they were dead ends. This practice of leaderless groups must be changed in this decade if small group ministry is to deal helpfully with the chaos and brokenness of human life. Where there is significant human depravity, a well-led faithful group can emerge from the ashes and show people how to follow Christ into a disciplined lifestyle.

2. The development of intentional small group leaders is crucial for the nurture of successful groups. Leadership development must include key small group skill development, group-dynamics awareness, the development of spiritual disciplines, situational-leadership frameworks, biblical foundations for leadership and the modeling guidance of a leader-mentor who demonstrates positive leadership practices.

3. Leadership is not learned through a book; it is learned through practice. The best small group leadership curriculum will never replace the woman or man who can lead by modeling and coaching. Small group leadership is caught, not taught. Learning to lead a group is a process of discipleship. Learning to exercise specific leadership gifts comes through experience, trial, error, correction and continuing practice.

4. Small group leadership generally is only as strong as its primary models and coaches. Therefore the church must be willing to seek out, train, empower and appoint to leadership key men and women who are gifted by God to lead the church into strong small group ministry. Small groups will never grow into their full God-gifted potential unless there are key church leaders who intentionally

empower other good small group leaders.

5. Good small group leaders must be taught the bright side and dark side of group leadership. Leaders need to be able to recognize the temptations and seductions of misdirected group power. Groups need to be coached to recognize patterns of tyranny or anarchy, resistance or control. Leaders need to have access to resources that will help them to deal with their own dark sides as well as help them to move groups out of negative behaviors. Leaders need to be able to recognize and admit their own tendencies toward dysfunctionality.

7

SMALL GROUP STRUCTURES

Moses sat as judge for the people, while the people stood around him from morning until evening. . . . Moses' father-in-law said to him, "What you are doing is not good. You will surely wear yourself out, both you and these people with you. For the task is too heavy for you; you cannot do it alone. Now listen to me. I will give you counsel, and God be with you! You should represent the people before God, and you should bring their cases before God; teach them the statute and instructions and make known to them the way they are to go and the things they are to do. You should also look for able men among all the people, men who fear God, are trustworthy, and hate dishonest gain; set such men over them as officers over thousands, hundreds, fifties and tens. Let them sit as judges for the people at all times; let them bring every important case to you, but decide every minor case themselves. So it will be easier for you, and they will bear the burden with you. If you do this, and God so commands you, then you will be able to endure, and all these people will go to their home in peace." (Ex 8:13, 17-23 NRSV)

As Moses and the people of God discovered during their exodus journey from Egypt to the Promised Land, leadership development and decentralized structuring are crucial to a community being rehumanized by the presence of God in their midst. The Exodus 18 intervention of the outside consultant/priest of Midian, Jethro, moved Moses to understand God's desire for this new nation of people. God had no interest in setting up a modified Egyptian governmental structure in Canaan. God wanted to implant a community of priests in the land of Abraham, Isaac and Jacob. To set this transformation into motion, God helped Moses set up new community-building disciplines and select community-empowering leaders to share in the initiation of the new community.

Leadership Development

Moses, as the primary redemptive leader, had to come to grips with the need to guide the people of God out from under their "kingly" expectations of leadership and into a new understanding of their "priestly" calling into mutual leadership and ministry. The people who had been born under the hand of Pharaoh had to be reborn and led to embrace the hand of Yahweh. An irony of this historical and pedagogical exodus was that Pharaoh would not allow the people to ascend to his exaltation, but God came down to be among the people, to meet them face to face. In order to accomplish this political decentralization and religious transformation, Moses had to create a structure of discipline that would continue to nurture face-to-face community and empower the motley nation of slaves to become leader-priests for one another.

Moses, however, grew up in the house of Pharaoh and suffered from the pharaonic complex of making the people dependent upon his own power and authority. Thus, he had to experience a personal transformation as a leader before he could lead the people into God's way of a more humanized community. The exodus was also about God's desire to purge Moses of the ghosts of Pharaoh's house and family system. For where there is no leader who envisions and models the way into God's promised land and community, there is no true spiritual exodus, only a continued wandering in the wilderness in frustration, loss and memories of a supposedly safe city.

The development of a healthy small group ministry structure has to do with the careful appointment and placement of key leadership. But as suggested in the last chapter, the leadership of a community is often tempted to keep authority and power centralized and centered in themselves. Moses, during the exodus, was haunted by this temptation. He often led as though the people needed only him as their leader. Not only was this an impossible role for one person to play, it was an inappropriate role, considering the call of God for the transformation and growth of this community. God had to confront Moses with the truth and action of divine character. God had to show Moses that Pharaoh's attempt to reach heaven looked much weaker than God's successful coming down to earth. While Pharaoh's leadership style was control and oppression, God's leadership style was empowerment. God would first empower Moses. And then God would help Moses empower the people.

In calling Moses to lead Israel out of Egypt, God's commitment to him was to make Moses "like God to Pharaoh" (Ex 7:1). The God who exists as Being in Community would "teach" Moses "what to say" (Ex 4:12) and what to do. When Pharaoh saw Moses, it would be as if he was looking directly into the face of God. Therefore, as God's incarnate ambassador, Moses could not play the autocratic sword-to-sword role in the presence of Pharaoh's tyranny, but instead, "cried out to the LORD" on Pharaoh's behalf (Ex 8:8-15). In so doing Moses demonstrated the kind of leadership God wanted him to display as model priest among the people in the wilderness. Pharaoh was the first leader to be shown God's full empowerment character in action, but he was too hardened to "let the people go" or to be transformed by what he saw of this God who empowers rather than controls. The more hardened Pharaoh became, the more gracious and merciful God acted. Even the "plagues" were graciously intervened in attempts to soften Pharaoh's controlling behavior and attitude.

The character of God builds new leaders who, in response, help the building of community-nurturing structures for the people of God. The leadership and structure of such a community must be formed out of the very nature of God in order to lead the people of God into building healthy face-to-face community. The priestly character of God made Moses to be a priest for Pharaoh and a priest for the people who were called to become a "kingdom of priests and a holy nation" (Ex 19:6). The wilderness journey was to be a wild retreat into leadership, courage and priesthood—a pilgrimage into full human community.

Jim and Carol Plueddemann develop this theme of pilgrimage and transformation through small groups in their book *Pilgrims in Progress: Growing Through Groups.* In reflecting upon the exodus experience they say:

> The Old Testament shows God at work in family groupings and other forms of small groups to accomplish his covenant purposes. When God delivered his chosen people from the slavery of Egypt, he could have taken them directly to the promised land. The distance from Egypt to Palestine was shorter than the miles from Philadelphia to New York, but God's purposes included far more than getting from one place to another. Taking the people out of Egypt was much easier than taking Egypt out of the people. And so a journey that could have been completed in a week of comfortable travel became a forty year pilgrimage.[1]

In order for such a massive transformation of human values and community to happen, Moses not only had to be the right kind of leader, but he had to be able to empower a whole new generation of leaders out of a motley group of people who had been slaves for four hundred years. The larger community had to be subdivided and had to nurture several new circles of community and leadership. This whole new structure had to focus upon the primary leadership and lordship of God. As Werner Jeanrond has said, "Leadership is a function of the Christian community and not a status over against it."[2] Leaders are called by God in the midst of the very community they lead. God calls primary and initiating leaders as servant leaders to empower expanding circles of leadership for the growing community. God appointed specific leaders to call forth the leadership gifts of all the people.

The key to the development of larger small group ministry structures is the careful discernment, selection, training, empowerment and support of leaders who will lead small groups with this same servant leadership character. Larger small group ministry structures are only possible if multiple layers or concentric circles of leadership are set into place, nurtured and empowered.

As we saw in an earlier chapter, in the faith community the ultimate leader is God, who exists as divine community. Even God does not hold all self-authority and self-power in one person. The power of God is ministered through multiple persons in the divine community. God's personal leadership profile is multiple leadership. The "I AM WHO I AM" is also a "WE ARE WHO WE ARE." Just as God leads from the midst of community, so God calls humanity to lead as leadership community for community—in teams, bands, squads or circles.

Moses, however, continued to be tempted to act as a Pharaoh-like god for the people of Israel. In Numbers 20:1-13, we read that the lack of water for the community at Kadesh led to much irritation and quarreling. Moses, trying to lift himself above the frustrations of the moment, did not act as their servant leader from God, pointing the people toward God as the source of the water (power). In striking the rock, Moses acted like Pharaoh, taking the place of God in the eyes of the people, acting as both source and judge. The striking of the rock called attention to Moses as if he were the source of his own authority. He took authority into his own hands just as Pharaoh would have done—and just as he had done in killing the Egyptian (Ex 2:11-14). As before, he became angry and abusive. He had learned well his control and abuse lessons while living in Pharaoh's house. But he had not yet fully learned "to be like God" for the people. This was a consistent and fatal flaw in the character of Moses. He was always tempted to become godlike (pharaohlike) before the people, rather than step aside and allow God to receive the primary attention as ultimate authority. The striking of the rock was such a drastic relapse into old behavior patterns, and such a visible misuse of power, that God would not permit Moses or Aaron to lead the people into the Promised Land. Aaron was coleader and copriest and, as such, was just as responsible to hold Moses accountable to model the character of God before the people. But Aaron's more codependent and slavelike passive support often contributed to the chronic return of Moses' pharaonic complex. They were not the leaders to nurture a nation of leader-priests in the midst of pagan abuses and feudal tribes.

Moses discovered that God wanted a human counterpart, an incarnate example. He discovered that God wanted to share the very intimate reality of divinity with him. God wanted Moses to be like God as one who helps other leaders become nurturers of healthy human community. God needed Moses to be the leader-priest who would empower other leader-priests. God as divine community would work through multiple human leaders in the midst of the community. Moses discovered that dependency upon one leader tends to move the whole community into demagoguery, the idolatry of human gods. The way of leadership in the presence of God is shared leadership. This is God's way and style of leadership. God desires to share authority and power with humanity so that humanity may share authority and power with one another.

The overarching temptation of humanity from the beginning was to "be like God, knowing good and evil" (Gen 3:5). Leadership is easily seduced into the lies: "Everybody needs me." "I must be here to judge right and wrong for everyone else." "I must be the center of this group." "This group can't survive without me." The community is easily seduced into the lie that "no one else can meet our needs." However, God calls larger communities to nurture communities of leaders who share leadership. Because God is an empowering God, community leadership is empowered through multiple expertise, multiple perspectives and multiple giftedness. God desires to lead the community through the gifts, skills and insights of many persons. God will not tolerate one pharaohlike person assuming all authority and power for the community. God promotes the exaltation of the powerless and the deprecation of the powerful.

The responsibility of *primary* leadership then is to identify, appoint and train other leaders for the community, as well as to establish disciplined structures in which such localized leadership can act. The primary leader's role is to work off center stage, to invite others to meet with God face to face, to train others to lead in the nature and way of God, to coach others to do God's will on the wilderness trail, to share the authority of God and to share the power of God. This is the call of the empowering leader—to be a leader for leaders, a leader of leaders and a leader of a leadership community who will then be empowered to lead all nations and peoples into the presence of the God who shares power with the meek and humble.

Moses' father-in-law, Jethro, "the priest of Midian," was God's coach sent to help Moses devise a structure of ministry and leadership development strategy that would reflect the character and nature of God. This new leadership framework would not look or act like Pharaoh's Egypt. In Exodus 18, Jethro's advice is for Moses to share the leadership load. If Moses could let go of the need to sit and serve as judge (leader) for all the people, others could share the leadership, and God could be seen as ultimate leader of the people instead of Moses. Moses could reflect the true nature of God who was not like Pharaoh. As a servant with the spirit of community, he could build a servant community. Moses' responsibility was to call the people to depend upon God. God would supply the authority and wisdom to empower multiple circles of leaders. Moses' leadership was to lead the people to God and teach the other appointed leaders to be dependent upon God and interdependent with one another.

Jethro's was a strategy and structure for the decentralization of power. In the decentralization of the community Moses put leaders in charge of smaller groups of people, created multiple layers of leadership, and recognized multiple circles of community. The larger community had to begin to function as several smaller groups together. The ongoing success of the larger community was dependent upon the increasing responsibility of these smaller groups to take charge of their own lives together before God. Jethro called for the leadership to be decentralized, multiplied and shared. The authority of God had to be shared. The responsibility to God for developing lives of integrity had to be widened and deepened. More people had to take ownership for the effectiveness and success of the community. God is the Lord who enables more and more of the people to exercise their gifts in leadership of the whole community. Such a structure of empowerment is reflective of the very nature of God.

Who then was Moses? What kind of leadership was Moses called to exercise? He was to be a leader in the midst of the leadership community of God. He was to decrease in power and visibility as other leaders increased in power and number. God desired the liberation and leadership of all the people. God had called a nation of slaves out of tyranny and into responsibility. God did not call them to exchange their codependency with Pharaoh for a codependency with Moses. The movement of exodus is not just a geographical movement, but a spiritual and psychological movement and a leadership empowerment movement. In this new community God was to be the Lord, the Source and Authority who existed as community and would share power and leadership with all the people.

In Exodus 19:3-6, we see that Israel was not called out of the presence and the tyranny of Pharaoh to be placed into the tyranny of Moses or some other king. Israel was called out from under the oppression of Pharaoh to become a nation of leaders, a "kingdom of priests," who were to share all good things together as the leadership community of God. God would empower them as a nation of priests to mediate the liberating shalom of God to one another and to all other peoples of the world.

The Structuring of Small Group Ministry

God's procedures for building structures for human community are in encircling, scattering, decentralizing and personalizing. The structures of humanmade culture are biased toward the pyramidal, centralized and impersonal. God builds face-to-face communities of human beings. Humanity builds cities and systems where the drive for productivity may ultimately rob people of their God-intended humanity. The structuring of small group ministry is about being sensitive to God's generic way of building human community.

As we move toward A.D. 2000, the turn of the millennium finds human culture and the people of God at a unique crossroads. Some would call this period an era of "paradigm shift" or "power shift." "Old patterns of power are fracturing along strange new lines. . . . This power shift does not merely transfer power. It transforms it."[3] Certain international megatrends destine this to be a period in which small group structures should prosper and grow. Alvin Toffler argues that the future in business and industry is in the development of "flex-firms," because "there is mounting evidence that giant firms, backbone of the smokestack economy, are too slow and maladaptive for today's highspeed business world."[4] These "flex-firms" are made of networks of small groups, whether families or hundreds of quality circles. Peter Drucker has commented that organizations are becoming "information-based," where "knowledge is specialized," "communication must be sophisticated," "people will have to control themselves," and "cross-functional teams are the key."[5] John Naisbitt has affirmed the megatrends of the industrial society becoming an informational society, centralized systems becoming more decentralized, institutional help giving way to self-help, representative democracies becoming participative democracies, hierarchies shifting to networks, and monolithic standards blooming into multiple options.[6] Rosabeth Moss Kanter has asserted that "task forces, quality circles, problem-solving groups or shared-responsibility teams" are "vehicles for greater participation at all levels," and are "an important part of an innovative company."[7]

Small group structures meet every one of these contemporary trends, shifts, swings, changes and demands. Small groups are flexible environments. And networks of groups create a climate for flexibility and rapid change. Small groups are spaces where people can offer help and support to one another. They can bring people together from various management levels and give them a place to understand one another. Small groups are great spaces for the focused exchange of key information and reflection for insight and meaning. They are good spaces to encourage creativity and innovation. Multiple small groups can easily network together. Small groups can provide a multioptional base to the various kinds of ministry and service an organization may wish to explore. Small groups are wonderful environments to empower persons who ordinarily have little power in a large organization. A larger organization networked through small groups can experience rapid metamorphosis (form change).

For all of these cultural and biblical reasons, the church of the twenty-first century needs to become a small group ministry network. Loren Mead, an Episcopal priest, church consultant and founder-president of the Alban Institute, sees a future where "the front door of the church is a door into mission territory," where there is a return to a more apostolic age style, where "the congregation has forever separated from the parish," where "there is a real ministry of the laity," and where the seventeen-hundred-year-old paradigm of institutional Christendom does not block the freedom of people to enter into community and ministry.[8]

Carl George, director of the Charles E. Fuller Institute of Evangelism and Church Growth, has carefully articulated the importance of small group ministry for the future church in his book *Prepare Your Church for the Future*, an introduction to the meta-church model. George identifies eight needs for the future church, which are best met through small group ministry structures: (1) the hunger for a personal touch, (2) the continual need for new options, (3) the need to have a place to interpret what's happening in the world, (4) a structure to help the church deal with rapid change, (5) a place for both women and men to lead in ministry, (6) a way to motivate every member in faith and ministry, (7) an organizational structure where people matter, and (8) a way for every member to receive personal care.[9]

As Jethro understood and Moses discovered, small groups provide access to hands-on ministry, study, mission, prayer and discipleship. In many ways, the coming paradigm of the church, as both Mead and George have discerned, will look much like the early apostolic church—networks of millions of small groups confederated into various- sized, structured and purposed organizations. As will be seen in part three of this book, the nature of the apostolic church was "wherever two or three could gather in the name of Jesus."

Paul Yonggi Cho has explained that we can view small groups as cells[10] of the larger bodies of God's people. Small groups are not the full and final word on the structure of complex human community. Small groups usually exist as parts of larger organisms of human community. Therefore, small groups are usually gathered together within some larger framework, network, structure or organization. The cells' relationship to the larger structure is usually developed in two directions: a larger body subdivided into smaller units, or smaller units joined together into a larger body. The key structural principles in building small group ministry structures are (1) leadership development, (2) the processes of empowerment, (3) the development of clear purposes for the group and (4) the administrative support structure.

Carl George's "meta-church" structure is an extrapolation from the Old Testament narrative of Jethro's advice to Moses (Ex 18). George names the new ministry model "meta" (change) because it demands "a change of mind" as well as "a change of form."[11] Like the Jethro structure, the meta model includes several distinct elements: (1) home-based small groups, (2) lay pastors who lead these home groups, (3) leadership gathering of lay pastors to be trained and led by the senior pastor, and (4) a large celebration gathering of all members of the church. The gathering of most of the members into various kinds of small groups makes the structure very adaptable to change; for as each new group is formed, it can be oriented according to the unique needs of those gathered into the group. Over a period of years, the metamorphosis of a church would occur through the creation of many new kinds of cells. The ethos of "the body" can gradually change. Such a cell system allows the whole body to grow as large or small as God so desires.

In George's meta model, Jethro's leadership prescriptives are followed in detail: leadership is layered to minister in concentric circles of groups and teams; the first layer contains small groups of ten with a leader; the next level is lay coaches who each train five leaders and oversee their five groups of ten; the third level are pastors who empower and oversee up to ten coaches. Each level of leadership selects and mentors an apprentice leader who learns the ministry through on-the-job training. The structure reflects the consultation of Jethro and the implementation of Moses: "He chose capable persons from all Israel and made them leaders of the people, officials over thousands, hundreds, fifties and tens. They served as judges for the people at all times. The difficult cases they brought to Moses, but the simple ones they decided themselves" (Ex 18:25-26).

It is important to discern the differences here between Jethro's model and setting up a hierarchy of management or a ranking militarylike system. Jethro encouraged Moses to localize the leadership with the people. He encouraged Moses to empower as many leaders as necessary so that no leader related to more than ten persons (family groups) at a time. It should be remembered that this structural consultation with Jethro occurred just before God told Moses to say to all Israel, "Now if you obey me fully and keep my covenant, then out of all nations you will be my treasured possession. Although the whole earth is mine, you will be for me a kingdom of priests and a holy nation" (Ex 19:5-6). Moses, like Jethro, was called to develop a network of priestlike leaders and groups so the people would care for one another. God would be their king-priest and Moses would be their chief priest.

The Sin of the Pyramid and Tower
Humanity has always been tempted to build pyramids and towers of power. From

a human perspective, the larger the pyramid, the greater the power. God's pattern for empowerment of humanity is not in the building of hierarchical power structures but in the gathering of priestly circles of face-to-face communities. In the pyramid everything supports and points to the top. In the circle everyone faces each other. The pyramid suggests that humanity may lift itself into heaven. The circle suggests that God must come down to earth. In the pyramid only one person at a time can be on the top. In the circle everyone is included as egalitarian members of the community. Such has been the provocative tension in the human search for God, authority and power since the beginning of time. How leaders use power builds or destroys human community. Much human activity is built on the misuse of power. Small groups are to be circles of mutual priesthood, where power is shared and care is reciprocated as every member of the group defers allegiance to God in their midst. Each person turns to a neighbor to administer the grace, mercy, peace and love of God. These are the circles in which there is only one law of love to practice, "love your neighbor as yourself" (Lev 19:18). This command in Leviticus is followed by the covenant affirmation that such a way of community is only found in the presence of Yahweh, the divine community who agrees, "I am the LORD."

In the first eleven chapters of Genesis, the human drive to build cities gushes out of Abel's murder and Cain's woundedness and culminates in the event of Babel (Gen 11:1-9). Cain's defensive avoidance in running away from the face of God (and the face of his dead brother) leads to the building of great cultures and powerful cities (Gen 4:17-22). Ham's broken relationship with Noah is also worked out through the building of great cities through the descendency of Cush and Nimrod (Gen 10:6-20). Many of these great cities were located on the plain of Shinar (Babylon). On this plain the people decided, "Come, let us build ourselves a city, with a tower that reaches to the heavens, so that we may make a name for ourselves and not be scattered over the face of the whole earth" (Gen 11:4). However, such a drive to reach heaven and rule with the gods was not what God desired for humanity: "But the LORD came down to see the city and the tower that the men were building" and said, " 'If as one people speaking the same language they have begun to do this, then nothing they plan to do will be impossible for them. Come, let us go down and confuse their language. . . .' So the LORD scattered them from there over all the earth, and they stopped building the city" (11:5-8). Clearly, God's intent for humanity was not to build self-serving cities with towers attempting to reach into heaven. From a biblical perspective the building of towering structures are human attempts at becoming more like God, of humanity trying to reach the realm where God inhabits and rules, of trying to become like God and trying to take God's place.

In the Babel narrative, it is very important to note that God "goes down" and "scatters." (It is also interesting to note the use of Genesis 1 language about God's plural identity, "let us go down.") While broken humanity tries to "build" structures to be like God, God is working to "scatter" (decentralize human power) them over the earth. While broken humanity is trying to "reach up" to heaven, God is "coming down" to earth.

The structures of human ingenuity often try to lift humanity up into heaven. But the structures of God are ways to help humanity face God on earth. Small groups are the scattering vehicle of a loving God. Monolithic and towering structures are the arrogant and egocentric pursuit of humanity. It's tough to be human in a highly structured, hierarchical and controlled system where the prime leaders of the culture are trying to be like gods. It is the nature of God to come down to face humanity and affirm the wonderful fullness of human community made complete by the presence of God on earth. This is why God ultimately makes the face-to-face small group circle of persons more important and powerful than all the superstructures of human ingenuity. From God's perspective there can be more real and healing power in a small group of humanity than in any of the great superstructures of human culture.

This is the trouble that Israel confronted in Egypt. The civilization of Egypt was also built by a descendant of the shame-based family of Ham (Gen 10:6).[12] Egypt enslaved Israel to build cities for Pharaoh (Ex 1:11-14). "But the more they were oppressed, the more they multiplied and spread; so the Egyptians came to dread the Israelites." While the scattered groups of Israel "multiplied and spread," Egypt tried to develop more and more control systems to bind them into restricted structures, to force them to yield to the power of Pharaoh's pyramids. The pinnacle structures of Pharaoh's Egypt were the great crypt-pyramids, the burial cities of the kings:

> The great cemeteries at Giza, laid out around the pyramid of Khufu, reflect vividly the way everything circulated around the king. . . . All the evidence suggests that it was in Khufu's reign that Egypt was most strictly centralized. The king . . . was Egypt; everyone else was subservient; everything planned was for the glory of the king; everything completely reflected this glory. The Great Pyramid is in every way the embodiment of this autocratic idea. It also offers the complete demonstration of what can be done when all resources are controlled by one man and directed solely for his purposes.[13]

While the exact time of Israel's enslavement is not known, the cultural suppositions about Egypt's centralized government and the symbolism of the power of the pyramid are universal in contrast to the biblical description of God's desire for human community. The exodus from enslavement in Egypt and the journey into the wilderness was to be a rehumanizing experience for God's people to bring them back into face-to-face relationship with God. For God came down to earth on Mount Horeb to establish a face-to-face community among the people of God. The exodus was also to be a liberation from the stifling and heavy structures of Egypt, to help the people come out from under the oppression of the weight and power of the pyramid, which was built on their backs as an enslaved people.

Such great Egyptian energy and ingenuity was invested in preparing for death—the death of one powerful man. God's great community-building structures are disciplines to be practiced for eternal life. The exodus, the Law, the multiple layers of leadership, the new groupings of people—all are community-building structures for life. Small group ministry structures must be community-building disciplines for the nurture of healthy human life, not the oppressive control systems for the protection of primary leaders.

■ SMALL GROUP MINISTRY IMPLICATIONS

1. Small group and relational ministry consultants are growing in numbers. Like Jethro, many of these individuals have emerged as advisory priest-leaders who know how to help organizations or motley groupings build disciplined structures into their ministry contexts. The key to good consultation is contextualization. Each small group ministry structure needs to be developed appropriately for its unique context. The consultant needs to understand how to help the organization or leader adjust small group structures and disciplines to fit their unique situation.

2. Like Moses, a primary and initiating leader of a small group ministry structure needs to have a communal experience and understanding of the nature and character of God. The leader's theology of ministry (perspective on how God does ministry) forms key assumptions about the nature and tools of ministry. These primary and initiating leaders are typically entrepreneurs. This means they do not usually enjoy managing the status quo. These entrepreneurial leaders are always looking for ways to start, grow or expand the structures of small group ministry. They must also be good models and coaches for small group leadership. They must be able to teach, show, coach and empower other leaders to build good groups. Schools, seminaries and churches need to look for such leaders, train them and support them to develop small group ministry structures wherever they go. There is a significant shortage of such leaders.

3. The church and parachurch organizations need to be attentive to the international phenomenon of decentralization and democratization. Empowerment is a secular demand today. The grass roots have grown tired of huge bureaucratic

and hierarchical control systems. This is particularly true in the church. Small groups are a vehicle of localizing and empowering the laity in ministry, of fulfilling the vision God shared with Moses of making God's people into a nation of priests. The purpose of small group ministry is to create a disciplined space to experience God face to face, encourage the community to practice healthy face-to-face relationships and empower a whole new generation of leader-priests who will venture out into a fragmented world carrying the love of God with them as individuals, couples and groups.

4. Small group ministry structures are built to help a group or organization go through an exodus journey together. These small group environments help members develop new spiritual disciplines, make personal and relational changes, and discover a promised new life together where the name of God permeates the community, and where God is known and named as divinity in community.

5. Small group ministry is not indigenous to the traditional structures of the institutional church. Pastors and laity are not generally trained or formed in the kinds of values that would enable small groups to be successful. The leaders of traditional structures must be willing to make the necessary adjustments to encourage small groups to flourish. One of the major value adjustments has to do with the nature of ministry. Institutional faith people have long associated ministry with something the institution does. However, this is not a true biblical or theological perspective. People do ministry. People do ministry in community. Human community is the environment that nurtures ministry. The people of God must pursue an ecology of ministry that preserves the core values of God's relationship with humanity and discerns the temptations of building power structures that oppress personal community. Organizational structures are only faithful as they support this building of human and divine community.

8

SMALL GROUP MINISTRY

Two are better than one, because they have a good reward for their toil. For if they fall, one will lift up the other; but woe to one who is alone and falls and does not have another to help. Again, if two lie together, they keep warm; but how can one keep warm alone? And though one might prevail against another, two will withstand one. A threefold cord is not quickly broken. (Eccles 4:9-12 NRSV)

Humanity was created as a ministry community. Their first ministry call was to serve creation, to serve one another, and to serve God. Small groups are the microcosms of humanity's call to minister together as community. Community establishes the foundation for mutual service. Where there is no community, there is no ministry. Where there is no ministry, there is no community.

Because a person can "sense" the presence of another through seeing, hearing, touching, smelling, tasting or discerning, there is then the desire to meet the other. There is also the desire to serve the other. This natural and created desire to know and serve was twisted in the Garden when the man and woman sought to become the center of the judgment of good and evil. The desire to know was skewed into the desire to judge and avoid. The result of such mutual judgment was a declaration of evil separation and hiddenness. The passing of judgment and condemnation shuts down the freedom and desire to minister to the other. Only the self is seen as worthy, and the other is seen as worthless.

The opposite of ministry is curse. The way of the curse is mutual condemnation and destruction. If we will not attend to one another, like Cain, we will destroy one another. Rather than attend to one another, humanity will reject and feel rejected by one another. This sense of fear and rejection isolates us from the God who created us and desires to attend to us. We refuse the attention of God and we hide from the attention of others. Human ministry is negated until God again comes close to us and touches us with a face-to-face encounter of the Spirit's presence. God reclaims us as ministering community when God as Ministering Community intervenes in our lives and shows us how to come together as a new community.

God brings together two or more people to reverse the pattern of the curse, nonministry and mutual destruction. Only God can reverse the tendency of humanity to avoid and to undermine community. Only God can restore the ministry of humanity in creation. This is the redemptive message of the Bible: God has brought ministry back into the midst of human violence and destruction. And the roots of this ministry are first seen where God ministers to individuals and empowers those people to turn to others and minister to them.

The ministry of God's faithful in the world is not a monolithic institution of one giant power structure, but is a network of interconnected and interdependent ministry groups who each experience the redemptive presence of God and pursue God's unique invitation into ministry through their personal experience of God's gracious presence. Such a call to ministry happens first in the micro sense and expands into the macro framework of interconnected and interdependent faith groups. These groups work together to minister in the name of the God who has first ministered to them. This is the experience of the people of God throughout the Old Testament, as exemplified by the leadership and model of Nehemiah, but more fully envisioned by the prophet Joel.

The Localization and Empowerment of Small Group Ministry

"You see the trouble we are in: Jerusalem lies in ruins, and its gates have been burned with fire. Come, let us rebuild the wall of Jerusalem, and we will no longer be in disgrace."

They replied, "Let us start rebuilding." (Neh 2:17-18)

The most striking reality of the rebuilding of Jerusalem's walls was that Nehemiah called every family group to work near their home and after their own style and skill. The detailed description of the craftsmanship of every family group is a trophy to Nehemiah's wisdom in being small-group-oriented and sensitive. The genius of Nehemiah's strategy was a *decentralization* of responsibility and a *localization* of the total effort. Various tribal and family groups came together, worked on a common project for a common goal, and brought their unique gifts and leadership to the project. Nehemiah was a networker of people groups. He was a macro group strategist. He, along with the family group leaders, developed a plan of shared building. His was a strategy of intergroup partnership with a common mission and a mutual ministry.

The interconnection and networking of many small groups together is the way to build and rebuild God's world. Macro leadership, after the character of God, is leadership that is able to bring diverse people groups together and encourage each group to build out of their own sense of call, their unique commitments, their particular skills and their special tools. This is contrasted with the pharaonic and heavy-handed style of intergroup leadership that tried to make all groups into one large crowd of slaves, under one human king.

In Exodus 1:8-14 (NRSV), we are reminded that the Pharaoh "who did not know Joseph" was a paradigmatic foil to Joseph. Joseph's style of leadership (Gen 41:33-57) was like that of Nehemiah and contrasted with the Pharaoh of Moses' day. He localized the growing and building effort. He worked with everyone to get the job done. He gave strong and authoritative direction to the ministry cooperative but did not set up a tyrannical dictatorship. The Pharaoh who enslaved the people did not understand ("did not know") the spirit, purpose, source, center or style of Joseph. Similarly, Nehemiah did not enter Jerusalem as a dictator, but as a directive leader and facilitator. In both cases the ministry work was for God and shared by the people as compassionate service.

Small groups (teams, bands, committees or platoons) are grouping methods for *decentralizing, localizing* and *democratizing* human work (ministry). The more power and authority given to the local small group to plan and accomplish the task, the more *ownership* the group will have in the completion and excellence of the task. Jethro understood this principle of leadership, judgment and decision-making. Nehemiah understood this principle in building. Joseph understood this principle in famine relief. The principle flows out of the very ministry character of God and the intention God gave to humanity in creation: share the power, responsibility, work and ministry with all people. Call every small band of humanity to share their personhood, gifts, skills and leadership. Call all humanity into shared dominion and care of the earth through small groups. It may be this networking of multitudes of God-centered small groups together that accomplishes the eternal reign of God in the world. It may be in the contemporary small group movement that the mystical character of God becomes visible as the political and ethical character of God.

Based upon the work of Johannes Metz, *Faith in History and Society: Towards a Practical Fundamental Theology,* Bernard Lee and Michael Cowan have suggested the long-term implications of base communities and liberation theology: small groups of laity will eventually change the character of national governments and world stewardship. While the political agenda of the liberationist base communities may be too strident or narrow for a complete ministry model, their methodology and process of ministry through small groups is generally consistent with a biblical foundation for ministry. The power of God will be demonstrated most dramatically in the world through the empowerment of small groups of laity in all countries and cities. Lee and Cowan have accurately and forcefully affirmed this dramatic historical and theological mandate, which God will create with or without official religious institutional support.

The transformation of the Chinese, Eastern European and other tyrannical governments in the world has been notably facilitated through the quiet development of thousands of small group meetings where faith and life are shared together. The natural movement of human democratization through the outworking of small groups flows from the very being and action of our Creator and Redeemer God. Yet this does not eliminate the need for overarching macro leaders who call these groups together and empower them to be, to go, to do. Moses and Nehemiah were leaders among leaders who called out the people and brought the diverse and motley groups together to minister cooperatively and interdependently.

Leadership that directs and facilitates such intergroup ministry cooperation must be sensitive to small group process. Such leadership knows how to issue an invitation to participate in the ministry. In Nehemiah 2:17-18, Nehemiah's invitation, "Come, let us rebuild the wall," was answered by the people, "Let us start rebuilding." This invitation recognizes the power of the plural from the start. Nehemiah knew how to involve the people in seeing the problem and discovering a solution because he had responded to God's character and ministry in his own life. He had participated in the confession of sin with the people (1:7) and prayed for the return of the people from exile. Nehemiah was a man *among* the people and *for* the people. He was one who embraced God's character as compassionate leadership community.

Faith leadership for ministry understands the nature of God as community and the core human hunger for community. Such macro leadership must know how to bring group leaders together, build consensus and implement a shared dominion as a way of life. Such leadership knows when to give up control and to allow more localized leadership to take the ministry lead. Such leadership knows how to stand aside and call attention to God as the center of all ministry relationships and tasks.

The Spirit's Ministry Is in Groups of Men and Women Together

I will pour out my Spirit on all people.

Your sons and daughters will prophesy,
　　your old men will dream dreams,
　　your young men will see visions.
Even on my servants, both men and women,
　　I will pour out my Spirit in those days. (Joel 2:28-29)
God desires to share the Spirit and ministry with all people, men and women, young and old, with all those who feel powerless. This is the prophetic and dramatic message of Joel: it is God's desire to give wisdom and vision for ministry to groups who include both men and women, young and old. This prophetic word involving all stages of men and women together in vision and ministry is retrospective of the original community implied in Genesis 1.

We remember in Genesis 1:26-28 that the shared dominion of the world by men and women was lost in the judgmentalism of the Garden. This loss of human empowerment was greatly recognized and beckoned back toward redemption according to Joel's prophecy. In the sharing of the Spirit and sharing of dreams and visions, Joel articulated what God wants human community to become—a new community of ministry.

In Exodus 20:14, we have also seen that the integrity of God's ministry character is reflected in healthy sexual relationships between men and women. Sexual balance, integrity and wholeness are implied in Joel's prophetic vision through the sharing of the Spirit. If the Spirit brings both men and women together for mutual dreaming and visioning in common groups, they would necessarily need healthy patterns of interaction with one another, particularly in the context of intimate group settings.

Joel advocates clearly for the visioning, strategic planning and ministry of groups of men and women together. The Spirit will call groups of men and women together to accomplish the redemption of God in the world.

Where cultural or religious parameters militate against this call of the Spirit to bring men and women and young and old together, the concern must be raised about the validity of the vision and the integrity of community to accurately reflect the image of God in character, purpose and mission. Will the liberating Spirit of God exercise a full width and breadth of ministry where members of the human male and female community are not free to live in redeemed relationships and to minister together?

This is a small group question. For if men and women cannot come together to share the Spirit's and vision for ministry in a small group, there is little hope of men and women sharing dominion of larger groups, societies or cultures. If only a male vision or a female vision determines the destiny and strategic plan of a small group, or the vision and structure of the small group ministry, there is little hope that the full character of God will be reflected in the world, or that the world will be fully served. If a small group is seen by men as women's turf, will men desire to discover the relational skills and processes needed to bring their souls and relationships into full humanity?

Gordon Dalbey has argued that the male abdication to women of relational and nurturing skills continues to drive a wedge in male-female relationships, blocking the full redemptive ministry of God in the world. The small group should be one of the redemptive laboratories for the restoration of healthy male-female relationships and their sharing of vision and dominion. There is a way into this redemptive community for both men and women, and it is through small group ministry.

Jesus is the *Way* into healthy male-female community and the *Leader* who will introduce the full process of building healthy community through small group experience. The redemption of fragmented divine-human, male-female community had to come through an *intervention*, a transcendent event of God breaking into broken human community to set things right. And as Martin Luther so aptly developed in his hymn text, this historical *intervention* came through the "right man." Luther's poem has sounded through human history, "Were not the right man on our side, a man of God's own choosing." That "right man" is the man who lived among and for the kind of shared community Joel envisioned, a community of men and women together empowered by the Spirit.[3] Jesus, as he lived in and among men and women, called them together to experience the nearness of God and gave them the power to do this ministry of the Spirit together.

■ SMALL GROUP MINISTRY IMPLICATIONS

1. Small groups are circles of and for ministry. Their directions of ministry are fourfold: ministry to God, ministry to one another, ministry to others outside the group and ministry to God's creation. Every small group needs to be guided into this holistic vision for life together. Many small groups exist only with the purpose of ministry to one another. This is a good place to begin, but growth of the group's life purpose is more fully seen as they move beyond themselves into the presence of God, the presence of outsiders and the presence of God's wider creation. Every group is called to minister in this four-dimensional relational ecology. Excellent vision will call forth excellent leadership and excellent ministering small groups. This four-dimensional vision should be shared and modeled for all small group leaders so they can carry the greater call of ministry to their groups.

2. Every small group will not be called to do every dimension of ministry. Small groups usually have a focused sense of call to one of these four dimensions of

ministry. However, long-term groups will tend to look for ministry opportunities beyond themselves. This is a sign of health and growth. Groups that stay cloistered to themselves for extended periods are probably not healthy and not experiencing spiritual growth. Spiritual maturity tends to move a person beyond oneself and move a group of people beyond themselves. While groups may have a focus in one dimension of ministry, they will tend more and more to look out into the wider world for their purpose and sense of mission.

3. Ministry is based upon the development of specific spiritual disciplines, both for the individual and for the group. Spiritual discipline is the practice of specific patterns of ministry to God, to one another, to others and to creation. Small groups need to decide which disciplines they will practice as individuals and which they will practice together as a group. The three main disciplines of small group ministry are face-to-face conversation, Bible study and prayer. These three are universal and deeply interrelated. The group's launching ministry discipline is to hold itself accountable to practice these three key ministry disciplines. Mutual accountability and empowerment are the group's way of saying "Amen" to the regular practice of key disciplines.

4. The mutual ministry of men and women together should be a part of the long-term ministry vision for every gathered group. This does not mean that there is no place for men's groups or women's groups. Such monosexual groups are helpful ministry environments, especially when the men or women are working on agendas that are unique to their sense of safety and growth. The expansion of the women's movement and the men's movement shows us the need for such monosexual group ministry. However, God's long-term call to mutual ministry is for men and women in ministry together. At some point men and women should risk ministry together within the same group context. The balanced small group ministry structure will have space for all three kinds of groups.

5. Small group gatherings will tend toward some form of homogeneity as they first start. We tend to be more comfortable with those with whom we have something in common. This common ground could be sex, marital status, age, children's ages, divorce, needs, interests or ministry concerns. Maturing people will tend to look for more diversity and risk-orientation in a group. Maturing groups will tend to expand their sense of diversity. The sign of ministry growth is a freedom and desire to minister among different kinds of people and in different kinds of places. Maturity tends to move the group toward greater risks of relationship and action outside the group's experienced comfort zone. Small groups need to be encouraged to exercise courage and take such increasing ministry risks.

6. Small groups should be encouraged to study biblical examples and situations

of ministry. While ministry-oriented studies have been written, many curricular small group Bible studies fall far short of helping a group consider the ministry implications of their Bible study. Ministry leadership needs to help groups develop their own ministry-oriented reflection questions if the prepared study fails to fully explore potential ministry implications.

Part Two

JESUS' SMALL GROUPS: GOSPEL FOUNDATIONS FOR SMALL GROUP MINISTRY

9

THE SMALL
GROUP
OF TWELVE

Jesus went up on a mountainside and called to him those he wanted. . . . He appointed twelve—designating them apostles—that they might be with him and that he might send them out to preach and to have authority to drive out demons. (Mk 3:13-15)

Cynthia was a middle-aged woman who had been fighting alcohol and drug addiction for most of her adult life. She had grown up in a family with a distant father and an addictive mother. She had been losing her war against addictions for several years when she entered the twelve-step program of Alcoholics Anonymous. This small group of recovering addicts helped her to admit that she could not control her own behavior. She needed to turn her life over to a higher power. After succeeding in recovery for several years, she was invited to a Christian small group that talked about Jesus Christ as their higher power. In this group Cynthia began to read the Gospels and learned to address Jesus as the One who could manage and direct her recovering life. After several weeks in the Christian group Cynthia exclaimed,

It finally makes sense to me. Jesus is the higher power. I needed a real person to be my higher power. I needed a person who could be here in this group with me. I needed a human being who could be God in my life. Other things or persons could not claim my attention as permanent higher powers because they had no ultimate power or authority. Jesus has become complete authority for my life, and now I need no other thing or person to be my source for living. I no longer need this recovery group to be God for me, because you have brought me into the presence of the only one who is God in the flesh. I meet Jesus in this group. We meet Jesus together. Whenever we get together Jesus is here.

As Cynthia discovered in her recovery group, Jesus is the key presence for the gathering—he gives ultimate purpose to the group. Jesus has complete authority for calling the group together. As the highest power on earth and in heaven, he is intimate with ultimate authority. Cynthia's experience and revelation in her small group is a parable of Christ's universal power wherever two or three come together.

Jesus as Small Group Leader

As we have seen in the first eight chapters, God's ministry presence in the world has consistently been expressed as a small group presence. Even when leading thousands, God's power is often more fully demonstrated when a smaller, more faithful group is gathered and sent on a mission of risk and faith. As the members of this smaller group act courageously, larger numbers of people are drawn into the reality of God's mighty acts in the world. The movement of God's Spirit in the world is a decentralizing and empowering flow through leaders who build new communities and call those communities to a pervasive priesthood, mediating God's presence to others.

The great leaders of the people of God in the Old Testament were iconoclastic models when compared to the prevalent parallel monolithic tyrannies, cities, nations and empires. God's vision for the nation of Israel was for them to be a people of shalom who treated other peoples with dignity, respect and assertive accountability to Yahweh. The tribal and small community expressions of Yahweh's presence continually affirmed that God's might was to be demonstrated through a humanizing community that would confront the structural facades of dehumanized systems, kingdoms and religions. Sensitive to this call to build human communities, God's primary leaders were confronted face to face with the powerful personal nature of a God who desired to be present with them and for them. God's request was that these leaders always would be present with and for God, modeling intimacy with God before the people, and calling the people to practice a similar community with God and with one another.

However, in Israel no leader had emerged who could completely model the power and fullness of such personal, vulnerable and empowering life among the people. No high priest was able to call all the people to become the nation of priests that God had envisioned them to be. Moses, along with models like Joseph and David, had shown Israel a leadership who knew God face to face, but they were terribly bound by the existing images and shadows of tyrannical pharaohs and kings who led systems of pyramids and hierarchies. No refined community-building model had been developed or demonstrated that could help leaders give away such personal and communal power from generation to generation. For humanity to find a way back to the Garden, there had to be a leader who could incarnate the character of God in human form and lead a community to be transformed by the power of the Spirit. All such human attempts at intimate and vulnerable community had fallen short. So Israel looked for the humanity, integrity and community of a Messiah.

Then came Jesus, the man who was the face, presence and community of God incarnated on earth. He was the man who drew others into intimacy with the "Father" as the "Son" in the "Spirit." Jesus was the long-awaited leader who would bring a small group together and demonstrate the immediate nearness of God's presence in divine community. Jesus called this demonstration of God's rule in community the "kingdom" of God. The small group community who gathered with Jesus in their midst was the visible "kingdom" on earth (Mk 1:15).[1] This new community was led by the "rule" of God, who measures the quality of life in different terms than do earthly kingdoms and leaders. God's desire was for this rule to become visible. And it could become real only if real humanity began to demonstrate it in everyday life. This was the purpose of the coming of Christ and the calling of the Twelve: to make God's full nature, character and purpose visible and active "on earth as it is in heaven."

The sabbath grainfield scene (Mk 2:23-28) from Jesus' life shows us how clearly his small group strategy and tactics worked to change the entire course of human history. Jesus' walk through the grainfields with his small group of disciples was an enactment of the nature of God's presence in and through the group on earth. The small group of disciples was picking raw grain (and probably eating it) on the sabbath. Jesus used this event as a parable of the nature of "priesthood," reflecting back on what David did with his band of outlaw men: "He entered the house of God and ate the consecrated bread, which is lawful only for priests to eat. And he also gave some to his companions" (Mk 2:26). Jesus, as had David, reaffirmed the ancient covenantal meaning of "faith community"—to become a "kingdom of (community) priests" on a journey together (Ex 19:6).

Calling the Small Group Together
This is a core value for the development of small group ministry—the calling together of a group to experience the intimacy of Jesus' vulnerable relationship with Abba God. This molds a group to become a model of God's dwelling place on earth. This original discipleship group existed in juxtaposition to their sur-

rounding culture and society. Jesus modeled God's way of transforming the world. He called out a small group of people to experience their own exodus journey together, to move from the enslavement of controlling social, political and religious patterns and to enter into the freedom of "pour[ing] new wine into new wineskins" (Mk 2:22). The faithful small group with Jesus in their midst was the visible demonstration of heaven come to earth.

The Australian small group ministry specialist John Mallison has asserted that Christ's key ministry strategy was a small group strategy. While Jesus ministered to thousands, he provided discipleship and shared ministry with twelve and a few others.[2] Jesus worked in groups of two or more (Mk 1:16-17), although his most frequently noted group was the Twelve. Jesus' mission was to demonstrate the nearness of God to alienated humanity. To do this he formed small group communities.

While Jesus did not live, travel or work alone (Mk 1:12), at times he chose to be alone. These were times of prayer, reflection and temptation, times when God and angels ministered to him. These were times when he invested in the community of heaven so that his community of earth would so reflect his heavenly connection. Jesus proclaimed and ministered in the midst of people because he received and revelled in the ministry of the community of heaven—God's communal and intimate presence. People were his ministry and mission. He intervened and completed the frustrated and unfinished work of God's creation. He reclaimed the "paradise lost"—the lost community of God with humanity and humanity with God.

In Mark 3 we see the beginnings and purpose of this small group of twelve which Jesus called together: (1) Jesus called to himself those he wanted; (2) Jesus appointed twelve; (3) Jesus wanted them to be with him; (4) Jesus sent them out to proclaim; and (5) Jesus sent them out to have authority.

As the Logos, Jesus called this small group into being and gave them "the right to become children of God—children born not of natural descent, nor of human decision or a husband's will, but born of God" (Jn 1:12-13). These were the new family of God, a family not by bloodline but by the Spirit. As the Word was made flesh, so this small group family of God was flesh. As the Spirit made Jesus the incarnate one (Lk 1:35), so the Spirit made this gathered group the incarnate community of Christ. His "word" was his nature, which was action and community. Christ formed the group to become Christ to the world. As Jesus' face shone among them and toward them, so their faces would shine as light together for one another and in the midst of a dark world. The one who was "with" God in community from the beginning was sent to be "with" a few so that the few could be with a few more in each expanding gathering.

Gerhard Lohfink has argued that because the circle of disciples was greater than twelve, including men and women, the concept of the Twelve was "a schematic element introduced by Matthew," not given the task of surrogate or replacement for Israel, but to represent Israel symbolically, to be what Israel was not able to become.[3] This view tends to reduce the importance of the practical and existential implications of Jesus working with a consistent small group over an extended period of time. However, Jesus specifically named twelve men to be this real group. Recognizing the constant and continuing references to the names of specific group members, it is clear that the group was not only a "symbolic" representation of Israel, but a strategic reenactment of God's primal pattern for humanity—the gathering of a small group community with God in their presence. This enactment harked all the way back to the Garden, the early covenantal families, and Moses' decentralization of a budding nation of priests.

The Twelve as Small Group

The Twelve were first called disciples, usually defined as "learners" or "followers." The etymology of the word implies "one who is being influenced."[4] As C. Norman Kraus has explained, "those who accepted [Jesus'] way were called *disciples* (followers, learners, apprentices), *Christians* (Christ's people), and *dedicated ones* (set apart to God, saints), to indicate their relation to Christ. They were to 'follow,' 'obey,' 'share in,' and 'imitate' Christ."[5] They were *mathētai* (students) of Jesus. As leader of the small learning and following group, Jesus was responsible for their purpose and actions.[6]

This practice of discipleship group relationships was dramatically illustrated in the recent movie *Dead Poets Society*. This film was a parable of the powerful transformation which can happen in such a group. The story is about a group of high school boys in an American prep school. The key character, a teacher of English poetry, is not just a teacher of concepts and ideas, but a teacher of life. The group of boys receives the vision for life from him, their poet mentor, forms a clandestine small group community, and reads the poetry (word) of their ancients. The model vision and direction of their poet mentor introduces the young men into the freedom of being a new community not bound by the traditions of the old prep school system. They begin to experience life in a new way and are changed even though their teacher is forced to leave. They discover the powerful possibility of gathering into a mutual learning and supportive community even without their mentor present. In their creedal affirmation of *carpe diem* (seize the day) they are moved to recognize a new center for their lives. The closing scene is a powerful affirmation of the group honoring their new leader who gave them a new framework for life. Standing atop their desks, they declaim the words of the poem "O Captain, My Captain." This case study of contemporary small group discipleship reaffirms the power of a charismatic person gathering human beings to a new life together. And so has Jesus' model of discipleship through small groups been reaffirmed thousands of times since the first century.

Jesus designated the Twelve to be *apostles*. An apostle is "one who is sent forth." The etymology of the word implies "one who is sent from." Jesus first called the small group to come and follow, then to go and minister.[7] In relationships with Jesus, this inner group of twelve grew out of discipleship into apostleship. The following and learning flowed into the being sent and ministering. Implied in the life-cycle of the faithful small group is the process of journey, growth, transformation and progression into ministry. Mission is always the fulfillment of learning.

In his overwhelming bestseller *The Master Plan of Evangelism*, Robert Coleman described this small group movement as eight stages of discipleship: selection, association, consecration, impartation, demonstration, delegation, supervision and reproduction. Coleman asserts the overarching importance of the Twelve as a small group community in their discipleship with Jesus.[8] He describes Jesus' small group strategy as the "principle of concentration":

> Here is the wisdom of his method . . . the fundamental principle of concentration upon those he intended to use. One cannot transform a world except as individuals in the world are transformed, and individuals cannot be changed except as they are molded in the hands of the Master. The necessity is apparent not only to select a few . . . but to keep the group small enough to be able to work effectively with them.[9]

An important historical affirmation of Robert Coleman's written insight is the practical and influential work of his brother, Lyman Coleman, who has been a significant leader in the Christian small group movement from the 1960s and into the 1990s. The Coleman brothers have consistently affirmed this key faith principle—that God changes people and history through the gathering and sending of small bands of ordinary people who demonstrate the realm of God on earth.

The Twelve did not remain static in their relationships with Jesus or with one another. Their life together with Jesus over two to three years reformed their experience, awareness and understanding of reality and their purpose for life. They came to discover the truth of Jesus' proclamation, "The kingdom of God is near" (Mk 1:15). The biblical image of "kingdom" is that realm where God is present and influential. Wherever Jesus lived, moved and acted he brought along his new family of heaven, that is, his intimate connection to Abba God and the angels of heaven.

This intimate connection to the familial community of the heavenly realm was dramatically demonstrated on the "mount of transfiguration" when he appeared before the disciples talking with Moses and Elijah (Mt 17:1-8). It comes as no surprise that "a bright cloud enveloped them, and a voice from the cloud said, 'This is my Son, whom I love; with him I am well pleased. Listen to him!' " (Mt 17:5). Where Jesus stood and walked, the entire community of heaven stood and walked with him. He represented heaven's community on earth. And he brought the Twelve, along with others, into the realm and relationship of his heavenly family.

The *realm* of God is the community of God among humanity and the human community in the presence of God. God's realm is the eternal community of real persons in relationship and work together. The realm of God was "near" the group because Jesus was in their presence and because they were brought into one another's presence by the God who desires to live in the midst of people. The gathering of the Twelve is foundational to the proclamation and demonstration of the gospel as good news: God is with us; God has come down to show us the way of salvation (Mk 1:1).

The good news about Jesus Christ, the Son of God, is that he came to bring God to all people and all people to one another. The good news is that God loves all human beings and has sent Jesus to proclaim, establish and enact the realm of God on earth. This enactment of the divine community was focused and launched in the group experience and ministry of the Twelve. There is no good news if humanity is not in community with God and if this community was not concretely modeled by Jesus among the Twelve. The good news is not Jesus alone as the rugged individual, but Jesus with people, especially Jesus with the Twelve.

The Twelve as a Healing Community

It is good news that God, through Jesus, can bring together any combination of persons to become a community to be healed and to bring healing to others. The community called and calling, healed and healing, forgiven and forgiving, reconciled and reconciling, is the community with Jesus and from Jesus to the world.

Stan had a bout with cancer. He had surgery and seemed to be in remission, but his fear about it recurring haunted him day and night. He felt alone and trapped in his fear. Even his strong faith in Christ could not overcome his isolating fear about dying of cancer. In desperation, Stan joined a support group with other cancer patients. Even though many in this group had no faith in Jesus Christ, Stan found his faith strengthened by being a part of the group. Stan was so impressed with his experience of the healing presence of Christ in this group with very few Christians that he decided to form a support group for cancer survivors that would focus upon the healing presence of Christ. In this healing community Stan began to more fully understand being present with Jesus in a small group. He felt that God had answered his prayer of loneliness by guiding him to start a group where Jesus was the acknowledged healing presence. Many others who joined this group shared their special experiences of Christ's healing presence in their lives through being a member of this support group.

The healing community of the gathered disciples was not only directed toward humanity but toward all creation. Paul Hanson has argued that the healed community will bring about a healed creation, that there is an intimate relationship between humanity and the physical universe which humanity without Christ is destroying.[10] The Twelve were the first microcosm of this good news community on earth as reality and action. The story of Jesus is the story of Jesus with the Twelve. "There is no real Jesus except as he is known through the kind of life he nurtured among his disciples."[11] The Twelve were the prototype and foundation of Jesus' universal call to all humanity to become small communities of disciples. As Stanley Hauerwas has said, "The universal can only be claimed through learning the particular form of discipleship required by this particular man."[12] The particular kind of discipleship to which Jesus called people was formed as a traveling community of twelve men surrounded by other groups of both women and men. Jesus' story is a narrative of small group discipleship.

Several theologians have called attention to the ethical and moral implications of Jesus' relationship with the disciples. However, few have called attention to the particularity of the Twelve as a generic and universal small group paradigm. Some have focused on the political act of Jesus in calling a community to be around him to be formed by his own character. But everything that has been said about the general "community of disciples" is also particularly and concretely true about the small group of twelve.[13]

So it is extremely important that the particular life of the Twelve is seen as reflective and fulfilling of the primal small group model God desired for creation from the beginning. The gospel is a story of God's realm coming to a few select people in a particular time and space to begin the reclamation of all creation.

As Hauerwas has said:

There is no way to know the Kingdom except by learning the story of Jesus. For his story defines the nature of how God rules and how such a rule creates a corresponding world and society. There is no way to talk about the social ethics of Christianity except as they are determined by the *form* of Jesus' life.[14]

To be a disciple is to be part of a new community, a new polity, which is formed on Jesus' obedience to the cross. The constitutions of this new polity are the Gospels. The Gospels are not just the depiction of a man, but they are manuals for the training necessary to be part of the new community. To be a *disciple* means to share Christ's story, to participate in the reality of God's rule.[15]

The Gospels can be likened to training manuals for small group life with Jesus. They describe the form, content and polity of Jesus' strategic ministry of intervention into old human institutions and systems. In establishing the Twelve, Jesus created a new prototype. C. Norman Kraus has suggested that Jesus' work with the disciples as a prototype was "authentic" to the original intent of God's desire for humanity to live in community.[16] The Twelve were a prototype group for the wider community of disciples. They were a beginning, but not a complete version of the prototype—they could not be a full prototype because they were all male. For from the beginning God created men and women to be in community together. Jesus' calling of twelve men was an act of intervention, that is, a corrective intervention to call humanity back to the authentic purpose of God— for men and women to live in harmony with God and with one another. He called the Twelve to follow him and to rediscover how to live with God, women, children and other men. The Twelve as a small group were not in themselves or by themselves the final prototype, but a launching pad, laboratory and mission group to form the initiative of this new prototype of human community. As Jesus walked with the Twelve, he gathered women to join them as extended family.

The twelve disciples became the twelve apostles, "the authenticated witnesses"[17] of Jesus' personal authority with God the Father. The Twelve could speak of Jesus from firsthand experience. They were in his small group together. They lived together. They shared pain together. They had conflicts with one another. They shared ministry together. They imitated Jesus together. They experienced the incarnate[18] shalom of God as human, accessible and vulnerable. They "received the commission and Spirit of witness to the original Word made flesh."[19] The relationship of the Twelve with Jesus was a validation of the realness of Jesus' humanity—that he was not just an apparition or a metaphysical fantasy. Kraus has argued that this is a key historical critique of docetism, that Jesus only "seemed like a human being." Life with the Twelve validated his full humanity because he validated their full humanity. A docetic Jesus would have no use for a specific small group with whom to live and love.[20]

Jesus, the man, lived and traveled with a small group of twelve men, around whom were many other groups of men and women. Jesus lived in constant and complete human encounter with a particular group of human beings. As Gerhard Lohfink has affirmed, these disciples were carefully selected, named and led by Jesus. This group had a new and unique future. They had to release the patterns and values of their past to adopt the character of Christ for their futures:

Thus Jesus required of his disciples a determined turning away from their own families. . . . Common life with Jesus took the place of family and of all previous ties. This common life meant more than merely being with a teacher, listening to him and observing him. . . . The disciples' community of life with Jesus was a community of destiny. It went so far that the disciples had to be prepared to suffer what Jesus suffered, if necessary, even persecution or execution.[21]

Today, following the model of Jesus with the Twelve, God continues to call small groups of men and women to gather around Christ, to give up previous connectional ties, to learn together the way of Jesus, and to allow their transformed life together to impact a world cut off from their Creator's primary intention and ultimate purpose. This is why the focus upon Jesus, the Christ, as ultimate small group leader is so pivotal to the meaning and practice of all human small groups. There is no redemptive gathering into a redeemed humanity unless Jesus continues to practice this ministry by the power of the Spirit throughout human history.

■ SMALL GROUP MINISTRY IMPLICATIONS

1. Small group leadership development should begin with the model of Jesus, who is the key small group leader for all Christians. The method and content of Jesus' leadership pattern should be understood by the key leader of any viable small group ministry. The key leader must understand the importance of an intentional imitation of Christ. Small group leadership development should look to the study of Jesus' leadership styles and patterns in the Gospels. Mark is the shortest and most concise small group narrative. Matthew is a discipleship manual. Luke is a ministry and mission manual. John is a teaching manual. All four Gospel models are small group training models, written for the apostolic house churches, the small groups of the early Christian movement.

2. The Christian small group is to be the visible realm of God in the world. Therefore it would be helpful for a group to study the nature and ministry of the "kingdom" as taught by Jesus. This could lead the group to talk about the radical nature of community as articulated by several authors quoted herein, like Stanley Hauerwas, Gerhard Lohfink, C. Norman Kraus, Robert Coleman, Edward Schillebeeckx and many others. The direct connection between the reality of the "kingdom" and the real life of the small group has to be consistently confirmed. One of the continuing problems of the contemporary church is the discontinuity between real, everyday human relationships and the teaching of Jesus. The serious small group must wrestle with Jesus as their primary authority and leader.

3. There are many small group ("disciple") scenes in the Gospels. A helpful small group study would be to go through the Gospels and collect these small group scenes, studying the implications of each as modeling patterns for small group life. Most typical small groups will see themselves through the attitudes and actions of the disciples as they read and reflect on each scene with Jesus. A group may even wish to develop a written study for other groups to use as they go through each Gospel small group case study.

4. A comparative study could be made of Jesus' leadership styles with key Old Testament leaders. Moses, David and others discussed in part one could be compared to Jesus. The comparisons could be extended to the real people in your group. As long as Jesus is seen as the primary model, any number of other biblical or contemporary leader examples could be compared.

5. A fruitful study series could also emerge out of the question, "Why were the Twelve all men?" Particularly, the Gospel of Luke could provide excellent small group discussion material to explore the issues of discipleship and ministry around the development of men and women in community with Jesus. Each member of the group would need to be open to admit sexual biases. This study would best be done in a mixed group of men and women who were willing to challenge one another's presuppositions and frameworks.

6. Every person in a small group has encountered many kinds of power structures and leadership styles. It might be helpful to encourage small groups to think about and discuss the kinds of power structures and leadership styles they have encountered personally. They might explore how these structures and persons have affected their lives. They might wish to share how their own views of and attitudes toward power and leadership have been formed by such models and experiences. It may be helpful to recommend some books on the use of power and authority. Two such books are *Real Power: Stages of Personal Power in Organizations* by Janet Hagberg[22] and *Zapp! The Lightning of Empowerment* by William C. Byham and Jeff Cox.[23]

10
GATHERING
THE SMALL GROUP

When he saw the crowds, [Jesus] went up on a mountainside and sat down. His disciples came to him, and he began to teach them, saying . . . "You have heard that it was said, 'Love your neighbor and hate your enemy.' But I tell you: Love your enemies and pray for those who persecute you, that you may be [children] of your Father in heaven." (Mt 5:1-2, 43-45)

They went to a place called Gethsemane, and Jesus said to his disciples, "Sit here while I pray." He took Peter, James and John along with him, and he began to be deeply distressed and troubled. "My soul is overwhelmed with sorrow to the point of death," he said to them. "Stay here and keep watch."

Going a little farther, he fell to the ground and prayed. . . . "*Abba*, Father," he said, "everything is possible for you. Take this cup from me. Yet not what I will, but what you will." (Mk 14:32-36)

Jesus gathered people. He not only called people to be with him, but his presence drew them into close proximity with each other. As they gathered around him, they too began to experience the personal presence of God, especially as they watched Jesus practice his relationship with Abba God. The gathering process of Jesus carried the feel of family—of being part of Abba's family. For Jesus, gathering and grouping was best imaged as family—human family.

Jesus also attracted crowds. Large groups gathered to hear him, see him, touch him, and watch him do miracles. Jesus' charisma drew the multitudes. But the crowd was seldom what moved or inspired Jesus to act and live. Jesus focused upon individuals and small groups; his attention was to the few because he loved the many. Jesus did not engage in a general discipleship ministry. While he proclaimed the nearness of the realm of God to vast numbers, he lived, worked and traveled with a few small groups. Jesus' intent was not to use the crowds to usher in the realm of heaven, but to gather the few in close proximity to himself.

Gathering around Jesus implied learning and changing, something not done well in a crowd. Jesus called his small groups to rethink their theology and purpose in life. He gathered them together to show them how to change and be like God. Their gathering was for "watching" the primary model of Jesus. Abba, the focus of the gathering, was the source of their strength to change. Jesus demonstrated that Abba could be their new parent and could show them a better way to live. Abba God could help them to do things their earthly parents could not and would not do. Abba could help them deal with the deepest pain, sorrow or terror in suffering and death. Abba could help them be released from the sins of their parents and ancestors.

Small groups who are gathered in the nature and character of Jesus live out a pattern he established with the disciples. They are called together by Jesus to watch, pray, learn, live, imitate and practice the disciplines and life that Jesus lived with Abba God. The gathering process is the beginning of discipleship. Unless the individuals come together in the presence of Jesus, there is no place or base for experiencing the realm of God on earth. The realm of God dwells in the hearts and relationships of real people who are gathered by Christ for a new kind of life together.

Gathering the Group in the Presence of God as Abba

Susan had been sexually abused as a child by her father. As she began to get in touch with the memories and feelings of this traumatic past, she joined a recovery group. As a long-term member of a church Susan had never trusted herself to be in a small group. She found most of the small groups to be superficial and preoccupied with triviality. Her past had many shadows and ghosts. She could find no safe place to explore these buried pains. She could not find a Christian community that would risk delving into the hard-to-reach parts of the soul. But she decided to try this recovery group.

She began to hear others in the group share pain in relationship with their parents. The group began to explore looking to God as a healthy parent to help them face the terror of their own experiences of dysfunctional parenting. Susan felt free for the first time to explore the hurt caused by her father. In the group she was able to experience God as the "loving father" who would not betray her. She was able to see Jesus as the loving brother who would not join in the generations of abusive men. She was able to look at other men in the group as friends instead of enemies. She was able to experience the group as a new family, her family. For the first time in her life she began to feel that she was in a safe household. Susan is one of thousands today who have found the gathering process of groups to be their new family and the parenting of God to be their new mother and/or father.

Two thousand years before Susan discovered her new family in a small group, Jesus called his group of twelve to live in the presence and parenting of God. Jesus is called the Son of God (Mk 1:1), a term that implies intimate community and familial relationship. Since Jesus was close to God, the disciples were brought close to God by being in his presence. They were invited to participate with Jesus in this sonship in the divine family. Jesus shared the familial intimacy of God with the Twelve, as well as with others. God was the progenitor of this new family, with Jesus as the first Son and the Twelve as adopted brothers. Jesus directed the disciples to enter into his model of sonship, to practice the new family system as he lived it. They were to imitate his life with God and his ministry with people. The calling of the first four disciples, two sets of brothers, suggested a reorientation of their primary familial relationships. The Mark text clearly points out that James and John "left" their father Zebedee. This implied a new familial attachment (Mk 1:16-20).

The metaphor and reality of "sonship" or being a "child" of God is rooted in the original experience of the covenant people of God in the Old Testament. The name of God was given to "the children of Israel" as a sign and downpayment of the reality intended. They started out as "children of Israel," bloodline descendants of Jacob. When they were mistreated in Egypt, "God heard their groaning and he remembered his covenant with Abraham, with Isaac and with Jacob. So God looked on the Israelites [children of Israel] and was concerned about them" (Ex 2:24-25). Israel saw itself not just as the family of Jacob, but as God's "children," as intimate members of God's family. In the Exodus narrative the identity of Israel as family moves from bloodline to spiritual covenant. They were to be as brothers and sisters to each other, not because of blood ties, but because God had rescued them, called them out, and gathered them together to become the people of God. They were a family, not by the will of Pharaoh, nor by the will of Jacob, nor by the will of Moses, but only by the will of God.

They were to live out the implications of life together as a loving family of families, not just tied together by common ancestry, but by the Spirit of God who called them together. God gathered them to become a family for one another first, and then as a welcoming family for the adoption of others into their community. They were to become a family who would welcome the whole world to join their family. From the beginning of the exodus, "many other people went up with them" (Ex 12:38). They were to experience God's presence in their midst as an adoptive and nurturing parent with an expanding household.

God's desire was to re-parent them as they traveled together on their journey to the Promised Land. And this divine parent's goal was to make them to be a nation of priests, that is, adult humanity who could minister God's presence for one another. They were to become priestly partners with God in the nurture of all creation. God's covenant was for them to be a family of priests through the Spirit and to be a family partnership in God's presence.

In completion of this same purpose, but in a more intimate manner, Jesus' sonship was a movement of God to come into the human arena. Jesus' intent was to gather humanity around himself as family, and to show them the way to be servants and partners together with Yahweh. They were to learn this first by joining Jesus in looking to Yahweh as Abba, the intimate Father. The Gospel of John asserts this: the Logos (Word), who "was with God in the beginning" (Jn 1:2), "came to that which was his own, but his own did not receive him. Yet to all who received him, to those who believed in his name, he gave the right to become children of God—children born not of natural descent, nor of human decision or a husband's will, but born of God" (Jn 1:11-13). God's eternal purpose is to make humanity into a new family where Jesus is the brother among a partnership of adult brothers and sisters. So God gathered people, not around biological or organizational roots, but around their common humanity and spirituality, around their common Creator and Redeemer. And Jesus was the initiating leader of their family gathering.

God did not try to gather the whole world around Jesus at this one major point in history. Jesus did not bring in God's realm by power or intimidation or manipulation of crowds or armies. God gathered a few—a few into small groups—around Jesus. And these few who gathered into small groups became the model and historical initiative of Jesus' way of gathering the whole world in every time and place. This is what covenant community is about: the people gathered by God to become a new family. This is why small group community is such an important tool and process in the development of God's eternal realm. People are most likely to gather together in small groups for the empowerment and fulfillment of their humanity as they enter into face-to-face relationships with God and with one another.

In the Bible the number "twelve" is a familial number. When twelve persons gather they can function together as if they are family. When twelve gather they can reach out to others and include them into their extended family. Twelve was a continuing symbol of God's adoption of Jacob's twelve sons. Thus Jesus continued that historical familial paradigm in calling twelve to gather with him. But the gathering of the Twelve was more than a symbolic fulfillment of those ancient family expectations—it was a paradigm of a divine methodology for re-gathering all humanity to God.

The twelve disciples became the new family of God—Jesus' family. This was not just the result of God's presence and call, but also the reflection of God's redemptive activity among the people. When Jesus was questioned about his family, "he looked at those seated in the circle around him and said, 'Here are my mother and my brothers! Whoever does God's will is my brother and sister and mother' " (Mk 3:34-35). The circle of followers became the new family, the family who acted out the ministry of God in the world. And the focal circle of this new divine-human arena was the Twelve, whom Jesus called to gather around himself. They were the small group who gathered in the presence of God and who made it possible for the glory of the Son to shine in their community.

Being the family of God means doing the will of God. Those who are intimately connected to God know God and know God's mind and will. They begin to think God's thoughts, develop God's heart and feel God's feelings. They desire God's way. They act out the family system of their new divine parent. They are a new small group defined by becoming a new family. Jesus showed them how to become a brother or sister by being the primary model of a brother and son who lived in intimate relationship with the Abba Father (Mk 14:35).

The Abba relationship of Jesus with God was most clearly articulated during his darkest moments of crisis and decision. This intimacy of Jesus with Abba was vulnerable, painful and deep. The disciples, in the same context of crisis, were not able to share the depth of this distress and intimacy with Jesus. They were not yet invested deeply enough in their own intimacy with Abba to enable them to share in the partnership (koinonia) of Jesus' suffering. While they had some experience in being family with Jesus, the small group had need of more mature sharing and intimacy with Abba to attain the level of Jesus' relationship. The Twelve had to grow into their intimacy with God. And their growth into God's familial intimacy was not immersed (baptized) into the depth and death of Jesus until after the resurrection and Pentecost.

Today, when a small group gathers "in the name of Jesus" they are being gathered by the one whom Jesus called Abba. They are being gathered to be formed into the way of the ancient children of God. They are gathered by a common parent and a common brother into a relationship with Abba as their center and model of family life. They are being exercised into the promise of God's eternal covenant which began with Abraham. They have access to the power of the same Spirit who empowered the relationship between Abba and the Son. When they come together they are the present reality of the realm of God "on earth as it is in heaven."

The gathered small group is called together by the same God who gathered Israel out of Egypt. They are gathered together to risk a journey into the unknown future with God in their midst. Gathered as a small group in Jesus' name, they become a visible family of God present in the world. This is not a guarantee of family bliss, but a covenant with God who desires to bring blessing to the group, and then abundant life through the group into the wider world. The gathering is only the beginning of their journey together. How the small group experiences Christ in their life together can transform them into the image of the Son who loved Abba and was loved by Abba.

The Selection and Gathering of the Twelve
According to Richard Peace, Jesus selected a "motley" group to be his disciples and apostles.[1] This term is very appropriate and important to the theological meaning of Jesus' small group and family. They were comprised of a combination of "clashing," "heterogeneous" and "diverse" cultural elements.[2] The group included Galilean fishermen (earthy and volatile), a tax collector (servant of the governmental establishment), a fiery nationalist (renigade from the oppressed establishment), one of "untroubled faith" (Andrew),[3] one of thoughtful reflection and prayer (John), the "doubtful" one (Thomas) and one (Judas) who eventually "betrayed" Jesus (Mk 3:13-18). The common bond between the Twelve was only the person of Jesus himself. This heterogeneous group of individuals and siblings from various political persuasions, emotional states and life purposes, came together around the charismatic leader—Jesus. John Mallison has argued that the diversity of the Twelve who found their union in Jesus was a "microcosm of the diversity of character of the church that was in the making. . . . The message of the first small group was that Christ does not overlook ordinary people."[4] In fact, Christ redeemed ordinary people in small group communities.

The small disciple group first formed around this key person, Jesus, who helped them develop common bonds of friendship and mission. The Twelve were called to be "with him" as a deliberate strategy. They were to share in his humanity, his vision, his way of life, his feelings, his values, his vulnerability, his temptations (Heb 4:15), his prayer and his rejection. But most of all, they were to partake of and share in the struggle, passion and benefits of his relationship with Abba God.

To bring the Twelve together, Jesus gathered a "scattered" group of somewhat nonrelated persons. The combined Gospels give an eclectic account of how Jesus gathered this original group. The first two to follow Jesus were disciples of John the Baptist (Jn 1:35-50). When Jesus asked them the question, "What do you want?" they responded by addressing him as "Teacher." Jesus invited them to "come and see" where he was staying, and they spent the day with him. Andrew, Peter's brother, was one of these original two. Andrew found Peter and persuaded him to join with him in following Jesus. In persuading Peter, Andrew used the rallying exclamation, "We have found the Messiah!"

Philip was recruited on the way to Galilee. Philip, Andrew and Peter were all from the same village of Bethsaida. Philip recruited Nathanael by appealing to him that Jesus was the fulfillment of the teaching of Moses, the Law and the Prophets. Nathanael was not impressed that Jesus was a native of Nazareth, but Philip suggested that he "come and see" for himself. To Nathanael's surprise, Jesus recognized his full character and nature from the beginning. Jesus had already observed Nathanael "under the fig tree" from a distance—he had "seen" (and understood) him. Nathanael's sudden recognition of and attraction to Jesus was evident as he exclaimed, "You are the Son of God; you are the King of Israel."

Jesus called the sons of Zebedee, James and John, out of the very presence of their father and the family business. He gathered all four fishermen (Andrew, Peter, James and John) with the invitation to become "fishers of [humanity]" (Mt 4:18-25). Matthew was gathered even as he sat "at the tax collector's booth"; Jesus then went to have dinner "at Matthew's house" with "many tax collectors and 'sinners' " (Mt 9:9-12). The details of the gathering of the other five are not revealed in the Gospels.

All the gathering process of the Twelve was accomplished as Jesus "went throughout Galilee, teaching, . . . preaching, . . . and healing" (Mt 4:23). The Twelve were gathered personally and individually from the "large crowds" who "followed him" from the whole region. Jesus' pattern of gathering the Twelve can be briefly summarized: they were hand-picked, gathered along the way, out of their everyday marketplace pursuits, away from their families, in spite of their diversity, because of their common attraction to Jesus, because of their faith in God, and because Jesus was going to teach them some things about life that they wanted to know. But the biggest reason they allowed themselves to be gathered was that Jesus presented them with a fresh hope for what life could be beyond what they had already experienced. This was their messianic expectation. These were ordinary people who sensed that they were being gathered to participate with an extraordinary person, in an extraordinary life journey. Their curiosity and excitement to discover life beyond their normal experience moved them to take the risk to "leave" and "follow." In their leaving and following, they were called together as a small group "on the way."

The gathering process that Jesus used with women seemed to follow different parameters. Luke says that Jesus "traveled about from one town and village to another. . . . The Twelve were with him, and also some women who had been cured of evil spirits and diseases: Mary (called Magdalene) from whom seven demons had come out; Joanna the wife of Cuza, the manager of Herod's household; Suzanna; and many others" (Lk 8:1-3). Women followed Jesus because he healed, forgave, respected and empowered them. This seems to be in some contrast to the reasons why the men gathered to Jesus. The men seem to be attracted by Jesus' charisma, teaching, power and influence. The women seem gathered toward Jesus' personal healing influence and touch in their lives. They gathered around Jesus "to support [Jesus and the Twelve] out of their own means." The women followed in thanksgiving, personal loyalty and support. Their common interest in Jesus was how he had transformed their personal and public lives. From Luke's perspective, the women were a source of financial support for the men.

The exact number of gathered women is not clearly known; however, John's record expands the list to include Jesus' mother Mary, Mary's sister and Mary the wife of Clopas (Jn 19:25). To this group Luke adds "the women who followed him from Galilee" (Lk 23:49), Mark adds Salome, and Matthew adds the mother of Zebedee's sons. We might also add to this group Mary and Martha, the sisters of Lazareth (the number of Marys makes the list somewhat chaotic). In any case it would be safe to say that the close cadre of women may have been about the same number as the Twelve.

Luke also says that Jesus "appointed seventy-two [seventy?] others" in addition to (including?) the Twelve "and sent them" ahead (Lk 10:1). These numbers present some interesting questions regarding Jesus' gathering and sending strategy: Were the women included in the sending of the seventy-two? Were the seventy-two formed in several extended small groups around the Twelve (for example, twelve groups of seven each, or six groups of fourteen each, or six groups of twelve each)? In any case, Jesus attracted several circles of followers who gathered to him for diverse reasons. Their universal and common ground was Jesus himself as he invested in his intimate relationship with Abba God. John's Gospel reveals what Jesus said about the general gathering of disciples: "No one can come to me unless the Father has enabled him [or her]" (Jn 6:65).

The small groups of men and women who have followed Jesus throughout history have been gathered in similar ways. They have been brought together because of their common interest in following Jesus, their common experience of being touched and healed by Jesus, their common desire to be taught by Jesus, their common interest in observing the model of Jesus, and their common desire to become members of a new family with Jesus, where God is their redemptive parent. Jesus continues to gather small groups of persons where he is the brother among brothers and sisters. He always establishes a new family where Abba is the warm and loving parent. These newly gathered small group families take the place and reform the patterns of our earthly mothers, fathers, sisters and brothers. The people who make up these small group communities are those, according to Jesus, who desire to do "the will of my Father in heaven." They are "my brother and sister and mother" (Mt 12:46-50). They are "the little flock" Jesus addressed when he said, "Life is more than food, and the body more than clothes. . . . But seek [God's] kingdom. . . . Do not be afraid, . . . for your Father has been pleased to give you the kingdom. Sell your possessions and give to the poor" (Lk 12:22-33). Jesus invites us to become a member of an eternal family where being and relationships are the food and material of Abba's household.

The Metamorphosis of Scattering and Regathering the Group

Jesus' gathering strategy also implied a scattering or falling away process. When Jesus began to teach, "unless you eat the flesh of the Son of Man and drink his blood, you have no life in you," from that time on "many of his disciples turned back and no longer followed him" (Jn 6:53-66). Just as gathering into face-to-face community initiates the redemptive process among people, so it is in the redemptive cycle of covenant community that every group will come to its time of being scattered. The scattering of a group is usually the result of a crisis or conflict. Most often this is precipitated by the loss of or disagreement with the group's primary leader who has enabled and empowered them to function well together. This loss of leadership presence or authority may be attitudinal, metaphorical, emotional or physical. The group may lose confidence in the leader or the leader may lose power with the group. The group may lose interest in having a particular kind of leader. The results are nearly the same. The scattering may be geographical—members leaving the group, or it may be emotional—the members of the group avoiding each other. Such an emotional scattering may reduce the group to a shadow or skeleton of its former vibrance. It may continue to meet, but the desire for growth, depth and intimacy has been lost. In any case the group has lost its cohesive factor—that person or ingredient which energized its life together. The scattering is the result of a loss of a gravitational center and dynamic, a loss of confidence, trust or identity.

The scattering process can also be the result of the group beginning to deal with the hard teachings and practices of Jesus. The excitement of the call to be gathered with one like Jesus who heals, cares and loves is often dampened by the realization of how hard such a life can become. To lay down one's life, to take up a cross, to follow Christ into suffering and death, to be willing to sell everything and give it to the poor, to be willing to stay married at high costs, to be willing to love children and not send them away, to be willing to live with others in a new family through difficult times—these are the hard ways of being with Jesus in the small group family. And these hard ways may cause the group to be scattered, to go "away sad" because of their "great wealth" (Mk 10:22), to give up being disciples together because they are not willing to "give up everything" (Lk 14:33), to want to "go and bury [their] father" or to "go back and say good-by to [their] family" (Lk 9:59-62). The gathering of the new family in Christ's love for Abba sometimes cannot stand the stress of the demands of discipleship together. So the group becomes scattered. And only the power of Christ can regather the scattered group.

Like the Twelve, the healthy small group lives with a fear of loss. The loss of temporal life together is inevitable. A member may die. A couple may leave. A rift may separate and push members apart. Some groups may continue to meet together for twenty years but their emotional lives become distanced. The loss and the scattering needs to be felt and faced by the group for the full possibility of resurrection and regathering. Yet many groups and members of small groups refuse to face this inevitable scattering. To face such fracture and fragmentation is to face the hurt and disillusionment of individual and group expectations. Groups who live in the fantasy that they will live "happily ever after" may not want to deal with the nagging signs that their group is disintegrating. Denial and avoidance are strong human covers. To deal with the scattering is to deal with the frailty, terror and shortness of life, with the reality that life is more than what this world has to offer, and with the growing awareness that human community is more a process of heaven than it is a demand on earth.

If the gathered group does not experience and recognize its state of being scattered, there is little possibility of it being regathered for a new life. Dissonance, loss, suffering, death and grief have a purpose in the life of an intimate community. Their purpose is to set the stage for hope, resurrection and new life. Eternal life becomes fully realized to the gathered community only as its temporal life and stability are lost. In the scattering, the group has to face itself, its limitations, its mistakes, its sin, its penultimate life together. No gathered human group is gathered forever as it is. Every group must go through periods of death and resurrection in order to come to grips with God's eternal will. The scattered group has the potential of being regathered as a fulfillment of the eternal covenant that God has established with humanity in Christ.

Fortunately for the human race, most of the Twelve dealt with the scattering of their small group after Jesus was removed from their center. The ultimate crisis of the motley twelve happened when Jesus was arrested and put on trial (Mk 14:50; 15:40). This could have been the end of their life together, but instead it was the end of their beginning life and the beginning of their new life together.

It was their necessary metamorphosis. As Jesus was arrested, tried, tortured and executed, the group scattered in fear for their lives. Their regathering was the resurrection and new beginning into a more mature and complete human community and spiritual partnership. This process of being gathered, scattered and regathered is a significant paradigm for persevering and maturing small group life.

During this crisis and transitional period of scattering, the contrast between the male and female groups who followed Jesus was most dramatic. During Jesus' crisis the eleven deserted and fled (Mk 14:50), but the women, "who had followed him from Galilee, stood at a distance, watching these things" (Lk 23:48). This group of women were the first to visit his tomb (Lk 23:55) and the first to experience and announce his resurrection (Lk 24:1-11). The women were already members of the scattered "outsiders" group. They had not been part of the Twelve. The scattering of the Twelve opened the possibility for the inclusion of others into the family circle.

As will be explored in part three, the ruptured and wounded Twelve became part of the empowered one hundred twenty on the day of Pentecost. The scattering of the initial small group erupted into an immediate tenfold increase, which, in turn, opened to a thirtyfold increase on Pentecost. Instead of one scattered and lost group, the Spirit birthed twelve groups of ten (one hundred twenty; Acts 1:15) and then another three hundred groups of ten (or two hundred groups of fifteen [three thousand]; see Acts 1:12—2:47). Scripture does not explain how the one hundred twenty of the upper room experienced the "all together in one place," or how they spread out into Jerusalem on the day of Pentecost, or how they began to form their house groups. A speculative possibility is that each of the Twelve launched a house gathering with nine others in a different part of Jerusalem. Another possibility was that sixty teams of two may have launched home groups throughout the city. This would have been consistent with their following of the model of Jesus to initiate a group that could minister and grow. It would also be consistent with the Jethro-Moses model of priestly communities in Exodus 19, of which they were surely aware, especially with their experiences of synagogue community patterns.

With the person of Jesus taken from the small group, they could no longer sustain their life together. The Twelve had too little in common and too little common strength to stay together when Jesus was gone. This crisis hints at the crucial nature of the group's gathered identity. The group existed only as long as Jesus was present for them and leading them. The removal of Jesus from the midst of the group sucked away the life-breath of the group. The group lived only as Jesus was present to live for the group. His appearance to and revisiting of the group, as well as the descent of his Spirit at Pentecost, was crucial to the continuity of the regathered group after the resurrection. Not until after the resurrection and Pentecost did the group of twelve (eleven) rediscover their identity together. In the resurrection and Pentecost the regrouped and reconstituted small group discovered that the Spirit of Jesus would always be present for them as they came together to do the will of God in the world.

The source of the Twelve's long-term cohesion is of primary importance to all human grouping. Common values, purpose or relationships hold groups together. It is of great importance to note that Christian group cohesion is centered in the presence of the person of Christ through the Spirit.[5] All other potential group bonding values failed to hold the group together during their identity crisis.

■ SMALL GROUP MINISTRY IMPLICATIONS

1. The process of gathering a small group happens in many ways. Groups can be gathered around many things: leaders, missions, topics, needs, ministries, styles, hurts, diseases, studies, issues and so forth. But from Christ's perspective, the group is gathered by God. If the Christian group is called around any of these secondary purposes, they still need to come to grips with their primary reason for gathering, to be together with Christ in the presence of God. Prayer is the primary discipline of the Christian group. Without prayer there is little hope that the group will come to grips with its primary purpose for gathering. However, this is not the typical prayer pattern of request, but prayer pattern for insight, purpose, identity and destiny. This is prayer for a deep experience of the presence of God in the midst of the group. This is prayer to experience the personal presence of Christ as the primary gathering center for the group. If a group cannot come to this place of discerning Christ as the gatherer, it will continue to struggle over secondary concerns about details, needs, desires and preferences.

2. Few small groups see themselves as family. The privatized and individualized culture in which we live does not move us to embrace gathering as family. The current wave of political concern may advocate for "family values," but the drive toward independence permeates society. Groups must consciously strive to practice group disciplines as family disciplines. The gathered Christian group is spiritual family. In the long run, spiritual family is more important and more powerful than bloodline family. Many Americans use bloodline connections to avoid spiritual family gatherings. The bloodline family may become a spiritual family, but an inclusive attitude develops as the group becomes spiritual family. Others outside the family bounds are included. The Christian small group family is always an extended family. The Christian group is always an embracing group from its center in Christ. Small group ministry must begin to define itself as

Christian spiritual family with a greater destiny than bloodlined family ties. This is a hard Christian value for many Christian small groups and families to embrace.

3. Given the strong directive of gathered groups to take on the character of the family of God, every group has to come to value the new parenting role of God in their midst. If they embrace Jesus as the model of the healthy elder brother who has a relationship with Abba Father, they must explore the "stuff" of their previous family experiences, including their experiences with parents and family values. The gathered small group around God as parent begins to exist as a countermodel to the families of origin of each member of the group. The new group meeting with the new parent (God) becomes a reorientation place in which to deal with the baggage and unexamined assumptions of families past and present. The new group is gathered by Christ to be a new family system, with new values, new relational dynamics and new disciplines. Sometimes the new family is so loaded down with the bad stuff from previous family systems that God is not permitted to be parent, Jesus is not permitted to be brother, and the group cannot embrace the possibilities of being a new family. Small group ministries must define a theology of family for their small groups to embrace and model.

4. In light of the need to embrace the gathered group as potential new family gathered by the elder brother Jesus in the presence of Abba Father, it would be good for churches and denominations to develop small group curriculum that helps a group embrace this family identity. Such a curriculum could study any number of New Testament texts to explore this idea of the group being a new family in Christ. For example, the Gospel of Mark could be examined to look at the Twelve in light of family systems and dynamics. In order for this to be complete, the relationship of the Twelve to the women would need to be explored up through and beyond the day of Pentecost. The discipleship of Jesus as elder brother did not stop with the Twelve at resurrection and ascension. It continued through the apostolic period.

5. Today a lot of "family" imagery and language is being used to described large gatherings of Christians. This is somewhat a breach of biblical history and theology. The family must be small enough to deal with its interpersonal life and dynamics. Large group gatherings are not "one family"; they are gatherings of many such families. The large church must deal with its need to help privatized and individualized Americans become family in Christ. This happens only when persons become close enough, vulnerable enough and interdependent enough to be called "family." Family imagery for large gatherings is often a sentimental trivialization of Christ's community unless there are many small group families

within the crowd who are experiencing an abundant life together. The large gathering is only family inasmuch as it is made up of many small group families. Such a superficial description and projection of "family" life betrays the work of Jesus with the "few" and the work of the apostles in the house gathering—the ecclesia. This is why large churches or large organizations must include networks of many small group families. The large group is only family as it encourages and supports its small groups to be family.

11
MODELING
GROUP LIFE

Jesus traveled about from one town and village to another, proclaiming the good news of the kingdom of God. The Twelve were with him, and also some women who had been cured of evil spirits and diseases: Mary (called Magdalene) from whom seven demons had come out; Joanna the wife of Cuza, the manager of Herod's household; Susanna; and many others. These women were helping to support them out of their own means. (Lk 8:1-3)

Allan was the typical successful American man of the fifties. He was young, good-looking, married (with two children), a rising sales executive of a major corporation, an excellent golfer and a churchgoer. He felt good about his life, and life was a wonderful experience for him. At church he was surrounded by many men just like himself and many families just like his. This looked like his world, his people and his style. His was a man's world. He was in control. But something was missing. He was successful, but he was unfulfilled—his life had little deeper meaning.

A new pastor came to Allan's church. Like the previous pastor, this man had a gift for preaching and much personal charisma. However, he did something different: he asked a few men and women like Allan to be in a small group with him and his wife. This was a new experience. This was not the normal church way—it was more personal and more intimate. When this group met with the pastor, they saw his real humanity. The pastor encouraged them to relax and be themselves and get in touch with their feelings in the group. But more importantly, he called the group to take the presence of Christ seriously. The pastor used his charisma and influence to call the group to experience the charisma and influence of Jesus. They first came because they liked the pastor. They stayed because they came to love Jesus Christ.

Allan had never seen or heard anything like this before. The pastor took him aside one day and said, "Allan, if you will allow Christ to be the primary influence in your life, you will begin to experience a dimension of reality that is beyond your wildest dreams." So, trusting in the model of this pastor, Allan began to practice the presence of Christ in his life. He began to experience a deeper reality of life. He began to know himself in a more complete way and to encounter others as a more present and alive person. He began to deal with his spouse and children in a more loving and humane way. He began to pray as a normal way of life, and to receive messages from God that he had not heard before. Allan became a new man. And the launch pad of his transformation was this small group he lived among for seven years.

At first, this young and charismatic pastor was Allan's primary model in life. The new relationships of the group were his new pattern for living. But after a couple of years, his focus shifted from the pastor to Jesus. He began to see the pastor as an ordinary human being, with gifts and flaws, with a bright side and a dark side. He began to understand the group as a community changed by the presence of Christ. He realized that the new life for him was not the result of the pastor or of this particular group, but because the pastor and group experienced the model of Christ among them as disciples. Allan lost interest in being a model of the successful American dream and became passionate about helping others to discover this graceful, abundant community life with Christ. He too, like the pastor, began to gather other men and women into small groups around the present Christ, modeling for them the Christ-present life.

Jesus lived and traveled with his small group just as Allan and others have experienced in faithful small groups. Luke states that two groups traveled with Jesus—the twelve men and an assortment of women (Luke names three women among "many others"). The focus of these two groups was upon Jesus. He was the center of their life together—their primary model and mentor. He not only brought the men together and the women together separately, he also brought the men's group and the women's group together. Their two small groups and the one larger entourage was a model of community, because they were with a model leader.

These communities gathered around Jesus were not models because of their perfection, power or charisma, but because of their curiosity, ordinariness, brokenness, diversity and willingness to stay together and follow Jesus. These were *voluntary* communities. They shared every aspect of life, but had only Jesus in common. Jesus' personal presence and teaching moved them to live together in ways not prevalent to the world in which they lived. Jesus called the women to live in dignity and self-awareness. He showed the men how to treat the women with respect. The women were free to support the men financially (Lk 8:3). The men were free to learn new ways of relating to the women. Both groups were called to experience life from God's viewpoint, as part of the kingdom.

The Model of Christ in the Group

The motley nature and heritage of the Twelve was foundational to the unique development of the group's character. Jesus was the source of the group's character. He defined the essential quality and nature and pattern of the group. Jesus' presence formed the life of the group. While the Twelve often wondered at his teaching and disagreed with his values, Jesus' charismatic presence and intimate relationship with Abba God was too powerful to ignore or to suppress.

David Prior has argued that Jesus' simple assertion, "Follow me," was a powerful illustration of his personal presence and power. What the Twelve found initially attractive in Jesus were his unusual healing and persuasive powers, his popularity and success.[1] Jesus' personal authority moved every dimension of their group life. The New Testament theologian James Dunn has reflected that Jesus' personal charisma, which grounded the authority of his teaching, must have been overwhelmingly apparent. People acted differently in his presence.[2] In every way Jesus was the formative character, personality, mind, heart and will of the small group of twelve.

This present and charismatic character of Jesus was an interventional call to a new kind of life together. Jesus beckoned the Twelve into a new purpose and new relationships, with new values, new perspectives and new character. He welcomed the Twelve to himself—to walk with him, watch him, imitate him, learn with him and take on his character. He became their future, their center of hope, their model of faith and their source of love. His community with "the Father" became their community with "the Father." His community with each of them became their community with one another.

When Jesus first encountered the Samaritan woman at Jacob's well, "his disciples had gone into the town to buy food" (Jn 4:8) and had left him alone to rest. Toward the end of this life-changing conversation, "his disciples returned and were surprised to find him talking with a woman" (Jn 4:27). Jesus offered a shocking model of openness and intimacy with a woman in a culture in which it was "forbidden to give a woman any greeting," where "one should not talk with a woman on the street, not even with his own wife, and certainly not with somebody else's wife, because of the gossip of men."[3] The Twelve must have felt the powerful rush on their values and feelings as they watched Jesus do and say things that were far outside the normal boundaries of their cultural and religious expression. Yet in this particular instance with the Samaritan woman, they kept silent, watching in wonderment, not asking the questions pounding in their minds, " 'What do you want?' or 'Why are you talking with her?' " (Jn 4:27).

Jesus' model of life created real tensions and conflict for the gathered disciples. Jesus beckoned the Twelve to follow him into foreign territory—the realm of God. Jesus invited them to experience new ways and roles for men and women. He showed them new patterns of human relationships and new perspectives on human institutions. He led them to places they had never been and feared to go. He asked them to see people in ways that they had not yet envisioned, and that might cost them to do so. Jesus' call to "Follow me" was a call to leave old values and measurements of character behind and to risk the exploration of new values, the embrace of new persons and the venture into new actions.

The first place Mark records that Jesus took the original small group of four Galilean fisherman was to Capernaum to encounter a demon-possessed man and experience an exorcism (Mk 1:21-28). This first adventure had to be an experience of cultural, psychological and theological shock. They were in a known place but confronted by a wild man who addressed their leader as Messiah, "the Holy One of God." They watched a confrontation between good and evil and an exorcism, the power of good over evil. They were astounded enough to declare the whole scene a "new teaching."

In affirmation of this kind of dramatic new experience, George Ladd, a New Testament theologian, suggested that Jesus drew his disciples into a bond of personal loyalty as distinguished from the typical rabbinic pattern of drawing disciples to be bound together by Torah. "The rabbis bound their disciples not to themselves but to the Torah; Jesus bound his disciples to himself. The rabbis offered something outside themselves; Jesus offered himself alone. . . . This relationship had no parallel in Judaism."[4]

Even though Jesus was a strong and charismatic leader, he was willing to live with the tension, clash and struggle of the wills of the Twelve. The Twelve had ideas, opinions, values and wills of their own (Mt 19). Jesus confronted their value systems but did not demand their absolute loyalty to his new values, thinking and action. He allowed them freedom for skepticism, disagreement, cynicism and fear. He allowed them to express their real humanity. But he did not leave them to this raw humanity. He called them to something beyond themselves. He gave them direction into a new way of life, a new dimension of life. He called them to change. He became more than their teacher and Lord; he became their friend and brother, and gave them direct access to God. As they watched and listened and imitated, the Twelve began to understand Jesus as their new and ultimate model of humanity and godly life.

While Mark's text reflects only some of the tension between Jesus and the Twelve, Matthew's text expresses several successive and intensive situations of conflict: views on divorce (Mt 19:10), on the value of children (Mt 19:13), on wealth and blessing (Mt 19:25) and on power and position (Mt 19:24). Matthew seems to portray the small disciple group in a constant state of values confrontation, where neither Jesus nor the disciples were afraid to speak their mind. Jesus' model and teaching were disturbing to the Twelve, and they were not afraid to express their frustration and anxieties. They did not seem to be intimidated by the charismatic strength or godlikeness of Jesus. And Jesus did not seem to demand blind acquiescence to his leadership or will. He seemed instead to desire and encourage openness and honesty from the rugged Twelve. He was willing to enter into the group's struggle of wills and not give in to the human temptation to suppress the disciples' flawed values.

So the sparks flew between Jesus and the Twelve as they were challenged by the one who "taught as one who had authority" (Mt 7:29). His authority was not controlling or oppressive, but impressive and expressive. He expected the group to change through spiritual rebirth and character redevelopment. Jesus did not demand mindless imitation. He was interested in the willing transformation of their characters. He would not control, manipulate, intimidate or terrorize their personhood or relationships. He was not a group tyrant. He was an assertive but gentle model. He was confident of his relationship and destiny with Abba God, and this confident modeling drew the curiosity of the Twelve into the wonderment of their own experimentation and imitation of Jesus' lifestyle.

The group's willingness to risk imitating the model of Jesus is somewhat humorously recounted in Matthew. The disciples were in a boat without Jesus, being tossed around in choppy seas. As Jesus walked out on the water during the darkest period of the night, the disciples were "terrified" because they thought that they had seen a ghost. Jesus' calming words, "Take courage! It is I. Don't be afraid," moved Peter to desire to go to where Jesus was, saying, "Lord, if it's you, . . . tell me to come to you on the water" (Mt 14:22-32). Jesus' positive invitation encouraged Peter out of the boat and onto the water, where he walked a few feet and then sank. His fear had overcome his desire to imitate. So it was with all the modeling Jesus did. The disciples could imitate him up to the point where their courage ran out and their fear took over. However, Jesus was there to meet them and catch them in their terrorized state. When the Holy Spirit came to them, their power to imitate, expand upon and extrapolate what Jesus did come into full bloom. But this fuller experience of the Spirit was after their beginning discipleship group experiences. In all things the real model of Jesus became their primary vision for how to live life. This model was made clear to them as they journeyed together as the small group of twelve. They discovered that being in the small group community was essential to the modeling and learning process.

The Twelve as a Model Group

If Jesus was the model leader for making the realm of God visible on earth, the Twelve together with him were to become the model community for making the realm of God even more visible. Jesus not only called the motley Twelve to be with him, he also called them to one another. They were a diverse small group of men who had never before traveled and lived together. Their model of life together was full of conflict and tension.

In assessing Matthew 5:1-2, Robert Guelich pointed out that the Gospel of Matthew is more descriptive of the character development of the disciples than is either Mark or Luke. This is particularly evident in the calling of the four fishermen (Mt 4:18-22) followed by the blessing texts, which are about the character of people who enter the realm of heaven (Mt 5:3-12).[5] The implication is that the gathered disciples are the arena in which God will work and move, where their character and model of life together will be transformed.

Jesus' model was a constant confrontation to their more limited and narrow view of life. The Twelve, in their anxiety during the storm, were confronted with a tired and sleeping Jesus who challenged their fear (Mk 4:35-41). The disciples, taking up the ministry of Jesus, were amazed that they too could drive out demons and heal people (Mk 6:7-13). They were confounded with Jesus' expectation that they should feed five thousand people with no money and little food (Mk 6:30-44). The hard-rowing, closed-minded Twelve were terrified by the sight of Jesus walking on water (Mk 6:45-52). In fact, Mark draws a connection between the Twelve's amazement of Jesus walking over the water and their inability to understand the meaning of his feeding five thousand with five loaves and two fish. Their understanding of reality and their participation in the realm of God with Jesus was confused, incomplete, narrow and myopic. Their model of life together was anything but a clear signal of harmonious and trusting human community. Rather, they modeled real and chaotic human relationships and attitudes.

The poverty of their model community was also visible in their thinking and learning. The more concrete-thinking Twelve missed the cosmic meaning of Jesus' teachings about spirituality. (Mk 8:14-21). The suffering and dying Jesus rebuked the messianic myopia of the Twelve (Mk 8:31—9:1). Day by day, event by event, confrontation by confrontation, turn by turn, teaching by teaching, the life of the Twelve was drawn into the new and astounding reality of Jesus and the realm of God. The Twelve were a model group with abundant flaws. Jesus drew them into character re-formation in spite of their ordinariness and stubbornness.

Their group was a model of real and ordinary persons, among an ordinary and diverse people. Their model leader led them into becoming a model group, not because they were perfect, but because Jesus was present with them. Their model life was accessible, touchable and understandable to surrounding groups. The fact that such a wonderful leader would walk among such ordinary people was a dramatic model of the nature of this realm of God and an encouragement to all human groups.

This model of character development—this process of discipleship—was a small group process. Jesus did not isolate his encounters with twelve individual disciples. There are few accounts of Jesus focusing one on one with individual disciples. The experiences and healings, the arguments and confrontations, were in the presence of the group of disciples. Jesus' call to discipleship was a call to be part of a small group. Their character formation took place in community, in their life together (Mk 8:27-38).

Peter's emotional declaration that Jesus was "the Christ" happened during a conversation with the Twelve together. This is followed by the most dramatic confrontation recorded between Jesus and Peter, with Jesus saying, "Get behind me, Satan." It is helpful to note the group dynamics of this encounter: while Peter took Jesus aside to rebuke him in private, Jesus rebuked Peter in front of everyone (Mt 16:21-28). The group's awareness of all the real issues of the realm of God was imperative. Even Jesus' suffering and death had to be shared and discussed by the whole group. Their model had to be immersed (baptized) into the painful reality. They had to be an example of a group that was not allowed to avoid conflict, deny death or trivialize trauma. If they were not going to be perfect (and they could not be), then they had to be fully human and openly flawed: vulnerable, fearful, obnoxious and defensive. What a great model these twelve motley men were as they journeyed with Jesus. They were real; they were human. Looking at them, any small group can say, "We can do this!"

The Twelve as Model Among Other Groups

Jesus ministered to and with the Twelve in order to minister to the multitude. The realm of God was present for the Twelve in order for them to be present as the realm of God among other groups of people. The Twelve were a small ministry group among several circles of people who hungered for, contributed to or inhibited their ministry.

David Prior has suggested that the ministry and community of Jesus be explained as concentric circles of persons who lived in increasing levels of intimacy with him. Moving from the inner circle to the outer circle, Prior has targeted six circles of community: John, the beloved; Peter, James and John, Mary, Martha and Lazarus; the Twelve; the Seventy; those who believed in him; and the crowds.[6] Jesus lived among these interlocking circles as the model and representative emissary of the realm of God. The groups gathered around him became models of life together centered in the new values of this "near" realm. They modeled life together for several other groups who observed Jesus and the disciples. Many of these outside groups looked to the inner groups as the plumbline of Jesus' call to repent and become part of the realm of God. Some of these other groups were the ever-present crowd, the women, the counterministry groups, Jesus' relatives, the disciples of John the Baptist and the little children.

The Ever-Present Crowd

The ever-present group around the Twelve was the "crowd" or "multitude." Jesus' charismatic presence, power and authority (Mk 1:22) attracted people of all kinds, from all places. With Jesus as the crowd-pleaser, the Twelve were often among them as observers, critics and, occasionally, reluctant servants. They were sometimes confined inside a home because whole neighborhoods gathered around, blocking their way out (Mk 1:33). When Jesus and the Twelve looked for retreat and solace, the crowd would do everything within their power to find them (Mk 6:30-44). The more Jesus healed, the more other people pushed in toward the Twelve to be healed (Mk 3:10). So Jesus and the disciples would often avoid the crowd and quietly leave an area (Mk 1:38).

The crowd functioned persistently as the ambivalent arena in which the Twelve could observe and learn. What Jesus said to the greater numbers in parables, he explained privately to them (Mk 4:10). Mark especially accents the secrecy of Jesus' teaching about the full implications of the realm of God. The realm was to be given to the Twelve, but hidden from the crowd. The Twelve were to become the living model so the crowd could see visible evidence of the realm of God. For example, the parabolic teaching suggested that the realm of God was a reality for the Twelve, but could be (and often would be) missed by the multitude. An implication of the parable of the soils is that the Twelve were the good soil—those who heard the word, accepted it and produced a crop (Mk 4:11-20). They were the deeply cultivated model in the midst of a shallow and weedy people. The process of community with Jesus was a sifting away from the rocky and hardened places of abused human patterns.

Life with Jesus enabled the Twelve to experience being and working in the reality (realm) of God. The Twelve with Jesus were God's kingdom come into being even in the midst of the earth's kingdoms. In describing how Jesus taught the Twelve to pray, Luke implies that God's realm will come where Jesus is in the midst of specially gathered human groups. The increased activity of group prayer was therefore in growing recognition of God's present realm and an increasing awareness of the people's hunger and God's desire to meet that hunger (Lk 11:1-12).

Jesus' relationship with Abba was the realm in their presence. With Abba he formed the disciples into a community and a family (Mk 3:35) to be the realm for one another as well as for others. "Whoever does the will of God" is in the family with Jesus. The group with Jesus is within near range of God's influence and power.

Out of the crowd and into the group came the hurting individuals to whom Jesus ministered. The crowd ignored them, but Jesus with the group invested in them. The disciples watched him deal with each person, family, village, system, power, institution and region. They watched and learned the ministries of exorcism, healing and forgiveness. Jesus practiced most ministry in their presence (Mk 9:14-29).

Ultimately, it was the crowd's condemnation of Jesus that precipitated the crucifixion (Mk 15:13) of the once popular leader. In this the crowd was manipulated by the religious and political enemies of Jesus. Further, the crowd pressures became so great that the remaining eleven disciples deserted Jesus and went into hiding. The crowd will never be the arena in which the realm of God is seen. The crowd will not be the arena where Jesus transforms people. Only the small group is where Jesus' "power is made perfect in weakness" (2 Cor 12:9).

The Women
Many of the individuals Jesus observed (Mk 12:41-44), touched and healed (Mk 5:30-33) were women. In doing so he became a wonderful personal model of the realm's male humanity. His model of maleness demanded a shift of the Twelve's sexual value systems. Jesus was their model of the "good" man who shared the good news that men were invited to be different in the realm of God. Jesus, the man, in the midst of an all-male small group, provided new ways for men to think and act in relationship with women (Mk 10:1-11). In such a dramatic shift of male values, Matthew described the disciples' reaction to Jesus' teaching on divorce: "If this is the situation between a husband and wife, it is better not to marry" (Mt 19:10).

Not only was Jesus willing to encounter the ordinary woman in her poverty and pain, but he was willing to risk the possible condemnation of inferred sexual misconduct in personal encounters with women (Mk 14:1-9). John's anti-gnostic Gospel text is more sensually expressive of such an encounter: "she poured it on Jesus' feet and wiped his feet with her hair" (Jn 12:1-3). Was there any faster way to get word out to the whole world than for Jesus to model the sexually liberating implications of the good news with the women?

Following Jesus' arrest, Scripture's focus on the attending presence of the male group of twelve shifted to a focus on the women's group (Mk 15:40-41, 47; 16:1-8, 9-11). Between the time the disciples deserted Jesus and when they were confronted by him after the resurrection, Mark suddenly and dramatically introduces the presence of the group of women who "had followed him and cared for his needs." They stayed with Jesus through his crucifixion, death, burial and resurrection. These women were the first to share the reality of the resurrection with the eleven men who had deserted Jesus. The remaining eleven men were confronted by the perseverance and faithfulness of the women's group. The men learned much about the passion, suffering, death and resurrection of Jesus from the women because the women stayed close by through the dark days. When they refused to believe the women's report, the resurrected Jesus rebuked them for "their stubborn refusal to believe those who had seen him after he had risen" (Mk 16:14). It is clear that the men's group did not come through the experience of the passion week as faithfully and loyally to Jesus as did the women's group.

The Counterministry Groups

While Jesus and the Twelve focused on the crowd and on individual hurting people, the foils to their ministry community were the groups of elders, chief priests (Mk 8:31), teachers of the law (Mk 2:6; 11:27), Pharisees (Mk 2:16), Herodians (Mk 3:6; 6:14-29; 8:15; 12:13), Sadducees (Mk 12:18) and the whole Sanhedrin (Mk 14:55). These counterministry groups were as omnipresent as the crowd, but in contrast to the crowd's ambivalent receptivity, these official religious and governing groups were present as the theological, ethical and legal critics and judges (Mk 2:7, 18, 24) of the activities of Jesus and the Twelve.

These counterministry groups were afraid of the crowd (Mk 11:18, 27-32), which they saw as having power they wanted to have and use. Jesus never affirmed the power of the crowd. The tense intergroup rivalries and fears between the official religio-political leaders, the Twelve and the crowd provided a dramatic background in which the disciples had to live and act as a small group (Mk 12:35-40).

Every movement of Jesus with the Twelve resulted in rather dramatic negative reactions from these institutional and official groups. The presence of the contrasting model of Jesus with the Twelve tended to call other kinds of group purposes into question. The existence of Jesus with the Twelve was a living critique and condemnation of all other religious, sexual, economic and political power systems and groups. They would either be transformed by Jesus' community or try to destroy it. There was no tolerance for coexistence. The counterministry groups were convinced that the Jesus-based groups had to be broken apart or their own institutional power systems would start collapsing.

Like the Twelve, the religio-political leader groups played an observational and critical role in relationship to the acts and words of Jesus. But in contrast to the Twelve, their constant questioning turned to inquisition and conspiracy (Mk 2:6). Like the healing and exorcism events among the crowds of ordinary people, the conversations and controversies between Jesus and the Pharisees became case studies for the Twelve to observe and discern.

Theological confrontation with the Pharisees occurred in the presence of the disciples' group. As Jesus went through the grainfields with the disciples, picking and eating grain on the sabbath, the Pharisees questioned his actions (Mk 2:23-24). The controversy was between Jesus and the Pharisees, but it was focused on the unusual and unacceptable actions of the group of Twelve who were following the model of Jesus. The values Jesus modeled with the small group of disciples were threatening to the more controlling religious system. The implication of the grainfield scene was that the small group with Jesus in its midst was a "sabbath" unto itself. The model of life this group demonstrated was a scandal to the ruling religious groups and powers. What could be done with a small group who had decided not to abide by the rules of the prevailing religious order? They had to be controlled or destroyed. Coexistence was a threat. Their liberating style of life was too attractive to ordinary people.

The Twelve were frequently at the center of these intergroup controversies and confrontations. It was often their action that these official groups condemned (Mk 2:18, 24). Hostile relations with the Pharisees were the source of much emotional frustration and distress for Jesus (Mk 3:5). Eventually the intense intergroup conflict with the principalities and powers developed into a homicidal conspiracy. The Twelve watched while the intergroup conflict escalated to its inevitable conclusion: the trial, torture and death of their leader. The Twelve lived and moved in the constant stress of countergroup surveillance, interrogation, harassment and oppression (Mk 3:22).

The Pharisee's ultimate accusation that Jesus was "demon-possessed" and that he had committed the unpardonable sin, blasphemy of God, which was punishable by death, had a traumatic effect on the Twelve. The risk to their lives grew each new day they were identified with Jesus. They came to exist as a hunted band of outlaws. And even one of their own succumbed to cashing in on the contract out on Jesus' life.

However, it is interesting to note there is no textual evidence to suggest that the disciples were afraid for their lives until Jesus made his final trip to Jerusalem. This lack of fear may have been a misguided sense of confidence that Jesus was practically invulnerable to human destruction. Their messianic expectation of Jesus' supernatural power may have jaded their sense of reality and vulnerability. Such is always a potential flaw of a cohesive group. Sometimes a group develops a sense of immortality and untouchability. Urban gangs often become so preoccupied with their charismatic leaders or group identities that they lose touch with the possibility of death and the fragility of life. The true faith-based group does not live in a state of denial about the constant threat of other groups, but chooses to live its fragile and vulnerable existence because Jesus has modeled the power of such servant and risk-taking leadership.

As Jesus set the direction of the Twelve "toward Jerusalem," the growing threat of countergroup conflict and Jesus' continued anticipation of being killed caused the Twelve to be "astonished" and the other followers to be "afraid" (Mk 10:32). The groups following Jesus increasingly realized the risk implied in going to Jerusalem. They were astonished that he would provoke such a confrontation and afraid that this could mean their own deaths as well. Being a part of this notorious group they finally realized was a matter of life and death. The meaning and cost of being in this model group with Jesus had become fully disclosed. The faithful small group was in increasing danger from the attack of other organizations, systems and institutions.

The Relatives of Jesus

Jesus' biological family also is contrasted with the Twelve (Mk 3:21, 31-35; 6:1-5). Like the counterministry group descriptions of the teachers of the law, the Nazarene relatives of Jesus were critical of and embarrassed by the ministry of Jesus. Unlike the Twelve, Jesus' family wanted to control him. They thought that he was "out of his mind." Like the teachers of the law, they thought that he was "demon-possessed." When his family called for him on one occasion, Jesus contrasted them with the circle of twelve around him, saying that his real family were those who "do God's will." This harsh critique of his blood-ties family was magnified when the Twelve visited Jesus' hometown, Nazareth, where his past neighbors and relatives "took offense at him." Then Jesus reflected to the Twelve: "Only in his hometown, among his relatives and in his own house is a prophet without honor." Jesus could not do any miracles there except lay hands on a few sick people and heal them. "He was amazed at their lack of faith" (Mk 6:4-6). The model of Jesus' life with the disciples was a source of embarrassment and irritation to his own family.

The Twelve (and others) became the real family of Jesus. They were the new model of family life, juxtaposed with the old bloodline groups that surrounded Jesus in the Hebrew culture. The only valued family group in the realm was the group that followed Jesus into mission and ministry and that exercised the faith (trust) of personal relationship with Jesus. Groups that misperceived the identity of Jesus as a "down-home" boy, who should still be under the control of his family system, missed the center of Jesus' nature and the new family nature of the near realm of God as transformed human community (Mk 6:2-3).

The neighbors and relatives of Jesus could not see his real purpose and personhood. They were caught up and bound by with their limited perception of what the world was about. They were lost in the old stereotypes and paradigms of how "good" families should behave. Was their attitude partly the result of some perception that Jesus was a "bastard" son? Or was it because of a common perception that families needed to tend to their own, to be servants of their past, and to perpetuate the good old ways and good ol' days? In either case, the new way of Jesus to adopt a wider, more diverse and motley group to be his model family was not well-loved by his blood relatives. And the endangered power brokers of the family system did not like what Jesus was modeling and teaching.

The Disciples of John the Baptist

Like Jesus, John was the charismatic and directional leader of a group of disciples (Mk 1:1-9; 2:18-20; 6:14-29). A. B. Bruce argued that many of Jesus' disciples were first disciples of John the Baptist.[7] But unlike John's group, the Twelve were more interactive with the ministry of Jesus. They grew from watching the ministry into participating in the ministry. While John's group seemed to be oriented toward a separate wilderness and ascetic lifestyle and ministry, where the crowds went out to them to be baptized in the Jordan River, the Twelve traveled to where the people lived and ministered to persons in the presence of their neighbors, families and friends. The Twelve were more relaxed and spontaneous in their group life, while John's group practiced careful disciplines of fasting and baptism. The Twelve had Jesus in their midst as the present realm, while John's group was proclaiming preparation for the "coming" realm. While both groups experienced the loss of their charismatic leaders, the eleven were sustained beyond that death into a resurrection and redeemed and renewed group life.

Perhaps the most striking and important point of contrast was that the eleven continued as a reconstituted and expanded group after Jesus' death and resurrection. In this special way, the ongoing life of the group was a resurrected life, a life out of death, a life out of brokenness and desertion. The life of the new Twelve after Jesus' resurrection was a new life, a new group relationship, a new group process, a new group beginning, a new shared understanding of ministry. This transformation of the new Twelve can be compared to Mark's last reflection about John's discipleship group: "John's disciples came and took his body and laid it in a tomb" (Mk 6:29). The stark ending of John's life and group ministry must be contrasted to Mark's jubilant descriptions of the resurrection and ascension:

You are looking for Jesus the Nazarene, who was crucified. He has risen! He is not here. See the place where they laid him. . . . 'He is going ahead of you into Galilee. There you will see him just as he told you.'. . . He was taken up to heaven and he sat at the right hand of God. . . . Then the disciples went out and preached everywhere, and the Lord worked with them and confirmed his word by the signs that accompanied it. (Mk 16:6-7, 19-20).

The group whose life is centered in the resurrected Christ does not have a dismal ending, but is in the constant state of a new beginning.

Jesus and the Little Children

Mark records two encounters between Jesus and little children (Mk 9:33-37; 10:13-16). In both cases, the Twelve are compared to the little children and found lacking. These encounters reveal two of the disciples' great misunderstandings about the nature of God's realm: (1) their need to decide which of them was the greatest next to Jesus, and (2) their need to control the focus and agenda of Jesus' ministry. Both confrontations around the children were loaded with major values differences between Jesus and the Twelve.

The first encounter was precipitated out of the Twelve's intragroup conflict. Jesus took aside one child to be an example of the kind of mutuality and hospitality the group should practice toward each other. Their welcoming of the child was equivalent to their willingness to welcome Jesus and the kind of welcome the disciples should have for one another. Jesus compared himself to the child to emphasize his weakness and desire to be the servant of the Twelve. The implication was that they should seek to serve one another and give up their need to control or outrank one another. In Jesus' group, positioning was not to be part of the heavenly value system.

The second encounter had to do with the desire of the Twelve to control Jesus' ministry agenda and to be an exclusive group. This encounter is found in the textual context of Jesus' teaching on sexual and monetary values in the realm of God. These were two very difficult value shifts for the Twelve to understand. From the perspective of the Hebrew adult male value system, women and children were not high priorities, but money and power were. Jesus turned the values of money, sex and power upside-down for the Twelve by giving women and children more value than money and just as much power as men.

Suggesting that the parallel concerns of business, marriage and government are money, sex and power, Richard Foster has accented their ethical and social dimensions. While Foster does not fully explore the interpersonal implications of these three minefields, he has suggested such unresolved values are the sources of human abuse behind most social and ethical problems. Where the issues of money, sex and power are so greatly covered and avoided, deep and intimate Christian community is unattainable. Where confessional prayer and interpersonal disclosure and dialogue could release many from the imprisonment of abusive patterns of business, marriage and government, the lack of confrontation on such key values does not provide the freedom to experience true human community.[8]

The children, like the women, were part of the poor and disenfranchised. By rebuking the Twelve and investing in the blessing of the children, Jesus was saying "No" to the exclusive and controlling male orientation of the group. They were not to be an exclusive male club, but an inclusive, gathering ministry group who embraced women and children as valuable members of the realm, even more important than themselves, and just as important as Jesus.

The one man Jesus encountered whom the disciples may have considered most eligible for entry into their group and the realm was "rich" and "righteous." But contrary again to the Twelve's understanding of the prerequisites for group membership, Jesus made it hard for this rich young leader to join the group. When the ideal recruit "went away sad," the Twelve were "astounded" and asked one another, "Who then can be saved?" (Mk 10:17-26). Who could possibly have the right credentials to join God's select group?

According to Jesus, the little children had the right stuff to join the group. The Twelve needed to learn how to welcome them rather than work at keeping them out. Those who considered themselves most eligible to join the Twelve would be the last to follow, while those seemingly least likely to join should be the first to be welcomed (Mk 10:31). It was a miracle and a wonder to see this group of thirteen men traveling throughout the Judean countryside surrounded by hundreds of women and children getting a substantial amount of Jesus' attention and being affirmed that they were every bit as important as the men.

The Transfiguration Group

The most unusual short-term small group in which Jesus participated was with Elijah and Moses on a "high mountain" while alone with the core group of three disciples, Peter, James and John (Mk 9:2). This wilderness expedition, comprised of the inner core group, implied an intimate experience not common to all the members of the larger disciples' group. Jesus was willing to risk the divisive potential of taking three away from the Twelve to experience together a unique event. Many would argue that this could have been a disastrous leadership miscalculation. When a *cohesive* group is subdivided in experience and connectivity with the leader, the whole group is often thrown off balance.

Group *cohesion* is a factor of mutual trust in a small group. If members of the same group are subdivided and led into diverse experiences, the subgroups are likely to become distrustful of one another. The inner group is perceived to have more influence with the leader and the outer group is perceived as having less power.[9]

The key questions here are: What was the purpose and implication of Jesus' desire and action to subdivide his band of twelve on this specific occasion? What was the purpose of identification with or relationship between the transfigured three and the ordinary three on the mountain?

Jesus' group appearance with Moses and Elijah could be understood as both historical and eschatological. Moses, the one through whom God gave the Law, and Elijah, the key representative of the prophets, were both historical figures among the people of God. Both left the face of the earth rather mysteriously (Deut 34:5-8; 2 Kings 2:1-12). The mystery of Moses' death is held in the words, "[God] buried him in Moab . . . but to this day no one knows where his grave is. Moses was a hundred and twenty years old when he died, yet his eyes were not weak nor his strength gone." Elijah's earthly end was even more dramatic and mysterious: "suddenly a chariot of fire and horses of fire appeared, . . . and Elijah went up to heaven in a whirlwind." Both were taken by God in the prime of physical health. Neither died typical or visible human deaths.

At this small group summit Jesus met and identified with two dead men who were visibly present and obviously alive. He experienced these brief moments of human community with the historical leadership of the people of God as they were "transfigured" together. They were "talking" together. They were brought together from two different realms, the heavenly and the earthly. This transfigured group was a model of how the earthly and ordinary was quickly (instantaneously) accessible to and in community with the extraordinary and eternal people of God. Jesus was showing the core group of three that their small group community was not limited to this earthly existence, but was in community with heaven forever. Theirs was not just a group "until death do us part," but a community beyond death, an eternal community of the people of God, into which Jesus had called them to live together. He was also showing the three that their ministry in community would have the impact of Moses, Elijah and Jesus together. The portals of heaven's power would be theirs as a group.

The three-on-three confrontation was frightening, but transforming. The core group of disciples had been reminded that their earthly community with Jesus was connected to an eternal community with him. Peter's way of dealing with the eternal community was to try to secure it as a historical and ongoing event. He wanted to erect three shelters to house and remember the three heavenly beings who had visited here. But Peter missed the long-term implications. The three disciples were being given a glimpse of the eternal community and ministry together of Moses, Elijah and Jesus. They too were participating and sharing in the community and ministry of the Law and Prophets through the eternal humanity of Jesus. What was in order here was not a celebration and remembrance of the past, but an ongoing participation with Jesus to be the community of God on earth as it is in heaven. They were to live risk-filled lives of faith together in community "down the mountain," not build shelters and become cloistered on the mountain. Theirs was to be a faith and ministry group down among the people with Jesus in their midst.

This awareness of the immediate presence of eternal community with Moses, Elijah and Jesus would be a source of encouragement for the disciples throughout their own ongoing ministry, suffering, death and resurrection. As Jesus told them, "the Son of Man must suffer much and be rejected. . . . Elijah has come, and they have done to him everything they wished" (Mk 9:12-13). The suffering and success of Moses, Elijah and Jesus was to be brought together in one group through Jesus who was leading the three disciples to share in this historical and eternal community of those who have been persecuted and rejected by the political and religious powers of their day. The heavenly three were a sign and model for the earthly three to remember and follow. And the whole community of heaven was present when Jesus was with them. Jesus brought the whole community of heaven to earth.

Another implication of this intergroup experience was the passing on of the historical mantles of Moses, Elijah and Jesus. At both death events of Moses and Elijah others inherited their ministry (Deut 34:9 and 2 Kings 2:9-15). Both Joshua and Elisha are given the spirit and the ministry of their mentors. The three disciples were on the mountain to inherit the historical and eternal ministry of the transfigured trio. This ongoing ministry of the small group was transferred through Jesus alone. He was the earthly three's connection to the eternal community. But this mantle was not being passed from one to one. The "powerful and awesome" deeds of Moses and Elijah were reflected in the prophetic and historic ministry of Jesus, a community ministry being passed to a community of disciples, three through one, one to three, three to twelve, twelve to one hundred twenty and on to thousands after the day of Pentecost. The power of the historical and heavenly community of God was to become the powerful ministry of the apostolic community on earth.

The three were the inner circle of the apostolic community to share their experience of the transforming and eternal power of Jesus with the ever-widening circles of the new prophetic communities to be established after the resurrection.

"As they were coming down the mountain, Jesus gave them orders not to tell anyone what they had seen until the Son of Man had risen from the dead" (Mk 9:9). The mountain experience of the three was to be shared with the wider community after they had experienced the resurrection. Like the fifty in the company of prophets who journeyed with Elijah and Elisha, the other nine disciples (and the many more) who traveled with Jesus watched his special relationship with the three, heard about the mountaintop experience, learned about the eternal community of the people of God, and began to participate in that inner community with Jesus after the resurrection. In this way the intimate experience of the three unfolded into the intimate experience of the many after the resurrection.

Jesus risked this more intimate relationship with the inner group of three not to make them an *elite* above the Twelve, but to make them an *elect* for the Twelve and for the many. The experience of the three (and then of the Twelve) has beckoned the many, not just during their earthly lives, but for subsequent generations of groups of the people of God. Just as Moses and Joshua, Elijah and Elisha were not to be an elite above the leaders and prophets of God, so the three with Jesus were to invite all the people of God into an intimate community of heaven on earth, to become partners in the new community of priests and prophets after the resurrection and Pentecost. The mountaintop three shared their intimate community with the inner core of three, who in turn would pass their community experience with Jesus to the greater community of the Twelve and "the many." While small groups have an earthly existence, in Christ they take on the mantle of being God's voice and ministry on earth wherever two or three gather. The intimate presence of heaven is passed from one group to another.

■ SMALL GROUP MINISTRY IMPLICATIONS

1. Every new and growing small group needs models of good leaders and good groups. These models may be in the group or known by the group. The chief individual model is usually a designated leader who guides the group in their life together. There may also be spiritual models after whom the individuals in the

group pattern their lives. Sometimes the group's leadership model and spiritual model are the same person. Groups should be formed with the modeling paradigm in mind. Modeling persons are those with small group knowledge, experience and wisdom. If the group has no such leadership model, the members may not be able to get in touch with Christ as their chief model. Such groups have little sense of destiny and direction.

2. New groups or less mature groups are at a vulnerable place of imitation. Charisma without maturity can be a dangerous thing for a leader of such a group. Such leaders will sway immature groups; for better or worse they will become the model that the group imitates. Charisma without maturity can lead to codependent, abusive or addictive behavior. The model leader can lead the group in the wrong direction. This is why it is very important that small group leaders are selected and appointed with discernment and training. The charisma of a misguided leader can harm a group and its individual members for years to come. The wrong leader can inoculate a potentially wonderful group against being in a small group at all.

3. An important role for the modeling leader is to teach and show the group how to have a good group experience. Natural charisma is a helpful attraction to catch the group's attention and confidence at the beginning. However, charisma by itself is not enough. This is one reason pastors often fail in their attempts to lead groups. Many pastors function solely as charismatic preachers and teachers. But without group experience and skill, charisma is not enough to give a group a strong sense of direction. As we will discover in the chapter on leadership, a good group leader knows how to use charisma to model a good group experience. Energy and humor are two important ingredients in the leader's charismatic exercising of directional modeling.

4. Eventually the model of the leader should shift to the incarnate model of the group as a whole. The mark of a good small group leader is the ability to transfer power and responsibility to the group. The fruit of the Spirit is for the group to take on the character and model of Christ as their leader, releasing dependency upon their original model and leader. A good leader knows when and how to wean the group from the substance of his or her charisma and strength. Eventually the group must begin to look to Christ as their chief model. For some groups this can happen during the first few meetings, while for other groups this transition may take one to two years. Model leaders must be prepared to lead new groups for enough time to help them through this transition of dependence. The healthy modeling process includes leading the group through these various stages of dependency and into interdependency.

5. The small group that models a vital life in Christ usually lives in stark

contrast to other religious or service groups around it. This contrast can be an invitation to a more full and complete human life as the realm of God and/or it can become a threat to the ongoing viability of how other groups function. Often there is a movement by the existing system to eliminate such a group. This movement to eradicate the healthier Christ-centered koinonia experience is a natural outcome of a confrontation of two worlds, the realm of God and the realm of human control. Principalities, systems, groups, clubs, organizations, governments or religious institutions which do not want to lose influence or control may see the faithful small group as a challenge to their kind of life. Even pastors have been known to stamp out small groups which do not buckle under their more controlling leadership. A healthy Christian small group is a threat to any group that does not want to face the reality of their need to dominate and control. There is a sense in which each faithful small group becomes a counter-culture if they are willing to allow Christ to be the focus of their formation and life together.

6. Small groups become cultures to themselves, for better or for worse. The dark side of this is becoming ingrown and insensitive to the wider world and becoming self-preserving at all costs. The group can become a "we" against a "they." Jesus worked hard at modeling the positive side of this new culture. A small group should become a culture *for* the benefit of others, not a vulture for the picking apart of others. The group's life in the Spirit of Christ should be a movement toward becoming a band of servant leaders. This sense of destiny and direction needs to be held up as a target and destination for the entire life of the group. Groups can become self-satisfied, protective and self-secure. Ministry and mission beyond the group should be an ever-possible and ever-probable fulfillment of their life together. Christ desires to take each group on a journey, to travel together into the places and among the peoples where individuals alone would not dare venture. Small groups are exodus bands who are moving from the control of life's negative systems to be servants of freedom with the present Christ. Group leaders need to understand the fullness of a healthy small group model: from discipleship into mission, from safety into risk, from old ways into new ways. This is the model of Christ among the disciples. The group's journey inward to Christ and one another must become a journey outward into the world.

12
LEADING THE SMALL GROUP

Then Jesus went with his disciples to a place called Gethsemane, and he said to them, "Sit here while I go over there and pray." He took Peter and the two sons of Zebedee along with him, and he began to be sorrowful and troubled. Then he said to them, "My soul is overwhelmed with sorrow to the point of death. Stay here and keep watch with me."

Going a little farther, he fell with his face to the ground and prayed. . . .

Then he returned to his disciples and found them sleeping. "Could you men not keep watch with me for one hour?" he asked Peter. "Watch and pray so that you will not fall into temptation. The spirit is willing, but the body is weak."

He went away a second time and prayed. . . .

When he came back, he again found them sleeping. . . . So he left them and went away once more and prayed the third time. . . .

Then he returned to the disciples. (Mt 26:36-45)

Jesus was a leader who prepared his small discipleship group to be leaders. Leadership is the art of influence, of taking initiative, of showing others where to go, what to do, how to act and how to think. Jesus' leadership was a continual calling of the group's attention to the primary authority of Abba God in their lives. Jesus led his small group in word and action, in prayer and planning, and called them to be even as he was, to do what he did, to watch like he watched. But the small group of disciples were not the leaders Jesus desired them to be until after Pentecost. In Gethsemane Jesus prayed to the Father for them, "so that they may have the full measure of my joy within them. . . . As you sent me into the world, I have sent them into the world. For them I sanctify myself, that they too may be truly sanctified" (Jn 17:13-19).

Jesus' leadership had to be experienced as well as taught. The group had to see it to believe it and follow it. The group was their arena of leadership discovery and development.

Leadership implies group process. If there is a leader, there must be at least one follower. Most initiatives of human leadership are ventured in the context of a small group. This is because leadership requires accessibility and nearness. While there is a kind of leadership that directs crowds and large groups, it is difficult to lead well from a distance. Face-to-face connections are important for successful long-term leadership. Followers need to be able to touch and see and feel their leaders. This can happen only when a leader is close enough to be encountered and experienced. Most helpful leadership happens in the midst of small bands of followers. Leaders of large groups usually lead a small group of leaders who lead other small groups. Leadership is therefore the leading of a small group or the leading of a small network of groups. Jesus understood this basic leadership rule: lead a small group of leaders who will in turn lead their small groups of leaders, who will lead the people. As we discussed earlier, Moses also discovered this rule of leadership. Leadership, to be effective, must be in the midst of a leadership community. Jesus selected and developed his own leadership community, and they changed the world.

A crucial leadership scene in the life of Jesus and the Twelve was Gethsemane. The crisis of the final hours of Jesus' life reveals a pattern of leadership he consistently used. First, he led the group where he wanted them to go. This meant he had to have a sense of leading within himself. He had learned to follow the inner direction of Abba. Second, he gave the group directions. Jesus led in word and action—leadership always combines word with action. Third, he led the smaller and more intimate core group a little farther than the others. But he always went a little farther himself than he took any of the members of the group. Fourth, he was always taking the initiative. He would not ask of them what he was not willing to experience himself. Fifth, he shared himself—his heart and his feelings—with them. He showed them who he really was, even in vulnerability, pain and sorrow. He did not protect them from the dark side of his spiritual life, but invited them to join him, watch him, and watch with him. Jesus allowed them the freedom to fail. When the small group of disciples did not meet his expectations, he was patient and understanding of their humanity and weakness. He gave them the space to be less than perfect. Yet he called them to be leaders of the Spirit. He taught and showed them how to pray, and led them into prayer. He revealed to them a deep intimacy and intensity of prayer. Finally, he patiently and repeatedly encouraged them to go the hard way of leadership. He called them beyond their comfort zones and led them where they did not want to go. He called them to experience what they did not yet have the capacity and discipline to experience. He continually called them to practice spiritual discipline and persevere in their practice.

Jesus was a leader *for* leaders and a leader *of* leaders who would lead many other groups. Jesus was a follower of Abba which made him a leader of humanity. He was the small group leader who used the small group as an arena in which to develop other leaders. Jesus often focused his leadership among a very small group of three: Peter, James and John.

Leading a Core Group

Of the Twelve Jesus gave special attention to the three, Peter, James and John. John Mallison has argued that Jesus spent more time with these three because they were the key leadership for the future.[1] It is possible that he invested more in these three because they were more aware of who he was and what he was about. He knew they were more likely to become the primary leaders and spokespersons of the Twelve after his death and resurrection.

The early church (ecclesia) seemed to affirm the primary importance of this core group. Peter's voice emerges frequently in Acts and the epistles of Peter, John speaks through a Gospel and set of three epistles. James is noted as a significant leader of the Jerusalem home church and "author" of the Epistle of James. The New Testament seems to give continued special recognition to these three men as key leaders in the new church, affirming that Jesus did something special with them that he did not do with the other Twelve. Simply, it may be that Jesus liked to be with the three more than the others.[2] The relationship of Jesus with the three was not always warm and friendly, however. Jesus had many edgy confrontations, especially with Peter. Peter was the one who first exclaimed that Jesus was the Messiah, only to be immediately rebuked by Jesus as "satanic" for trying to dissuade him from his destiny of suffering and death (Mk 8:29-33).

Since Andrew was one of the first four disciples, he was perhaps the most conspicuous disciple not included in this inner core group. Yet there is no apparent biblical reason for Andrew's absence from the core group. Peter, James and John seem to be characterized as having more assertiveness, aggressiveness and drive to be a part of the inner circle. Peter often took the primary role as spokesperson for the Twelve and the three. James and John had an assertive mother who conspired with them to ask of Jesus to be at the right and left side. This was an arrogant request, but it showed their initiative, ambition and willingness to take risks and lead.

The three formed around Jesus as the inner group of the Twelve. They were with Jesus from the beginning of his ministry (Mk 1:16). The three were with Jesus when he healed Peter's mother-in-law (Mk 1:29-31). They took the initiative to go out looking for Jesus when he was in solitary prayer (Mk 1:35-39). The three were probably with Jesus when he called the tax collector, Levi, and went to eat with him at Levi's house with other tax collectors and "sinners" (Mk 2:13-17).

On several occasions, Jesus invited only the three to accompany him. One of these was an invitation to the house of Jairus to be in the room with him, Jairus and Jairus' wife when their daughter was raised from the dead (Mk 5:35-43). The Gospel of Mark does not explain the secrecy attached to this scene, but simply says "he gave them strict orders not to let anyone know about this." They were also alone with Jesus on the mountain when he appeared transfigured with Moses and Elijah and they heard the "voice from the cloud" affirming Jesus as beloved Son. Again, Jesus asked the group to keep the confidentiality of the experience among themselves (Mk 9:2-13). If this imperative included the confidentiality of the three not to tell the rest of the Twelve, Jesus had the intention to layer the knowledge and awareness of the three amidst the Twelve. Only speculation can answer the question, Why would Jesus want to keep such an amazing happening from the rest of the Twelve? Why were only the three with Jesus at such important moments? In any case, it is clear that Jesus had a special relationship with this core group and they emerged as primary leaders of the future expanding small group movement called *ecclesia*, or church.

The three were included in the innermost life, thoughts and feelings of Jesus while the other nine had more limited contact. The splitting away of the three from the rest of the Twelve seemed to be a source of group irritation. The nine left behind when Jesus and the three went up the mountain did not have the spiritual maturity to accomplish an exorcism (Mk 9:14-37). This raises the question as to whether there was a gap between the spiritual maturity of the three and the rest of the Twelve. One wonders whether the layered relationship, the relative status of the three and the other nine, had taken its toll on the cohesive ministry of the Twelve. Would the argument over "who was the greatest" have happened if the three had not been given special attention and relationship with Jesus? Would Judas have betrayed Jesus if he had been included in the inner three or if the Twelve had been more evenly interdependent? Did Jesus use this separation as a designation of friendship and trial to test the commitments of the whole group?

It was after the heady mountaintop event that James and John had the audacity to ask for special privileges and status in their relationship with Jesus. This caused the other disciples to be "indignant" with them and gave Jesus an opportunity for some theological reflection on the nature of servant leadership (Mk 10:35-45). James and John had a misunderstanding of the nature and privilege of their inner relationship with Jesus. They tried to impose a secular view of leadership upon the friendship nature of the realm of God, where there were to be no tyrannical leaders. They wanted to set up a hierarchy of power even among the Twelve. (One can wonder what Peter thought about this power play.) Did Jesus use the particularization of the three from the Twelve to provide an opportunity to teach kingdom leadership and shared power? He must have known that the existence of the inner group would eventually cause hard feelings and temptations to hoard position and power.

Peter seemed to be more observant, more vocal and more risk oriented than the others. Jesus quite often played off Peter's rash comments and initiatives, almost as though his leadership was a counterinitiative to Peter's misdirected attempts at leadership. For example, Peter recognized that the fig tree which Jesus cursed had withered (Mk 11:21), giving Jesus an opportunity to speak to the Twelve about the intimate relationship between prayer and faith. Jesus used Peter's observation as an opportunity to address the whole group. The smaller group provided a more intimate and more interactive environment than the arena of the Twelve.

In a noteworthy shift of the profile of the inner grouping, the original four disciples (the three plus Andrew) approached Jesus as he sat on the Mount of Olives, opposite the temple, to ask him privately about the sequence and meaning of his expectation of future events (Mk 13:3-4). Again, in this situation the question emerges whether the inner group had some continuing hope that they would be in the inner circle of leadership if Jesus planned to overthrow the existing political system in Jerusalem. From their perspective, they probably thought that since they were the "original" four disciples, they were the most probable inner group to rule with Jesus in the coming of the new kingdom. This could help explain Peter's denial of Jesus after Jesus was captured and sent to trial (Mk 14:27-31, 66-72). Maybe it was not until that moment that Peter understood the deep frustration of his own ambition (shared by the other two or three), that he had been hoping for a conquering Messiah rather than a dying one, and that he thought he would be a shareholder and insider in the new ruling group.

In any case, Jesus took the three along with him to Gethsemane to share in his deep distress and sorrow, but they fell asleep and deserted him at his moment of crisis (Mk 14:32-42). Their lack of personal support for Jesus in his most intense hour of pain is amazing in light of their seeming intimacy and close friendship. After all the special attention Jesus gave to the inner group, it is amazing they were not mature enough to participate in what Jesus was feeling.

While he was preparing to be separated from his most loved friends and be killed, the three could not bear that such a powerful and charismatic leader would make himself so vulnerable to death. Their sleep may have reflected a numbness (and extreme denial) at the point when Jesus was most vulnerable. That Jesus' full passion was inaccessible to them may have been the result of their inability to share at this time the deep pain of what God was asking Jesus to endure. No matter how close to Jesus the three had become, they were not close enough to know the full humanity of Jesus. No matter how capable a leader Jesus had been, he was still not able to lead them fully into the place where he had to go. There was still a chasm of intimacy and a flawed chemistry in their human bonding. Not until after Jesus' death and resurrection was the Spirit able to complete the leadership task Jesus could not fulfill in his finite humanity.

This realization of Jesus' limitations should caution every human leader of a group to be aware that there are things that only the Spirit can lead a group to accomplish and individual members to understand. Such ultimate leadership influence is primarily a spiritual reality, not just a matter of good modeling, great training and perfect planning. Such a realization should take the heavy burden off small group leaders. Only the Spirit is able to complete the development of fine leadership. Even Jesus himself was not able to lead the group where they would not go or could not understand to go.

After Jesus' arrest Peter was the first of the three to recognize and feel the deep pain and sorrow of his lack of trust in the leadership of Jesus (Mk 14:72). Peter's brokenness in the absence and loss of Jesus was finally a recognition of his intimate loss and the vulnerability of his relationship with Jesus. Peter grieved the loss of his friend and mentor, but more fully grieved the recognition of his own cowardice and disloyal behavior. After the resurrection, his deep sorrow was met by the angel's insistence to the women that Peter be specifically told about the resurrection of Jesus (Mk 16:7). Even in death and desertion, Jesus attended to the emotional needs of his followers.

The inner core of the Twelve consistently experienced more of the personal reality and heart of Jesus. They were the ones to feel the deepest loss of separation at his death, and exaltation at his resurrection. The paradox of the inner three was that while they were not called to rule with Jesus in the worldly sense, they were called to serve with Jesus in the heavenly sense. Their rule was through their friendship and intimate community. Jesus used their experience of intimacy to beckon others into future intimate community with the risen Lord (Acts 1:11-15). Jesus led them into closeness so that they would be able to lead others into deeper community with Abba and with one another by the power of the Spirit. Jesus led the inner core of three disciples who led the Twelve, who, in turn, gathered with the one hundred twenty, who led the expanding circles of ecclesia (church).

Jesus' Situational Leadership of the Twelve

Paul Hersey and Ken Blanchard are the authors of a seminal book on the theory of situational leadership entitled *The Management of Organizational Behavior: Utilizing Human Resources.* In this book they describe the necessity of leadership to meet groups and individuals at their unique levels of maturity in skills, desire, ability and attitudes. Their theory suggests that people at different levels of maturity need different styles of leadership. Jesus seemed to understand and model a similar leadership methodology, adjusting his leadership style as his small group of disciples walked with him and learned with him. He used different leadership styles with the crowd, with the women and with his enemies than he used with the Twelve.

Without the varying leadership styles of Jesus and his initiating, directing and sustaining presence, the Twelve could not have been a cohesive discipleship group.[3] Once Jesus called them together their common bond was his presence as leader (Mk 3:13). Jesus situationally shifted the focus of the group from his personal presence to their interpersonal faith. Jesus' first group leadership act was to "call" twelve to be with him and to follow him. While Jesus himself remained the continuity for the group's bonding, over the weeks and months he shifted his leadership style gradually and intentionally. In the end Jesus became the absent and delegating leader of the Twelve through the presence and power of his Spirit (Mt 28:18-20).

The trinitarian baptismal benediction at the end of the Gospel of Matthew may signify a fulfilled leadership progression in the life of the Twelve by the situational leadership of God. God's leadership initiative was that the Father sent the Son, and the Son sent the Spirit (or the Father and Son sent the Spirit together). The disciples' maturing process may have been connected first to an awareness of the new parenthood of God, second to the experience of Jesus as the Son and their partner-brother, and third to the Spirit coming into their community to make them full partners and mutual priests. Jesus' affirmation, "Surely I am with you always, to the very end of the age," was made possible by the sending of the Spirit to be Jesus' ongoing presence among them. The Spirit came when the eleven were gathered in the upper room for prayer and reflection among one hundred twenty men and women (Acts 1:13-15). There the Spirit succeeded and completed the leadership work first of Abba, then of Jesus.

It was in the presence of the Spirit that the fulfillment of Jesus' leadership came to bloom. He no longer led the Twelve from outside but moved to lead from

within their hearts and between their relationships. This group leadership movement from Jesus to the Spirit, from without to within, is key to the maturing
eschatological call and identity of all postresurrection Christian groups. Every
group in Christ has the destined potential to experience the intrinsic leadership
of the Spirit in the maturing process of their community together.

As it was for the leadership and character formation of the Twelve, so it can
be for every group that is called together in the name of Jesus (Mt 18:18-20). The
"binding" or bonding process on earth is attached to that which is true in heaven.
Where two or three come together with Jesus in their midst, they are in the
presence and realm of God. The coming together of the group on earth is simultaneous to their coming together in heaven. Jesus is the continuing leader who
brings people together in twos or threes—in small groups. Jesus initially calls the
group to God as Abba, but finally in maturity, calls the group to the spirit within
them. The maturational movement of Jesus' leadership is from God as parent
(dependence) to God as Spirit (interdependence). And Jesus himself models this
full continuum of small group discipleship and leadership development.

Jesus may initially call the group together through the charismatic presence of
one strong human leader, but it is the Spirit's maturing desire and work to move
that faithful group into a leadership of interdependence upon the Spirit of Jesus.
In the Gospel of John there is a connection between the going away of Jesus and
the coming of the Spirit. This is a situational leadership movement (Jn 14:16-31).
The charismatic leader Jesus had to leave so that the Spirit could give leadership
charismata to the whole group of twelve and beyond. Jesus finished his earthly
leadership task by announcing to the Twelve that the Spirit "will guide you into
all truth" (Jn 16:13).

In the ongoing life together of the Twelve, their group maturity and situations
changed. Their leadership needs shifted. Their personal characters and task com-
petencies matured. They matured in their awareness of how and where Jesus was
leading them. But it was not until the Spirit came into them and among them
that they fully understood the purpose of Jesus' direction and leadership. Jesus
wanted each member of the group to become as he was, full of the Spirit, attentive to Abba, but empowering of those who followed together.

Empirical research of small group behavior has affirmed the relationship between group growth and maturity and aggressive leadership styles. The highly
directive early leadership style of Jesus among the Twelve transitioned into a final
and completely delegating style. The coming of the Spirit made possible the
completion of the ongoing process of spiritual maturity which empowered the
Twelve to be interdependent with one another and lead others in the name of
Jesus. They no longer needed to be dependent upon the finite direction of the

present and human Jesus.[4] As we trace the leadership character and style of Jesus through the Gospel of Mark it becomes clear that Jesus, the strong human leader (Mk 1:17), became Jesus, the Spirit of shared leadership (Mk 16:17).

Between the beginning and the ending of the Gospels is a shift of emphasis upon who is doing the ministry and the leadership. Jesus' "Come, follow me, and I will make you fishers of [humanity]" becomes "In my name they will drive out demons; they will speak in new tongues; they will pick up snakes with their hands; and when they drink deadly poison, it will not hurt them at all; they will place their hands on sick people and they will get well" (Mk 16:17-18). The emphasis on the leadership and ministry of the human Jesus shifted to an emphasis on the people who do leadership and ministry in the name of Jesus (see table one).

In reviewing the actions of Jesus' various leadership styles, it is important to note how he adjusted his leadership style as he led the Twelve on the way to Jerusalem. The early Jesus called persons to himself. The later Jesus called the disciples to take responsibility for the ministry. As John Mallison has said, "Jesus chose to share his ministry with others, not delegating in order to help him cope with the growing demands, but to develop future leaders."[5] And Robert Coleman has affirmed that this process of group leadership and ministry delegation is a mandate for Christian discipleship.[6] Jesus came to share the power and authority of the realm of God with all those who follow him.

Jesus' determination to share leadership authority and power, first with the Twelve (Lk 9:1-2), then with the seventy-two (Lk 10:1-11), then with the one hundred twenty (Acts 1:15—2:4), and finally with all who are afar off (three thousand on the first day of Pentecost, Acts 2:14-21, 38-41) is foundational to the meaning, purpose, goal and process of his leadership among the Twelve. Of all the Gospels, Luke is most clear about this revolutionary practice and concept of a leader sharing power with wider and wider groups of persons. Shared and empowered leadership development is unique to the good news of Jesus' discipleship model.

In his book *Jesus and Power* David Prior argues that Jesus modeled and taught the Twelve a nongrasping view of power (see Mt 11:12; Jn 6:15; Phil 2:6). Prior maintains that Jesus' leadership style and use of power was counter to every cultural norm of "getting, grabbing, keeping, snatching, controlling and retaliating." He became a leader who saw power "in terms of giving, serving, welcoming, forgiving." To follow the model of Jesus is "to be a servant of all, to give himself away, to walk the way of the cross." Prior sees Luke articulating five leadership themes in Jesus' radical call to servant power: facing up to failure; dealing with competitiveness; avoiding the divisive spirit; denouncing racial prejudice; and

Table One
Jesus' Situational Group Leadership Styles

1. Jesus was the group leader with a strong identity and mission (Mk 1:11, 15).

2. Jesus was the group leader who was tempted and proven (Mk 1:12-13).

3. Jesus was the initiating and designating group leader (Mk 1:16-20).

4. Jesus was the group leader with charisma and authority (Mk 1:21-28).

5. Jesus was the teaching group leader (Mk 1:21).

6. Jesus was the praying group leader (Mk 1:35).

7. Jesus was the directive group leader (Mk 1:38).

8. Jesus was the forgiving and healing group leader (Mk 2:9).

9. Jesus was the discerning group leader (Mk 2:8).

10. Jesus was the risk-taking group leader (Mk 2:13-17).

11. Jesus was the celebrant group leader (Mk 2:18-22).

12. Jesus was the value-setting and liberating group leader (Mk 2:27).

13. Jesus was the popular group leader (Mk 3:7).

14. Jesus was the group leader who was the brother (Mk 3:31-35).

15. Jesus was the group leader who put away evil and fear (Mk 4:40).

16. Jesus was the leader who subdivided the group (Mk 5:37).

17. Jesus was the leader who traveled with his group (Mk 6:1).

18. Jesus was the group leader who gave away authority to his group (Mk 6:7).

19. Jesus was the leader who sent the group out in teams (Mk 6:7-11).

20. Jesus was the compassionate group leader (Mk 6:31-42).

21. Jesus was the leader who called the group into ministry (Mk 6:37).

22. Jesus was the inductive and theological group leader (Mk 8:27-30).

23. Jesus was the confrontational group leader (Mk 8:33).

24. Jesus was the patient and enduring group leader (Mk 9:14-19).

25. Jesus was the model servant leader of the group (Mk 9:33-37).

26. Jesus was the model activist leader for the group (Mk 11:15-18).

27. Jesus was the group leader who followed God's leading (Mk 12:17).

28. Jesus was the group leader who loved God and people (Mk 12:28-34).

29. Jesus was the group leader who valued women and men (Mk 14:3-9).

30. Jesus was the leader who gave himself for the group (Mk 14:22-24).

31. Jesus was the leader who gave his ministry to the group (Mk 16:15-18).

following with a whole heart.[7] According to Jesus, power was not to be snatched away and held on to, but to be given away and to be shared with anyone who desired to become a member of the realm of God. While this model of power-sharing began with the Twelve, they were key to it being distributed at Pentecost to many different groups of people (Acts 2:5-12).

The Twelve were present on Pentecost among the one hundred twenty Galileans who on Pentecost spoke the languages of many diverse people groups. This is a dramatic example of how God shares power with all people. Language, speech and hearing are communication power, which is leadership power. The sharing of language is a symbol of shared power and leadership. The people said, "We hear them declaring the wonders of God in our own tongues." What does this mean? God is not just the God of the Jews. Jesus is not just the leader of the Twelve. Jesus is the Lord for all and Lord of all. Jesus is the Lord who gives power and authority to all. But before Jesus had the freedom to share power with all, he had to be willing to recognize all power came from Abba. This is the hard preparation for healthy group leadership. He had to deal with the temptations of human leadership and leadership systems to control and manipulate people for one's own ends. Jesus had to deal with these temptations before he could be the servant leader after the heart of God, and before he could lead others to become the servant leaders of God.

The Leadership Temptations of Jesus and the Twelve

Before Jesus could begin his liberating and empowering leadership of the group of twelve he had to work through his own personal temptations to gather people and power to himself (Mk 1:12-13; Mt 4:1-11; Lk 4:1-12). Mark simply mentions the temptation period of Jesus in the wilderness, while Matthew and Luke develop the three specific temptations. It is interesting to note that Matthew and Luke switch the order of the second and third temptations, those having to deal with political power and religious power. For Matthew the final (and ultimate?) temptation was secular rule, to be godlike before all the kingdoms of the world. For Luke the final (and ultimate?) temptation was religious rule, to be godlike before the people of God, Israel. These divergent emphases may reflect the redactional concerns of Matthew and Luke, one a focused critique of political power, the other a focused critique of religious power. But to be a good small group leader both lessons must be faced for there are political and religious leadership temptations in all small groups.

The three satanic temptations of Jesus had to do with group leadership and power. Before Jesus could call the Twelve to follow him, he had to identify and work through the world's systemic drive to seduce group leaders into the misuse of power. For if Jesus could not be the empowering servant leader of the Twelve, he could never be the empowering Servant Lord of the nations (Is 52:13-15; 61:1-11). Isaiah declared, it was the Servant who was to have his total identity in "the Spirit of the Sovereign LORD," who could therefore be free to "preach good news to the poor. . . . To proclaim freedom for the captives and release . . . for the prisoners." Jesus discovered that his true identity was determined by his receptive presence and relationship with the Father who was the primary source of his power. As Jesus refused to tap into any other "higher power" source (including himself or Satan) he was freed to lead others to Abba as the key authority for their lives and groups.

As the work of Abraham Maslow might suggest, the wilderness experience of temptation was a process of *individuation* or *self-actualization* for Jesus as a human leader. In developing faith implications from Maslow's work, James Fowler has suggested that there is a faith stage (stage six: universalizing faith) that reflects the completing of individuation and self-actualization. If self-actualization is the preeminent fulfillment and completion of human identity and need, Jesus was working through his ultimate and cosmic identity in the wilderness. He desired to find his completed self as the Son, fully actualized in community and relationship to Abba God. He therefore had no further need to gather power to himself. He had developed complete trust through his intimate relationship with and empowerment from the "Father." Even in the most adverse and lonely situations, cut off from the community of the three or the Twelve, cut off from the face of Abba, he was still able to say on the cross of his leadership task, "It is finished."

In Luke (4:13-30) the period of wilderness temptation is followed by Jesus' return visit to Nazareth, where, in the synagogue, amid his family and the community of his childhood, he identified himself not as Jesus of Nazareth, but as the messianic Servant of God. His first demonstration of being completely confident and actualized in trust with the Abba God was to risk and experience the total rejection of his human family and village of origin as well as his religious heritage. With no human rootage or bonds to hold him captive, the completely self-actualized Jesus, "in the power of the Spirit," could go on to have authority over evil (Lk 4:31-37) and authority to call persons to himself without need to own, control or manipulate groups of ordinary women and men.[8] Jesus had to know who he was, even in the most lonely and alienating environments. And he discovered his full identity in the presence and intimate community of the Father before he could help or lead any human group to discover who they were in the (presence and community) realm of God (Lk 4:3, 9). This man, whose community was securely attached to divine community, could weather whatever human systems offered as temptations. He could lead any human group without succumbing to the political intrigue of the group's power dynamics.

Satan's seductive approach to Jesus both at the beginning and the end was, "If you are the Son of God . . ." If you know who you are, then take all the human power that is rightly yours. Be the human leader everyone wants you to be. Become the most influential and powerful leader in the history of humanity. The three temptations called Jesus to deal with the key temptations of all human leaders. The three temptations of Jesus were leadership temptations no matter what the size of the group to be led.

In his book *In the Name of Jesus* Henri Nouwen examines the three temptations of Jesus as primary and universal temptations of human group leadership. The leadership discussion is somewhat autobiographical of Nouwen's own leadership journey to move "from Harvard to L'Arche, from the best and the brightest, wanting to rule the world, to men and women who had few or no words and were considered, at best, marginal to the needs of our society."[9] Nouwen suggests that because Jesus worked through his own personal identity and leadership temptations, he was then able to lead a small group of men to also work through their personal identities and leadership temptations.

Nouwen explains Jesus' three leadership temptations as the temptation to be relevant, the temptation to be spectacular and the temptation to be powerful. Through his dialogical interaction between the texts of Matthew 4 and John 21, Nouwen claims the temptations as common to every human leader. These are common to both religious and secular leadership contexts.[10] Wherever two or three are gathered members of the group will be tempted like Jesus to abuse their group power.

We can articulate these three leadership temptations in light of the small group context as (1) the temptation to provide for all the needs and desires of the group, (2) the temptation to be the sole source of governing power and authority for the group, and (3) the temptation to be the sole authority of meaning and purpose for the group. In the context of group network leadership, group systems leadership or small group program management the three temptations become the (1) temptation to provide for the needs of all the groups, (2) the temptation to have the primary governing authority and power over all the groups, and (3) the temptation to become the theological center and lord of the whole group system or program. These three temptations are reminiscent of the Moses' syndrome in Exodus 18. Moses' temptation, as Jethro so confronted him, was to have everyone dependent upon himself. Jesus—and all leaders—face a similar group systems temptation: to have all people and groups dependent upon one human authority. Each temptation has its unique small group consequences.

The Temptation to Meet All the Needs of the Group

Small group leaders are often tempted to "make it happen," or to meet the needs for all members of their group. Group members will often treat the leader as though he or she is the only source of "bread" (of truth, of expertise, of direction, of balance, of control, of influence, of biblical knowledge) for the group. While these desires are seldom spoken, the group may imply they want the leader to "turn these stones into bread," "turn these chairs into family," "turn these Bibles into mature lives," or "turn these group dynamics into Christian community."

In *Life Together* Dietrich Bonhoeffer strongly affirmed that Christian community is the gift of God and cannot be produced through human ingenuity.[11] Small group leaders must learn to lay aside all such temptation to provide the messianic expectations of themselves and their groups.

Nouwen has argued that this first temptation of Jesus was "to be relevant," to give people what they wanted. Accordingly he says, "the Christian leader of the future is called to be completely *irrelevant* and to stand in this world with nothing to offer but his or her own vulnerable self." While Nouwen's call to irrelevancy may seem a bit overstated, it is consistent with the nature of Jesus' leadership pattern that what group leaders have to give is their being, their relationship to God, and their love for group members. Expertise and skill are integral to Nouwen's call to irrelevance. The core value of good group leadership is the personal and relational character of the leader. Not the ability of the leader to meet everyone's need. If the desire to provide for the needs of the group usurps the leader's freedom to be God's person in the group, the leader will succumb to the first temptation.[12] As Jesus said, "Human beings live not by bread alone, but by every word that comes from the mouth of God."[13] A small group can not be sustained and nurtured to maturity solely through the knowledge and expertise of the leader, but through the leader's willingness to listen to the voice of God and help the group learn to listen and respond to the voice of God.

Nouwen has also written that "obedience" is the leadership of listening.

The word *obedience* has so many negative connotations in our society. It makes us think of authority figures who impose their wills against our desires. It makes us remember unhappy childhood events or hard tasks performed under threats of punishment. But none of this applies to Jesus' *obedience*. His obedience means a total, fearless *listening* to his loving Father.[14]

The group leader who listens to the voice of God is the leader who does not lead out of demand but out of loving relationship. The good group leader will not permit the expectations of the group to block out the quiet voice of the Spirit of God.

Along this same theme Nouwen continues,

> We are usually surrounded by so much inner and outer *noise* that it is hard
> to truly *hear* our God when he is speaking to us. . . . Thus our lives have
> become *absurd*. In the word *absurd* we find the Latin word *surdus* which means
> *deaf*. A spiritual life requires discipline because we need to learn to *listen* to God,
> who constantly speaks but we seldom hear. . . . The word *obedient* comes from
> the Latin word *audier*, which means *listening*.[15]

As the small group leader learns to listen for and be open to the voice of the Spirit
of Christ, he or she will not be tempted to "turn the group stones into bread"
but instead will "listen to the voice of God" to discern which things (patterns,
skills, disciplines) are best for the group to practice. Group leadership competence
must emerge out of a disciplined practice of the leader's listening faith. As Nouw-
en has cautioned, leadership skill, competence, efficiency or directiveness must
not be driven by secular values of success and productivity, but by the primary
value that a listening love directs the leader and the group.[16]

Jesus did empower the Twelve to provide abundant food for multiple thousands of people, but the provision and sharing of the bread was a sensitive and
listening service of the small group of twelve to Jesus in the midst of the larger
group's need (Mk 6:30-44; 8:1-9). In both Gospel scenes of the feeding of the
multitudes, sufficient food was produced out of insufficient reserves. There were
plenty of stones around for Jesus to pick up and turn into bread, but he chose
to work through the distribution of the gifts of the small discipleship group. Jesus
turned the need of the crowd into an opportunity for the small disciple's group
to discover a dependency upon God's surprising provision. The small group already had the basic resource—their relationship with God and one another. Their
willingness to listen, obey and act as a servant community met the multitudes'
greater need.

The listening leader can help the willing small group to meet the needs of
greater numbers of people. Such leadership is not just a matter of the group's
personal wealth, power, skill or competency, but of the group's willingness to
listen to God and serve together. The way to such sensitive service is through

> union with God in prayer . . . so that every word spoken, every advice given
> and every strategy developed can come from a heart that knows God intimate-
> ly. . . . Leadership must be rooted in the permanent, intimate relationship with
> the incarnate Word, Jesus . . . to find there the source for [the group's] words,
> advice and guidance. Through the discipline of contemplative prayer, Chris-
> tian leaders have to learn to listen again and again to the voice of love and
> to find there the wisdom and courage to address whatever issue (need) pre-
> sents itself to [the group].[17]

The small group leader's temptation to use personal expertise and power to meet group needs can be redirected as the leader is willing to listen for the voice of God in the midst of the group.

The Temptation to Be the Group's Controlling Manager

Human groups live in constant struggle for power and control. Roberta Hestenes has pointed out that all groups go through stages. Long-term groups have a life cycle that includes periods of struggle for power and control. It is tempting during such chaotic times for a small group leader to hold onto the power and control of the group, or to position for gathering more power and control, "to control complex situations, confused emotions and anxious minds . . . to feel safe in an unpredictable climate . . . have moments in which [one] clamps down and tells everyone to shut up, get in line, listen . . . and believe."[18] This stormy period is worsened if other group members are also trying to lay hold of the group for permanent control or power.

Nouwen has framed the second leadership temptation of Jesus as the desire for control—the desire to lead but not be led, the desire to be the godlike boss or tyrannical executive of the group—the temptation of power. The desire to control or manipulate the group process and to execute unilateral or monolithic decisions is a significant dimension of this second temptation. This temptation is often most apparent in a leader who oversees multiple structures or groups, such as a senior pastor or small group pastor. The exercise of autocratic authority over large numbers tends to override the hearing of the still small voice and the "being led" dimension of the leader's authority.[19]

The misuse of group executive and administrative power is a constant temptation for all secular and religious leaders. Why is this such a pervasive temptation? As Nouwen observes, "Maybe it is that power offers an easy substitute for the hard task of love . . . easier to be God than to love God, easier to control people than to love people, easier to own life than to love life."[20] Such an executive and administrative orientation in a small group is often disguised as a desire to keep the process going, stay with the set agenda or make the product happen. When the group agenda is maintained and the group work is produced at the expense of sensitivity to persons and relationships, the leader has given in to the seduction of the second temptation. The task has become more important than persons or community. Law has snuffed out grace. Truth has stifled love. Or orthodoxy has buried orthopraxy. Condemnation is loosed on the group in the form of a demanding parent who wants perfection but cannot give love.

The *distributive actions* theory of group leadership describes that every group member can exercise leadership by performing a role for either the maintenance of relationships or the accomplishment of the task. All small group situations reveal a constant tension between these polarities of task and relationship. From the secular perspective of social psychology and group theory there is a nontheological orientation to valuing a balance between both of these polarities. But from a biblical and theological perspective, emphasis on task accomplishment always exists under the judgment of the law of love. From God's perspective, productivity must be a servant of community. The value of human being and relationship in the Garden had precedence over the work of gardening. It is in the context of a "type A" work ethic that friendships, marriages and community are sacrificed on the desks of successful but lonely executives who may gain the whole world but lose their own souls.[21] In the realm of God the main task of the group is to grant high value to persons and relationships.

Reflecting on the recent history of American crusade evangelism, Richard Halverson, chaplain of the U.S. Senate, has lamented the institutional and executive orientation to "produce converts" but not "nurture Christian community and discipleship." He suggested that the future of evangelicalism lies "in the awakening of the Christian community to assertive and loving discipleship, and being willing to let go of the idolatry to numbers and productivity."[22] Small group leadership must be committed to the care and maturity of persons. Evangelism must be a servant of loving community. The small group leader must become a servant who has more love for people than drivenness to get through all the agenda. Agendas are spiritual disciplines to be flexed and adjusted according to the voice of the Spirit and the law of love in Jesus Christ.

For Jesus, the man, and for the Twelve, as men, dealing with these temptations was a watershed for masculine leadership maturity. Throughout history an abusive male orientation has been to wield executive, administrative or task control while neglecting the nurture and skill of interpersonal sensitivity—that is, to get the job done at the expense of redeeming human life.

Gordon Dalbey has pointed out in his book *The Healing of the Masculine Soul* that men have tended to abdicate responsibility for relational skill and human nurture to women. As a result they may be threatened by the ability of women to build more intimate relationships and personal human networks. Dalbey says that in fear men build

> systems of law and institutional hierarchies which reduce relationship to some
> manageable form. Similarly, we men may seek to allay our fear of a living God
> by writing elaborate "systematic theologies," believing we can use those theologies to keep the "hound of heaven" on a leash of rationality.[23]

With the potential of such one-sided purposes overtaking groups, small group leadership should include both men and women who understand the importance of getting the task accomplished is always secondary to the long-term redemption of the humanity and community of the group. This of course does not mean that some women do not have similar disabilities in controlling groups, but because of sustained cultural influence and elongated patterns of abuse, men seem to be more tempted to move in this totalitarian direction.

This tension was illustrated in a December 1990 article in *Working Woman*, entitled "The Career, the Husband, the Kids and Everything." The frequently stated concern of working women is to find creative ways of balancing careers and relationships. As the article suggested, the feminist movement may have sold out to the addictive and abusive patterns of the male culture in this concern for success in the corporate and professional world. Many women have become successful by learning to play the male game as well as or better than men. But, like some men, they may have lost their human souls in the process.[24] Similar concerns for men in community are being raised by the men's movement through such writers as Robert Bly.

The man Jesus clearly pointed in a new direction for the Twelve, the seventy and the one hundred twenty men and women together. The temptation for one person to control one group or a network of groups is a satanic movement. The keeping of the first commandment, "Worship the Lord God, and serve him only" (Mt 4:8-10), is a covenant commitment to community. The gracious movement of the Holy Spirit in human life is away from task-oriented control systems and toward the growth of community with God, men and women. As Nouwen has warned,

> The temptation of power is greatest when intimacy is a threat. Much Christian leadership is exercised by people who do not know how to develop healthy, intimate relationships and have opted for power and control instead. Many Christian empire-builders have been people unable to give and receive love.[25]

Such empire-building is often the result of the adolescent and independent action of a person who has become autonomous but not learned the value of interdependence. Often mature small group leadership has been defined as the ability to make independent decisions. But this is more an adolescent behavior sustained when adults give in to the second temptation. In *The Modern Practice of Adult Education*, Malcolm Knowles, building on Maslow's "hierarchy of human needs," declared that the mission of adult education is to help individuals "achieve complete self-identity through the development of their full potentialities. . . . Self-development is a universal human need . . . an ultimate need of individuals is to mature." Knowles has defined the chief movement of maturity as growth from dependence to autonomy.[26]

From a relational and theological perspective the word *autonomy* does not adequately describe the process of human maturation. The full movement is from dependence upon to interdependence with God and other human beings. The "self-actualized" person, like Jesus, is indeed "separate" but chooses to "live among." The developmental movement from dependence to independence is parallel to the growth from childhood to adolescence. However, the developmental movement to adulthood and self-actualized leadership is the freedom to be an interdependent participant in adult community and decision-making. Hersey and Blanchard have said that "the intent of *situational* leadership is to enable *follower control* or self-leadership. This places the primary leader in interdependent leadership relations with *mature* followers. They together become a leadership community."[27]

Good group leaders are best grown in leadership communities where mutuality and interdependence are highly valued. If the value system of good leadership is the ability to lead independently (the "it's lonely at the top" syndrome), the maturity of the leader will be locked in at the stage of adolescence. But if leadership is valued as in the model of Jesus, as the ability to function interdependently with God (and with others), then maturity is the freedom to grow into a truly self-actualized adulthood in the midst of both the heavenly and earthly communities.

Nouwen defines leadership as "the ability and willingness to be led where you would rather not go." He portrays the typical secular view of mature leadership by saying, "When you were young you were dependent and could not go where you wanted, but when you grow old you will be able to make your own decisions, go your own way and control your own destiny." There is an interconnection here with the leadership perspectives in Knowles and Hersey and Blanchard. The freedom for leaders to be interdependent is a sign of leadership maturity, which is the freedom to be mutually led by the Spirit.[28]

The temptation is to be a leader who has independent vision and makes independent decisions rather than the spiritually mature servant leader who, as Nouwen says, "is being led to unknown, undesirable and painful places." In these places in the group's life the leader is not in control, but must willingly defer to God who has the higher view. This is "a leadership of powerlessness and humility." Nouwen is also quick to assert that this is not a "*psychologically* weak, passive victim or spineless leadership," but an *assertive* love of Christ and people.[29]

Such a frustrated expectation may account partially for the desertion of the eleven when Jesus was arrested, tried, tortured and crucified. The showing of the powerlessness of the group's leader at a crucial point where "great" male leaders should struggle to prove themselves—by pulling out a sword and fighting for independence (Mk 14:43-51)—was more than eleven virile men could comprehend. But not for the women who "watched from a distance," who had often been led by men into pain and abuse (Mk 15:40-41).

The hope for healthy Christian small groups lies in group leaders who "are willing to be led" by the Spirit, not for independent group executives who demand a following of their decisions and process with little sensitivity to divine and human relationships. As Nouwen has suggested, the temptation to exercise a demonic and independent leadership style must be exorcised by the leader's commitment to "strenuous theological reflection" that "will allow [the group] to discern where [they] are being led." To avoid being seduced into the limited values of the behavioral sciences, where "little true theology" is learned, the group must learn to think theologically, "to discern from moment to moment how God acts in human history and how the personal, communal events that occur during our lives can make us more and more sensitive to the ways in which we are led to the cross and through the cross to the resurrection."[30]

But even among theologically reflective leadership and groups, there is a temptation for a group leader to exercise abusive power. This is the substance of the third (Luke text) leadership temptation.

Temptation to Be the Group's Sole Theological Authority

Consistent with Nouwen's leadership perspective, small group leaders are not called to "rugged and *spectacular* individualism, stardom, heroism, self-made dominance" or group process "stunt" work, but to "communal" and "mutual" experience and ministry. Leaders were not sent out alone by Jesus, but in small group teams of two or more.[31]

Christian small groups are tempted to look for that one great Bible teacher to "show and tell" them everything they need to know about faith and life. Groups can be seduced into thinking that only this one great charismatic teacher can direct the group into deep spiritual wisdom, insight, maturity and ministry. Jesus did not call leaders to minister alone, or to do theological reflection and teaching alone. As the Twelve ministered with and to one another, so also they were called to minister to and with others.

The temptation of a group leader is to minister alone, to lead from the perspective and vision of one, in the skill and expertise of one. But healthy small group leadership is about leaders who lead *among* leaders, who minister *with* ministers, who share theological reflection *among* the group. As Jesus himself modeled, it is God who does the ministry. And God ministers in the midst of the ministering group (Mk 1:14-28).

In the first chapter of Mark the order of events in Jesus' life was a movement from the lonely period of wilderness temptation to the calling of the first four disciples (the original small ministry group) to the first act of ministry in Capernaum (Mk 1:14-28). From Mark's perspective Jesus did no ministry without the shared ethos of an accompanying small group. This order of Jesus' ministry plan is shared by Matthew, who describes Jesus preaching in Galilee and calling the first four disciples before healing the sick. Luke suggests that Jesus performed some limited healing (of Simon's mother-in-law) before he called the first four. The Gospel of John also has the calling of the first disciples before the healing ministry is undertaken. There is strong and consistent evidence, therefore, that the healing ministry of Jesus was somehow dependent upon and bound to the presence of a small group of disciples. Jesus seemed to heal only when accompanied by a ministry group. From the beginning Jesus was teaching the Twelve and others that healing, forgiveness and ministry are community expressions. As Nouwen has said, "Whenever we minister together, it is easier for people to recognize that we do not come in our own name, but in the name of Jesus who sent us."[32]

As demonstrated many times in the Old Testament, the temptation for a group to focus all theological and political power and authority in the one leader was called idolatry. In Exodus 20 and 1 Samuel 8, the clashing community values of "have no other gods" and "give us a king" are continually lurking behind a group's expectations. But Jesus himself would not take away Abba God's primary place of authority in the group. He refused to be their king as determined by human standards. He was their teacher-servant and their friend. As Nouwen so clearly articulates,

> As Jesus ministers so he wants us to minister . . . not as professionals who know their clients' problems and take care of them, but as vulnerable brothers and sisters who know and are known, who care and are cared for, who forgive and are being forgiven, who love and are being loved. Somehow we have come to believe that good leadership requires a safe distance from those we are called to lead. Medicine, psychiatry and social work all offer us models in which service takes place in a one-way direction. Someone serves, someone else is being served, and be sure not to mix up the roles! But how can anyone lay down his life for those with whom he is not even allowed to enter into deep personal relationship? Laying down your life means making your own faith and doubt, hope and despair, joy and sadness, courage and fear available to others as a way of getting in touch with the Lord of life. We are not the healers, we are not the reconcilers, we are not the givers of life. We are sinful, broken, vulnerable people who need as much care as anyone we care for. . . . Therefore, true ministry is mutual . . . mutuality can only be seen as a weakness and dangerous form of role confusion. The leadership about which Jesus speaks is of a radically different kind from the leadership offered by the world.

It is a servant leadership . . . in which the leader is a vulnerable servant who needs the people as much as they need him or her.[33]

The antidote for small group leader idolatry is confession and forgiveness.[34] Confession and forgiveness help the group deal with the temptation to idolize the strong Christian leader who has no desire to nurture the group's mutual and spiritual leadership.

Among Christians, a misunderstood concept of strength undermines this movement toward mutuality, confession and forgiveness. Too often the person perceived as a strong leader is the person who demands center attention, has a self-centered purpose and vision, makes autocratic decisions, practices relational insensitivity and convinces the group that he or she has the best intentions for the whole group. Such leaders are not oriented to help the group understand that they are just as vulnerable and sinful as the rest of the group. The leader who does not choose or is not permitted to live in mutual ministry, theological accountability and relational submission with the group is destined to ongoing immaturity, isolation and idolatry. The leader's immaturity is often exalted as strength and the group's immaturity is often affirmed as teachability, but all continue to be imprisoned in their exclusivity, polarity and isolation from one another and from God. The healthy small group and leader should not give in to the temptation to have or be the solo and so-called strong spiritual leader. The healthy group and leader need to enter into mutual confession and vulnerability, embracing the strengths and weaknesses of each group member, not permitting any one member to emerge as the group's solo theological expert, king, savior or lord.

An Antidote to Group Leadership Temptations

The way to avoid seduction into any of the three leadership temptations is to enter into the leadership prayer of Jesus: "Lead us not into temptation, but deliver us from the evil one" (Mt 6:9-13; Lk 11:2-4). Luke portrays the Twelve watching Jesus at prayer and asking him to teach them to pray. The group learned to pray by watching and listening to their leader at prayer. In this context of prayer they are shown how to avoid temptation. Just as Jesus chose the Twelve after an extensive time of prayer (Lk 6:12-16), so he led them to avoid temptation by investing much time in prayer together (Lk 22:39-53).

Twice while Jesus was in prayer with the disciples on the Mount of Olives he said to them, "Pray so that you will not fall into temptation." But they fell asleep—and also fell into the temptations to control the situation. They became combative for control to defend their leader and themselves. They deserted Jesus when they perceived him as a weak leader. For the Twelve, at that moment of learning the way of kingdom leadership, "darkness reigned."

As Luke described these dark events, so also he described the movement of the eleven into more self-awareness and prayer. After the disciples had been tempted that night on the Mount of Olives and they watched the resurrected Jesus ascend into heaven on that same Mount, they returned to Jerusalem to be "joined together constantly in prayer" and to wait for God to give them the gift of the Spirit (Acts 1:10-14).

The eleven moved from the prayerless and powerless seduction of evil's effect on their leadership to a prayerful and powerful willingness to be led by the Spirit. In prayer they discovered how to be like their group leader, Jesus, who prayed "as a regular response to situations of crisis and decision."[35] The small group of disciples learned to practice their leadership and community in prayer. Their words and actions emerged out of intimacy with the Spirit and one another. The way for the new leaders to avoid temptation and allow the "kingdom to come" was to develop intimacy with God and with one another. So they developed the mutual trust of the group in the power of the Spirit to pray "all together in one place" (Acts 2:1).

Just as prayer is a demonstration of covenant by the small group to live in intimacy with God and with one another, so it is for group leaders. And in this intimate presence and trust of the Spirit, leaders are able to meet and overcome the temptations to misuse theological, communal and personal power. They learn to share the group's ministry of the prophetic and the visionary, the dreaming among the men and the women, and the young and the old (Acts 2:17-21; Joel 2:28-32). This is the way to mature group leadership, to interdependence upon the Spirit, to mutual self-actualization of personhood, and to participation in the leadership and group ministry of Jesus. The community of prayer is a discipline of leadership to deal with the temptations of abusing leadership.

■ SMALL GROUP MINISTRY IMPLICATIONS

1. The leader needs to be a personal practitioner of small group life. Leaders need to have self-awareness of their own abilities and disabilities as a group leader. They need to have a directional vision about the full meaning and implications of small group ministry as an action of the Holy Spirit and the realm of God. A leader needs to be able to understand the particular cultural context of the group ministry and be able to adjust the ministry model to fit the needs and opportunities of the context.

2. Leading a small group is both easy and difficult. If a group is practicing mutual and interdependent behavior, the formal leader may have little need to take initiative and give direction. The group may do this for one another. How-

ever, if the group tends to be greatly dependent upon the vision and knowledge of a leader, group leadership is much more demanding. The leader of a more dependent group must be able to move the group into less and less dependence on the leader and increased dependence on the Holy Spirit and one another. This is very hard work—helping a group to maturity takes patience and perseverance. The leader must have a strong sense of purpose and direction. This kind of leadership demands a mature leader. Mutual groups do not demand the same intensity of leadership as dependent groups. This is even more intense in a group full of dysfunctional, addictive, abused or recovering persons. Such groups need leaders of confident experience and assertive powers.

3. Leader goals are different for short-term versus long-term groups. Leading a short-term group generally takes less knowledge of life cycles, periodic evaluations, interventions, confrontations, recovenanting procedures or maturational patterns. The short-term group can function quite well with a prepared curriculum. However, the healthy long-term group demands a leader who can take the group through life-cycle changes, periodic evaluations and numerous corrections of vision and direction. The leader of the long-term group needs to be able to wean the group from her or his dominant presence and help the group take on the responsibility of sharing the load and joy of leadership. The long-term group will not reach their personal, relational or spiritual maturity if the leader does not understand how to let go of the group's authority and power and empower others to take it.

4. As Max DePree has said, "Leadership is an art."[36] Small group leadership is both skill and art. The good small group leader commits to learning the skills and practicing the art. This is a lifetime commitment and process. Small group leadership skills can and should be used in all arenas of human gathering—not just for the church group, but for teams, friendship, marriage, counseling, psychotherapy, committees, families and boards. This is leadership for being completely human. It is good therefore to call all people of faith to an intentional process of developing their small group skills and art. This is not just a program, but a way of life.

5. Small group leaders must become aware of and deal with their temptations of power and control. Group leaders have biases, seductive tendencies, controlling styles, dysfunctional patterns and defective knowledge. Ongoing leader accountability, reflection, feedback and affirmation are key to the maturity of a small group leader. Leaders need to be in circles of affirmation and accountability to become more aware and more skilled. This means the primary leader of a small group network needs the same kind of ongoing accountability and development. Ongoing leader support groups may help to accomplish this. A good small group

leader should be growing up in the stature of Jesus Christ. Leadership is a commitment to move beyond status quo and to run against the inertia of groups who resist venturing into the deeper community with Christ in the realm of God.

6. Encourage small group leaders to read the Gospels and see Jesus as a model of small group leadership. If leaders can develop this mindset of seeing Jesus as their primary model of good group leadership, they will have a lifetime target for which to shoot. This will also develop their observational and interpretative skills as a Bible study leader.

7. Leadership is what any member of a small group can and should do. The good group leader will encourage other members of the group to take appropriate initiatives of leadership. The freedom, responsibility and privilege of leadership action should be shared with all group members. As soon as the initial leader begins to give permission for others to take leadership initiative, they become empowerment leaders for the group. As we have seen, Jesus was not afraid to encourage the disciples to speak up and take initiative. The many potential leadership actions for group members should be outlined so members can choose to activate them: asking good questions, leading a discussion, observing the group dynamics, leading group prayer, preparing the place of meeting, hospitality, planning a special event or meal, making contact with the individual members, etc.

13
OBSERVING SMALL GROUP DYNAMICS

When evening came, [Jesus] said to his disciples, "Let us go over to the other side." Leaving the crowd behind, they took him along, just as he was, in the boat. There were also other boats with him. A furious squall came up, and the waves broke over the boat, so that it was nearly swamped. Jesus was in the stern, sleeping on a cushion. The disciples woke him and said to him, "Teacher, don't you care if we drown?"

He got up, rebuked the wind and said to the waves, "Quiet! Be still!" Then the wind died down and it was completely calm.

He said to his disciples, "Why are you so afraid? Do you still have no faith?"

They were terrified and asked each other, "Who is this? Even the wind and the waves obey him!" (Mk 4:35-41)

When Jesus was with the Twelve, he was deeply aware of their feelings, moods, reactions and intentions. Jesus used his observation of the group dynamics and individual behavior of the Twelve as a foundation to confront them with themselves, their values, their biases and their motivations for action. He also used the dynamics of the Twelve to teach the wider collection of disciples about the nature of God and what God desires of people together. The nature of the realm of God, as Jesus taught it, was a striking contrast to the typical behavior of the Twelve. Jesus' keen observational discipline was the preparatory platform for his calling of people away from their fear-bound worldview to embrace a faith-filled immersion into the realm of God.

The disciples in turn were also keenly aware of Jesus' attitudes and actions as he traveled with them. Everything he said and did was worthy of their observation. The writings of the Gospels are the result of the observations and re-membrances of Jesus by the disciples. The group's memories of Jesus in their midst helped them later to reflect more fully on the full nature of God's realm and the complete nature of Jesus' ministry life. Their observational and reflec-tional awareness of Jesus in their presence was the foundation for their own ministry. As they watched the model of Jesus, they imitated his character and spirit themselves.

The Importance of Observation

In reviewing the action, discipline and practice of Jesus with the Twelve and the Twelve with Jesus, it is clear that small group observational practice was a core discipline of discovering the mystery of the presence of the realm of God at work in the world. If God's actions could not be observed and contrasted with typical human reactions, the disciples could not have apprehended the purpose and min-istry of Christ among them. But they did. Their observational awareness has been the foundational theological stuff upon which the church has been centered and built. And this basic human discipline, empowered by the constant presence of the Holy Spirit, continues to help gatherings of faithful people be aware of Christ in their presence. Groups become poignantly aware when their narrow and sinful human actions undermine the ongoing ministry of Christ in their group and in the world. Spiritual and relational observation gets us in touch with both the light side and the dark side of a group's reality.

Observation is the art of watching and understanding the interpersonal dy-namics and patterns of human relationships. It is a community discipline that has a particular importance in small group life. Each group has its own unique way of relating and behaving. Each time the same group gathers, the different set-tings, moods, circumstances and purposes will tend to lead the group to explore new patterns of relating. Observation is an inductive skill that allows the group being watched to speak for itself. Observation allows—and in fact, expects—the Spirit to bring insight about the meaning and practice of the group's life, to bring light to what is really going on in the group.

This is why it is extremely helpful to observe Jesus with the Twelve. They were on a journey together of constantly changing environments and experiences. They lived out a complete group life cycle. Their interactive patterns were three-dimen-sional. Their group was in constant flux—at different times different persons emerged in relationship with Jesus, and some had no visibility at all. Over the extent of their group life together certain persons seemed to behave consistently, while others went through changes of attitude and character. Through the Gos-pels, we see the flaws and frustrations of several disciples. We see how Jesus interacted with each in a unique way, and how he interacted with the whole group.

Biblical exegesis is also a discipline that observes the persons, relationships, events and words of God's people. It includes the process of doing group case studies on gatherings and interpersonal dynamics of biblical people. While the people observed are not currently alive as a contemporary group, they were real people in real groups. In exegesis there is the need to observe authors who themselves also practiced observational skills as they reflected and relived and retold the stories. All of Scripture is a multi-layered compilation of the group observations of the key events, attitudes and actions of God's people throughout salvation history. The Gospels in particular are lessons in the observation and reflection of dynamics where Jesus is in the midst of the group. The original observers were the early apostles, authors and compilers of these observation events and teachings of Jesus. The historical observers have been God's people, the readers of the Gospels, throughout history, who have been empowered by the Holy Spirit to see and understand what was happening between Jesus, the Twelve and the wider world in which they lived, moved and had their being.

The typical small group observational process follows a classic inductive study methodology: observation, interpretation and application. These three stages in the observational process include: (1) noting what is happening in the group's life together, (2) interpreting what this behavior means, and (3) making needed changes to improve the group's life together. These three observational steps are *recording, reflection* and *re-action*. These three stages of observation attend to the dynamics of the group. Observation allows the group to speak for themselves and allows the group observers the freedom to interpret for themselves what these observations mean. As in any classic inductive situation, there is a primary source which in observation is the whole group. God is active and present in the group's life. This observational process helps us to see what God is doing in the group.

Recording is the process of attending to the facts of the relational dynamics of the group. A note is made, that the disciples woke Jesus. *Reflection* is the process of discovering what this recorded fact might mean. The disciples seem to be frightened and dependent upon Jesus to intervene on their behalf.

The third stage in the observational sequence is *re-action*. Now that we see *what* is happening, and we think we understand *why* it is happening, we need to decide *what to do* about this behavior pattern. How do we help the disciple's group to be less fearful and not as dependent upon Jesus? For the faithful small group, this is always wrapped inside the greater question, What is God asking us to change about or do with our group? Good observation leads to re-action and change. Faithful observation leads to transformation. God gives groups the capacity to be reflective so they can be changed by the power of the Spirit into the image and community of Christ. This is what the journey of the Twelve with Jesus in the Gospels is about: God changes people who walk together with Christ in small groups.

This transformational process begins with the practice of intentional observational disciplines. The absence of such reflectional discipline has kept many small groups from experiencing the powerful transforming presence of the Holy Spirit. On the other side, a sterile exercise of such observational techniques also can rob the group of their potential transformational implications. Good observation occurs when the mind, heart, spirit and body are engaged and working together. This integration of the whole person is like a well-composed and well-arranged song. When the melody, harmony, rhythm and dynamics are orchestrated and artistically joined with the words, the whole presentation makes a dramatic impact with its complete performance. This three-dimensional group observational art is both a skill to be learned and a gift of God.

In his book *The Spirit of the Disciplines* Dallas Willard differentiates between two kinds of spiritual disciplines: abstinence and engagement. In the arena of engagement, Willard includes fellowship (koinonia) as an important spiritual discipline. In order for koinonia to be vital and passionate, the special koinonia disciplines of communal recording, reflection and reaction must be exercised. Willard says that "the disciplines of engagement counteract tendencies to sins of omission. Life . . . does not derive its power of growth and development from withdrawal but from action—from engagement."[1] Observation of the behavior of persons with one another in a small group context helps the leader and the group to prepare themselves for change and transformation, for new action in the realm of God.

Observation is a key discipline of engagement. In order to engage another or a group, one must intentionally receive all the signals that they communicate, both verbally and nonverbally. Observation is the process of being "aware" of what others are communicating. Without this special discipline of receptivity, there can be no real sense of the "body" of Christ, the "community" interaction, the face of others.

Observation implies accountability. The fulfillment of recording and reflecting upon group behavior is that members of the group call the group to attend to its positive and negative patterns of communication. Affirmation of the good stuff going on in the group is as important as critiquing and changing the bad stuff. In either case, observational leadership is an accountability to watch what the group is doing, calling the group to reflect about the meaning of its behavior patterns, and asking the group to re-act to form a healthier dynamic for its life together.

Spiritual observation must be empowered by the Holy Spirit. Just as Jesus observed the behaviors of the Twelve and others, so the Holy Spirit can enable the disciples of Jesus to observe the life of their group as the "body" of Christ. The Holy Spirit can sustain the observational reflection, discernment and accountability of a small group that desires to walk in the way with Christ. The Spirit gives special insight to group patterns and individual members' behavior. The Spirit brings about the transformational possibility of intimate life together as it helps the group to become more self-conscious and self-aware. And as the Spirit helps the group become aware of its own flaws and graces, the group is more empowered to turn out into the world as a "light" for healthy relationships and psyches. Without this reflective spiritual practice and empowerment, the small group is left to tread over and over its own tracks as it circles around and around in a status quo wilderness or, worse yet, pursues a malevolent decline.

Israel wandered in the wilderness for forty years because the people refused to become self-aware of their dysfunctional group dynamics. They feared going on and venturing into new territory. This would challenge their set patterns of behavior and force them to exercise faith. To cross into the Promised Land meant risk, danger and threat to their desire for individual and group security. Every small group is confronted by such an "exodus" journey. Will the group wander in a long-term safe wilderness together, or will they move on into new territory, take the necessary risks, meet the interpersonal giants and experience the abundant life of a group that has the faith and courage to meet new challenges?

As we observe in the Gospels, Jesus' leadership of the Twelve led them where they feared to go. Instead of wandering in the wilderness of structured and safe Judaism, Jesus called them back to their faith roots in Yahweh as Abba who intervened in their lives and moved them to leave their comfortable prisons of law and confining order. Jesus led his group into confrontation with their individual and group values. He led them to observe the reality of the destitution of human life all around them. He led them into the intervening action of God in their lives. He brought the realm of God close to them as they grew close to one another. And he taught them to watch and observe life through his eyes, the eyes of the Spirit of God. Jesus and the Twelve were the observant exodus group that *did* experience transformation.

Observation, therefore, has a confrontational dimension. If things are not well with the group, someone needs to have the courage to confront the group with the negative reality. If poor behavior is observed but not confronted, the group may enter a more rapid rate of decline, because members of the group will know the truth but not call the group to embrace and act on it. The result is dissonance. The group becomes aware, but is unwilling or unable to deal with its awareness. Without the confrontation and call to change, the group will slide into denial, decline or self-destruction. Confrontation brings the possibility of renewal and change. Confrontation introduces the possibility of transformation, or new life. Gracious confrontation is a gift of the Holy Spirit and a reenactment of the personal ministry of Jesus.

Observation also has a confessional dimension. Confrontation without confession, forgiveness and repentance is double indemnity. For the group to change they must find new solutions for the betterment of their life together. If the group fails to change it must also deal with the heat of the confrontation without the release of tension. Confrontation without constructive change will cause the group to explode and fragment. Observation must be the beginning of the road to change. Confrontation is speaking the recorded dysfunction. Confession is the admission that there is a need for change. Repentance is the re-action of change. While many Christians may practice this behavior personally and individually, much of the American church is not well prepared to practice these disciplines corporately. The small group can be a safe place to rehearse the spiritual disciplines of confrontation, confession, forgiveness and repentance, which could eventually transform even larger bodies of Christ.

M. Scott Peck has argued for a similar extension of observation, reflection and accountability as peacemaking disciplines in his book *The Different Drum:*

Communication takes many forms: written and oral or verbal and nonverbal. Similarly, there are many standards by which we can judge the effectiveness of communication. Is it clear or unclear, verbose or precise, thorough or limited, prosaic or poetic? These are just a few of the parameters for such judgment. There is one standard, however, that takes precedence over all others: does communication lead to greater or lesser understanding among human beings? If communication improves the quality of the relationship between two or more people, we must judge it from an overall standpoint to be effective. On the other hand, if it creates confusion, misunderstanding, distortions, suspicion, or antipathy, in human relations, we must conclude it to be ineffective. . . . The overall purpose of human communication is—or should be—reconciliation. It should ultimately serve to lower or remove the walls and barriers of misunderstanding that unduly separate human beings one from another. . . . Confrontive, even angry communication is sometimes necessary to bring into focus the clear reality of those barriers before they can be knocked down. In the process of community building . . . individual differences must first be allowed to surface and be fought over so that the group can ultimately learn to accept, celebrate and transcend them. . . . When people confronting each other with their differences lose sight of reconciliation, they began to act as if their purpose in being together is merely to fight with each

other. The reality, however, is that the proper task of communication is to
create love and harmony among us. It is peacemaking.[2]
Observation of small group behavior is the foundation for personal and corporate
spiritual transformation. The very discipline of observation and reflection around
the biblical narratives of Jesus with the Twelve can enable faithful small groups
to better understand how the Holy Spirit may be working with them to observe
what is happening in their own groups. This is the model of observation being
practiced in this book: to watch what God does in Scripture with the small groups
of gathered faithful, and discern what God might have us do as contemporary
expressions of such faithful gathering. The primary biblical focus of this discipline
of observation is the life Jesus had with the Twelve. These observations of Jesus
with the Twelve give Christian small groups the freedom to observe and explore
the possible implications of their behavior for themselves.

Observing the Group Experience of the Twelve

To read the Gospels is to observe the group behavior of Jesus with the Twelve
as well as Jesus with other small and large groups. The Gospels also contain many
personal observations of the apostles and others. Through their observations and
ours, with the help of the watchful and interpreting presence of the Holy Spirit,
we can glean much insight from studying the group behavior patterns of Jesus'
small band of disciples.

Jesus and the Twelve traveled and lived together for many months. They
exchanged human values, ideas, pain, frustration, fear, hope, dreams and conflicts common to all people. The amount and intensity of time invested together
as a group was substantially more than is experienced by a typical Western
culture small group. Most modern small group experiences pale in comparison
to the depth of life together between Jesus and the Twelve.

While Dietrich Bonhoeffer did not do an extensive exegetical analysis of Jesus
with the Twelve, he did note the importance of "life together" in Christ as a main
emphasis of New Testament theology.[3] When Bonhoeffer read the Gospels he
became aware of the importance of seeing Jesus at the center of the gathered
community. This led him to see the disciples as a case study of Christian life
together. His observations of this special small group discipleship life led him to
write his greatest works, *Act and Being, The Community of the Saints, The Cost of
Discipleship* and *Life Together*. His observations also moved him to form a close
Christian community and develop the courage to stand against Nazism. This kind
of intense passion for life together can be better understood by making a recording or list of several events in the life of the Twelve with Jesus and reflecting
on the meaning of their behavior with one another (see table two):

Table Two
The Small Group Experience of the Twelve with Jesus

1. The group visited in the home of a group member (Mk 1:29).

2. Jesus healed a group member's relative (Mk 1:30-31).

3. The group searched for Jesus who wanted periods to be alone (Mk 1:35-37).

4. The group lived occasionally with Jesus in isolated places (Mk 1:45).

5. The group visited in the home of the socially unacceptable (Mk 2:15).

6. The group was questioned by officials about their activities and behavior (Mk 2:16).

7. The group lived under constant outside scrutiny and criticism (Mk 2:18).

8. The group was accused of breaking the Law (Mk 2:24).

9. The group was often pressed by large expecting crowds (Mk 3:7-10).

10. The group took up the message and ministry of Jesus (Mk 3:13-15).

11. The group often went hungry for lack of space or time to eat (Mk 3:20).

12. The group became the new family of Jesus (Mk 3:31-34).

13. The group was taught secrets that the crowd could not bear to hear (Mk 4:10).

14. The group often lived in danger and fear of the physical elements (Mk 4:37-38).

15. The group experienced the power of Jesus over the elements (Mk 4:39-41).

16. The group watched Jesus heal and exorcise evil spirits (Mk 5:1-13).

17. The group was asked to leave villages and regions (Mk 5:17).

18. The group shared in rigorous travel (Mk 5:21).

19. The group coped with Jesus' intense sense of reality (Mk 5:30-34).

20. The group saw Jesus rejected by his own home town and family (Mk 6:1-6).

21. Jesus sent the group out to heal and exorcise evil spirits (Mk 6:7-13).

22. The group reported back to Jesus about their ministry experiences (Mk 6:30).

23. The group was called away by Jesus to rest (Mk 6:31).

24. The group was asked to feed large crowds with few resources (Mk 6:37).

25. The group was sent out alone without Jesus (Mk 6:45).

26. The group was shocked by Jesus' surprising words and actions (Mk 6:49-50).

27. The group watched Jesus in conflict with religio-political leaders (Mk 7:5-12).

28. The group missed the point of Jesus' teaching (Mk 7:17-19).

29. The group served the crowd at the direction of Jesus (Mk 8:6-8).

30. The group entered into dialogue, discussion and questions with Jesus (Mk 8:16).

31. While the group traveled they discussed the identity and mission of Jesus (Mk 8:27).

32. The group was asked to keep the confidentiality of Jesus (Mk 8:30).

33. The group entered into conflict with Jesus, his purpose and direction (Mk 8:31-33).

34. The group sometimes failed to accomplish the ministry of Jesus (Mk 9:17-29).

35. The group asked Jesus for insight about how to do healing (Mk 9:28-29).

36. The group was often alone when taught by Jesus (Mk 9:30-31).

37. The group often misunderstood the teaching of Jesus (Mk 9:32).

38. The group argued about who was their best leader next to Jesus (Mk 9:33-34).

39. Jesus gave situational instruction to the group (Mk 9:35-37).

40. The group defended the ministry and mission of Jesus (Mk 9:38-41).

41. The group did theological reflection with Jesus (Mk 10:10).

42. Jesus and the group entered into conflict over their differing values (Mk 10:13-16).

43. The group often questioned the validity of Jesus' teaching (Mk 10:23-26).

44. The group was surprised with Jesus' direction (Mk 10:32).

45. The group entered into hostile jockeying for leadership positions (Mk 10:35-45).

46. Jesus directed group members to perform specific actions and words (Mk 11:1-6).

47. The group observed the power of Jesus' words to effect change (Mk 11:13-25).

48. The group participated in an observational learning process with Jesus (Mk 12:41-44).

49. The group practiced observation and reflection with Jesus (Mk 13:1-4).

50. One of the group plotted to undermine Jesus' leadership (Mk 14:10-11).

51. The group prepared for and participated in special celebrations (Mk 14:12-16).

52. The group regularly ate together (Mk 14:18).

53. Jesus confronted the group with the truth about themselves and the world (Mk 14:18-21).

54. Jesus led the group through the meaning of their experiences together (Mk 14:22-25).

55. The group sang together (Mk 14:26).

56. Jesus confronted the group with their lack of loyalty and faithfulness (Mk 14:27-31).

57. The group struggled with Jesus in the midst of his great sorrow (Mk 14:32-34).

58. The group fell asleep in the face of Jesus' most difficult emotional pain (Mk 14:35-41).

59. The group fought with governing authorities on Jesus' behalf (Mk 14:43-48).

60. The group deserted Jesus when he was arrested (Mk 14:50-72).

61. The dispersed group heard from women that Jesus had risen from the dead (Mk 16:7).

62. After his resurrection Jesus confronted the group about their lack of trust (Mk 16:14).

63. Jesus gave away authority and power to the group when he left them (Mk 16:15-20).

64. Jesus continued to be present with the group by the power of the Spirit (Acts 1:8).

We can understand the life together and the group dynamics of Jesus and the Twelve as three-dimensional in comparison with what seems to be an often two-dimensional life of a modern Christian small group. The time, space, movement, emotion and intensity of their life together illustrate the third dimension often missing in modern small group expressions of Christian community. American groups often tend to be more passive and rational in their approach to faith and life. Such is probably a reflection of our preoccupation with facts, words and ideas rather than our freedom to feel, move, act and work with one another as a faith community.

George Barna has suggested that "20-25 million [American] adults are involved in small groups." The typical American small group meets once per week for two hours in the home of one of its members ("people involved in groups that met weekly were substantially more satisfied with their group experience than those who met less often"). However, there is little tendency or time for the group to be together outside these short cloistered experiences. Their brevity of time together contributes to the shallowness and rationality of the typical American small group Bible study.

Cloistered Catholic and Anglican intentional communities seem to have much more time, space and movement together as a group. This is also true of the Intentional Christian Communities or Base Communities that are active in Latin America.[4] These intentional and base communities live more of everyday life together like Jesus did with the Twelve. This is often possible because of their more rural and localized living situations. As full-time communities every dimension of their life together is rehearsed in light of the gospel of Jesus Christ (notwithstanding their unique political view of the gospel which many evangelical Christians find difficult to support).

As we observe the relative divergent amounts of time invested in being in a small group that meets weekly or being in a full-time community like Jesus had with the Twelve, it is easy to see why the typical two-hour-per-week Western culture small group does not have the same impact on society that full community groups can have. If the typical American small group meets for approximately two hours per week for a life span of two years, they've had about 160 hours of life together. When we compare this to Jesus' time with the Twelve—all day, every day, for three years—even allowing some time apart—the Twelve may have had as many as nine thousand hours of life together. This simple observation could explain why modern discipleship falls far short of the life transformational possibilities Christ can bring to a group together on the way.

The Twelve were a family on the move, a mission group. They were an itinerant band of men, surrounded by other bands of men and women, who followed one charismatic person, imitating his message and ministry. But the lessons learned in the group process of the Twelve give much to inform our process of small group experience today. The human relationship dynamics, the leadership styles, the theological framework, the motivation, the training, the learning processes, the crisis, conflict and confrontation, the power struggles, and the interplay of relationships and tasks are all reflected in the life of the Twelve together with Jesus. We can therefore argue that the life of the thirteen together is a foundational theological, ecclesiastical and educational paradigm for all Christian groups to observe, consider and imitate.

According to Richard Peace, group research has confirmed that the number thirteen is an optimal size for a mission group. Peace believes that Jesus was intentional in the modeling of the Twelve to be a primary paradigm for how the church was to "go into all the world and make disciples of all people groups." It is historically evident that the experience of the Twelve with Jesus has been an ongoing experience of Christians in many times and places. The argument of the thirteen as being a primary paradigm for universal Christian ministry has historical, educational, and even theological validity. Given the ongoing practice of the apostles and Paul in establishing ecclesia (churches) as small group house gatherings, the continuing small group practice after Jesus' resurrection was intentional, immediate and effective in many diverse parts of the world.[5]

Jesus and the Twelve as Mutual Observers

When we look back to the beginning of this chapter at the case study of Jesus with the disciples in the boat (Mk 4:35-41), we can catch a brief glimpse of the personal observational skills of Jesus and the Twelve. The Twelve observed Jesus asleep and his terrifying powers over nature, while Jesus observed their fear and lack of faith. As in all small group situations, the members of this group were constantly watching one another and assessing the meaning of the other's actions on their own lives. However, in this case, the Twelve seemed to feel Jesus was not paying close enough attention to their life-threatening situation. On the other hand, Jesus felt that the Twelve were not paying close attention to his response to the situation. He was totally relaxed. From his perspective there was no danger. As much as the Twelve thought they were understanding Jesus, they were so preoccupied and blinded by their own fears that they were unable to pay attention to Jesus and understand who he was in their midst.

This is a temptation of every small group and gathered community. The small group can become so narrowed by their own limited fear-bounded observational skills that they lose the sight and meaning of Jesus with them in their midst. They panic and forget to exercise their faith. This is a kind of observational practice without spiritual discipline. Observational work in the faith dynamics of a group demands giving attention to the constant presence of Christ, not just to the behavioral practices of the group. The Holy Spirit gives special observational discernment to a group that attends to observing the work of Jesus in their midst.

When a small group senses that they have been left alone by Christ, fear becomes an overriding reality of group life. Their observational skills become jaded and they fail to see the complete picture. Because Jesus seems to be "asleep" the group may misread the threat to their safety and panic. They may begin to devour one another as they overreact or underreact emotionally.

The spirituality of observation disciplines demands a continual reaffirmation that, in fact, Christ is with the group. The group's perception that he is asleep in the midst of their turmoil may not mean that they are going to suffer ship-wreck, but that they need to pray and wait out the storm together. They may need to continue to "bail" the water. If the Twelve had not awakened Jesus, would they have been blown away? The group was not in the danger they perceived. Jesus was asleep. All was well, even in the midst of the wild storm. Jesus did care. The disciples had missed the key observation: Jesus was with them in the boat. His sleep should have sent them a message of "If I'm relaxed through this mess, you should be too." But they missed the message and became preoccupied with their own fear. Their trust in Christ was overcome by their feeling of inadequacy in their troubled circumstance. Faithful observation and reflection may often give way to *groupthink* and paranoia.

Fortunately, God is gracious to the limited-awareness (faithless) group. When they miss the obvious presence of Christ and panic about the viability of their life together, Jesus observes their fear and panic. Christ is able to calm their waters and settle their spirits. The Spirit can restore their sanity as soon as they see Christ as an active group member again. It would be hoped that the next time the group endures a storm they will take some time to remember this scene and note that Christ is with them even in the midst of their trouble. Maybe the next time they can have more trust and ride the storm out together. After all, if in the midst of chaos, Jesus seems to be relaxed and asleep, so the group can learn to relax and struggle together in spite of the wildness of life.

■ SMALL GROUP MINISTRY IMPLICATIONS

1. Since the Gospels include narratives of Jesus' relationship with the Twelve, groups can use these pericopes (sections) as case studies in group dynamics. The process of studying these narratives is similar to doing group observation, albeit from a distance and through the eyes of the authors and translators. Observation of a group always has a bias from the eye of the observer. Each group that reflects

together about the behavior of Jesus and the Twelve will perceive different and distinct patterns of relationship and action. Each group will read into the narrative their own bias and experience. But this is not necessarily bad. This is what makes the story, the event, and the reality of the gospel such a powerful and transforming experience. The Holy Spirit is present to help any group do transformational observation of the group dynamics of the Twelve. So encourage small groups to read the Gospels, observe Jesus' relationship with the Twelve, and reflect upon their own life together in light of this primary historical model for Christian small group life.

2. There are several kinds of observational techniques for tracking small group interaction. Several textbooks on small group life have sections on observational techniques. See *Small Group Communication in Organizations* by H. Lloyd Goodall Jr. (William C. Brown, 1990) or *Joining Together* by David W. and Frank P. Johnson (Prentice Hall, 1991), as well as several others. When training small group leaders such observational techniques are helpful to encourage them to watch carefully what is going on in the group. However, such observational technique practice should be reserved for controlled settings and training groups. The use of such "technology" can be unnerving and undermining for a typical church small group. Encourage leaders to develop and nourish their observational disciplines and discernments. Healthy groups are nurtured along by leaders who are sensitive to what is happening in the group. Groups that have little or no observational and reflectional leadership will eventually (sooner rather than later) fall apart. Groups that have too much technical observational activity will become bored. It is generally best that leaders have a place to go to discuss their observations and get a reality check. It is good for leaders to call groups to reflect upon their life together on a periodic basis. For a fuller discussion on this point, see the chapter on evaluations.

3. A specific way small group leaders can do consistent observation is by keeping a journal of the group's life together. After each meeting, the leader could take a few minutes to reflect back upon the conversations, feelings, moods, events and frustrations of the group, and write down brief observations in a journal. This journal could be brought to occasional meetings (with the agreement of the group) and the leader could lead the group in some observations and reflections of their life together. Of course, the group needs to know that the journal will be held in confidence along with their life together.

4. To help learn the value of observation as a normal group discipline, it might be helpful to train group leaders in some observational case studies of Jesus and the Twelve in the Gospels. This could also work occasionally within the small groups themselves. Two or three curricular case studies could be prepared to help

each group practice their observational skills by exploring the Gospel scene. The storm scene analysis at the end of this chapter could be used as an example of how to do this.

5. No matter how good the technical observational skills of the leader or the group, there is no substitute for spiritual discernment, which comes of deepening personal and relational faith in Christ. The Spirit enables us to observe things that the rational and pragmatic mind will miss. Small group leaders need to develop both sets of leadership skills—the disciplines of group observation and the spiritual disciplines of Christian community. But, above all, they need to attend to the deepening of their sense of spiritual discernment. Spiritual discernment is nurtured in dialogue and prayer with God, with a select few and with a leadership partnership in a small group.

14
TRAINING SMALL GROUP LEADERS

[Jesus] called his twelve disciples to him and gave them authority to drive out evil spirits and to heal every disease and sickness. . . . These twelve Jesus sent out with . . . instructions. (Mt 10:1, 5)

The Australian small group leader John Mallison has said that "intimacy with Jesus is the best of all teachers."[1] He has further described Jesus as "the living lecture."[2] As Scripture itself asserts, he is "the way, the truth and the life" (Jn 14:6). Jesus lived for the Twelve so that the Twelve could live for the world. He trained the Twelve so that the Twelve could lead the church into Christian discipleship and change the world forever.

Fascinatingly, Mallison quotes Fidel Castro in affirming Jesus' discipleship strategy: "I began my revolution with 82 men. If I had to do it again, I would do it with 10 or 15 men and absolute faith. It does not matter how small you are, providing you have faith and a plan of action." Mallison points out that the disciplined, focused action of a few dedicated people can change the course of human history, while "undisciplined mobs achieve little."[3]

The small group of twelve who walked with Jesus has multiplied into hundreds and thousands of small groups throughout history who have met and ministered in his name.

Called to Follow
Richard Peace has suggested that the phrase "in his name" is the key identity for

all groups who, like the Twelve, follow after Jesus. Just as Jesus was in the presence of the Twelve, giving them purpose, identity and power for mission and ministry, so he is in the presence of every group gathering that calls Jesus their leader and Lord. The "name" identifies the nature, character, being and mission of the group. Groups that meet "in the name" are reliving the experience of the Twelve in their contemporary context. They are reenacting the ongoing ministry of the Twelve after the resurrection and Pentecost.[4] The focus of the training of the Twelve was Jesus, the man, not an idea, not a method, not an ideology, not a system or curriculum. All these are servants to the man Jesus and his relationship with God as Abba.

When Jesus said to the Twelve, "Follow me," he was calling them into a training mission that was not an experimental mission, but the real thing. He did not take them to a secluded place and give them an introduction to discipleship method and strategy. He walked with them into the real world, to learn in the real transactions of life, to experience the real crises of encounter, to be confronted with the immediate and costly implications of acting out the realm of God in the world. The group of twelve was the experiment and the real world the laboratory. The chemistry of real persons in reaction to Jesus was often volatile and explosive. While some were bonded to the realm of God, others mixed with the realm like oil and water. While some were receptive, others were indignant. While some understood, others were insensitive. While some pleaded for mercy, others pleaded for retribution. While some were healed, others were killed. While the immediate implications of "Follow me" were excitement, success and popularity,[5] it was not long before the Twelve experienced the dark side of their discipleship training and the call to suffering.[6]

The watershed for the life of the small group of twelve was their recognition that Jesus was indeed Messiah and was determined to be a suffering Messiah, thus calling them as a group to participate in his suffering (Mk 8:27-38). Their training as representatives of the realm of God meant that they had to embrace the implications of the counter-value system their small group represented to the power structures and family systems around them. The training had to include a clear signal from Jesus "to follow," to be "with him" if the group was to suffer. The wrenching paradox of the climax of Jesus' life with the Twelve was that they were living with the powerful Son of God who would also be the weak, vulnerable and dying Servant. While he trained them to minister "in his name," he showed them that the primary way of his ministry was through "taking up the cross." While Jesus was resolutely "setting his face toward Jerusalem," the group was adamant about their opposition to his intentional vulnerability and ultimate goal (Mk 8:32). Peter acted as spokesperson for the whole group when he rebuked Jesus for choosing such a way.

The group's training in ministry climaxed in its observation of the suffering, rejection and death of their leader. Their ability to understand and receive gladly this unexpected twist of mission did not happen until after Pentecost. Then the redeemed Twelve (Mk 14:10-11) entered more willingly into their leader's process of suffering and death, as did many members of their following groups. It was ironic that while Judas precipitated the suffering and death of Jesus and the disciples, he was the first to suffer and die—not out of commitment to the mission of Jesus, but out of ambivalence or opposition to his mission.

But before they accepted his suffering and death, the Twelve deserted their training leader and aborted their training mission (Mk 14:50; 15:40). Although the men deserted Jesus in his suffering and death, the group of women continued with him through to the end to see him suffer and die. The small group of women were alone at the tomb to be the first to discover the risen Jesus. In some ways, these women were a more willing training group during the dark times. Gordon Dalbey has suggested that men are quick to withdraw from the demonstrations of human weakness in the church that women will often embrace. Some say that this is a function of female culturalization, and others say that this is the result of women learning to live and thrive in weakness and suffering. It may be possible that Jesus' call to *suffering* discipleship is more readily acceptable among women than among men. Dalbey therefore recommends that the church is called to create a place for authentic Christian manhood, the kind demonstrated by Jesus, a "redeemed toughness."

Dalbey's call to male toughness is consistent with Jesus' call for the Twelve "to take up their cross." This tough call did not come easily for the Twelve. Their betrayal and desertion suggest that the women had more courage to follow Jesus to the cross. But after Pentecost, the Spirit gave new courage and toughness to the eleven men who had failed to take on the mantle of suffering. As Dalbey has suggested, there is a certain heroic triumphalism in the male call to war that the invitation to crucifixion does not sustain.[7] Only in the context of safe small group life may it be possible for many men and women to sustain this tough training and taking up the cross of Christ.

Jesus' call to discipleship was an invitation to small group training. His method of preparing disciples was to put them into small groups. Both men and women who followed Jesus were among groups who saw Jesus as their core leader. Why did Jesus need to train anyone? He was preparing to die. What was the purpose of this three-year small group training program for the Twelve and others? The answer to these questions are found in the very nature of God, humanity and the church. Jesus had to point men and women in a new direction. He wanted to reintroduce them to the real nature of God. He wanted them to experience the best environment in which they could have their humanity restored to God's full intention. He wanted them to be prepared to accomplish an impossible mission of changing the world. The only way to accomplish all of this eternal mission was to gather the men and women together into new small communities and train them through a phenomenal apprenticeship of life together and life for others. The training of the Twelve was a theological, existential and ecclesiastical boot camp, an arena in which to live life, practice new behaviors and support one another to go a new direction. Jesus knew that the small group was the ideal arena in which to redirect broken humanity, train for changed lives, and commission for an eternal vision. It was only in the small group with Jesus that heaven and earth came together and that a new humanity could be formed.

The Call in Modern Context

Jan had never led a small group before in her life. She had never been in an intentional small group community. But suddenly she found herself in the new members class of the church she wanted to join. She thought that they were going to learn about the denomination of the church and about its governmental structure, but she discovered that they were getting to know one another and discussing how they felt about God. Jan was the senior executive of her department. She had graduated magna cum laude. She had avoided church because she had experienced it as an obnoxious male ego camp. But this church was different. This group experience was unique. She appreciated how women were valued here. She noticed how her desire to ask questions and not settle for quick answers was welcomed. Gradually, Jan developed trust for the group leader. Jan soon discovered that Jesus had led both men and women into discipleship and apostleship. Jan found that her natural relational and inquiring spirit was helpful foundation to her being prepared to lead a faith group. Jan's new members group had been an apprenticeship with an excellent mentor. And now she wanted to open the same pathway to faith in Christ for others. So she started a small group at the office for both men and women to talk about faith and learn about Jesus.

Jan's experience was an introduction to basic small group discipleship. She was launched on her way into leading small groups through the training example of her new members group leader. By being in a group, Jan discovered how to lead a group. By being in a group that focused on Jesus, Jan discovered how to come to know Christ and to live in Christ. She found that she needed to be with a small group of Christian friends who could be her faith family. By being in a small group, Jan discovered that Jesus was her brother and friend, God was like a loving Father (and Mother), and the church was a circle of real human beings. Jan's small group life had begun with a solid introduction because it had been led by a trained and prepared leader who knew Jesus. And with Jan, the cycle of the training of the Twelve had run another turn in the cycle of the redemption of humanity.

As Jan discovered, the group training patterns of Jesus in the Gospels reveal some key values that are transferable to most cultural contexts. These core values, when practiced in the power of the Spirit, help perpetuate the ministry and mission of Christ in all times and places.

Ten Training Values of Jesus with the Twelve

As the Twelve journeyed with Jesus, watched Jesus, listened to Jesus, questioned Jesus, argued with Jesus, and imitated Jesus, certain values emerged as important and integral to their life together as a small group who was the new family of God. These are key concerns for all future groups that meet "in the name of Jesus." It was while they were on the way that Jesus invited the Twelve and others to experience these values. And the Spirit of Christ continues today to confront groups with similar values that meet together to follow Christ. The discipleship pattern of Jesus with the Twelve is the foundational discipleship model for every small group that comes together with Jesus as Lord. The discipleship of the Twelve has beckoned all Christian small groups into their life together and their implications for ministry with Christ.

Surveying the many experiences of the Twelve, ten key values stand out as intrinsic to Christian discipleship and small group leader development: (1) the centrality of Jesus in the group, (2) the heterogeneous culture of the group, (3) the invitation of the group to ministry and mission, (4) the sharing of life together in the group, (5) the group as community for others, (6) the group as countermodel to the structures and systems of the religious and political world, (7) the group as invitation for men and women to live life together, (8) the group as new and eternal family, (9) the group as new model for human empowerment, and (10) the group as failed and restored community. While many other values emerge in the study of the training of the Twelve, these ten will be explored to beckon other Christian small groups into a more vital christological pattern and practice for small group leader training.

1. *The centrality of Jesus in the group.* Jesus called all the disciples to follow him (Mk 1:17). In doing so the Twelve were called to focus on the centrality of Jesus' relationship with Abba God. Every group that calls itself *Christian* must be formed with Jesus and Abba God through the Spirit as center of the community. The Twelve looked to Jesus as their director, model, teacher, brother and friend. Without Jesus there would have been no small group of twelve disciples or apostles. Without Jesus there are no other potential gatherings of the people of God.

Without Jesus there was no clear way to intimacy with God as Abba. Jesus has called all groups of humanity to recognize their presence with him before the Living God. This is their "nearness" to the realm of God.

2. *The heterogeneous culture of the group.* Jesus did not call these twelve persons together because of their common interests or common culture. Rather, he brought together those who had little in common except their common humanity and his leadership. Small groups that come together in Christ are not primarily together because of common culture. Any common values in the small group except Jesus are of secondary importance and can become idolatrous blocks to the centrality of Jesus as the common bond. Each person, when called by Christ, brings his or her own personal culture to the group. But the mandates and values of individual human cultures exist under the judgment of the present and common Lord. Every individual knee shall bend, every human culture should bow to Christ as Lord and center of the small group. The heterogeneity of human cultures in any Christian small group is joined across all barriers and values because Jesus is the common relationship, the new culture and the bonding presence of the group. To call people together from heterogeneous cultural backgrounds and experiences, there must be a common purpose and person in whom each of the members finds a connection. In Jesus, the common purpose is incarnate in the person who is the Son of Abba God.

3. *The invitation of the group to ministry and mission.* The Twelve were called into mission at the very beginning of their relationship with Jesus. When they followed him they followed Jesus into his ministry and mission. Their group existed only as a group *on the way* to Jerusalem, the cross and the resurrection. On the way Jesus worked with them in proclamation and ministry. Christian small groups are on the way with Christ and are called into ministry along the way. The small group is not "in Christ" if it is not in mission or in ministry. In following his ministry and mission the small group will encounter intimidating, frightening and disillusioning events and experiences. The ministry of the group is its action and reaction in Christ to the interruptive, the critical and the confrontational. The events along the way are both binding and threatening to the group's life. The small group will always discover that their humanity together is inadequate to these confrontations and crises. But Jesus is more than adequate. Through confrontation with trouble, Jesus trains a group to come together, speak the truth in love to each other, and move on together as a more cohesive community.

The ministry and mission in the small group is focused and nourished through the discipline of prayer, that is, the constant and continuing interaction and reflection with God through the model of Jesus as Son. Prayer is the centering ministry of Jesus and the primary ministry that he calls the group to learn and to practice. Prayer is the most difficult, demanding and intimate ministry of the group with Jesus. Without the intentional discipline of prayer the small group will not be successful in the sharing of the ministry with Jesus. For example, because the Twelve had not learned the depth of the ministry of prayer the nine were not able to exorcise the demon in a boy. Jesus performed the exorcism, but called the Twelve to be more serious about their discipline of prayer (Mk 9:14-29).

4. *The sharing of life together in the group.* The Twelve lived together and traveled together for several months. They ate together and went on retreat together (Mk 6:31). But in all their mutual sharing of life, there was the constant outside demand of the crowd to share life beyond themselves (Mk 9:35-44). The crowd was always around, demanding attention even when the Twelve were trying to be alone with Jesus. The life they had with Jesus was constantly being tapped to be a life for others. Jesus with the Twelve was simultaneously Jesus for all. The life together of the small group was under constant mandate to be a life *shared* with all who would come and ask to be fed. The group lived in constant tension of life for itself and life for others. The group was a training ground where they learned to live life together so they could have the freedom and power to share life with others.

5. *The group as positive community for others.* The Twelve were called to live a model life separated to Christ yet among all others. These other human communities, organizations, and small groups are full of negative and abusive patterns. In their book *The Addictive Organization* Anne Wilson Schaef and Diane Fassel describe the relationship between personal and organizational addictions. This discussion is interwoven with the concept of family systems.[8] Schaef and Wilson connect the presence of healthy or addictive leaders to the development of healthy or addictive communities and organizations. Jesus was a healthy leader who developed a healthy community while in the presence of many human systems which were abusive and addictive, perpetrated and perpetuated by abused and addicted leaders. Jesus came to be one healthy human being in long-term relationship with specific small groups of people. Whether among the Twelve, the women, the seventy, the one hundred twenty, or all inclusive, Jesus was the central driving force for their existence. The relationship Jesus had with his groups was unique and transforming.

When the good news of Jesus was shared with wider groups of people, an intrinsic implication of the goodness of the news was that Jesus gave human beings, both men and women, a new way to live life together. He gave them a radical new framework for human community: a new model, a new paradigm, a new way, a new family. The primary meaning of *radical* is "of or from the root or roots; going to the foundation or source of something."[9] The good news that Jesus lived was a radical recall to the origins of God and humanity. Jesus was the source of the way back to genuine human community. Jesus is the source of any and all healthy group life.

Gerhard Lohfink (like many others) has argued that the Twelve were simply a symbolic gathering to represent a new Israel. But this interpretation of the value of the Twelve does not adequately proclaim that the disciples were the particular beginning of a new family gathered around Jesus. Many who track the numbers and symbols of Israel's prophetic fulfillment through Jesus' life account the rational rather than the relational dimensions of the gospel. However, it is important to salvation history that Jesus be seen as gathering a new small group family around himself and drawing them into intimate relationship with Abba.[10] There are significant dimensions to the particularity of the number of the thirteen together which reveal God's plan for saving the human race and all of creation.

This small group was a strategic rethinking of God's vision for human relationships. It was a recalling of humanity to the center of divine creation order: "It is not good for the man [or woman] to be alone" (Gen 2). The Twelve were called to life *with* Jesus and *with* one another. The old way of being together was in need of repairing and remodeling. Jesus showed us a new way of being with God and with one another through the experience of the Twelve and others. The nearness of the realm of God (Mk 1:15) is an intimacy with God and an intimacy among the people God loves. The model of Jesus with the Twelve is a transforming small group community paradigm in history and eternity, "on earth as it is in heaven." The training had to be in a small group because the small group was a quantitative and qualitative environment for the church to be in the world with Jesus.

6. *The group as countermodel to the structures of the world.* Just as Jesus with the Twelve is a healthy paradigm for human community, it was also a counterparadigm for all other human forms of community, structure, organization and institution. Schaef and Fassel argue that there must be a better way for human beings to be together in positive and healthy relationships. Jesus' relationship to small groups of men and women articulates a theological and christological vision for this new human community. Many secular and nonchristological critiques of human structures and relationships are left with a clear articulation of the bad news of systemic human sin but give unclear direction and vision as to how to attain the good news. Some defer to the practice of the Twelve Steps of Alcoholics Anonymous as a core process for attaining healthy organizational life. The underlying foundation of the Twelve Steps is a strong theology and an implied Christology and Incarnation. We must ask ourselves the question, Who was the

first to show us the way back from the lost systems of the world?[11]

The small group of the Twelve was a countercommunity in the midst of other religio-political human structures: Roman, Pharisaic, Sadduccean, patriarchal, paternal and so on. The living "Yes" of Jesus' life with the Twelve was a present judgment of "No" upon other systems of human relationships. As Karl Barth declared,

> God the Creator did not say No, nor Yes and No, but Yes to what he created. There is, of course, a divine No as well: the necessary rejection of everything which by His own nature God cannot be; and consequently the necessary rejection of everything which again by His own nature God cannot will and create, and cannot even tolerate as a reality distinct from Himself.[12]

The existence of the Twelve was more than a symbol of a new Israel. They were an eternal declaration of Christ's yes as a model of community moving in a healthy direction because they were led by a man who followed Abba God in that right direction. And they were small enough to be in intimate contact with this one special man to have their lives transformed. Like Lohfink, James Dunn has argued it is doubtful that

> we should speak of Jesus' disciples as a "community." There is no clear dividing line between those who literally followed Jesus and the wider circle of discipleship. . . . The twelve's primary function as "the twelve" was to symbolize the eschatological people of God in it's totality . . . there is no evidence that they were regarded or acted as functionaries constituting a community gathered around Jesus.[13]

Such a strong ambivalence about the communal and group cohesion of the Twelve seems to run counter to the particularity of Jesus' work with small groups of disciples and tends to undermine what Bonhoeffer and others have found to be consistently true: Disciples are best trained and formed in one-on-one and small group community. While agreeing that the number twelve does carry a symbolic fulfillment for Israel's twelve tribes, Dunn (and other scholars) seem to miss something crucial about the radical nature of the Twelve with Jesus. The original twelve were the twelve sons of Jacob—a family. Jesus called the new twelve to be a new family. The ancient family of Jacob demonstrated significant sexual and spiritual brokenness: selling their brother into slavery and massacring whole villages of vulnerable people. The new family of Jesus was called away from such a destructive life pattern. They were to be the family of the reconciled as well as the reconciling family. They had to be small and they had to be unique (separate) to Christ.

The small group size of the disciples provided a special dynamic for the real working of this new family life. These unique relational dynamics (small group dynamics) are not possible in larger groups or as isolated individuals. The small group of twelve provided entrée to the larger groupings of the seventy and the one hundred twenty and the crowd as a "way" of community. The Gospel narratives reflect specific group dynamics of the Twelve and the new kind of life Jesus wanted them to live together.

When one follows a symbol long enough, that symbol takes on a life of its own. The symbol of the Twelve has become transformational in and of itself. It is not just Jesus alone as the individual who ushered in salvation, but it is Jesus with the three, Jesus with the Twelve, Jesus with the seventy, Jesus with the one hundred twenty. It was Jesus with the Twelve in the midst of the crowd that was the present and active realm of heaven on earth. It was the thirteen together among the women and others that unveiled the communal nature of the realm and made clear the radical nature of how God desired humanity to come together "on earth as it is in heaven." The nature of the realm and the essence of the good news is "Emmanuel, God with us." It was this presence of Jesus in the midst of the Twelve that established them as a countermodel to the world around them. They were being trained as counterculture to be a new visible community in which Jesus' relation to Abba God formed the core group values.

It is possible that some Western theologians and church leaders have suffered from a biased perspective bound by individualism and institutionalism in the interpretation of the gospel. Many church leaders miss the communal nature of Jesus' and the Spirit's ministry. The Western church still lacks an understanding of family systems and the importance of Jesus showing not just his own individual humanity but a communal humanity as a new and redemptive family system.

The thirteen with the women (Lk 8) were a beginning order of a new human community that God would make to last forever. This new community would eventually put to death or transform all other inadequate human made structures and systems. As in the model of Dietrich Bonhoeffer's life teaching and sacrificial death, there is an affirmation of a pattern of life together with Jesus and the Twelve that is an ongoing critique of any human attempt to organize itself without Jesus as the elder brother/friend and God as Abba parent.[14] The training of the Twelve was only possible as Jesus allowed God to be their parent and as he was able to become their true friend and brother. The experiment of counterculture community and training would have failed if Jesus had stepped into the traditional role of paternal expert or king and insisted that the Twelve be his "subjects" or simply "symbols" of a prophetic fulfillment.

As it was with the Twelve, there is with every small group an "already" and a "not yet" aspect to this common "kingdom" in Christ. Expanding the work of Geerhardus Vos, George Ladd once said, "The church lives between the times;

the old age goes on, but the powers of the new age have irrupted into the old age." Every small group gathered in the name of Jesus like the Twelve is an ecclesia of heaven on earth.[15] The group is increasingly beckoned into the presence and relationship with Jesus, but the old cultural baggage continues to weigh heavily on group members. The Twelve struggled and disagreed about many things, but Jesus was their common point of relationship. Jesus drew them into more maturity and completeness of the Spirit to become a new community culture. Theirs was a new culture where Jesus was the pivotal influence and defined the nature of the new culture which created and nurtured this realm of God's nature, presence and influence. The Twelve were trained by both the individual who was Jesus and the community who was Jesus.

7. *The group as invitation for men and women to live life together.* The assumption of Jesus' selection of twelve men to be the "symbolic" center of the new Israel and the apostolic community has often been a stumbling block for the encouragement of men and women to be together in community and ministry. As many have throughout salvation history, we must ask ourselves the question, Why did Jesus call twelve *men?* Why were there no women in this core training group if Jesus was trying to bring women and men together to be a leadership community?

It seems we do avoid dealing with the Twelve as a real community partly because they were an all-male group. James Dunn has made the specific point that "the immediate circle of those who followed Jesus was certainly wider than *the twelve* and included women."[16] A selection of men and women together would have sent a much clearer message about an expected codominion and shared ministry to following generations.

A potential answer to this dilemma of why the Twelve were an all-male group may be emerging from the growing study and reflection in family systems theory. Edwin Friedman represents a new movement of relational theologians and therapists who realize that individuals are formed, deformed and reformed through communal group process, mostly in early family life. This need for a family systems reformation has a direct connection to the value of small group ministry for men as they learn a new way of looking at the world, of looking at God, of looking at other men, of looking at women and of looking at children.[17]

Given the foundational grid of a family systems perspective, it is possible that Jesus called these twelve men to a new understanding of their masculinity. In the group he was providing a model of human relationships as defined by the Fatherhood of God and the Sonship of Jesus. The male disciples needed the group (family) experience with Jesus to be intentional about release from an unhealthy family history of enslavement to and dependence upon negative patriarchal and paternalistic modeling of their fathers and institutional leaders. They needed to experience and embrace a new model of how men could relate to God, to one another, to women and to children. The grouping of the twelve men around Jesus as friend and brother helped them to refocus their understanding of God as loving, accessible, gracious and forgiving Abba Father. Jesus' personal experience of Abba was as one who invited both men and women to follow together. As James Dunn has pointed out,

> Jesus' calling on God as "Father" (Abba) was the language of experience rather than a formal address . . . that Jesus' abba-prayer expressed an unusual and unprecedented sense of intimacy with God . . . that Jesus certainly taught his disciples to pray the same way . . . that their use of abba was somehow dependent on their relationship with Jesus, that their abba was derivative from Jesus' abba.[18]

Dunn's perspective is that Jesus drew the disciples into the intimate circle of community between himself and the Father. The Twelve and, even more so, the three had unique access to this new male familial intimacy. Their close proximity as men to this new kind of Father-Son relationship had a profound impact upon their relationships with one another, with women, with Gentiles, with children, with family and with organizational systems. They learned in their small group with Jesus to be men with new values, new skills, new characters, new intentions, new purposes and new patterns of relationships. They learned a new way from the "men" of the divine family, the Son and the Father. But this new way was inclusive of many who had been disenfranchised and sidelined by the old way. The new maleness of intimacy and wholeness between Abba and Son drew the men's group into radical redefinition and reformation of a communal vision and experience.

There was an intentional inclusion of women, who provided financial support (Lk 8:1-3), and a constant calling of attention to children as the primary model of humanity for the Father's realm (Mk 10:13-16). All of this suggests that Jesus called men around himself as an inner circle to give them a strong, clear and historic message that their traditional and sin-bound masculine cultural perspectives had to be transformed radically. This radical transformation could only be accomplished through the intentional experience of being in a small male group empowered as a new family system, a cultural experiment of Abba's realm. This radical value group had to run, by origin and destiny, counter to the pattern established from ancient times (Gen 35). As Joseph had to show his brothers a new, more vulnerable and forgiving way of life, so Jesus had to show his brothers a transformed way of living which invited all humanity into the inner circle of intimacy with the Son and the Father.

Jesus was in no way reestablishing, reenacting or reaffirming the dominant male patriarchal family system of history. There was a paradox in Jesus' action and ministry which many have missed over the centuries. He took what seemed to be an old patriarchal model and redirected it. Out of himself as the model son and new center, he trained his twelve men inwardly through the transformation of their primitive male attitudes and habits, and outwardly to embrace a partnership with the women in the upper room and at Pentecost. With the retrained twelve who were joined together with the women, Jesus has transformed the entire human race forever.

8. *The group as new and eternal family.* Jesus called the group of twelve into training to be a new kind of family (Mk 3:31-35; 10:29-31), to grasp and reflect this nature of the realm of God. This new family community was to learn and practice the will of God "on earth as it is in heaven." They were not to be defined by biological or cultural relationships, but by the intimacy of God's presence and direction. And in this way it was an eternal family, for it had been established by the eternal God whom Jesus knew intimately as Abba (Daddy). This eternal family was brought together "on earth" by Jesus as an elder brother, the one who brought the rest of the family back to the Father.

Any new small group gathering of the people of God becomes a real demonstration of this new and eternal family "wherever two or three" join together with their brother Jesus and address God as their accessible and loving parent. The presence among the group of the resurrected Christ makes them an eternal community. Even though their gathering is on earth, their prime existence is in heaven. Their home is where Jesus and Abba love each other. As they gather in the temporality of time and space, they are beckoned into the transcendence of Jesus at the right hand of God. For Jesus said, "Whatever you bind on earth will be bound in heaven, and whatever you loose on earth will be loosed in heaven. . . . If two of you on earth agree about anything you ask for, it will be done for you by my Father in heaven. For where two or three come together in my name, there am I with them" (Mt 18:18-20). Every Christian small group has a dual citizenship. Every Christian small group has two homes. Every group gathered with Christ is learning to transfer their primary residence from earth to heaven, from biological and cultural ties to spiritual ties.

9. *The group as space for human empowerment.* After the Twelve were scattered, they were reconstituted through a new experience of empowerment. They could not make the group work on their own initiative and power. But only through a new experience of God's power exercised out of their brokenness and powerlessness was the group given the mutual courage to regather. This resurrected group power came through their willingness to accept the Spirit of Jesus as the "higher power" of their lives personally and corporately. They learned the powerful na-

ture and name of Jesus was once-for-all demonstrated as a willingness to suffer and die. They learned to be open to receive this power by being servants and experts at letting go (Mk 10:42-45). The Twelve were constituted as a group from the beginning only because Jesus had called them to follow him. They were only reconstituted as a group after the resurrection because they were reconnected and recommitted to a continued mutual following of Jesus, not as one on earth, but as their brother and Lord in heaven. The power to be a group, to be a family, to be a people, was possible only because Jesus and Abba continued to be *with* them in resurrection and Spirit. The group reformed because the power of the relationship Jesus had with the Father was now through the Spirit. Jesus, the trainer, had prepared the group for interdependent leadership. The group went through a kind of graduation and was promoted from dependence upon an earthly leader to a partnership with a heavenly leader. The power to do ministry was then not limited to Jesus' acts but was an empowerment of the apostles' acts.

So the ongoing Twelve did not exist as an independent leadership community unto themselves. By the experience and empowerment of the upper room intervention of the Holy Spirit, the Twelve became the one hundred twenty. The small group became a network of small groups that launched ever-increasing numbers of ecclesia (home gatherings) in Jerusalem, Judea, Samaria and the uttermost regions of the world. The empowered Twelve became interdependent with the empowered one hundred twenty, which included the women and many other disciples. The Twelve as male community were scattered only to be regathered as a newer community of men and women together empowered to do ministry. The power of the resurrection was a power that called the Twelve beyond where they were with the earthly Jesus and launched them into where they should go with the heavenly Jesus. Their restored and expanded community was much greater and influential than their original gathering with Jesus. The training transition had to do with their receptivity to let go of a visible and touchable leader on earth, and welcome a spiritual and discernible leader of heaven who would become incarnate and visible only as they faithfully gathered as a community of men and women together.

10. *The group as broken and resurrected community.* The small group of twelve whom Jesus called together was both scattered (Mk 14:50) and regathered (Mk 16:7). The experience of the resurrected Christ sustained the Twelve (and then only eleven of the Twelve) after the death of their leader. The experience of being the Twelve, of being the new family with Jesus, did not fully make sense to them until after Jesus continued to live on with them into the eternal side of his humanity.

The small group of disciples came back together after they realized that what

Jesus was calling them to live had both earthly and heavenly dimensions. The earthly life of the group would be lived in a kind of scattering and brokenness; the heavenly life would be lived in eternal togetherness. The group was not limited to relationships "until death do us part," but would be sustained as heavenly family forever and ever. The resurrection of the man Jesus, their brother, was a resurrection for and of the whole group. And the resurrected Twelve embraced and participated with the newly formed and empowered one hundred twenty. The resurrected Twelve were called to expand their family and expand the numbers of families. They were called to go into all the world to form vast numbers of small faith groups (Mt 28:19). Their call to make disciples became synonymous with the call to start small communities of believers who would be disciples together. Their resurrected brother, by the power of his Spirit, would go with them into the rest of the world to form more and more new families. As these ecclesia were formed, torn, scattered and reformed, an expanding number of small disciple groups would look to God as their primary Abba, Jesus as their elder brother and the Spirit as their teacher. The Twelve (with others) would be recorded and remembered as the model discipleship family. And so it will be forever and ever that the Twelve were trained to be gathered, scattered and regathered as a pattern of resurrection community building initiated by Jesus and sustained by the Spirit.

■ SMALL GROUP MINISTRY IMPLICATIONS

1. Small group leaders must be trained by being in good model groups and in real group situations. Classroom training of small group leaders can be informational but not formational. Good leaders need to be formed and reformed in the context of real groups. As we have seen in the model of Jesus with the Twelve and Jesus with the women, he launched the small group movement of the early church by forming groups and forming men and women to be together in groups. Small group leadership development is about making disciples first and leaders second. Personal and relational spiritual disciplines are only learned in safe, affirming, supportive and accountable group situations. Small group leaders should be trained by being in small groups.

2. Good leaders need to be trained by a good primary leader. The primary leader, whether laity or clergy, needs to be a person of long-term experience in small group life. Technical expertise and theological knowledge is no substitute for being in the real group laboratory with Jesus, the Spirit and real people. Real groups have all sorts of rough edges and surprises that perfectionistic theorists never touch. The primary trainer needs to be in constant touch with real people in real groups. Small group authority comes from being in small groups. In a

church, parachurch or other organization, the primary modeling for being in small groups needs to go all the way to the top (or all the way to the center). If being in a group is the nature of God, no human leader should avoid training and life in a group. If Jesus invested so much in a few, then primary leaders also need to invest a lot in a few. Such practice of leadership development is not a common pattern in the church. Seminaries and churches must start investing greater energy in the development of leaders who are discipleship oriented and small group savvy.

3. Both men and women should be small group leaders—especially women. As Paul Yonggi Cho has discovered in Korea, the best group leaders are often women. Many of the greatest primary small group trainers in the Western world are women. The women's international culture is generally more personal, more intimate and more relational. Men can learn much from women about being in community together. Men and women should be trained together as group leaders. This is the way the Spirit came at Pentecost and the way the Spirit will continue to be released to the church. Jesus led the way for bringing women and men together in ministry. Small group ministry is the safe place to begin such an interdependent working together. The evangelical church must open itself to women and men in partnership and leadership especially in the development of ecclesia as the church.

4. Small group leaders should be trained in seeing the Gospels as a primary source for their content, purpose and direction. Some proponents of the Myers-Briggs Personality Inventory have suggested that each of the four Gospels tends to appeal to one of the four major personality groups. Depending upon the personality makeup of your leadership group, you may want to use the Gospel text most likely to connect with them. In any case, small group leaders should have a clear connection in their minds and experience of how important Jesus' relationship with the disciples was to forming good small group life. The Gospel of Matthew seems to be the most intentional discipleship manual of the four Gospels. A curriculum built upon Matthew may be a good place to begin. However, Mark is the shortest and most concise; Luke is so clearly completed in the Acts; and John teaches and reveals to us so much depth in koinonia and agape. All four Gospels are key to a balanced long-term biblical foundation for small group leadership training.

5. Small groups and small group ministry structures should not be launched until an intentional leader training program has been established. It is absolutely fatal to begin a small group ministry by putting the whole population or congregation into groups, especially geographical groups, before good leaders have been trained. Good groups need good leaders—carefully selected and trained leaders.

Jesus invested years in training the Twelve and several months in training the women. Leadership development should be the number one priority of a long-term small group ministry. Therefore, start small with a few well-selected and trained leaders, and grow the small group ministry carefully. Excellence in small group leadership will go a long way to nurture the entire life of your congregation or organization.

6. There are many technical and practical things to model and teach small group leaders. Many books have been published on the training and development of good groups. All these disciplines and technical skills need to be taught and practiced. However, there is no substitute for spiritual and relational maturity in a small group leader. The technical skills can be learned along the way, but unless there is a foundational commitment and understanding to relational life in Jesus Christ, all the technical education will be lost in a basic lack of spiritual openness, humility and discernment. The open and spiritually aware person will eventually learn the way of intentional Christian community, but the group technocrat may never learn the way of the Spirit. Teach leaders spiritual disciplines before they learn group technique. This is where discipleship begins in Christ. Small group leadership is, first of all, a spiritual discipline centered in the model of Jesus.

7. The technical expertise of small group process and dynamics must be servant to the Spirit and the Word. Sacramental community life is always bound to a focus on Christ, the empowerment of the Spirit and the authority of Scripture as the Word. The pragmatics of small group games, skills, curricula and education must be submissive to the living presence of Christ in the group. As in all disciplines of life, we must learn and practice the disciplines before the Spirit can use them for the best. Small group leadership disciplines must be servants of the Spirit. Small group leaders must see their primary empowerment coming from the Spirit, not from their technical knowledge of groups.

8. The greatest leadership disciplines are personal prayer and Bible study, which must be expanded to include relational prayer, Bible study and interpersonal sharing. Small groups are about relationships—developing relationships with God and with other human beings. Continually call small group leaders to these core disciplines and to Jesus who modeled them.

15

EMPOWERING SMALL GROUP MEMBERS

When [Jesus] was alone, the Twelve and the others around him asked him about the parables. He told them, "The secret of the kingdom of God has been given to you. But to those on the outside everything is said in parables so that, 'they may be ever seeing but never perceiving, and ever hearing but never understanding; otherwise they might turn and be forgiven.' " (Mk 4:10-12)

Tom was a member of a men's group. A corporate lawyer, he was having some trouble with his boss, who treated him and the other senior employees badly. Tom shared his frustration and anxiety with his group. His boss was the kind of person who was vindictive and would probably fire Tom if he confronted him. Tom could not afford this. Corporate legal positions were tough to find and he had a family to support. Yet he could hardly stand by and watch his boss abuse people day after day. Tom continued to seek the support, prayer and guidance of his group. After several meetings, the group finally said, "We'll stand by you to confront your boss. If you lose your job, we'll help you. We'll either help you get your job back or we'll help you find a new one. In any case we'll support you financially if you lose your job. We'll get you through this."

Tom hesitated for a few more days. He wondered if he was blowing the whole thing out of proportion. However, during the next week, Tom's boss was caught in a financial crisis in the company and demanded that Tom cover up for him if he wanted to keep his job. This did it for Tom. He confronted his boss with his abusive and manipulative behavior, said he would not tolerate it anymore for himself or for others, and he would not lie for him. Tom then went to the president of the company and told him the whole thing. Tom did not lose his job, but he was moved to another part of the company. His boss continued in the company, but in a less influential position. Tom thanked his group for giving him the courage to take the risk and do the intervention.

Tom, like thousands of people of faith, found it difficult to put his faith into action. He did not want to take the risk and endanger his job. Yet he increasingly realized that his tolerance of a bad situation was allowing the abuse to continue unabated. Tom's small group stuck with him, supported and encouraged him to take the risk. The group's faith and trust in Christ and in one another empowered him to take an initiative in risk he would not have taken on his own. As Tom discovered, small group community is a key to personal, spiritual and political empowerment. Empowerment is the basis for the freedom and courage to take action. Empowerment best happens in the supportive safety of a small group.

The Secret of the Realm

According to Mark's Gospel, Jesus wanted the Twelve to understand the secret of the realm of God. Jesus wanted the disciples to have the special power of such intimate knowledge about the nature of God and God's way of ministry in the world. Much has been said about the nature of this "secret." But when using a community hermeneutic it is important to observe and reflect upon the context and group dynamics of this situation in which Jesus spoke these amazing words, "The secret of the kingdom of God has been given to you."

At the beginning of Mark 4 we observe that Jesus is teaching by the lake. A large crowd is gathered. To the whole crowd Jesus tells the parable of the four soils: the beaten path soil, the shallow, rocky soil, the weedy soil and the good soil. Much has been said by commentators about the nature of these four soils as they symbolize life. Here the concern is mainly with the nature of the good soil where the seed takes root, that is, where the word of God is best heard, accepted, and productive of vastly fruitful crops.

It is important to note in the textual context of this parable what is happening in the group dynamics around Jesus. While he spoke the parable to the crowd, he was alone with the Twelve and a few other disciples when he explained it. The shifting size and attitude of the groups around Jesus seem to parallel the progressive identification of the types of soil. The larger gathering of the crowd represents the essence of the three poor soil groups: (1) as soon as some of them heard these words of Jesus, Satan took away the words; (2) others heard Jesus' words with joy, but the words took no deep root because of their immediate preoccupations and trouble, and (3) for still others the everyday worries, deceits and seductions of life choked out their interest in knowing more about the realm of God. This is why the crowd dissipates, leaving only a few true disciples to hear the full story. So it was that the words of Jesus evaporated for most along with the disbanding of the larger crowd. The unrooted and shallow expectations and behavior of the crowd is never the nurturing environment for spiritual growth. But not so with the smaller gathered community of the Twelve and a few others who traveled with Jesus. The good soil of their small group community and closeness with Jesus empowered them to hang in there for a more complete explanation when they were alone with Jesus. It was in the very nature of their being together with Jesus as an ongoing close-knit and small group community that provided the nurturing and empowering context for them to become the good soil for hearing, accepting and growing in the knowledge and way of God. Their intimate trust in Jesus motivated them to hear him out. They were the living testimony of validation to Jesus' parable. The crowd was the continuing example of untilled, unkept and unfruitful soil.

The small discipleship group gathered in the presence of Jesus is the best soil to nurture the growth of God's realm. Only when the small group gets alone with Jesus, away from the busyness and superficiality of the crowd, is the secret of the realm of God revealed. And this secret was given to the Twelve and to other small groups of disciples who followed and gathered around Jesus. These small groups allowed Jesus to work their ground of understanding, fertilize their minds and water their spirits so their actions could match these new seeds of thinking. The secret of the realm of God is the revelation that "wherever two or more are gathered" in Jesus' name, Jesus is there with them, God is present, and heaven's realm is active and visible. In the context of intimate community with Jesus, God's secrets are revealed and understood.

What is it about the small discipleship group that makes it such a nurturing environment for planting and growing the realm of God on earth? Personal and intimate contact with Jesus and with those who know Jesus *is* the nurturing process. Living in the presence of Jesus, knowing him personally, seeing him continuously in action, staying with him day and night, day after day, week after week, month after month, year after year, having recurring and frequent reminders of his way and word—these are the nurturing components of "good soil." Living among others who also watch Jesus in life and ministry, who also talk with Jesus about his life and ministry, and being among a few who share the freedom to imitate Jesus' style—these are the ingredients of fertile ground for growth and action. It is in the small group community that there is openness, receptivity, encouragement and the willingness to risk a new way of life. The small discipleship group is the most fertile ground for the seeds of Jesus' life with

Abba to be planted, watered, nurtured, cultivated, grown, blossomed and allowed to bear fruit as risk, adventure, confession, forgiveness, repentance and transformation.

Only in the intimate and close-knit small group of disciples can modeling, sharing, questioning, confronting, discussion, accountability, observation, commissioning, gifting, affirming and sending take place. Only in the close community can the explanations about the realm of God make sense, for the realm is about the liberation and restoration of humanity for human community. It was in the smaller gatherings of real people around Jesus that the secrets of the realm made sense and that the invisible realm became visible, touchable, knowable and real.

Jesus' Small Group Strategy for Empowerment

To better understand Jesus' unusual strategy of revealing the secret of the true nature of God's realm, it is important to look at the contrast between the religious institutional practices of his times and his small group approach to empowerment. Jesus did not come into the world to build another political or religious organization. His strategy was to call human beings into relationship with himself and with one another. His methodology was the establishment of small group communities—the primary of which was that with the Twelve. The historical foils of Jesus' strategy were the political-military structures of the Roman government and the religio-political structures of the Hebrew government. In both governmental systems the primary methodology of decision-making and action was a hierarchical power structure. These "principalities and powers" systems granted power through positional definitions of hierarchical responsibility and influence. Empowerment of participants in these systems was not nearly as important as control and manipulation.

These institutional power structures were established to make sure individuals and groups worked within the boundaries of certain well-defined patterns of behavior, decision-making and action. They were not so much interested in affirming the humanity of their constituents as in making sure the people remained tuned to a specific and narrow set of values and practices. They needed to make sure that the people were obedient to the systems and lived contentedly within the walls of their well-defined institutional life. Those who obeyed these detailed and confining norms were affirmed and promoted as successful in the system. Those who allowed their humanity to question and confront the system were contained or eliminated. This is the essence of sin-bound systems, institutions and organizations. Unless human community in Christ is free to transform the structure, the structure will try to crush the community.

A classic environment for such power-down, controlling male systems was the Roman military. In Luke 7:1-10 the story of the Roman centurion sheds some light on this relationship between community, faith and empowerment. The centurion's "valued" servant was "sick and about to die." The centurion had heard of Jesus and sent for him. Yet *how* he contacted Jesus comes as a surprise. He did not send his soldiers to order Jesus to come to him; he sent some Jewish elders to "ask" that Jesus come. And these good Jews did not demand for Jesus to come, but "pleaded earnestly" with him. Their argument to convince Jesus was not a threat of what would happen if he did not come, but an appeal based on the centurion's "love" for the nation of Israel and his gift of building their synagogue. Jesus was convinced to go. But there is a second surprise in the story. Jesus had not even reached the centurion's home when he was confronted by another group, "friends" of the centurion, who bring an amazing statement from the centurion:

"Lord, don't trouble yourself, for I do not deserve to have you come under my roof. That is why I did not even consider myself worthy to come to you. But say the word, and my servant will be healed. For I myself am a man under authority, with soldiers under me. . . ."

When Jesus heard this, he was amazed at him, and turning to the crowd following him, he said, "I tell you, I have not found such great faith even in Israel." (Lk 7:6-9)

When the friends returned to the centurion's house, they found the servant well.

This story is about the contrast between traditional institutional power and empowerment through networks of human friends and community. The centurion did not use military position and influence to convince or manipulate Jesus to act on his behalf; he used faithful friends and a loving community. In fact, even though he was a man of high rank, he did not see himself as worthy of being in the presence of Jesus. Jesus, a man of no rank, had only his relationship with God and his love for humanity to accomplish his work. The centurion understood this in a way that others around Jesus did not seem to understand. The centurion had discovered that the empowerment of personal community, of having friends, was more powerful than being a military leader. Military power could not heal his beloved servant—only love and trust could. He had learned the disciplines of personal empowerment by becoming a loving participant in a faith community. He had learned to depend upon his friends. He had learned to love his servants and to serve them as his intimate friends. The centurion understood that the key to empowerment and healing was a loving community in touch with a healing God. Jesus saw this as "amazing" faith. This is one of the great ironic events in the life of Jesus. The centurion had personally experienced the great paradox of power. Try to control the community and life is lost. Learn to serve the community and life is gained. The religious leaders of Israel had missed it completely. The secret of the kingdom belonged to the centurion.

Jesus, like the centurion, did not practice containment or control with his disciples as a movement from the outside. His was an invitation to a voluntary community. His was a community of friends, a family of brothers and sisters. His was an appeal, not to live by the exterior rules of Rome or of Israel, but to live by the rule of God from within. His was a community of human beings, both men and women, who wanted to be together, who wanted to be with him, and who desired to live out of inner motivation to be in relationship with God. For Jesus, personal and relational power—human power—were the primary values that moved these small communities to obedience and action. For the Roman and Hebrew governing powers, such personal and relational inner motivation could not be trusted. After all, every person and every group may have different motivations and desires. To be without some form of outside control, boundary, rule or order was a threat to these powerful systems. But Jesus did not come into the world to set up another outside boundary system. He entered the world to live among people, to be an example of God's desire for personal relationship and community with humanity, and to demonstrate that the kingdom of God was "within" and "among" them: "Once, having been asked by the Pharisees when the kingdom of God would come, Jesus replied, 'The kingdom of God does not come with your careful observation, nor will people say, "Here it is," or "There it is," because the kingdom of God is within [among] you' " (Lk 17:20-21).

The Pharisees could only comprehend the establishment of another competitive institutional power structure where rule was externally exercised. But Jesus invited his small discipleship groups to be ruled from the inside out, to be empowered by God's internal presence in their lives and in their relationships. This is what face-to-face community can do. It can empower persons to discover and do what God has motivated them to be and do. Jesus' small groups were places to discover not what they had to do, but what God was calling them to do. His small groups were spaces to develop the discipline of inner and intra listening for the voice of God. He taught the groups to listen to the still small voice within them and to listen to one another as they together discerned which direction God was leading them to go. Such is the ultimate way of human empowerment—to be guided by the Spirit from the inside out rather than be driven by demands of power structures from the outside in.

Jesus demonstrated this kind of personal empowerment from God. The Gospel of Matthew, at the end of the Sermon on the Mount, accents this inner motivation of empowerment in reflecting the response of people to Jesus' teaching:

"When Jesus had finished saying these things, the crowds were amazed at his teaching, because he taught as one who had authority, and not as their teachers of the law" (Mt 7:28).

Jesus taught with "authority," that is, in Greek, *exousia*, or "out of the essence of his being." His source of authority was out of himself, out of his inner being. He taught as one who had inner empowerment to say and do what he said and did. His authority was a stark contrast to the power brokers of religious and political structures who said and did things because some outside authority source—the Law, Moses, Caesar or others—directed, manipulated or controlled them. Jesus modeled such a way of empowerment for those who walked with him in small groups. They were close enough to see that he had his own motivation and authority. He was not bound by some outside system in order to act, but by an inner strength. Within, he was one with the Father. He was a servant of the realm of God within. With such a power from "within" no outside authority could stifle Jesus' passion to do the will of the Father. As the Gospel of John affirms,

The Son can do nothing by himself; he can do only what he sees his Father doing, because whatever the Father does the Son also does. For the Father loves the Son and shows him all he does. . . .

For as the Father has life in himself, so he has granted the Son to have life in himself. And he has given him authority to judge because he is the Son of Man. . . .

By myself I can do nothing; I judge only as I hear, and my judgment is just, for I seek not to please myself but him who sent me. (Jn 5:19-20, 26-27, 30)

The Empowered Destiny of the Twelve

The personal and intimate relationship of Jesus with the Father gave him the inner power to speak and act. Jesus beckoned his small groups of disciples to share with him in this experience of empowerment, to enter with him into the presence of the Father and to receive their own inner empowerment.

To explore this contrast of internal and external empowerment more fully, it is helpful to interact with the writing of Peter Block in his book *The Empowered Manager*, as a contemporary commentary on and illustration of Jesus' empowerment strategy. Block has argued that

our acute awareness of the political moves of others, especially those above us in the organization, is in part an expression of our dependency. I fear those that I feel dependent upon. If you have power over me it makes me cautious and watchful. . . . This unbalanced way of viewing the political dynamics and possibilities around us stems from the experience of being in a low-power position. Since we all have bosses, we experience ourselves as reacting to people and events outside ourselves. This results in a reluctance to take full responsibility for our own actions. . . . How we choose drives us in either an entrepreneurial or a bureaucratic direction. . . . We choose between maintenance and greatness . . . between caution and courage . . . between dependency and autonomy.[1]

To use Block's terms, because Jesus was empowered by a *higher* source who gave him inner confidence, he did not need to be a cautious and dependent maintainer of the lower bureaucratic status quo. Instead, he was freed to be an entrepreneurial person of inner strength, greatness, courage and autonomy. His empowerment was from God. God's Spirit lived within him and he was able to speak and act *exousia*, out of the very essence of his being and intimacy with the Father.

Those who gathered around and walked with Jesus saw that he was not dependent upon or afraid of outside controlling forces. The small groups he lived among could sense that he was not cautious about protecting himself from Rome or Jerusalem. They could see that he had no fear of other authorities. They experienced his freedom to do whatever God wanted, flying in the face of existing power structures. And they were the recipients of this same source and commitment of empowerment from Jesus that Jesus received from the Father. This empowerment happened for them as they walked day after day in the face-to-face presence of their empowering leader who had an intimate confidence in his empowering "Abba."

This message of Jesus' empowerment was articulated clearly for the Twelve from the beginning of their early discipleship through the ascension, Pentecost and beyond. Jesus wanted them to have the same inner power that he had received from the Father: "Come, follow me, . . . and I will make you fishers of [people]" (Mt 4:19). Jesus' intent from the beginning was to use the group experience as a place and way of empowerment, to help them become persons of inner motivation and authority like himself, to help them become free to seek out and save other men and women from the controlling and oppressive systems and patterns of evil institutions and leaders. He wanted them to receive the same power that he had received from the Father. As Jesus prepared to ascend into heaven, he said to the eleven:

All authority in heaven and on earth has been given to me. Therefore go and make disciples of all nations, baptizing them in the name of the Father and of the Son and of the Holy Spirit, and teaching them to obey everything I have commanded you. And surely I am with you always, to the very end of the age. (Mt 28:18-20)

You will receive power when the Holy Spirit comes on you; and you will

be my witnesses in Jerusalem, and in all Judea and Samaria, and to the ends
of the earth. (Acts 1:8)

Such empowerment is about human beings being encouraged to be really human,
to get in touch with the essence of their being and calling. It is about people
discovering that they are gifted and capable. It is about self-motivation and the
freedom to choose one's destiny as a gift of God. It is about having a vision of
the future and seeing how God can help accomplish that future. It is about
believing that God really cares about an individual. It is about believing that I
have something to contribute to God's realm. It is about discovering that the vast
God of creation and the universe is interested in an individual and a small group
of ordinary people. Empowerment is about each one giving away the best he or
she has to another, and helping the next person accomplish even greater things
than the first. Empowerment is about being a partner, not an employee, soldier
or slave, with God. Empowerment is experiencing Jesus as the older brother who
serves us and helps us to do more than we can possibly think or imagine.

Empowerment is about the process of change. Change comes at high cost and
high investment. It comes slowly in the midst of continuous affirmation, encouragement and reminding. The realm of God is the arena in which people are helped
to see life in a new way, to practice the new way of life, to talk about the new
way of life, and to help one another pursue the new way of life. The small group
is a safe place to experience the support of God and God's people. Small groups
are good places to get to know Jesus and to feel the empowerment flow from
him to us to me.

Jesus used many tools and techniques of empowerment as he walked among
the Twelve and the other groups of disciples. These are the tools of the realm
of God—the tools of small group community. Many tools of empowerment can
be used while living life together: modeling, observing, sharing, questioning,
conversing, confronting, reflecting, encouraging, affirming, critiquing and coaching.

Empowerment is not a function of the crowd. The crowd is where proclama-
tions and announcements are made. In Luke's scene between Jesus and the centurion, it was to the crowd who followed him that he turned and announced that
he had not seen such faith in all of Israel. Jesus announced and proclaimed to the
crowd, but he forgave and healed individuals in communities. The crowd watched
from a distance, but the disciples were empowered within close quarters. Jesus
talked to the crowd; he *touched* the few close at hand. Jesus noted at the incident
of the healing of the woman with chronic hemorrhaging, "Someone touched me;
I know that power has gone out from me" (Lk 8:46). Power flowed out of Jesus
to those who came in close proximity to him, to those who were near him, or

those to whom he was near. Empowerment is the pattern of Jesus' ministry for those who desire to participate in the realm of heaven. Jesus empowered those whom he loved and those who loved him. Jesus empowered persons who valued living as loving humanity among friends. He empowered people who wanted to know God more intimately. He empowered people who had given up trying to control everything in their lives. But he cursed those who tried to hold on to power or to manipulate the power of the crowd. The crowd cried out for Jesus' death while the small groups of followers watched their loving friend suffer and die. Empowerment is an action and experience of intimate community. People are empowered by the Spirit when they are part of a small group who meet together in the spirit and nature of Jesus.

After they had been disoriented and scattered by Jesus' arrest, trial, execution and death, the small group of disciples came back together when they realized what Jesus was calling them to live out had both earthly and heavenly dimensions. The earthly life of the group would be lived in weakness and vulnerability; the heavenly life would be lived in an eternal togetherness and power. The group was not limited to relationships "until death do us part," but forever and ever. The resurrection of the man Jesus, their brother, was a resurrection for and of the whole group. And the resurrected Twelve participated with the resurrected and empowered one hundred twenty. The resurrected Twelve were called to expand their family and numbers of families of small faith groups into "all nations" (Mt 28:19). The call to make disciples became synonymous with the call to start small communities of believers who would be disciples together. Their resurrected Lord, by the power of his Spirit, would go with them into the rest of the world to form more new families—more small groups. These gatherings of the faithful would look to God as their new parent-father, to Jesus as their elder brother, to the Spirit as their teacher and to the Twelve (with others) as their model discipleship family.

The destiny of the apostolic Twelve and one hundred twenty was to establish new communities where heaven's rule could be recognized on earth. To accomplish this mission they would place themselves in harm's way, for the principalities and the powers of the world would not like the resulting ebb of controlling influence that the gravitational attraction of these new small house communities created. So their temporal destiny included persecution, oppression, suffering and death, but their eternal destiny envisioned community in the presence of Christ forever and ever. They were empowered to launch rippling concentric circles of empowerment through networks of small groups who would, by their life together, be the light of God as they gathered in diverse places around the world.

Jesus' Recognition and Affirmation of Small Group Life

On two distinct occasions in the Gospels Jesus called direct attention to the empowering importance of the small group. Much of his teaching about relationships and community was nonspecific about the numerical size of the community. However, in these two situations Jesus clearly identified the number and affirmed the active faith of the small group. In one case, an encounter situation, Jesus talked about the importance of group faith. In the second case, a teaching situation, he focused on the importance of his presence in a group to accomplish acts of faith.

> Some men came, bringing to him a paralytic, carried by four of them. Since they could not get him to Jesus because of the crowd, they made an opening in the roof above Jesus and, after digging through it, lowered the mat the paralyzed man was lying on. When Jesus saw their faith, he said to the paralytic, "Son, your sins are forgiven." (Mk 2:3-5)

The specificity of these four men in action, ingenuity and faith, combined with the calling of attention to *their* faith, is a dramatic affirmation for the importance of the active faith of a small group. The New Testament scholar C. S. Mann has pointed out that it was unusual to have such a detailed description of a group encounter. This was probably the result of an eyewitness account.[2] The size and impact of the small group who took the risk were a model for Jesus of how a faith community can precipitate the intervention of God's realm.

This small group of four carried the paralytic to see Jesus. When they could not find a way into the house through the crowd, they somehow got the paralytic up on the roof of the crowded house. They decided to dig through the roof[3] (and do damage to someone else's property). They were willing to disrupt the gathering as they lowered the paralytic into the midst of Jesus and the crowd. Jesus recognized their risky action as "faith." The small group prompted the healing and forgiveness of their paralytic friend and set the stage for a major theological confrontation between Jesus and the teachers of the Law. They provided an opportunity for Jesus to connect the granting of forgiveness with the giving of healing, and inspired him to declare his intimate relationship with God.

The active, persistent and risk-taking faith of this small group led to the physical and spiritual transformation of the paralytic. But it was also the paralytic's willingness to be carried to Jesus through rather difficult and traumatic conditions that was integral to the faith venture. The faith of the five (or more) together revealed several very important aspects of the character of Jesus, the realm of God and the conflict with Israel's religio-political system. The faith of this small group was confrontational. Their faith was demonstrated in a willingness to break down barriers, even to do physical damage to a house if necessary, to get their friend to Jesus. They refused to accept the common social assumption that disability was the result of sin, even when in the presence of the teachers of the Law who could have them cut off from the rest of the community for associating with a "sinner." The healing of their friend was more important to them than concern over any social stigma attached to them or the disabled man.[4]

This group together made the difficult decision to risk themselves for the healing of their friend. Their mutual trust and servant spirit was made visible to the whole community (and history's faith community) as a model of the value and impact a small group of friends can have upon an individual and the surrounding society.

The second case of Jesus' direct attention to small group ministry was a pivotal statement in his teaching on the nature of the church:

Whatever you bind on earth will be bound in heaven, and whatever you loose on earth will be loosed in heaven. . . . If two of you on earth agree about anything you ask for, it will be done for you by my Father in heaven. For where two or three come together in my name, there am I with them. (Mt 18:18-20)

This teaching is found within the context of Jesus' response to a question from the Twelve, "Who is the greatest in the kingdom of heaven?" (Mt 18:1). One of the themes with which this portion of Jesus' teaching deals is the importance of mutuality, community and accountability among the disciples. His emphasis upon the smallest, the least, the sinful and the indebted provided a pointed opportunity for Jesus to talk about forgiveness and joint ownership of faithful action. The words *church* (ecclesia, v. 17) and *assembly* (v. 20) are contextually identified with the promise that "wherever two or three are gathered" Jesus will be present with them in their gathering. Such a small group gathering has exceptional influence, power and accountability.

Jesus' response to the disciples in this context suggested that there was not one who was greatest, but that "wherever two or three are gathered"—wherever there is a small group gathered in childlikeness, agreement, forgiveness, reclamation and reconciliation—Jesus in their midst would bring greatness to them together. The emphasis here is on the increasing value of the individual who voluntarily chooses to join together with others (Mt 18:12-14). The value to God of "one" brought back to the "ninety-nine" is great. The individual brought back into the community is of great value to God and to God's group as long as the spirit of accountability, reconciliation, reclamation and forgiveness is present. The individual is made more complete by being a part of God's realm which is being among a family of close friends. The group adds value to the individual, and the individual brings value to the group.

The greatness of the kingdom of heaven is a greatness of inviting and including individuals, no matter how insignificant, pagan, or indebted, in the gathering of faith, small or large. Wherever there is agreement (mutual trust and faith) between even two or three, there God will show the greatness of Jesus through them.

From Jesus' perspective, it is the faith of a small group of reclaimed and reclaiming persons who will make heavenly things happen in the world. They will participate in the processes of "binding" and "loosing" on earth because they together are in touch with heaven's agenda and order. Not just the select few are important and great in heaven, but every individual who is willing to gather with God and with others is important and great.

The small group is the microcosm of God's community intention for the whole world: to be together, to be assembled, to be with Jesus, to be in agreement, to be like children, to be welcoming, to be humble, to be reclaiming, to be listening, to be confronting, and to be reconciling (Mt 18:1-20), are all trademarks of the faithful group with Jesus.

Jesus called the Twelve and those who gather "in his name" to act as agents of reclamation and reconciliation for as long as it takes the alienated world to turn and come around. They gather together to be empowered by the Spirit to live a new kind of life together that announces to the world that Jesus Christ is the risen Lord who lives in their gathered midst. As Christ empowers the small group to meet, they are empowered to change earth and heaven.

The small group that reflects such life together is like heaven on earth. And the good news of Jesus Christ is that this heavenly presence continues as an empowered, more complete humanity wherever two or three come together in the presence of Jesus, who is the complete man who lives in eternal intimacy with Abba.

As Robert Slocum has written in *Maximize Your Ministry*, the people of God are called to become a people of "heart," and the way to empower Christians is to be members of small groups who share their heart before God and before one another. This gives individual men and women courage and power to venture into an alien world as "scattered pilgrims," because they have a "gathering place" that knows them, encourages them, loves them and holds them accountable to be the most whole and fulfilled persons on the face of the earth. God's ultimate purpose of empowerment is not the creation of a new society but the freeing and empowerment of a complete humanity who lives in the world as participants with Jesus' close presence near the heart of God.[5]

■ SMALL GROUP MINISTRY IMPLICATIONS

1. Just as Jesus' intention was to empower the apostles for ministry, so it

should be the intent of Christian groups to empower their members for discipleship and mission. This needs to be a clear goal articulated for every small group and small group leader. The process of empowerment needs to be modeled then by primary leaders. Members of groups should be coached into careful prayer, reflection, study, sharing, decision-making, planning and action. Members should be able to dream their dreams and share their visions in the safety of small group life.

2. Empowerment in the small group should happen in several ways and at several levels. There should be empowerment for all arenas of life: personal spirituality, ethics and vision; family, marriage, lifestyle, singleness and parenting; work, education and corporate ethics; church life, calling, giftedness, mission, and so on. There should be space in a small group to deal with every aspect of life as to be lived in the presence of the empowering Lord. Not only individuals, but subgroups and whole groups together should be empowered to accomplish ministry through the mutual support of all gathered around Christ in the group.

3. Small groups should do biblical studies about how God has empowered various persons and groups: Abraham to venture to an unknown land; Sarah to have a child; Joseph to live through repetitive oppression and enslavement; David to stay alive while in the sights of Saul; Deborah to lead with Barak; Job to survive personal devastation; Jesus to endure the pain of betrayal, rejection and the cross; Paul to weather numerous shipwrecks and abuses. Each of these was part of a supportive community who were on the journey together.

4. Groups could also be encouraged to read books on empowerment like Peter Block's *The Empowered Manager*, Steven Covey's *The Seven Habits of Successful People*, William Byham and Jeff Cox's *Zapp! The Lightning of Empowerment*. The discussions around such books should be led by persons who have been empowered to ask good discussion questions that call the group to deal with the guts and heart of their lives individually and together. Good books read but accompanied by bad discussion questions are a poor investment of group time. The key to transformational study is the quality of the questions and the freedom of the group to share their thoughts and feelings without fear of criticism or judgment. Empowerment allows each individual the space to wrestle with his or her own stuff in the faces of a trusted group.

5. Small group leaders should be encouraged, affirmed and held accountable to practice the disciplines of empowerment in their group. The temptation for a leader to control or dominate needs to be checked. Such demand or manipulation kills the spirit of empowerment. Leader training needs to model an empowerment style. This means that progressive situational leadership styles

like those articulated by Hersey and Blanchard should be modeled and taught. This falls to the primary teacher/coach to understand and implement. It is usually the pastor, director or manager who first of all needs to model an empowerment lifestyle for the larger community as well as the small group.

6. A group should have access to a list of opportunities which they could be empowered to accomplish in local service and mission: being Christian at work; developing loving parental patterns, taking the group to the local soup kitchen; accomplishing a special mission project together; venturing into a short-term cross cultural mission trip together; committing to pray consistently for a person or group in trouble; becoming a leadership group that commits itself to starting other small groups in various places. Training, encouragement and ongoing support is a must for the empowerment of growing, long-term small group ministry programs.

16
MOBILIZING THE SMALL GROUP FOR MINISTRY

Jesus went around teaching from village to village. Calling the Twelve to him, he sent them out two by two and gave them authority over evil spirits.

These were his instructions: "Take nothing for the journey except a staff—no bread, no bag, no money in your belts. Wear sandals but not an extra tunic. Whenever you enter a house, stay there until you leave that town. And if any place will not welcome you or listen to you, shake the dust off your feet when you leave, as a testimony against them."

They went out and preached that people should repent. They drove out many demons and anointed many sick people with oil and healed them. (Mk 6:6-13)

Empowerment is for ministry. Discipleship always moves toward ministry and mission. In salvation history God's people have been gathered for restoration and empowerment and sent out into mission. The small group is the gathering space to help people experience forgiveness, healing, encouragement, affirmation, trust and courage. This is preparation to be sent back out into a hostile and alienated world that needs to hear, see and touch the presence of Christ lived out through empowered individuals and groups. Jesus' early call to discipleship, "Follow me, and I will make you fishers of men [and women]," is an invitation to gather, to journey together, and to go out and minister to other hurting people. Every gathered group of disciples is in some way called to go out and fish, to seek others who also need the presence of Christ in their life. Jesus sent his small group of twelve out into ministry to share in his mission. The calling of the Twelve to follow was also a calling to participate in the ministry of Jesus.

James Dunn has suggested that the disciples were given charismatic power not only

> for the service and upbuilding of the community, but to enable them to share in Jesus' mission. . . . It is only as they shared in his mission that the disciples shared in his authority and charismatic power. . . . Those who gathered round him did so to share in that task, to follow him in his mission, and for no other reason.[1]

Jesus gave the Twelve his *authority*. As we have already noted, this term *exousia* means "out of one's essence or being." Jesus' "authority was charismatic in the sense that it was immediately received from God, or rather was the immediate authority of God." That is, his authority was the authority of God, out of the very essence, being and character of God.[2] Jesus received this essence as he communed with Abba. There is an intimate connection here between the deeds of Jesus and the being-essence of Jesus. In classical systematic theology this is commonly differentiated as the person and the work of Jesus.[3] The authority of Jesus was unique but transferable. He did not hold tightly to that authority, but gave it away to the small group of twelve, to be exercised in partnerships of two. He used his authority to mobilize the small groups of disciples into teams of twos.

What was the connection between this exercise of authority and the ministry of the Twelve in pairs? Why didn't Jesus send the Twelve out one by one? Mark states that the authority was given to the Twelve and the works were to be accomplished two by two. The seventy-two were also sent out two by two (Lk 10:1-12). Jesus was consistent regarding this pattern of forming mission-ministry teams. While he himself seemed to function alone (although he was usually with the disciples in ministry) at times (Mk 1; Lk 4), his disciples were expected to minister in teams (very small groups). This teaming order seemed to be connected with the giving of authority. The implication of the giving of this *exousia* to groups of twelve and two may be that such power could (should?) only be used as they shared in partnership relationships, in communities of mutual faith and accountability.

If the essence and being of God is plural, that is, if God exists and works in and through divine community, then the Father's essence was expressed as intimate relationship with and through the Son. The authority and mighty works were accomplished through their community—the relationship of the Father with the Son and of the Father through the Son. The same authority and similar mighty works could be accomplished only in the relationship of Jesus with and through the Twelve and others. The need for grouping and pairing for the sharing and release of the authority and mighty works was what Jesus wanted the Twelve to understand. Such authority existed only through intimate relationships of faith. Trusting and empowering interpersonal partnerships had to be grown and made visible to others—those between the disciples and him, and the disciples with one another in intimate relationship with the Father. The authority of God was given out of community to community and through community. The smallest formation of this divine community is two by two. Only through groups of faithful persons together does God accomplish ministry. God exists to do ministry as the divine community of the Father with the Son through the Spirit. Thus, it seems more than symbolic that Jesus gave authority to small groups and pairs. There is a universal mission of God for *exousia* and *dunameis* (authority and action) to be shared through human community from divine community with Jesus as the pivotal (common) connection.

Another way to look at this movement and mobilization of service and mission out of community is to explore the simple Johannine confession: "God is love" (1 Jn 4:16). Love is the action of care toward and for another being. The very nature of God is to engage beingness in the encounter of valuing another. Love is not possible as a solo activity. Love is only visible in community, where at least one person may feel and act upon love for another. God's very essence is to act toward another in a helping (serving) and completing (healing) way.

Love is mission and ministry. Love must have an intention to reach out to another as encounter, embrace and empowerment. Only God could say to humanity "it is not good for the man to be alone" (Gen 2:18), because God's essence is not to be alone, but to be in community. God's mission flows out of this essence. God's nature is love. God's being is community. God's mission is to assert love and create community. God's authority (*exousia*) is to empower (give away) the divine essence of love and establish new communities.

Community can only create community. The love of Abba for Jesus had to move to mobilize new communities. The "twos" of apostleship were bound by the nature of their Source and Spirit to establish God's new communities whenever they could establish a locus of love in a household. As Jesus said to the apostolic groups of two as he was sending them out, "Whenever you enter a house, stay there until you leave that town" (Mk 6:10). This team "beachhead" of visible love, this "seed" of community planted in a "welcoming" and receptive household was the visible, touchable, knowable and imitable reality of loving divine community planted (tabernacled) among humanity to show us the way and nature of God.

1 John describes this apostolic mission of love:

We declare to you what was from the beginning, . . . what we have seen with our eyes, what we have looked at and touched with our hands, concerning the word of life . . . we declare to you what we have seen and heard so that you

also may have [koinonia] with us; and truly our [koinonia] is with the Father
and his Son Jesus Christ. (1 Jn 1:1-3 NRSV)
These apostolic seeds of the small communities (twos) of divine community were
scattered out among the villages and towns to be planted in households who were
receptive (fertile) to their message and visible mutual love. These twos of apostles
brought not only healing and exorcism, but the incarnate proclamation of divine
community as they modeled community together. Their mission was an extrapolation of their love partnership which they had seen modeled by Jesus and Abba
toward them. They were simply loving others even as they had seen Jesus loved
by Abba and felt Jesus' love for them.

The apostolic healing and exorcism of evil was a direct product of the presence
of loving community. Where the incarnate love of Abba and Jesus warmed the
household the apostles were able to heal and cast off evil, and the people were
free to welcome God's loving presence in them and between them. The apostolic
mission could only be accomplished as the small seed group planted a small faith
household and did the work of heaven on earth: love, confront, repent, forgive,
heal, cast out, empower.

The ministry of the Twelve was to proclaim the "nearness" of the realm of God,
exorcise evil spirits and heal the sick. As a small group they were participants in
the administration of God's healing grace to broken human community. They
extended the ministry of Jesus. They learned about the communal and intimate
nature of God as well as the nature of human brokenness through the process
of sharing and doing ministry with Jesus. They together were the realm in action.
As a small group and six subdivided teams they shared and continued Jesus'
mission and ministry to the wider human community. The ministry included
proclamation for repentance, exorcism of evil spirits, and healing of the sick. They
had no visible means of support except their faith in Jesus, their relationship with
one another, and their dependence upon others to accept, support and care for
them. Their ministry was dependent upon community with Jesus, with one another, and with a receptive few in a specific household. It was dependent upon the
relationship, trust, vulnerability and receptivity of a few households in the wider
society. They literally had to live on love through being in love. Their ministry
was of heaven's realm and for heaven's realm. Theirs was a ministry for the healing
of persons and relationships out of their own beings and relationships. Their
ministry was an immersion with Jesus at the dramatic intersection of the divine
community coming to dwell among human communities.

The Group's Resistance to Jesus' Mission
There are many negative examples of Jesus working with the Twelve to do

ministry. Some of these ministry situations were the feeding of the four and five thousands (Mk 6:30-44; 8:1-9), the failed exorcism by the nine disciples of the boy with an evil spirit (Mk 9:14-29), the restraint of the little children from Jesus (Mk 10:13-16), the struggles for group power (Mk 9:33-37; 10:35-45), the attempt to stop the ministry of others (Mk 9:38-41), the betrayal of Judas (Mk 14:10-11, 18-21), Peter's denial, the desertion of the eleven (Mk 14:27-31, 50, 66-72), the sleeping of the three through the painful prayer of Jesus (Mk 14:32-42), and their lack of faith and their stubbornness after the resurrection (Mk 16:9-14). In every case the disciples resisted the invitation and action to ministry. In some situations they simply failed.

In both feeding situations, the Twelve were initially unwilling to carry out the ministry of Jesus. They lacked the vision and confidence to fulfill what was needed except as they submitted to the direction of Jesus. However, they discovered there was always more than enough of God's provision for the people and for themselves. Their needs as a small group were met abundantly as they did ministry for the wider human community. As the group was willing to follow Jesus into ministry and mission, they found that their personal and relational needs were powerfully met.

Mark documents at least nine other situations in which the Twelve acted as counterministry to the mission and purpose of Jesus. In these situations the Twelve bungled or blocked what Jesus was trying to accomplish for others. They not only were unable to do his ministry but often tried to stop it. As a group they sometimes became servants of evil against Jesus. But inevitably they opened themselves to the correction and redirection of Jesus. They learned the way of ministry through failure, disability and stubbornness. The small group of twelve was a mission laboratory for ministry experimentation, both good and bad. In failure and success the Twelve learned to do ministry in the presence, power and character of Jesus and the Father.

A small group's resistance to participation in the ministry and mission of the loving community of the Son and Abba is a natural part of the group's need to realize the powerful transforming movement of God's Spirit to make them into a mission community.

Sin was a constant restraint to the Twelve, inhibiting their free embrace of the nature and purpose of Jesus. For all individuals and groups sin is still a pervasive prison from which to be released. The mission of every group is to allow the Spirit of Jesus and Abba to overcome their resistance and alienation from God, each other and the world outside. If the group is not able to experience the liberating life of Jesus with Abba in their immediate relationships, how can they possibly take that loving community into a hostile world?

The group must allow the community and intimacy of Jesus with Abba in their midst to break the chains of fear, shame, guilt, anger, abuse, numbness, alienation and isolation which engulf their spirits, cut them off from one another and disable their desire to partner with Christ. The resistance is only overcome as the Spirit gives each the desire and freedom to speak the truth in love, to confess the dark side, be welcomed and forgiven, and venture into intimacy as partners in divine community.

Resistance to intimacy is a sign the Spirit is working with the group to risk engagement and encounter.

The process of the Spirit as demonstrated in Jesus' patient working with the Twelve is to persevere until all resistance is dissolved and the group becomes community. Community is a gift of the Spirit who has overcome sin. Sin is condemnation. Love is confrontation and forgiveness. The spirit of condemnation is overcome in the group by the growing seeds of the Spirit of love and grace.

Once the law of the Son's gracious loving community with Abba permeates the inner life of the group, the small group has the foundation and cornerstone to participate with Jesus in the mission of planting new loving communities. Resistance is the death throes of condemnation being condemned by gracious reconciliation between persons.

The Twelve began to see this in Jesus and practice it for themselves. As grace transformed their relationships with each other, they were able to turn to others outside the circle and plant new seeds of loving community. The resistant group was transformed by the presence of Jesus with Abba so their newly reconciled partnerships could plant seeds of reconciliation in other households.

The Twelve (still in the ambivalence of lessening resistance and growing grace) were empowered two by two, relationship by relationship, to share this communal power of Jesus with Abba. And so they were mobilized by Jesus to go into the countryside with their mustard seeds of God's community on earth.

The Future Impact of the Twelve

After the Lord Jesus had spoken to them, he was taken up into heaven and he sat at the right hand of God. Then the disciples went out and preached everywhere, and the Lord worked with them and confirmed his word by the signs that accompanied it. (Mk 16:19-20)

In the mobilization of this divine community of love there are profound implications for small groups as the continuing ministry order of Jesus after the resurrection and Pentecost.

The positive historical impact of Jesus' work with the small groups of Twelve and other disciples is beyond human comprehension. Human history and eternity have been transformed through the life of Jesus with this small group. Jesus did not use traditional political and religious systems to change the world. He used a small group. This small group of twelve became the seventy, which became the one hundred twenty, which became the thousands composed of many small groups multiplied in homes throughout the Roman Empire. The original small group became the millions of small groups that have met in the name of Jesus throughout human history. Human institutions and structures were and will continue to be transformed through the forgiving, reconciling and transforming relationships of communities of people who gather in the nature and character of Jesus with the Twelve.

But the multiplied Christian small groups throughout history have flourished with an absent leader, a Lord who sits "at the right hand of God," who works through the influence of his Spirit, not through the physical presence of his humanity. The world has been transformed by a leader who is not calling attention to himself, but has and always will call attention to his relationship and intimacy with God, the Father, the redeeming parent of humanity who establishes new households of divine community where Jesus is affirmed as divine human Lord:

> Power and rule belong only to the God whom the disciples may address as *abba*. If there no longer exist for them the kind and caring fathers of the past, but only the one Father in heaven, then it is all the more true that authoritarian fathers exercising power have gone out of existence. . . . Patriarchal domination is no longer permissible in the new family.[4]

Jesus' eternal relationship with Abba (God the Father) is the foundation of all healthy human community. The Spirit of Jesus does not draw attention to himself but to God, the eternal parent of every small group family gathered in the name of Jesus. This is the God who makes all such groups to be new families, replacing the old familial structures and bonds that imprison humanity with new bonds of freedom where Jesus is the elder brother. The future of God and of humanity is a future of small groups, of new families, with a new parent whose Being is plural and who lives as community. The future of humanity is a future with Christ in small groups of people, wherever two or three or more come together in his name, in his Spirit.

And wherever the Spirit of Jesus lives in the community of a small group of men and women, there is a real demonstration of the realm and domain of God. For the realm of God is made up of loving and mutual human relationships patterned after the way Jesus lived with the Twelve, which is the way and nature of the realm forever and ever. Heaven is glimpsed on earth where a small group of men and women come together with Jesus in the Spirit. That small group is a direct connection between the "right hand of God," and the active work of God in the world.

And so the group that meets together in the presence of the risen Lord Jesus is empowered through the community of Son and Father which is the Spirit. Through the reconciled and loving human relationships of being a community, a small group together goes to "proclaim" (Mk 1:4) this gospel that Jesus calls humanity into new relationships, new community and new life together. The Greek word *kerusso* is too often translated as "preach." This presents a reduction of the full meaning of the group's mission. Particularly in Protestant churches the word *preach* is too narrowly defined and modeled. It is more appropriate to use the word *proclaim*, which includes the demonstration of good news and opens a way of venturing into wider ministry methods and means declaring the life of the whole community. Too often people see present-day preaching as the activity of one professional or expert. Proclamation, on the other hand, must carry the imaging of everything the community or small group does individually or corporately to share the good news of Christ. This corporate sharing of life together, this reconciled community, these peaceful relationships, these forgiven persons and healed relationships, are the full proclamation in word and deed. Preaching must b- carried by the visual and real workings of loving community lest the body of Christ become a gnosticized mannequin embedded with loudspeakers.

The community *is* the proclamation. The small group meeting "in Christ" is the visible realm of God. The word must have a community of confirmation, a place and space where the signs of the realm are visible, where men and women are healed where people love one another, where evil is exorcised, where Scripture is free to address hurts of people, where the Spirit is active in both word and deed, where the work of Jesus continues to be as evident as it was when he walked among the Twelve. It is people in small groups, two or more sharing and working together, who are the authentic practitioners and proclaimers of the ongoing ministry of Jesus.

It will never be the formal institution or the humanly engineered structure that accomplishes the real ministry of Jesus. Karl Barth criticized not only the institutional forms in which the church appears but also the community forms. As he saw it, the community can enter a process of inner decomposition, either of alienation (secularization) or self-glorification (sacralization). In either case, the community can lose its centered identity in the life of Jesus, taking on a lifeless formality and loveless agenda. Such a self-styled agenda can be institutional (formal) or relational (informal).[5] The pursuit of structured community driven only by psychotherapeutic theories and parameters but lacking the presence of the mystery of God's Spirit and lacking the core model of Jesus' relationship with

Abba is both a secularization and a desacralization. Human systems must be in submission to this eternal reality of Jesus with Abba.

As it was with the Twelve, it will always be Jesus working with a few people in small groups of various kinds, different sizes and combinations of persons, to do the work of God. As formal human structures are formed and reformed to be free to support this structuring of the Spirit through human networks and groups, so the church will be free to be an ongoing expression of Jesus and the Twelve on earth as it is with God in heaven.

■ SMALL GROUP MINISTRY IMPLICATIONS

1. Ministry and mission should be goals of every group gathered in Christ. This ministry should be directed both inwardly and outwardly. Eventually every group needs to consider the outward implications of its life in Christ. This should be asserted and stated over and over again. American Christian groups have a tendency to become so wrapped up in their own personal faith agendas that they forget to be salt and light participants in a larger set of world systems. This cocooning effect is a form of avoidance, withdrawal and denial. The world is a tough place. The group must be a safe and supportive place to help the members go out into the world in the name of Jesus. Small group warm fuzzies must fuel courage for the group to venture into hostile places.

2. Small groups do not come to the practice of mutual ministry through cordial passivity. Humanity tends toward independence or dependence or codependence, not interdependence. The small group leader needs to model a style of mutuality and to call the group into mutuality. This takes preparation, planning and practice. It also takes training and intentionality. Mutual ministry is an invitation by key leadership to "come and share with me."

3. Resistance and conflict are realities of life together. The way a group deals with these can become a major source of power or frustration in its practice of ministry. If the conflict is processed and reconciled in helpful ways, the group will be able to apply those same patterns and skills in other arenas of life: friendship, work, marriage, family, education. If the ways of dealing with conflict are not handled well, the group will not be empowered to practice healthy patterns of reconciliation outside of itself. Groups will tend to carry their functional or dysfunctional life beyond themselves. The group must become a safe place to reorient members to healthier patterns of relationship.

4. There is a connection between a group's sense of authority (of being in Christ) and their freedom to take action. If a group receives the message from its leader or the leader of its parent organization that the group has no authority, most likely they will not act. One of the greatest gifts primary leadership can give

to encourage the maturity of small groups is to give away authority like Jesus did. This process of giving authority to groups needs to be modeled and practiced carefully. Sensitivity to the group's ability to receive empowerment is crucial. A maturing group's authority to act should less and less be based upon the will and direction of a manager, pastor or leader, and more and more grounded in their own intimate community in Christ.

5. The human exercise of authority is always flawed. The disciples and apostles were far from perfect. They made mistakes. Groups need to have the freedom to make mistakes and to deal with their flaws. Confession and reflection are important interpersonal disciplines to be practiced in the helpful exercise of ministry and mission. Groups need time for reflection, observation and evaluation if they are going to become healthier on their ministry way together. Leaders need a place to go to share with other leaders about their concerns and frustrations. These retreat outlets will allow them the freedom to reengage with the group and take it into another level of ministry together. Growing freedom to venture into mission flows out of the group's time invested in reflection on their motives, values, relationships and purpose.

6. Small groups are new families. Old negative family patterns of communication can and should be changed in a healthy long-term group. This establishment of the small group as new family is one of the key ministries of small groups in a dysfunctional world of dysfunctional families. One of the greatest gifts a good group can give to its networks is a new way of being healthy family together. This is what Jesus was able to show to the men and women who followed him. This is a key foundation for small group ministry and mission.

Part Three

THE CHURCH
AS MULTIPLE GROUPS:
APOSTOLIC FOUNDATIONS FOR
SMALL GROUP MINISTRY

17

THE ECCLESIA
AS AN EXTENSION
OF THE TWELVE

Now that same day [of the resurrection] two of them were going to a village called Emmaus. . . . They were talking with each other about everything that had happened. As they talked and discussed these things with each other, Jesus himself came up and walked along with them; but they were kept from recognizing him.

He asked them, "What are you discussing together as you walk along?"

They stood still, their faces downcast. . . .

"About Jesus of Nazareth," they replied. . . . "Some of our women amazed us. They went to the tomb early this morning but didn't find his body. . . . Some of our companions went to the tomb and found it just as the women had said. . . ."

And beginning with Moses and all the Prophets, he explained to them what was said in all the Scriptures concerning himself. . . .

They urged him strongly, "Stay with us. . . ." So he went in to stay with them.

When he was at the table with them, he took bread, gave thanks, broke it and began to give it to them. Then their eyes were opened and they recognized him, and he disappeared from their sight. They asked each other, "Were not our hearts burning within us while he talked with us on the road and opened the Scriptures to us?". . .

The two told what had happened on the way, and how Jesus was recognized by them when he broke the bread. (Lk 24:13-17, 19, 22-24, 27, 29-32, 35)

The smallest Christian group is two persons together with Jesus meeting them (Mt 18:19-20) in their hopes and fears. The Emmaus Road is an explicit case study of Jesus' teaching and modeling about the nature of Christian community. Where two persons are together and reckoning with the reality and person of Christ, Jesus is suddenly and immediately present. In reflecting on the words of the Christmas carol "O Little Town of Bethlehem," "the hopes and fears of all the years are met in thee tonight," Richard Mouw, president of Fuller Theological Seminary, once said that it is in the presence of Christ's humanity, the baby Jesus, that all the "hopes and fears" of humanity are focused. The present Christ is the center of all human community. This was particularly true for the two on the road to Emmaus who experienced the emotions of hope and fear when Jesus met them and walked with them.

The Small Group Reality of the Resurrection

The Emmaus Road is a postresurrection paradigm of life together with Jesus. The smallest common denominator for small group ministry is where two people share life together around their personal faith experience with Christ, their reflections on Scripture, and their breaking of bread.

Recognizing the importance of the Emmaus Road scene, the United Methodist Church adopted it as a primary paradigm for personal and corporate renewal. In their model, persons are called away on retreat together where, in conversation, the breaking of bread and reflection together around the Scriptures, individuals are often moved to new or renewed awareness of the presence of Christ. The Spirit comes to them in their experience of retreat community.

In such an intimate moment of relationship the resurrected Jesus appeared with the two while they were on the way to Emmaus. In their honest and painful exchange of the dramatic and traumatic, in their reasoning together about the Scripture, and in their eating together, the reality of the present and resurrected Jesus became clear to them. Luke said, "Their eyes were opened and they recognized him, and he disappeared from their sight" (Lk 24:31). And in that recognition of Jesus' real presence, they came to understand that Jesus continued to be present with them in their relationships and community even though he disappeared physically from their immediate sight. The resurrected Christ is present where two or more gather or walk together, sharing humanity which flows to and from the heart of Jesus.

The continuing presence of Jesus is *the* important reality. The community of the Spirit of Jesus grew from the resurrection community encounters into the Pentecost community empowerment, from the community of Jesus with the Twelve to the community of Jesus with the two on the road to Emmaus, to the community of the one hundred twenty in the upper room and into the midst of the house churches. In all times and places, the continuity of community experience with Jesus is "wherever two or three [or more] come together in [his] name." Their eyes are opened to see that he *is* present in such a way that their hearts burn within them. Wherever a small group comes together to explore the meaning and purpose of Jesus' life, they discover that his life is present with them and between them as they share life together on the way. Jesus joins them when they come together. Their coming together reflects his very character and community. The story of Jesus has become their story. Their coming together becomes the "body" of Christ on earth.

The powerful reality of the resurrection was present for a family whose young son died on Maundy Thursday. They went to his room in the morning to discover that he was not breathing. In panic and terror they called their neighbors, one of whom was a pastor. The son died in spite of attempts by a neighbor to administer CPR. But there was something unusual about the whole event. While the family had nominal faith, the neighbors had an intimate trust in Christ. The neighbor sensed that the dying child was trying to communicate something important to his stricken parents. In the small group gathering, even in the midst of the disaster, the neighbor sensed the presence of Christ.

Just three days later on Easter Sunday, the distraught couple again called their Christian neighbors, pleading with them to come back as quickly as possible. The pastor left a full house of relatives and rushed over. The couple had an Easter visitor, a woman who was a casual friend of the family. She was beside herself with excitement and anxiety. She had written a long note that she felt was a special message from God, but she believed that the pastor had to be the one to read it to the family. The pastor, in a state of skeptical wonderment, read the note. But as the pastor read, she sensed the presence of the resurrected Christ near at hand. The words of the note were as if they were from the dead child's own mouth—words only the child and the parents would understand for each other. The essence of the message was, "Mom and Dad, I'm OK. You did the best you could with me. You loved me. But now I want you to know I'm in a safe place where I'm loved."

It was as though in the intimate faith-family gathering the resurrected Christ had given the child a special way to share with his parents in the midst of the tragedy. Where the small group of family and friends were gathered, they sensed both the resurrected Christ and child were present.

We hear such a story with skeptical wonderment. The event, like the Emmaus Road, was for the small group, but the story is for the wider church. Wherever two or three gather in the nature and spirit of Christ, the resurrected Jesus is present. A significant portion of the Emmaus gathering was about facing the pain and feeling the anxiety of the suffering and death of Jesus. Whenever a group deals with death and dying, Christ is not far away. The small group is the powerful arena where we can face the stark reality of suffering and death and feel the presence of the resurrected Christ.

The Story-Formed Community

As Stanley Hauerwas has said, "Good and just societies require a narrative [story-event] which helps them know the truth about existence and fight the constant temptation to self-deception."[1] Hauerwas has argued strongly that the story of Christ, the experience of Christ, forms the "character of the community," for it is a community around a special and unique character, Jesus of Nazareth. For the Emmaus two it was their discussion about the life story of Jesus which culminated in the climactic breaking of bread, that opened their eyes on the journey to Emmaus. And in that event they realized they were no longer cut off from Jesus. If they had not been struggling with their experience of Jesus, they may not have had their eyes opened. They may have continued in their skeptical wonderment and sense of abandonment.

Christian small groups must be formed by the narrative of the Scripture which pivots around the life of Jesus. Friendships, marriages, families and small groups discover their social and ethical values as they reflect and act together around the story of the people of God made complete in the story of Jesus. Neither doctrine nor theological principle ultimately forms the real life of the relationship or community. It is formed by the reality of life together that has been personally experienced and practiced in the presence of the resurrected Jesus.

Stanley Hauerwas uses the novel *Watership Down* as a paradigm of the "story-formed community."

> We must challenge ourselves to be the kind of community where such a story can be told and manifested by a people formed in accordance with it. . . . Without trying to claim a strong continuity between rabbits and us, I think at least the suggestion that we, no less than rabbits, depend on narratives to guide us has been made.[2]

Hauerwas believes that human beings are formed by experiencing and sharing a specific story. This commitment to follow the story is formative as the group reenacts and learns a new model for being a family system.

As the Emmaus two walked out their experience with Jesus, they came to understand the key to their openness to new life was Jesus there in their midst. This was most clear as they shared the meal with Jesus. Their beingness and relationship took on new meaning and passion when they realized that Jesus was *with* them. They understood that their relationship had become a meeting place of heaven on earth, where intimacy with God had released the possibility of intimacy between persons. Jesus had come to initiate a new community—a new way for two or more human beings to relate to God and to one another.

As C. Norman Kraus has affirmed, "Jesus gave new importance and dignity to the individual. . . . Jesus came to establish authentic community. . . . Life in the

Spirit is a life of new openness to others in a fellowship of reconciliation."[3] Kraus understands that Jesus "authenticates" the identity and reality of this new story-formed community. The person and relationships of Jesus become the formative model of how the rest of the community should relate and act. The Christian small group is the micro "story-formed community," even where only two are on the road together with Jesus.

The climactic and revelatory event of the Emmaus microcommunity, and of every Christian community since, is the "breaking of the bread." Meals, which are most often shared in small groups, gather people into face-to-face encounters. By eating together, their common humanity is affirmed. It is often at the point where the symbolic body of Jesus, the loaf, is broken and shared that the community realizes that *they* have become the ongoing body of Jesus. Jesus becomes known and the group walks on together in the Spirit.

At the very point of Jesus' breaking the bread, the two recognized him, and he disappeared from their sight. The two realized that their relationship and conversation, their ongoing community and ministry, their "burning hearts," were the continuing presence and body of Jesus. Their microgroup was where Jesus lived as long as they shared life, Scripture and bread together, as long as they had Jesus in common (Lk 24:30-31).

The apostle Paul worked out this theology of the "body" more completely in his letters to the Corinthians. As Paul declared, the climactic recognition of the community is that Jesus' body was "given" and continues to be shared so that more and more humanity may participate in his body. Wherever the bread is broken, wherever Jesus is acknowledged, wherever Jesus appears unexpectedly, those gathered discover that they are Jesus' community. They recognize that their continued sharing is the ongoing character, life, event and story of Jesus.

The passion of the group's life together, that is, the "burning" of their hearts, was the result of being with Jesus. This was their experience of the ministry of the "word and sacrament." Understanding the theological and relational foundations of word and sacrament, structure, formality and liturgy are disciplines of community practiced to provide a free way into the warmth and reality of real people together. They share food, discuss Scripture and meet Jesus face to face. If the formal disciplines of word and sacrament do not lead to this freedom of real life together, there is no reality of human community with Christ. In fact, the liturgy and structure of discipline can become idolatrous rather than a means of grace. Geoffrey Wainwright, as well as other liturgical theologians, has refocused the meaning of the Eucharist toward its primal relational roots. Wainwright has said, for instance, that "sacrifice is the loving surrender of self to the Other."[4]

Sometimes church leaders are seduced by a temptation of maintaining institutional icons. They may argue for the continuity of formal practices of word and sacrament but fail to call for the substance of such life to be seen in the ordinariness of everyday human community. Such institutionalists may have a hard time seeing the Emmaus Road as a real eucharistic sacrifice of word and sacrament. But it is clear in Scripture that event and symbol must be simultaneous. It is in the historical event where real life and symbol come together. The resurrected Jesus is present at the sharing of the real meals of gathered groups. As Paul said to the Corinthians, if this is not recognized, there's little point in practicing the formal symbol (1 Cor 11:29).

While on the road, the three shared themselves with one another in conversation and food. Jesus provided the leadership and vision for the other two to see life from a new perspective. Their beings were stirred. Their passions were aroused. Their humanity was freed. Their relationships were intensified. Their microgroup became an event of transcendent life together, life beyond typical human bounds, yet life as ordinary humanity. The two knew they had been with Jesus and with one another. They would never again be the same; their eyes had been opened. As they met together, the community in heaven had met their community on earth.

The theologian Ray Anderson has argued that it is being present with other real human beings that gives an individual the experience of the Spirit and the reality of God. He has declared that

> the kenotic [hidden] community is formed of actual people who have their place in the community, not by virtue of their capacity to love or their maturity of spirit, but by virtue of their common humanity with Christ and the reality of the Holy Spirit which comes as a gift. When the Holy Spirit assumes the historical existence of the other man as the form of Christ for me, a cripple is no less real than a whole person.[5]

If this is true that the community continues as the incarnational presence of Christ in the world, then it is as the individual experiences the real community of persons gathered in the name and story of Jesus that God's real presence is experienced in the world. The incarnation of Christ is experienced through the incarnational community, the small group, where two or three gather, like the Emmaus group. The two together continued the spirit, attitude and community of the three even though Jesus was no longer visible. They continued to experience the transcendence of the three as they met together "in the name of Jesus."

Because they had personally experienced life together with the resurrected Jesus, the two saw all of life differently, including the value, role and integrity of women. This new male understanding and openness to women was a direct result of their personal postresurrection experiences with Jesus in community. The women were right—Jesus had been raised from the dead (Lk 24:24). Their eyes were opened to the model of Jesus, who entered fully into community trust with women as readily as he did with men. So the men and women of the postresurrection community gathered in the upper room for sharing life, for discussing the Scripture, for exploring their past with Jesus, for continuing to affirm their current life with the invisible Jesus through prayer (Acts 1:12—2:1). The Emmaus two contributed to the openness of the upper room one hundred twenty, and to the wider formation of local house groups.

The resurrected power of Christ expanded from a microgroup of three to a macrogroup of three thousand to a metanetwork of millions of small groups throughout salvation history. Carl George uses the term *meta-church* to describe multiple small groups that exist together within a common unifying principle or structure—that is, they exist alongside or with one another. "Meta" (as in metamorphosis) implies change. "The term *Meta-Church* . . . signifies both a *change of mind* about how ministry is to be done and a *change of form* in the infrastructure of the church."[6] Such a network of small groups as a structure has a chameleon-like ability to adjust to change quickly. This metagroup idea finds its roots in the New Testament pattern of house groups. These ecclesia (gathering) existed side by side all around the city of Jerusalem and beyond. However, today this pattern of the adjustable and flexible church structure exists in some tension with Christendom's seventeen-hundred-year-old practice of church defined by the tight structures of buildings, liturgy and institutional life.

The experience of the Emmaus group was multiplied a hundredfold as home groups expanded throughout Jerusalem, Judea, Samaria and the world. The resurrected presence and spirit of Jesus was the center and heart of every new group:

All the believers were one in heart and mind. No one claimed that any of his [her] possessions was his [her] own, but they shared everything they had. With great power the apostles continued to testify to the resurrection of the Lord Jesus, and much grace was upon them all. There were no needy persons among them. For from time to time those who owned lands or houses sold them, brought the money from the sales and put it at the apostles' feet, and it was distributed to anyone as he had need.

Great fear seized the whole church and all who heard about these events. (Acts 4:32-35; 5:11)

According to the apostles, the development of the ongoing gathering and meeting of the people who believed in Jesus was the continuing and extending ministry responsibility of the Lord Jesus Christ himself. Jesus' ministry did not stop with his earthly ministry in death, resurrection and ascension. The apostolic community understood that Jesus continued to "call out" those to be saved. It was Jesus' continued activity in the world that added to the ecclesia day by day. The gathering of persons into the temple courts and homes was the result of Jesus' continued action in the world. Jesus was still calling people to be in community together. His resurrection and ascension removed his physical presence from the one group so that he could be present in multiple groups, simultaneously, by the power of the Spirit. And each new group was a new incarnation of Jesus' presence and character on earth.

The Jesus Character of Early Christian Small Groups

These early Christian small groups developed a unique character from being together and having everything "in common" (Acts 2:44). This was demonstrated in their expression of "gladness" and "simplicity of heart" (Acts 2:46). This character of life together formed their character of moral behavior with one another and with the wider world. The intentional imitation of the twelve apostles' life with Jesus set the environment for the formation of their new life and their new character in Christ. Hauerwas has described it this way:

> Moral life entails by imitating another. . . . The Christian life requires a transformation of the self that can only be accomplished through direction from a master. The problem lies not in knowing *what* we must do, but *how* we are to do it. And the how is learned only by watching and following.[7]

Hauerwas argues that healthy moral development comes through the imitation of healthy moral behavior. As the apostles imitated Jesus, so the ecclesia imitated the life of the Twelve with Jesus. The apostles' community and character were formed as they lived life together in memory of their life with Jesus and Jesus' life with Abba Father.

Such healthy character formation could happen only in a community that had a consistent and ongoing healthy center. Jesus was the character center of every ecclesia. And the apostles were present to reinforce and affirm, in being, word and action, what they had learned from Jesus. Jesus had shared everything with the Twelve (even more than they could bear or understand) and had lived life as model and mentor before them in gladness and simplicity.

Jesus, through his Spirit (Jn 14-17), continued to be the personal and relational presence through whom the character of the small Christian groups were formed. He was the one in whom they lived and moved and had their being (Acts 17:28). It was not just Jesus the suffering and dying man who was able to transform the character of the Twelve, but the resurrected Jesus through the power of the Spirit. The Spirit launched the beginning of the transformation while the

Twelve were gathered in the upper room as part of the one hundred twenty.

As Kraus has noted, Jesus gave them their "authentic selfhood," both individually and corporately. This "awareness of one's new individual identity before God inevitably and necessarily involves one in community. Life in the Spirit is a life of new openness to others in a fellowship of reconciliation."[8] The character of the individual was formed by the character of the group, which was formed by the character of Jesus who walked with the Twelve.

Jesus had initiated a new family system. The apostles had been *formed* before the resurrection and *transformed* after Pentecost by the presence of Jesus. This was the key to their family system. In this experience of transformation with the one hundred twenty in the upper room, they were able to give birth to ecclesia in the same identity and character of Jesus. Jesus' story and Spirit lived on in the newly formed small group communities.

It would be an interesting study to compare the process of transformation in the upper room with that which often happens in twelve-step groups. In what ways did the Spirit act as an "agent of intervention" among the Twelve and between the men and women to give them the freedom to create new communities without being loaded down with the old baggage of their arguments with Jesus? Something happened in the community of the upper room that drew them into confrontation with the way Jesus accomplished character transformation and taught them about how to change. For after Pentecost they were changed, and they formed change-oriented house communities.

The health of the apostles flowed from the fullness of the Spirit (Acts 2:1-4). Being "all together in one place" preceded being "filled with the Holy Spirit." The apostolic community reached a point of committed (covenant) togetherness after fifty days of postresurrection prayer and group discussion. In the midst of this sharing of life together the Holy Spirit was freed to be overtly demonstrated. The dramatic ecstatic effects of the Spirit came out of intimate community with God and the people of God. The maturing health of the group in the upper room was demonstrated in their freedom of expression so that every person in the crowd heard them "speaking in their own language." This potentially *exclusive* group addressed the plurality of the city in a free and *inclusive* manner. Such freedom of group expression and invitation could only come from God's welcoming Spirit at work in the health of the group. As Hauerwas has affirmed,

> Moral growth involves a constant conversation between our stories that allows us to live appropriate to the character of our existence. By learning to make their lives conform to God's way, Christians claim that they are provided with a self that is a story that enables conversation to continue in a truthful manner.[9]

The Christ narrative forms the life pattern of the small Christian community. The character of the apostles together with Jesus became the character of the ecclesia. The narrative of Jesus became the narrative of the apostles, which became the narrative of the multiple ecclesia. Healthy community birthed healthy community because their stories were consistent and continuous with Jesus' story. Jesus' moral character became the real moral character of each ecclesia. The "fruit" (Gal 5:13-26) of their life together was the direct result of their life with Jesus through the Spirit, reinforced through the words, relationships and actions of the apostles who had also learned from watching Jesus with Abba as the pattern of the Spirit.

There is a bright and dark side to every Christian small group gathering. The patterns of sin are in conflict with the essential character of the group's Spirit-formed identity. Only through persistent disciplined intentionality can a small group enter into the healing process of the Spirit. This is not the group's ability to make the Spirit work but the group's intention to provide space to give the Spirit freedom to work. This is the crucifixion process articulated by the apostle Paul in Galatians. The group crucifies (disciplines) the acts of sin and sets aside an intentional space for the gift of the Spirit to intervene (Gal 3).

The work of Jesus in demonstrating character formation became the how of the Spirit in accomplishing character transformation. Jesus provided the words and the life as the *content*, but the Spirit provided the desire and the direction of Jesus as *process* and *presence*.

Each ecclesia, then, through the power of the Spirit could fully form the real character of Jesus and be the body of Christ. Whereas Jesus with the Twelve was a complete expression of this group character, each ecclesia could also be a full expression of his moral character. Sin, however, continued to be a real and present danger simultaneous to the ecclesia expression of new life. By putting on the character of Christ as a community, each small gathering of Christians was able to impact persons, marriages, families, institutions and governments to override the resistance of sin through their individual and corporate presence. They became Christ's presence in the world, drawing many into the good news community and disturbing the status quo of social networks.

As Bernard Lee and Michael Cowan have said in their book about house churches, *Dangerous Memories,*

> When members of a house church all choose to change their lifestyle, the subculture of their *koinonia* provides a sustaining and encouraging context. . . . Banding together for empowerment and networking with other groups for still greater empowerment . . . we are building mediating structures. What we cannot do alone we can often do together.[10]

The liberationists, like Lee and Cowan, see the ecclesia as a strategy and structure for intentional political change. And so it can and should be. While the early church may not have had such a strong intentional political agenda as their defining purpose for gathering, the political impact of their gathering was definitely perceived and resisted. Wherever two or three gather in the name of Jesus, there will be moral and political implications. But this was not the primary reason for believers to come together. Rather, their primary reason for gathering was to express the beingness, the nature, the character and the community of God in the world, and to live up to the intended nature of humanity in creation. When all else about human grouping is said and done, God's comment on the nature of humanity still rings as the overwhelming call to ecclesia: "It is not good for [humanity] to be alone" (Gen 2:18). Where people continue to gather in the nature and character of Jesus with the Twelve, the earth will be more transformed by the realm of heaven, more salt is sprinkled and more light is shined.

■ SMALL GROUP MINISTRY IMPLICATIONS

1. Small groups should study the connection between Jesus' relationship with the Twelve and the development of apostolic ecclesia. This could be a sequential study of Luke and Acts or thematic study of Mark and a Pauline letter. In whatever way, Christians must come to grips with our New Testament roots of life in small groups. When they see small groups as a continuation of the ministry of Jesus and the apostles, their ministry value in the organized church will take on primary significance. Otherwise, small group ministry may continue to be reduced to a ministry technique or gimmick with superficial or secondary value.

2. We need to interpret biblical texts with a community hermeneutic rather than a privatist hermeneutic. Such a community hermeneutic laid across the text of New Testament passages will bring meaning and value to our Christian origins as being rooted in small group life. Such a privatist hermeneutic runs deep in American cultural blood, but we are coming more and more into a period of history where this bias will not carry the church. The Western church has had the privilege of being carried on unstated community assumptions. Such ordinary community disciplines of family, town and small church are crumbling under the weight of an individualistic scientific society. There are few "natural" communities left. If the church is not developing intentional small group communities, there may be no community left in the West. The rise of Twelve-Step groups is a strong sign that our culture is starved for healing communities.

3. Another helpful study would be Jesus' relationship with the Father (Abba God). It's one thing for us to say Jesus is present in the small group; it's another to understand Jesus as in relationship with God as Abba. When Jesus is present

wherever two or three gather together, Jesus is present as intimate relationship with the Father. The relationship of Jesus with Abba defines who the Spirit is. Small groups must begin to study and meditate on their existence as sustained by Jesus with the Father—that the Holy Spirit is by nature a Spirit of divine community who calls forth human community. This again is tough to see in a privatistic and individualistic world. We must start affirming the every nature of God as divinity in community. This gives small group ministry a solid theological foundation and puts Jesus into the midst of every Christian group as the one who brings us to God as gracious "Daddy."

4. Small groups need to be encouraged to tell their "group" experiences of God. Too often, when people are asked to share their personal experiences of God, the focus is on individualistic mystical events where no one else is present to confirm or reflect upon the event. Such personal experiences of God are fine, but too often people miss the possibility of looking for experiences where others were present to confirm the event. Every small group who gathers in the name of Jesus may have an experience together where they sensed God was present. Groups should be encouraged to tell these stories and examine the implications of the experience for their faith development.

5. Members of a group could be asked to share the key stories of their families of origin. What are the memories they have and stories they learned which helped form their sense of being a part of a special family? Such a question could also be asked of their relationship to the town or church where they grew up or the church where they now participate. Every group and organization has its own oral tradition of stories about its beginnings, its troubles, its victories and its experiences of God. Groups should give lots of time to the sharing of stories. This is what gives foundation to their common sense of humanity as well as a shared vision for the future.

18

SMALL GROUP DIRECTION AND DISCIPLINES

Those who accepted [Peter's] message were baptized. . . .
   They devoted themselves to the apostles' teaching and to the fellowship, to the breaking of bread and to prayer. (Acts 2:41-42)

The apostles were those who had had a personal encounter with the risen Jesus, who had personally sent them out into the world to start other groups of followers. The word *apostle*, says James Dunn, means "delegate, envoy or messenger," one with the "authority to represent [Jesus'] community elsewhere" and to set up "local communities" of Jesus in other places. They had three unique attributes: "they had been commissioned personally by the risen Jesus in a resurrection appearance," "they were missionaries and church founders," and they had "a distinctively and decisively eschatological role."[1] The apostles were called to start small Christian communities (small groups). Their authority for beginning these small communities of believers was Jesus himself, who founded an original community of twelve men, related to other small disciple groups. These groups expanded into multiple group clusters of one hundred twenty men and women before Pentecost.

It was important for these new small communities of Christians to focus upon the discipline and direction of the apostles, who carried the group story and the community experience of Jesus. They had lived with Jesus, walked with Jesus, talked with Jesus, and argued with Jesus. They had to be able to transfer both the message and experience (medium) of being with Jesus to the new groups.

Their group life with Jesus *was* their message. The experience (medium) of the Twelve, the seventy and the one hundred twenty was the experimental context where the teaching of Jesus could take on real meaning, real relationship, real personhood and real community. The apostles taught with authority because they taught from personal and communal experience. They had experienced Jesus' message as his medium. The new group communities they started needed the apostolic discipline of both experience and teaching, word and sacrament, that came out of direct contact with Jesus.

This discipline of personal experience was behind the polemical response to Gnosticism in John's first epistle:

That which was from the beginning, which we have *heard*, which we have *seen* with our eyes, which we have *looked* at and our hands have *touched*—this we *proclaim* concerning the Word of life. The life *appeared;* we have *seen* it and testify to it, and we proclaim to you the eternal life, which was with the Father and has appeared to us. We proclaim to you what we have *seen* and *heard,* so that you also may have *fellowship* with us. And our *fellowship* is with the Father and with his Son, Jesus Christ. (1 Jn 1:1-3, italics mine)

The apostolic drive for firsthand encounter through personal, touchable and concrete evidence was absolutely necessary for the continuity and consistency of the real human fellowships who gathered in the name (nature and way) of Jesus. Jesus' life with the apostles was a real human fellowship, which means that the small group fellowship of Christians needed to be a real human fellowship, a flesh-and-blood community of healing and reconciling persons, men and women, young and old, Gentile and Jew. The teaching of the apostles was the teaching and life of Jesus through firsthand face-to-face experience. Jesus' communal life was both the direction and discipline of every ecclesia.

This apostolic treasure of firsthand instruction and experience with Jesus was sustained through the ongoing mutual and supportive grouping of the apostles in Jerusalem. They continued to minister, teach, heal and confront in partnership (koinonia) together. The Twelve called together the larger group of disciples in order to pick seven "to wait on tables" so that the apostles could give their "attention to prayer and the ministry of the word" (Acts 5:12—6:7). Even the apostle Paul went to Jerusalem to meet with the core apostolic group to hold dialogue on the question of circumcision.

The community of the Twelve was the center of theological and christological integrity for all the small Christian communities being formed in both the Jewish and Gentile worlds (Acts 15:1-35). The dialogical and experiential grouping process of the Twelve was an important *community of reflection,* where each was held accountable to maintain integrity with the life and words of Jesus. As this apostolic group continued to hold itself in mutual accountability and integrity, the other newly birthed small groups maintained their discipline of listening carefully to the disciples' teaching, which was considered a direct word and life pattern from the resurrected Jesus himself.

The Disciplines of Early Christian Small Groups

For these small groups of Christians to be able to sustain a new way of life in both the pagan and religiously closed societies of Jerusalem, they had to adopt and practice simple but definitive community-building disciplines. Luke's summary of these universal and key small group disciplines included devotion to "the apostles' teaching and to the fellowship, to the breaking of bread and to prayer" (Acts 2:42). We know that these four acts are key group disciplines because of Luke's use of the term *devoted*, which means "continuing steadily, intensively, with focus, strong purpose and intentionality."

Without the consistent and recurring practice of these crucial disciplines the new home-gathered communities would dissolve into pervasive and oppressive urban cultures. But instead, through the diligent (devoted) practice of every day discipline, these small Christian communities began to attract more and more attention, transforming the very culture that sought to wipe them out. These groups were living examples of the realm of heaven coming to "tent" on earth, transforming human systems even while these same systems developed more oppressive techniques to rid themselves of the mobile heavenly communities.

These earthly communities, these ecclesia, received their identity and purpose from the risen Lord who sat in the presence of Abba God in heaven. "In Greek *ecclesia* was a familiar word. From the fifth century B.C. onwards it referred to the regular 'assembly' of citizens in a city to decide matters affecting their welfare."[2] The communities of believers became family along with the Son who lives in eternal community with the Father and works to bring brothers and sisters into his new heavenly family through the ambassadorship of apostles and the foreign consulates of small local households on earth.

Bernard Lee and Michael Cowan have said that "the key to the vision of Jesus is that the parenthood of God makes us all sisters and brothers. God's parenthood puts an end to human patriarchy. . . . God's parenthood is a critical subversion of all structures of domination."[3] While Lee and Cowan represent a liberationist strategy for the formation and purpose of small groups as "base communities," their theological understanding of Jesus' role as elder brother is key to the understanding of the ongoing need for small group ministry patterned after the foundations of the ecclesia in Acts 2. If there is no locally identifiable new family of two or more who gather in the name of Jesus, there can be no ongoing expression of the good news incarnate. Unless there are established beachheads of small house groups in the cities and towns, there is no hope of God occupying the whole land. The continuing incarnation of Jesus comes through the Spirit who ushers a plurality of incarnate groups into culture and society. It is Jesus meeting with two or more that is both the mind and the method of the gospel.

The practices and ethics of these Christ-centered ecclesia were earth-directed, but their source, values and center of discipline were heavenward. The apostle Paul said that Christ "is the head [source] of the body, the ecclesia" (Col 1:18). The Greek word *kephalē* can mean "head" or "source." It carries the descriptive image of "head waters" or "source of flow" or "center of relationships," and does not reflect a hierarchical image of "control from above," "dominance from higher up," or manipulation. As Robert Banks has noted, this passage brings ecclesia and *kephalē* together: "He is the *kephalē* of the body, the ecclesia."[4] Unfortunately, too often the spatial and geographical concepts of height and position have been confused with the relational concept of center and source. This is key to the understanding of ecclesia *not* being an organization and structure with Jesus at the top, but being a gathering of human beings with Jesus in their midst.

The commitment of the ecclesia to regular gathering was their core discipline. Gathering allowed them a consistent practice of the four key disciplines of Christian community. As Donald Postema has so clearly affirmed, discipline creates space for encounter with God, with creation, with self and with others.[5]

Without this core discipline of gathering, there is no such thing as "the church." Christ now has an earthly "body" if there is a small group who forms it. American individualism sometimes flies in the face of this when a person says, "I can worship God on my own. I don't need a church." Such a statement misses the core value and key purpose of "church" as face-to-face gathering and that God can only be known fully in community as community.

The Discipline of the Apostles' Teaching

Unfortunately, when those who are products of the Western concept of classroom education hear the word *teaching*, we bring a very strong image and bias to this biblical term and pattern. The teaching of Jesus and the apostles was *exousia*, "out of the very essence of who they were" (Mt 7:28-29). Their teaching was their experience of Abba God in relationship with Jesus and with them by the power of the Spirit who made them to be "Christ" together. The apostles' teaching had to be a group experience pouring out of a group experience. Their memories of being with Jesus in a group were reflected and mediated through their ongoing group which were shared as interpreted story in the context of house groups. They would have had no teaching except that they continued to invest in small group life. Their teaching was their life together, using the fullness of their mental, emotional and physical capacities as human beings in community.

Learning is a relational process. Learning is dialogical and experimental. Learning is an integrated experience of a whole person among whole people. Learning is a communal, familial and tribal process from a center and source flowing to fertile and tilled ground.

Andrew was in a Bible study group, but he was frustrated. He felt as though he was not growing. Their group had a great teacher who knew the Bible well and could tell them all sorts of important information about what it said and what it meant. Their group met once a week in the home of the teacher. But Andrew, after two years in the group, realized they never talked about everyday life. Additionally, there was little discussion, and every time he asked a question he felt that the teacher discounted his concerns. Andrew felt he wasn't a very spiritual person because he had so many questions. The other members of the group seemed to understand and accept everything the teacher said. Andrew was increasingly sad about being in the group and he was thinking of dropping out. As he thought about his hunger "to know" he realized he wanted to be in a group where there was less teaching and more sharing about the real issues of life.

Andrew's experience can be multiplied a million times in Western Christendom today because study groups and institutional churches have a very cerebral, didactic, rational, informational and objective orientation to the teaching of the Bible. Such an attitude was not true of the apostolic small group communities. As the apostles gathered people together, life was their foundation and field of instruction. Like Jesus, they told stories and led gutsy discussions. They encouraged curiosity and affirmed questions. Arguing, debating, confronting, challenging, reflecting, sharing, feeling and planning to act were all part of the group process. They practiced noncondemning responses to the wondering, the inquiring, and the conflicting. They wanted real men and women to have a safe place to deal with the hard questions of life. And in all the discussion and teaching, they pointed to Jesus' life as the center and source of the community. They were, like Jesus, more interested in formation of lives and relationships than they were in getting people to accept the right information.

There was and is no New Testament discipline of teaching that is not group bound. For the apostles, the only true learning environment was that which they had experienced with Jesus, the small group in conversation about real life.

The Discipline of Community

The word *community* is one way to translate the Greek term *koinōnia*. The context of Acts suggests that *koinōnia* was a general descriptive word for the gospel's impact on all aspects of human relationships. In Christ every human activity and intention was guided by the law of love: love God, love neighbor, love self. The apostles understood that the essence of life "in the name of Jesus" was the emerging reality of reconciled relationships.

Just as Jesus built human community wherever he ministered through his teaching and his life, the apostles, who imitated Jesus, were builders of ecclesia (gathering). The apostle Paul advocated and incarnated this reconciling, relational, personal community-building attitude of Jesus: "For Christ's love compels us, because we are convinced that one died for all. . . . And he died for all, that those who live should no longer live for themselves but for him" (2 Cor 5:14-15). And living for Jesus demands that we live for others after the model of Jesus (2 Cor 5:17-21).

The apostles also understood that the reality of reconciliation would not happen unless there was *intentionality* and *space* to *practice* the *disciplines* of reconciled relationships. From the model of Jesus they understood this *disciplined space* to be in small groups of persons who came together around the real person of Jesus. While these groups were not intentionally limited in numerical size, they started small, honoring Jesus' parameter, wherever two or three came together (assembled or gathered) there was ecclesia. The disciplines of coming together and of going together were apostolic because they were Jesus' group disciplines.

The process of sending groups into mission was also consistent with Jesus' strategy. The Jerusalem apostolic group called together the whole network of ecclesia to choose a subgroup to go to Antioch with Paul and Barnabas. This team gathered the Antioch assembly together to encourage and strengthen them. Paul and Barnabas remained with them to teach and proclaim the word of the Lord. The disciplines of teaching, proclamation and community building were always practiced by mission teams who themselves acted together (see Acts 15:22-23, 30-35).

Just as Jesus had originally sent them, the apostles went out from a larger group to travel in twos, threes and fours. The apostles (sent ones) traveled and ministered together in community—in small mission groups. While they practiced the disciplines of community building among one another, they also modeled and taught others to practice these same disciplines of human reconciliation through small- and medium-sized groups. The apostolic team ministry, by example, called new believers to practice the law of love as they observed the apostles practicing the law of love. It was this constant display of concrete apostolic reality, of real Christian community, alongside the words of the Lord, which taught the believers in various cities what it meant to follow Jesus. The apostolic mission was the portable community of Jesus who birthed other groups.

Paul called upon the Philippian ecclesia (church) to "join with others in following my example" and "live according to the *pattern* we gave to you" (Phil 3:17). This was the *example* of a person living in intimate relationship to Christ and the *pattern* of living in community with one another. These are the two dimensions of the Christian discipline of community, a balance of word (teaching or *didachē*) and sacrament (community or *koinōnia*).

"Word" in the Refomed tradition is often understood to mean the written and verbal explanation of the gospel, often losing its existential meaning as the person and work (community) of the historical Jesus who lived in real human relationships. This is the intended polemic against Gnosticism in John's Gospel, "the Word became flesh and made his dwelling among us" (Jn 1:14). From our inheritance of rationalism and empiricism of the Enlightenment (and before that in scholasticism) there has been an ongoing tendency in Western theological thought to reduce the full humanity and community of Jesus to a ministry of the written or spoken word. Such has been an ongoing modified form of Gnosticism. Thankfully, the modern existential pragmatics of the social sciences seem to be calling the Christian faith back to its primal roots in the full spirituality of human community. This modern movement of "human potential" is one of the pressures placed upon classic theology to again find its center and balance in the full humanity and community of Jesus. The real disciplines and elements of Christian community were partly, if not greatly, lost in the Reformation. One of Bonhoeffer's greatest contributions to the Reformed faith was his articulation (in *The Communion of Saints* and *Life Together)* of the need for a Christology that recognizes Jesus in the reality of everyday life together. Jesus is only fully visible in real community.

The word *sacrament* has to do with "an oath of allegiance . . . a mutual contribution made by two parties."[6] The covenantal root of the concept of sacrament is the basis for the discipline of community, that wherever two or more come together in mutual commitment to Christ and to one another, there is the real presence of Christ. This formed the fullness of Jesus' and the apostles' teaching. These two group disciplines found their integrative and unifying fulfillment in the specific sacramental event of the group's "breaking of the bread."

The Discipline of the Breaking of Bread
For the small groups of early Christian community, the intentional discipline and practice of breaking bread was foundational. The definition and purpose of the breaking of bread had to do with the very nature and being of their human community.[7] To be in an ecclesia was to be a participant in the shared breaking of bread. The apostles gathered believers together around the centrality of the

Person of Jesus, who had gathered them around the table of the Last Supper.

Jesus had first broken the bread with the twelve apostles. Whether he did so with only the Twelve (Mt 26:20; Mk 14:17) or with more (Lk 22:14, "his apostles," James Dunn and others would say the Twelve and others), the importance here is that a small group of apostles was present with Jesus in a home. The apostolic repetition of the discipline of breaking bread in homes was an ongoing reenactment of the place and spirit of the Last Supper, which they had shared in a "guest room," or a "large upper room" of a "home" in Jerusalem (Lk 22:10-12). The shared meal was a continuing return to the scene of the group event and an ongoing portrayal of the story. For the early ecclesia the breaking of the bread was deeply attached to their meeting as small groups in homes.

This third discipline of the early Christian small groups, like the others, was deeply rooted in the historical reality of the apostles with Jesus. The place, the ethos, the feelings, the conversation and the exact words of Jesus were recalled every time the apostles led the meal. This pattern of physical, spatial and geographical reenactment was rooted in Hebrew history. Jesus had intentionally tied the celebration and reenactment of the Passover to his own breaking of bread. The Passover meal was originally a small group home event. The Lord's Supper was a home event in continuity with the Exodus story (Ex 12; Lk 22:7).

As Eric Voegelin reminded us, the Hebrew practice of spiritual discipline was for *recall* (remember) and *replay* (reenact). Voegelin's philosophical apologetic and critique of what he called apocalyptic-gnostic thinkers whose "purpose of abolishing a 'past history' of mankind" relates to this discussion of the nature of small group as sacramental community. Voegelin argued that the "remembering" and "reenacting" in consciousness of the true historical past—the real events of the past—is of prime importance to maintaining our human sense of identity, balance and direction. "The historical dimension at issue was not a piece of 'past history' but the permanent presence of the process of reality in which man participates with his conscious existence." The ongoing practice of meeting in small groups in the presence of Christ is a continuing affirmation of the historical reality of the life, death and resurrection of Jesus with the Twelve and the early apostolic communities.[8] The words of Jesus at the last supper, "Do this in remembrance of me" (Lk 22:19) is a call to small group life.

The re-*doing*-ness of the breaking of bread was deeply and intimately connected to the re-*doing*-ness of the meeting together in homes and the re-*doing*-ness of the small group community, the ecclesia. Today we are again moved to ask the crucial question, Is this special call to the re-*doing*-ness of the breaking of bread in homes a radical and historical critique of the institutionalization and clericalization of the breaking of bread in larger religious gatherings and buildings? The small group celebration of the supper would be in direct conflict with most current Catholic and Protestant practice. In such organizational systems the Lord's Supper is ordinarily performed in the sanctuary with an ordained minister or priest. This Christendom practice continues to raise questions about group size, place of practice, intimacy of community and historical rootedness. Biblical foundations strongly suggest the need for a return to intentional small group celebrations of the Lord's Supper wherever two or three come together in Christ (homes, work, schools). For religious institutionalists this is a tough movement.

In the small group communities, the sharing of a general meal together was directly connected to the sharing of the Lord's Supper. Eating together affirmed the importance of the group's mutual and interdependent economic and physical sustenance. These were no longer separate individuals who had no connection to or responsibility for one another. These were now people who were bound together for human community, for food, for money, for touch, for survival, for salvation, for growth and for preparation for earthly ministry. The sharing of the meal was integral and central to the expression of a totally shared life. If a member of the group had no food nor money to buy food, the rest of the group shared their money and food. The individual's bread became the community's bread because all bread came from God.

The Lord's Prayer uses bread as a specific symbol for the total daily physical and economic needs of the community of disciples: "Give *us* each day *our* daily bread" (Lk 11:3, italics mine). Jesus also taught the apostles to feed those who were hungry in smaller groups. When confronted with the hunger of the multitude, Jesus told the Twelve, "You give them something to eat" (Lk 9:13). Jesus gave the apostles direction to divide the crowd into smaller groups of about fifty. This was a numerical and spatial movement from which the Twelve learned a universal strategy for ministry: Do not try to minister to the whole crowd at one time. Serve the people in smaller groups. Feed the people when they are in more intimate communities. The division of the crowd paralleled the division of the post-Pentecost Jerusalem crowd into smaller groups for the breaking of bread in their homes. The sharing of food, in the life of Jesus, was distinctively a small group experience.

The apostle Paul's strong theological and christological centering of all meals in the meal of Jesus with the Twelve is a very important foundation for all small Christian gatherings:

When you come together, it is not the Lord's Supper you eat, for as you eat, each of you goes ahead without waiting for anybody else. One remains hungry; another gets drunk. . . . Do you despise the [ecclesia] of God and humiliate those who have nothing? What shall I say to you?

For anyone who eats and drinks without recognizing the body of the Lord eats and drinks judgment. . . .

When you come together to eat, wait for each other. (1 Cor 11:20-22, 29, 33)

The meal of the gathering is a measure of the intention, integrity and maturity of the small group. And the communal reality and value of all meals should be measured against the spirit and discipline of the Lord's Supper. The gathering must be sensitive to every member of the group, where every member is looking out for the needs of every other member.

The enactment of the Lord's Supper gave focus and ultimate meaning to the more general practice of eating meals together. The mere sharing of food with others was not enough. The sharing had to be rooted in the event of Jesus breaking bread with the apostles. The Lord's Supper defined the meaning and direction for all other suppers: Jesus was in the midst of the house group, which was the physical body of the risen Lord. The members of the group were called to feed one another, to live for one another, to serve one another, and to love one another.

It is no accident that the Gospel of John places Jesus' teaching about washing one another's feet and loving one another in the context of the Lord's Supper (Jn 13). The shared meal was the focused event around which all other sharing and serving of the body should happen. Friends and family share meals and life together. Intimacy exists as a way of life in the household where people show deep affection for one another, fight with one another, and plan to lay down their lives for one another. The meal is the central sacrifice of the sacrificial community.

The sharing of the meal was to be a reflection of this intimate and loving community. The abuse of mealtime was a visible insensitivity to Jesus, who presided at every meal. All meals were to be measured by the rule of the one meal that bridged earth and heaven, today and forever. As James Dunn has pointed out, "In so far as it (the common meal) harked back to the fellowship meals of Jesus' ministry, particularly the last, it would almost certainly carry the same note of eschatological expectation (Luke 22:18, 'from now on I shall not drink of the fruit of the vine until the Kingdom of God comes')."[9]

The small group or house ecclesia was the concrete space and place where the spiritual discipline of breaking bread was to be practiced and critiqued. The small group ecclesia was also the space where a glimpse of God's future for humanity could be seen, where men and women, adults and children, free and slave could relate with one another based upon the new values, new character and new hope of forgiveness and reconciliation. The Christian small group was to be a foretaste of the meals of heaven.

The Discipline of Prayer

The fourth group discipline which the apostolic groups practiced was prayer. The discipline of prayer gave the other group disciplines direction and meaning. This prayer discipline was specifically a group discipline and not a private discipline. While Jesus had taught the Twelve to pray (Lk 11:1-4), their practice of prayer had little content or intensity until their communal experience in the upper room. When the Twelve gathered with the one hundred others in ecclesia "they all joined together constantly in prayer" (Acts 1:14).

There is no evidence that when the Twelve were with Jesus they had any regular practice of prayer, individually or corporately. When the three were with Jesus on the Mount of Olives he called them to "pray so that you will not fall into temptation," but he later found them asleep (Lk 22:45-46). Also, when the other nine disciples failed in their attempt to exorcise a demon from a boy, Jesus pointed out that "this kind can come out only by prayer" (Mk 9:28-29).

In the upper room this group discipline of prayer was learned "with the women." The women had been passionate participants in the suffering and death of Jesus (Lk 23:27, 49, 55). It is possible that the women were experienced in the group discipline of prayer before going into the upper room. Could it be that their model of group prayer was formative for the Twelve men in the upper room? Luke's Gospel, far beyond the emphasis of the other synoptic Gospels, emphasizes the reflective and passionate character of Mary, the mother of Jesus, even including her poetry (Lk 1:26-56). Luke suggests that she was already a disciplined person of reflection and prayer. Perhaps Mary was instrumental in teaching the Twelve the discipline of prayer in the upper room group.

It was in the midst of this shared discipline of men and women together in prayer that the Spirit of Jesus came in fulfillment of Joel's prophetic message: "Your sons and daughters will prophesy. . . . Even on my servants, both men and women, I will pour out my spirit in those days" (Acts 2:17-18). Even as the discipline of prayer was shared by men and women, so the Spirit was given to men and women together in the group. And it was men and women together from the group who shared the good news of the resurrection throughout the whole city of Jerusalem. The "amazement" and "perplexity" of the citizens may have been partially the result of seeing both women and men participating together in such a public display of passion, intensity, emotion, and common purpose.

After learning the discipline of prayer in the upper room with men and women together, the apostles helped new believers to form household groups of men and women, young and old, who practiced this group discipline of prayer together. The learned experience of the power of group prayer became a major component of the life of every small group ecclesia that met in the homes and courts. The groups' discipline of prayer came out of continuity with the apostles' experience of prayer, which had been nurtured by the prayer life of Jesus. "The prayer of primitive Christianity finds its starting point and center in the prayer of Jesus." But beyond this, "as with the continuation of the common meal, so in prayer, the first Christians were not merely doing as Jesus did, but doing it in conscious reference to and continuing dependence upon Jesus."[10]

The four small group disciplines of the early house ecclesia were mutually interwoven into the fabric of their being together. The apostles' teaching informed the character and meaning of the koinonia, the breaking of bread and the prayers. The shared meal added substance and symbol to the community. And prayer centered the community in the intimacy of the Son with Abba God. The four disciplines were founded in the historical continuity of the life of Jesus with the Twelve. The practice of these four small group disciplines gave the ecclesia the character and courage to practice its ministry, which had been passed on from Jesus with the Twelve to the ecclesia. The ecclesia, practicing the four disciplines of Jesus, became small groups open to the formation of Christ's life among them. Their receptivity to being guided together and to being directed into the future was a product of an apostolic attitude which undergirded all their experience. They were encouraged to listen, discuss and respond to Jesus as a voluntary experience of their own curiosity. Theirs was an inductive experience of Christ totally embraced as their own.

The Small Group as Inductive Community

Now the Bereans were of more noble character than the Thessalonians, for they received the message with great eagerness and examined the Scriptures every day to see if what Paul said was true. Many of the Jews believed, as did also a number of prominent Greek women and many Greek men. (Acts 17:11-12)

The strategic plan of going to the Jewish synagogue (assembly) of a particular town or city was Paul's regular practice for forming new gatherings of Christian believers. At the synagogue, Paul "reasoned with them from the Scriptures, explaining and proving that the Christ had to suffer and rise from the dead" (Acts 17:2-3). Those who had assembled in the tradition of Jewish culture and religion became those who were called by Christ to gather as ecclesia. The movement between synagogue and ecclesia often called for a radical regrouping of the men with the women since they were generally separated in the synagogue. The ecclesia, made up of Jews and Gentiles, men and women, were founded around a traditional process of building community through biblical, theological and experiential reflection.

Among the ecclesia the original sources for faith exploration were the Old Testament Scriptures and the apostles' firsthand experience with Jesus. Just as Jesus led the apostles to experience his being and teaching through communal reflection of the Old Testament Scriptures, so the apostles expected the small house groups to meet together to share their reflections of Jesus and his relationship with the Father. The ecclesia were formed out of firsthand experience with the apostles, who had firsthand experience with Christ as he taught, ministered, suffered, died and rose from the grave. Unlike the synagogues where the Scriptures were interpreted through several layers of Jewish commentary, the ecclesia called its members to the immediate and personal experience of the apostles with Jesus, to firsthand contact with the biblical texts, and to firsthand charismatic experience of the Spirit. These firsthand experiences were reflective of the inductive nature of Jesus' community and apostolic ecclesia.

Small Group Communion

Induction is the process of allowing a source, an experience, an event, a person, or a text to speak for itself. The Holy Spirit is the great inductive agent of Christ in the small group community. The Spirit must be given the freedom to teach the group and its members what Christ desires for the group to know and understand. Induction is a tough group discipline because much of Western educational theory is built upon a hermeneutic of deduction, that is, having an expert interpret the primary sources and tell the group what they mean. Deduction is an honorable and helpful discipline if practiced within the greater arena of an inductive ethic. If expert deduction controls the thought of a group, the Spirit is greatly limited in its freedom to teach and empower.

This was a source of constant tension in apostolic authority. The apostles were called by Jesus to call together small groups, teach them the inductive disciplines of community in Christ and to let them go (with some guidance) by the direction of the Spirit. The Spirit's ethic and attitude of inductive learning and empowerment had to balance the leadership temptation of the apostles to control the ecclesia and stifle their creative and personal sense of divine direction. The apostles were to be group spiritual directors, not CEOs of controlled systems.

From an educational perspective deduction is in polarity with induction. Induction is the process of allowing an original source to speak for itself. Deduction is the process of an expert summarizing and systematizing what the original said, which forces the learner first to understand the summary and system of the expert. Induction allows the learner to encounter the source firsthand.[11] In the case of ecclesia, induction was a key to the "noble character" of the Bereans, demonstrated by their direct scriptural and charismatic encounter with word and Spirit. Deduction, the temptation to defer to a human system in relating to God, was part of the Thessalonian syndrome (Acts 17:1-9). Why were the Thessalonians so jealous except that their closed system was being threatened by this new, firsthand experience with God?

The *charismata* as inductive experiences were the "ongoing creative events," the immediate mutual ministries of the Spirit at work in and through the ecclesia. As Dunn has said, the

> charismata are the living actions of the body of Christ. The body of Christ only comes to realization in any place through the manifestations of grace. . . . Christian community exists only in the interplay of charismatic community, in the concrete realizations of grace, in the actual being and doing for others in word and deed.[12]

The apostles did not want to inhibit believers from personally and corporately exploring their new life of the Spirit. Instead, they wanted the ecclesia to have the freedom to exercise the *exousia* of Jesus as their own *exousia*. And this could only happen as they were willing to risk firsthand encounters with the Spirit. They demonstrated their community hermeneutic by calling each ecclesia to explore primary faith sources personally and inductively. The house groups reasoned together with the apostles about their experience with Jesus and their understanding of Scripture. They experienced life in the Spirit together as a community. In sum, their three primary inductive sources were the apostles' life with Jesus, the Hebrew Scriptures and their charismatic experience of the Spirit with one another in community. These three resources—the present Lord Jesus Christ, those present persons in mutual ministry of the group through the Spirit, and the Scriptures—have continued to be the primary inductive sources for the ecclesia throughout salvation history.

For each of these primary inductive sources in the historic life of the Christian small group, there is a parallel small group discipline to be learned and practiced. These three disciplines are the discipline of participating in the prayer of Jesus with the Father, the discipline of studying and the discipline of sharing life together (koinonia) as mutual ministry of those in the Spirit.

Paul *reasoned* with the Thessalonians and *examined* the Scriptures with the Bereans. These reciprocal movements of face-to-face dialogue and firsthand biblical examination were examples of the inductive community discipline which the apostles called the ecclesia to practice. This was no lecture method, no one-way communication, no deductive systematic theology. The apostles expected the members of the ecclesia to participate with them in the ongoing discovery of the meaning of Christ's life and resurrection. They met together around the texts of Scripture. Their authority was not in their official expertise, but in their personal experience.

As Luke commented about the Bereans, the "nobility" of Christian community lies in its personal eagerness to receive and examine the inductive sources of the group's life and to experience life together for themselves as a body called and connected. The underlying values which drove such a nobility of openness and responsiveness were the desire to know God personally and corporately, the willingness to learn together as a community, the determination to embrace experts (apostles) into mutuality, and the practice of the group to be interdependent upon one another's knowledge, ideas, opinions, thinking, disciplines, perspectives and wisdom. These were small groups who sought with all their heart to find God. As Jeremiah prophesied, " 'You will call upon me and come and pray to me, and I will listen to you. You will seek me and find me when you seek me with all your heart. I will be found by you,' declares the LORD" (Jer 29:12-14). The dwelling place of God is in community with a curious, seeking and noble people.

Such interdependent inductive learning enabled the Spirit, not the apostle, to be the primary teacher. The Spirit called the apostolic community to remember all that Jesus did and taught (Jn 14:26). The Spirit called the community to do the ministry of Jesus' life at work through them (Jn 16:5-15). The Spirit was the "advocate" and the empowerer of mutual ministry. Such interdependent experience and learning in the Spirit leads into interdependent ministry in the Spirit.

Robert Banks argues that the interdependence of the Christian community is the result of dependence on Christ and independence from outside social values and systems. This empowerment had to do with the apostles' understanding of charismatic authority. They taught that their authority existed in the centering of the gospel in Christ and the working of the Spirit in the life of the ecclesia. Christ was the primary authority of the group. Theirs was an authority alongside, not above, the ecclesia. They became partners in ministry as quickly as possible. The apostle only had authority as focused in the person and ministry of Christ.[13]

The inductive presence of the Spirit in the ecclesia as "counselor" and "teacher" reorients a small group away from typical human values of authority. The human leader of the group, specifically the apostle, was never allowed the place of lordship in the group. For every ecclesia there was only one Lord and one "source" of the body's direction, one ultimate leader of the group—the Spirit of Christ. This made all other group leaders penultimate sources of authority. Their leadership was to call the community to dependence on Christ and to interdependence with one another. The nobility of the ecclesia was inherited from its princely

Leader and Lord, Jesus Christ, who himself worked through various members of the group to minister to and to teach each other. Jesus was no Lord of control, manipulation and intimidation, but a Lord of love who invited a willing group of followers to accept responsibility for their life together.

Too much giving of authority to a secondary source, even to an apostle, would have undermined this delicate learning relationship and process. Deferring to "expert" human authority, apart from Christ, moves a group away from its primary relationship with the Spirit and Scripture, creating a dependence upon the more deductive and limited systems of that human authority. For the apostolic expert to become the primary authority was to move the Spirit out of its central role. The community would then lose its noble calling of inductive discovery of the word and ministry if it sought its identity and life in the deductive system formed by human ingenuity and strategy, no matter how brilliant, how influential, how attractive or how powerful.

This was Paul's major concern for the Galatian ecclesia (see Gal 1—3). They had so easily given up their direct dependence on the Spirit and the gospel to lean upon the secondary authority of Jewish law. This human system would rob them of their primary dependence on Christ and their mutual interdependence in the Spirit. To give up dependence upon the Spirit was to accept dependence upon a human system and upon those who taught such a system. According to Paul, even the apostle Peter was guilty of bowing to such a human system and running away from the freedom of the gospel. Complete deductive dependence on the expert or theological system robs the ecclesia of an inductive interdependence with the Spirit. The apostle must be a mutual participant with the community of those who exercise their nobility of interdependent learning and ministering. The directive leadership of the apostle was always to be submissive to the guidance of the Spirit among the group. The group always lives between these two poles of authority as they exist in creative tension under the primary direction of the Spirit, assisted by secondary adjustments by individual group members.

The ecclesia were inductively and intuitively countercultural because they experienced firsthand the reality of God's presence in the world. Wherever the apostles proclaimed the gospel and formed a new small house group they introduced the inevitable dissonance with existing cultural patterns. The new creation and inductive authority of the Spirit was often seen as subversive to the established deductive authority of the law. Such tension with existing principalities and authorities was a strong reason Jesus was crucified and the ecclesia were persecuted. The mutual submission of the group to one another out of reverence for Christ implied that existing systems and authorities lost primary control over their lives together and as individuals.

This may be the reason the apostolic epistles admonish the ecclesia to "submit . . . to every authority instituted among [humanity]" (1 Pet 2:13). In some cases the ecclesia wrongly assumed their freedom of mutuality could be imposed upon the outside world. They might use their experience of the Spirit to refuse to live peacefully with the existing hierarchical paternal and controlling systems. Rather than submit to the abuse of the system as Jesus did, they were tempted to transform the human system through militant, rebellious or vindictive actions. Such reaction by ecclesia would look like anarchy to a controlling governing power. Eventually these outside religious and political systems lost their authority, power and control over the house communities. Such a loss of influence and control moved them to attack the apostles and to persecute the groups.

The personal, relational and ethical values of the members of the ecclesia were being directed and transformed by the presence of Christ through the power of the Spirit. Their patterns of thinking about human relationships and institutions were changed through a continuous inductive experience of life together in Christ. They lost their need to be conformed to the patterns of the world as they intentionally helped one another to be conformed to the pattern of Christ. Their inductive learning of Christ through the Spirit caused them to be a transformed human community. They became a small group of people who lived for one another through the law of love. As Dietrich Bonhoeffer said, "In the community of the Spirit there burns the bright love of brotherly service, *agape*."[14]

■ SMALL GROUP MINISTRY IMPLICATIONS

1. Many groups only exist because someone brought them together, but no one ever said why they were together. Every small group needs to define its purpose. This defining purpose should be examined by the group at least once per year. The development and review of the purpose can be formal or informal processes, but each group must invest in these regular disciplines. The purpose may be as simple as "we are together to grow in Christ," but then the group must define for themselves what this means and how they will know if it is accomplished. Groups who have no defining purpose will be reduced to the purpose of the strongest members or meet aimlessly forever. Undefined groups usually have a short life.

2. Every group has to invest in a set of mutual disciplines in order for the group to work. These disciplines may include dates, times, agendas, Bible study, prayer, sharing, listening, singing, asking questions, reading and so on. The group needs to agree upon the disciplines they want to share together. If there is not agreement upon the shared disciplines eventually some members of the group will grow frustrated that their commitment and investment are being undervalued

by other group members who refuse to participate in the key disciplines. This often happens in a Bible study group around the discipline of advance preparation before the meeting. Some do their homework and others may not. Soon this disparity of commitment undermines the integrity of the group covenant.

3. Many Christian groups invest in Bible study as their primary discipline, but they miss the importance of the apostolic discipline of personal and communal experience with Christ. Some groups today think there is no good way to help a group get in touch with their immediate experience of God so they only invest in how biblical people were in touch with God. This reluctance is partly due to the fear that "experience" will take the place of the authority of the Bible as the "word." And this is a legitimate concern. However, to reject the current experience of Christ as the present and immediate redemptive community of the Spirit, and only look to the past story of the people of God in Scripture, is to undermine the powerful gift of the Spirit to act today. In every gathered group there is always a creative tension between Scripture as the historical Word and Spirit as the present Word. How God is active right now in the group must always be weighed against the measure of Christ in Scripture. But a group must be free to look and reflect upon God's immediate action and their sense of God's immediate presence. There must be a strong and growing existential sense of God's communal presence as the group wrestles with the meaning of the biblical text. This ambivalence is one reason why groups often avoid investing substantial time in the "application" phase of inductive Bible study. They lose the connection between their current life together and the biblical record of God's faithfulness.

4. Small groups need to take lots of time to be communities of reflection. God is active and present, but if the group does not stop to reflect upon what God is saying and doing in the group, they may miss the precious gift of their life together—the chance to see God at work close at hand. Journaling is a helpful discipline in this process of reflection. Keeping a group journal as well as keeping individual journals can help a group get in touch with their sense of God's voice and activity. There is a lot of stuff each person is sensing each day as well as the substance of the group's meeting together that provides abundant food for mutual spiritual reflection and direction. It would be good for small group leadership training to include some ways to help a group do this kind of spiritual reflection.

5. There is an intimate relationship between the frequency and intensity of a small group's meeting schedule and the potential depth a group may experience in their life together. It is somewhat obvious that groups who meet only occasionally will not share the same sense of being the "family" of Christ as those who meet more frequently or for longer durations. A small group retreat where the group meets for an intense period of ten to twenty hours together may have

more long-term impact than ten biweekly meetings of two hours each. Especially today, when schedules are so tough to coordinate, a group may prosper more from fewer and longer meetings than from an occasional schedule drawn out over many months. It is also true that small groups who meet every week tend to experience a stronger bonding process than those who meet every other week. Some of this has to do with the purpose of the group and what tasks the group is trying to accomplish.

19

SMALL GROUP
AS FORMATIONAL AND
TRANSFORMATIONAL
COMMUNITY

I urge you, brothers [and sisters], in view of God's mercy, to offer your bodies as living sacrifices, holy and pleasing to God—this is your spiritual act of worship. Do not conform any longer to the pattern of this world, but be transformed by the renewing of your mind. . . .

Do not think of yourself more highly than you ought, but rather think of yourself with sober judgment. . . . So in Christ we who are many form one body, and each member belongs to all the others. We have different gifts, according to the grace given us. . . .

Be devoted to one another in [familial] love. Honor one another above yourselves. (Rom 12:1-3, 5-6, 10)

Living as a participant member of the body of Christ changes one's values and lifestyle. Because Jesus is the preeminent member of the ecclesia, the group members follow his thinking and model to see themselves and one another through new eyes—the eyes (and mind) of Christ. As reflected in Romans 12, this transformation comes about through the small group's exercise of good thinking, mutual sacrifice, healthy self-awareness, sharing personal gifts and expression of familial love. As the small group practices thoughtful and mutual relationships, it becomes a transforming space, community and family system.

The Small Group as Family System

Families form the character, ethics, beliefs and relational patterns of each human being. Family systems are created and nurtured by strong persons (and relationships) who establish clear patterns of behavior. Every human being grows up as a participant in several different family systems that affect one's personal and relational values in different ways. Edwin Friedman, in his book *Generation to Generation*, points out that every human being is rooted in families of origin, for better or for worse. Friedman has suggested that the movement from linear (one-dimensional) thinking about how people form to systems (two- and three-dimensional) thinking is the pivotal paradigm shift. This essentially is a shift from seeing life as formative through "content" to seeing life as formative through "process."[1]

Every new relationship and group sets up a new arena for an unfolding family system. Humanity as a whole family system looks back (theologically speaking) to Adam and Eve (and the Noahic family) as the originators of our general human family system. Exploring the human family system in the biblical account of Genesis strongly suggests that the general human system has deep fragmentation and woundedness. Men and women seem to exist as crosscultural elements in a human family system cut off from community with God and mutual relationships. Sin binds every human group until God is able to intervene into the group life to redeem its values and bring healing and reconciliation to participant relationships.

Every new small group gathering is a new family system, a gathering of persons who each brings his or her own family systems, values, attitudes and patterns of group behavior into the new group. Particularly during times of increased stress and tension, group members tend to withdraw into unredeemed practices of previous family systems, especially those from their family of origin. Group behavior will tend to be driven by the family behaviors of each group member, but most strongly by primary and influential group leaders. Leadership forms the primary values of each new family system.

The Forming and Transforming Presence of Small Group Leadership

Primary group leaders affect the patterns of group life, the primary values of group behavior and the group's primary relational dynamics. As the leader lives and acts, so the group tends to imitate and react. Groups take on the patterns of their effective leaders over extended periods of time, both in areas of healing and of continuing hurt. Every Christian group is caught between the beckoning of God as Abba Father, the ultimate new family parent, and human leaders as penultimate influences or temporal family parents. Leaders make or break groups because of their own experiences of healing or hurt from their families of origin. Biblically, our human family brokenness goes all the way back to Adam and Eve.

Whether we see Adam and Eve as historical persons or generic archetypes of the beginning of human society, the theological foundation is still the same: in the beginning the human family system entered into relational chaos because of their self-determination to find their way without God and without one another. The foundational theology of the human family system is that "all have sinned." All have grown up in some form of abusive family system. None, except one, has been nurtured by the pervasive presence of God as parent and family. Humanity is in desperate need of a new family system to intervene. And that new family system comes through Jesus.

Leaders nurture patterns of healing or perpetuate abuse depending on their ability to receive forgiveness and healing out of their previous family systems. In looking at the first eleven chapters of Genesis it is easy to see that abusive leaders tend to birth abusive groups. In looking at the Gospels it is just as easy to see that healed leaders tend to nurture groups where forgiveness, healing and transformation are normative. As Friedman has said,

> To the extent that we can learn to define ourselves within the emotional triangles of our families of origin, to that same extent will we have the increased capacity to do this in any of our other relationship systems. And in the process of doing so, our position in that set of interlocking triangles will become converted from a source of stress to a source of strength and survival. . . . We can see most clearly how leadership can become a more fundamental healing modality than expertise, both for others and ourselves.[2]

Friedman sees that leaders in their modeling of life and group behavior affect groups more than does the exercise of professional expertise or group skill. Pastors or group leaders who are well skilled in group dynamics may not be the most helpful group leaders. The more helpful leaders may be the relatively unskilled persons who have experienced healing and recovery from negative or abusive family patterns and have learned to live a new kind of relational shalom. This is why most twelve-step groups are not led by professionals but by those persons who have experienced sustained healing from their addictive or codependent behavior. However, a combination of a healed *and* skilled small group leader is optimal.

God as the Transforming Parent of the Small Group Family

Before his own transformation in Christ, Saul "ravaged" or "eliminated" the ecclesia, "going from house to house," dragging men and women off to prison (Acts 8:1-3). The transformed Paul understood his own dysfunction to be the result of a life of addiction and imprisonment in an errant Jewish religious system. His personal spiritual imprisonment had fed his need to control and imprison members of the ecclesia who were successfully escaping the imprisonment of his religious system. Since these followers of Jesus chose not to stay in his spiritual prison, Saul put them into physical prisons. There was and is always an irony here. Those who began to practice the new life of Christ in ecclesia, having been liberated from the old prison of legalism have often been thrown into political and physical prison by those who could not bear their practice of liberated life together in the ecclesia of Jesus Christ. Human organizations tend to isolate or persecute any who would dare live outside their predetermined boundaries.

Paradoxically, the transformed apostle Paul continually called the ecclesia to experience freedom and stop perpetuating the abuses of families of origin. He intentionally planted new ecclesia with Jesus in their midst. For Paul, Jesus was their elder brother and Leader, the Lord who lived and demonstrated a healthy relationship with Abba God. Jesus called the original Twelve to imitate his relationship with God as "Daddy." In calling the fishermen, Matthew says the disciples "immediately . . . left the boat and their father and followed him" (Mt 4:22). Then, soon afterward, on the mount Jesus taught them to address God as "Our Father in heaven" (Mt 6:9).

This intentional turning of the Twelve and other disciples to God as Abba was an act of "intervention" to stop the negative patterns of their previous fathers (parents) and families of origin. Only within the realm of a new loving and transforming parent, a new family and a new model of life together could God initiate in Christ the transformation of the whole human family system. Christ was like the antidote injected into the relational stream of the dying human family system. As Jesus and the Twelve formed new and increasingly healthy family groups, the wider human family showed new vital signs.

Jesus as the Transforming Brother of the Small Group Family
The transformational thinking and behavior that Paul called the ecclesia to practice intentionally was that same model and behavior the apostles had learned with Jesus. It was a breaking of conformity with the existing systems of the culture and society to embrace the transformation of a new way to be humanity together. As ecclesia, the new community and new family gathered with Jesus as brother and God as Abba.

Paul noted in his letter to the Romans that the continuing process of becoming a "transformed" community was facilitated by individual members of the ecclesia who would personally practice the behavioral model of Jesus to be "living sacrifices" (Rom 12:1-2). As he continually deferred to the renewing parenthood of God, Jesus initiated God's way of calling humanity into mutual loving relationships. Leaders of the small house ecclesia were called to be like Jesus and to participate as mutual restored and gifted members of the group, who joined together into the Spirit's empowerment to become like Jesus, to become the "body" of Christ together.

As Paul said to the Philippian ecclesia, "Your attitude should be the same as that of Christ Jesus" (Phil 2:5). This intentional patterning of group members to imitate Jesus' relationship with Abba God meant that they would work hard at developing healthier self-awareness and allowing the Spirit to give them a new kind of life together. This self-awareness came from their meeting together in honesty, confession, repentance and compassion. They trusted one another enough to confess their fear and sin and receive from one another honest feedback about their strengths and weaknesses, their sin and their graces.

Bonhoeffer understood the need for a divine intervention into the circle and cycle of abuse. The intervention for him came through the process of personal and intimate confession and forgiveness between members of a small Christian community. Christ was mediated as the members of the community imitated the attitude and compassion of Christ to one another:

> Who can give us the certainty that, in the confession and the forgiveness of our sins, we are not dealing with ourselves but with the living God? God gives us this certainty through our brother. Our brother breaks the circle of self-deception. A man who confesses his sins in the presence of a brother knows that he is no longer alone with himself. He experiences the presence of God in the reality of the other person.[3]

Human Transformation as a Small Group Process

The courage of group members to enter into honest self-awareness, confession and confrontation is made possible through the determination of each member to honor another above oneself and to be devoted to one another as a loving family (Rom 12:10). The ecclesia were not like other social groups. Rather, they cared for one another in such striking contrast to the practice of other social systems that people flocked into them when they saw the unusual working of their love. This is the new family motivation in the letter of 1 John as a call to a new loving community: "This is the message you have heard from the beginning: We should love one another. Do not be like Cain, who belonged to the evil one and murdered his brother." "Everyone who loves has been born of God and knows God" (1 Jn 3:11-12; 4:7). The new family shows the world an alternative to the way of Cain—the way of Christ.

This family love was most visible in ecclesia as individual members were willing to lay down their lives for other group members. They were willing to be "living sacrifices." Their love was demonstrated in mutual sacrifice. They were to be people as concerned about others as they were about themselves.

Such an attitude of mutual sacrifice has seldom been prevalent among Americans. Quoting the French sociologist Alexis de Tocqueville, who reflected upon the nature of American life in the 1830s, Robert Bellah and others have raised this concern about the isolational tendency among Americans as a way of life:

Individualism is a calm and considered feeling which disposes each citizen to isolate himself from the mass of his fellows and withdraw into the circle of family and friends; with this little society formed to his taste he gladly leaves the greater society to look after itself. . . . There are more and more people who . . . have gained or kept enough wealth and enough understanding to look after their own needs. Such folk owe no man anything and hardly expect anything from anybody. They form the habit of thinking of themselves in isolation and imagine that their whole destiny is in their hands.[4]

Such an attitude of isolational individualism (anarchy) is as inhuman as religious or governmental abuse of the ecclesia (tyranny). Both controlling patterns of life miss the nature and need of humanity which the gospel meets: that persons are forgiven, healed and enabled to develop compassion for wider groups of humanity by experiencing the forgiveness, healing and compassion of a loving group of family and friends. These redeemed people, then, are not compelled to run a closed system, but can nurture an open community in the confidence, trust and care of God as loving Abba.

The ecclesia were willing to share their possessions, themselves and their special human gifts with one another so that the whole group might benefit from the presence of every member. They were able to become a transformed community because Jesus was the central person and paradigm of their mutual thinking, sacrifice, gifts and love. As he instructed the disciples, the love of the ecclesia was to be demonstrated in mutual sacrifice and love:

As the Father has loved me, so have I loved you. . . . My command is this: Love each other as I have loved you. Greater love has no one than this, that he lays down his life for his friends. . . . I no longer call you servants. . . . Instead, I have called you friends, for everything that I learned from my Father I have made known to you. . . . This is my command: Love each other. (Jn 15:9, 12-13, 15, 17)

The freedom to practice a new law of love, transformed from the law of isolation and individualism, can only be experienced in the context of a new small group community.

Human Community as Transformed by Divine Community

Spiritual transformation is a process of human community formed and reformed through the presence of divine community. Group members are empowered to help one another embrace God's transforming power. The Spirit's power to effect human change is mediated through the ability of group members to see themselves through God's eyes and mind and act on behalf of the Holy Spirit who is a community Spirit. They help one another to see the truth of their beings and relationships in light of Jesus' intimate relationship with the Father. As Jesus has ongoing intimacy with the Father, so the Spirit enables the disciples of Jesus in the ecclesia to share in his divine relationship and community. This participation with Jesus in the communal life with the Father enables the Christian small group to be a transforming family system for the forgiveness, healing and maturity of group members.

Karl Barth argued that "Jesus Christ *is* the community," but "the community *is not* Jesus Christ."[5] Every small group meeting in the name of Jesus is enabled by the Spirit to participate in the existing relationship of Jesus with Abba God. The center and beckoning presence of the group is Jesus as he has an intimate relationship with the Father. It is the work of the Spirit to enable the small group community to be transformed, to become like Jesus and to share more fully in his intimate community with Abba. This is what ecclesia is about: a small group being drawn into a divine arena to share the love of the Father for Jesus and the love of Jesus for the Father.

The Small Group as Maturational Community

Live a life worthy of the calling you have received. Be completely humble and gentle; be patient, bearing with one another in love. Make every effort to keep the unity of the Spirit through the bond of peace.

But to each of us grace has been given as Christ apportioned it . . . to prepare God's people for works of service, so that the body of Christ may be built up until we all reach unity in the faith and in the knowledge of the Son of God and become mature, attaining to the whole measure of the fullness of Christ. (Eph 4:1-3, 7, 12-13)

Human spiritual maturity is the fruit of healthy relationships with God and with the people of God. Such maturity is attained only through the process and experience of real people who care for one another in gatherings of two or more persons. Wherever two or three persons come together there is either a raising or a rending of humanity and human relationships. The small group either responds positively to the Spirit's invitation to enter into the realm of God or runs away with a pervasive fear of entrance into the divine presence. Fear of facing God's loving presence destroys humanity and human relationships. The small group is either moving toward Jesus, becoming like Jesus, becoming more mature, or it is moving away from Jesus, resisting the presence of Jesus with the Father, and continuing in spiritual infancy and immaturity.

This is the thrust of the apostolic admonition to "become mature *(teleion)*" and "no longer be infants." Maturity and infancy are oppositional movements to and from Jesus. Maturity is based in the "knowledge of the Son of God" and the "fullness of Christ." Knowledge and fullness are the fruit of long-term intimate relationship with Jesus and the Father. Maturity is a product of the daily experience of a small group of people who meet face to face with God's face-to-face community in Christ and with one another through the facing power of the Spirit.

Spiritual growth is the process and product of being in community. Isolated individuals cannot grow spiritually. Spirit demands community. Persons grow when they are in relationship with God and with one another. We remain in spiritual infancy when we refuse to participate in community (koinonia).

In referring to Bonhoeffer's *Sanctorum Communio*, Karl Barth pointed out that "the upbuilding of the community is the community of saints."[6] Wherever two or three saints come together, God builds their eternal community as they willingly open themselves to Christ and to one another. Christians who cannot relate to one another in face-to-face situations are missing the reality, hope and growth of the *sanctorum communio*, the communion of saints. To be together with other Christians in a small group is to open oneself to being formed and transformed in Christ. The very act of intentional gathering around Jesus is an act of courage and mutual growth.

As the writer of the letter to the Hebrews argued, the main way to "spur one another on toward love and good deeds" is through "meeting together" (Heb 10:24-25). People who do not meet together do not have a space or place to help one another do the good things of Jesus' ministry. Righteousness flows directly out of community. It is the fruit of face-to-face human encounters where confession and forgiveness are practiced. Justice is the outward product of groups who practice the law of love within their own group context. Paul Hanson has intensified this by saying that

> being related to the living God renders most conventional ways of dealing with injustice unsatisfactory, for they are largely determined by myopic self-interest. Being an agent of healing requires of the community of faith a clear discernment of God's presence in the world, and an unswerving commitment to the transformation of personal habits, family patterns, and social and political structures until they conform to the standard of righteousness manifested by God's creative, redemptive activity on behalf of all creatures.[7]

The changed and matured habits and relationships of the gathered community in Christ provides a base for them to practice the same matured habits and relationship skills in the larger society. As a small group is able to grow together the members are empowered to take their maturity into the world to accomplish the gospel ministry. As the group learns to practice the righteousness of Jesus within its own community so it is empowered to practice the compassion and justice of Jesus in the world. As the group is willing to accept healing it becomes an agent of healing in the world.

Facing another human being can be a courageous act of reconciliation and self-disclosure. Lillian Ruben has stated that men, in particular, seem to have a profound fear of intimacy. She suggests that it is an amazing act of bravery for some men to look into the eyes of their friends or spouses and tell them about their feelings. This is so difficult for some men that they bury their emotions and eventually lose them entirely.[8] Admitting in the safety and confidence of a small group that one needs to become a loving human being can be a transforming, life-changing self-recognition and self-disclosure.

Em Griffin has argued that healthy self-disclosure must be reciprocal. "There is a quid pro quo."[9] But this means that someone must have the courage to take the initiative and another must have the courage to follow. These mutual acts of courage are transformational. For a man to admit his fear of a woman because she is skilled in human relationship building is to admit his disability, weakness and need for help. Gordon Dalbey has registered such a special concern for men by suggesting that men fear and resent women for their relational competency.[10] Only the high trust and safe environment of a small group will help men regain their relational confidence.

The growth and maturity of group intimacy must be interwoven with the growth of intimacy between each group member and God. Anne Wilson Schaef has suggested that personal and relational growth are simultaneous and interdependent. Growth cannot occur between two persons if the individual is not growing in self-awareness and personal honesty. One needs to be honest with oneself before one can be honest with another. While Schaef's perspective is predominantly psychological, from a theological point of view self-honesty and group honesty are mutual movements of the work of the Spirit. There is no real honesty unless the God of Truth is participating in the growth of individuals and their mutual relationships. Schaef has said: "True intimacy is a process that grows over time. It is a process of knowing and being known, and it requires openness and willingness from each person involved."[11] This process of "knowing and being known" is the primary ministry of God's Spirit among humanity. The knowing and being known is essentially the spirituality of community.

A maturing community comes about when each member of the small group has something to give to every other member. As affirmed in Ephesians: To each small group member Christ gives a portion of grace to prepare every group member for mutual service so that the small group may be built up until, in the unity of mutual faith and trust with Christ and with one another, the group becomes mature, attaining the fullness of Christ's being and relationship with the Father and with the disciples (Eph 4:7-13, paraphrased).

Every group member is given a portion of grace to share and to self-disclose with the rest of the group; no one member can have enough grace to produce the complete identity, integrity and fulfillment of the person of Jesus. Jesus' body has been broken and distributed. All group members must participate in bringing his body back together, in bringing unity to his body. Every member contributes to or deducts from the full humanity of Christ in the group. The full measure of Christ is found in groups who have allowed themselves to become fully disclosed to Christ and to one another. In these small groups nothing has been held back or hidden. Em Griffin has said, "In the process of letting someone else get to know me, I discover who I am. . . . We can't get to know ourselves through introspection." Griffin has asserted that we are hungry to share ourselves so that we can know ourselves.[12] As we share ourselves with Christ and with others who live in Christ, we are able to receive the gifted completeness to our humanity as they share themselves with us and reflect our sharing back to us.

Apportioned grace at work in the small group enables each member to share the whole gift of his or her humanity. Grace is given to be shared. All the brokenness of being and relationship has to be disclosed, forgiven and healed. This is the way to maturity in Christ. This is the ministry of reconciliation, which is simultaneous to the process of growth and maturity. Paul described the ministry of reconciliation to the Corinthians and ended with the plea that they not "receive God's grace in vain" (2 Cor 5:11—6:1). They had to share themselves with God and with one another. They needed to be reconciled to God and to one another. Then they were to go out from the safe group and be reconciled to others who were even more hostile. This is the process of transformation. This is the intervention of justice. It can happen only when two or three come together and allow the character of Christ to rule their relationships.

Human maturity cannot be attained without the working of intimate community between Christ and at least two human beings. Maturity comes through the relational transactions of grace, truth and trust. The mature group is the one that has the courage to share their gracious relationships and community with an unreceptive and hostile society. The mature group is like the mature Jesus. They are willing to lay down their lives to touch an unreceptive and hostile world. The mature group shows and shares their trust in God and in one another by offering their mutual humility, gentleness and love to the alien and the stranger. In the mature group, personal concerns have been transformed into public concerns. Life together has become a life for others. As Paul Hanson has affirmed:

An asocial private piety is simply unbiblical. Where God's people are present in the world, they are present on behalf of the God of righteousness, and thus on behalf of those who suffer from discrimination, poverty, and injustice. They are a people who no longer distinguish between their personal needs and the needs of others. Ministering to the least esteemed or most despised human is thus a concrete act of attending to their most urgent personal concern.[13]

The mutual courage of the confessing and forgiving small group is released to become a prophetic and confronting ministry to the world.

The translator of Dietrich Bonhoeffer's *Life Together*, John Doberstein, pointed out that Bonhoeffer's theology and experience of a shared common life with twenty-five vicars led him to participate in political and military resistance and attempt the overthrow of Hitler: "The sin of respectable people reveals itself in flight from responsibility."[14] The sin of immature and unchanged people who have not learned the grace of deeply valuing other human beings is manifest in their inability and unwillingness to lay down their life for others. Bonhoeffer's deep valuing of humanity and his courage to risk death came as an abundant overflow of his transforming experience of Christian community.

Small group maturity is demonstrated as the freedom and desire to go into the world with the learned compassion of the body of Christ. Hanson put it this way:

In the political arena, the community of faith represents a prophetic perspective that opposes every form of idolatry and rationalization of greed and special privilege, and proclaims the alternative order of universal justice, equality and peace. This stance involves risk-taking and sometimes danger.[15]

What Hanson sees as the call of every Christian community to be a prophetic presence can be understood to be the courageous action of a mature Christian community that has been willing to face one another and now has the courage to face the stark reality of the darker world. Mature love is both confrontational and reconciling, prophetic and priestly. The mature small group will find that its prophetic ministry flows out of its interpersonal and mutual growth, where its members together have experienced the gracious intervention and reconciliation of Jesus Christ.

Anne Wilson Schaef and Diane Fassel have said that the courage and insight to intervene in an addictive organization usually comes about through an experience of personal intervention in a small group context. Those who have faced their addictive behavior in a small group are better able to confront addictive behavior in a larger organization. Together a group can model this insight by confessing their own addictions before venturing out to intervene in the addictions of corporations. As these two women confessed together, "It is important to note here that the really vital thrust of our learning truly came from personal involvement in recovery from our co-dependence."[16] As Schaef and Fassel have personally experienced, a growing and maturing ecclesia will seek ways to demonstrate its mature life together in the larger society.

A report to the General Assembly of the Presbyterian Church (USA) states, "Faith and the life of faith—as well as growth and transformation in relation to them—are communal before they are individual. . . . The process of coming to faith and growing in the life of faith is fundamentally a process of participation." Growth and maturity are a product of life together. There are thirteen "practices and disciplines" that have been the "means of grace" in church history through which Christian groups may experience and express the way of maturity. This report suggested some of these practices are

> struggling together to become conscious of and understand the nature of the context in which we live; criticizing and resisting all those powers and patterns (both within the church and in the world as a whole) that destroy human beings, corrode human community, and injure God's creation; working together to maintain and create social structures and instructions which will sustain life in the world in ways that accord with God's will.[17]

The maturing small group will have a transforming effect upon the larger society in which it lives and moves and has its being. There is a direct relation between the maturity of a small group and its members' desire and courage to venture into an alienated world with the experience of koinonia. Such maturity is the fruit of a group of people who have shared life together over the long haul, who have practiced the mutuality of "one-anothering" described and requested so frequently through the New Testament Epistles. These apostolic ecclesia were groups of people who became mature through the daily disciplines of "one-anothering" in Christ. They were formed in discipline and transformed in the Spirit who gives the gift of eternal life on earth as it is in heaven.

■ SMALL GROUP MINISTRY IMPLICATIONS

1. It may be helpful for a group to spend some time thinking about the differences between "formational" group experiences and "informational" group experiences. A formational experience is something that helps the group form behavioral or skill patterns which are modeled after Christ and the apostles. This has more to do with discipleship than with belief. Formation has to do with changing patterns. Information is what is needed to help the group understand why the formational process is so important. Bible study can provide information

about the faith. Learning how to use the Bible as a tool provides a formational discipline to help the group live the faith. From a rationalistic enlightenment heritage, Westerners have a tendency to mistake information for formation. Formational leaders teach people "how to fish," while informational leaders teach facts about fishing. Jesus did both. He gave the crowd information. He led the disciples through formational experiences. Formation has to do with being in touch with real life—intellect, volition, emotion and physical action. Groups interested in formation need to be led through feeling and doing as well as thinking.

2. Since small groups are family systems, it is helpful to guide the group to see their family behavior patterns. Groups, like families, are not often aware of their interpersonal roles and relationship patterns. Leaders of group networks need to help group leaders become aware of their family dynamics. The foundation for looking at a group's immediate relational patterns is developing an awareness of each member's family of origin patterns. If a group can share about their personal roles and patterns growing up, they may be able to help one another face the dark side of these patterns and experience the redemption of Christ as they practice new behaviors in a confident and trust-filled new family where Jesus and Abba are the preeminent model of intimacy. The group will need to reflect upon themselves as a family system and think of how their family is being influenced by Christ's relationship with God as Abba. These are probably new thoughts for most church members. Careful preparation will need to be given to leaders and groups to help them think about their group as a family.

3. Leaders, in many ways, are "heads" of the family in their small groups. Their headship is like a braintrust of thoughts and emotions about how to live together. They bring with them their own family of origin patterns, both for better or for worse. Small group leaders must be helped to see their leadership styles in continuity with their families and cultures of origin. They are who they are in the small group family because of an accumulation of all their previous group and family experiences. They bring with them their "hopes and fears for all the years" of family and group dynamics. Every group has several types of family leadership. The "formal" leadership roles of a group may not be as influential as the "informal" leadership roles. The formal roles may be as Bible study leader, the informal role may be as group "energizer." In such a case the informal role may have more impact on the success of the group as family than the formal one. Small group network leadership must be able to discern the subtleties of such family roles working in the group.

4. Small group members should be trained to sense dysfunctional behavior and ask for interventive help when their group family becomes dysfunctional. Leaders need to be especially sensitive to seeing negative patterns of behavior. Every

long-term small group at some point in its life together may need to confront negative family dynamics. Every group member and relationship is bound by sin. Speaking the truth in love means that leaders and members must be able to confront dysfunctional group behavior. Such confrontation is tough, and most run away from such assertive action. In many cases, groups may need to turn to outside help for support. In most cases, the outside consultant should help the group confront itself rather than intervene from the outside. Long-term small group community will only grow more healthy in Christ if the group has the courage to speak the truth in love. Otherwise the group will implode—retreat into denial and superficial cordiality—or explode around their dysfunction.

5. To see God as a good new parent for the group may be a stretch for some members. If some have bad images of their father or mother, to address God with such imagery may perpetuate negative or abusive memories. This is especially true if a person had an abusive father. If God is addressed as Father by the group, it could hurt this person's sense of intimacy with God. These issues of transference of feelings about parents to God are complex, but real for many today. Such subtle awareness of a group's family relationships with Jesus as brother and God as parent may demand the counsel and insight of a licensed counselor or psychologist. While these are theological foundations for small group ministry, there are profound psychological implications in all group dynamics. The world of small group ministry demands much more sophistication today than ever before. There are more relational landmines along the road to community, but there is also more potential healing and recovery of the fullness of life in Jesus Christ.

20
MUTUAL MINISTRY IN THE SMALL GROUP

Set your hearts on things above. . . . Set your minds on things above. . . . Your life is now hidden with Christ in God. . . .
   Put to death, therefore, whatever belongs to your earthly nature. . . .
   Clothe yourselves with compassion, kindness, humility, gentleness and patience. Bear with each other and forgive whatever grievances you may have against one another. Forgive as the Lord forgave you. . . .
   Let the peace of Christ rule in your hearts, since as members of one body you were called to peace. And be thankful. Let the word of Christ dwell in you richly as you teach and admonish one another with all wisdom, and as you sing . . . with gratitude in your hearts. (Col 3:1-3, 5, 12-13, 15-16)

In *Life Together*, Dietrich Bonhoeffer named seven mutual ministries he felt were necessary to the nurture of the Christian community: the ministry of holding one's tongue, the ministry of meekness, the ministry of listening, the ministry of helpfulness, the ministry of bearing, the ministry of proclaiming and the ministry of authority. Bonhoeffer's list was a consolidation of the many "one another" statements in the apostolic letters to the small group ecclesia. (See table three, "One-Anothering in Christ.") Since the letters were written by the apostles to the ecclesia, their fundamental assumption was that the members of the house church would minister to one another as they grew in their knowledge of Jesus, who had taught the twelve disciples to be a mutual ministry community. Mutuality was an apostolic expectation of the small house groups from the beginning. From the start they "had all things in common."

Table Three
One-Anothering in Christ

Romans	12:5	Belong to one another*
	12:10	Be devoted to one another
	12:10	Honor one another
	12:16	Live in harmony with one another
	12:18	Live at peace with one another*
	15:7	Accept one another
1 Corinthians	1:10	Agree with one another
	10:24	Look out for one another*
	12:25	Have equal concern for one another*
	16:20	Greet one another with a holy kiss
Galatians	5:13	Serve one another
	6:1	Carry one another's burdens*
Ephesians	4:2	Bear with one another*
	4:25	Speak truthfully with one another*
	4:32	Be kind to one another
	4:32	Be compassionate to one another
	4:32	Forgive one another
	5:19	Speak to one another with psalms, hymns and spiritual songs
	5:21	Submit to one another
Philippians	2:4	Look to the interests of one another*
Colossians	3:13	Bear with one another*
	3:13	Forgive one another
	3:16	Teach one another
	3:16	Admonish one another
1 Thessalonians	4:9	Love one another*
	4:18	Encourage one another*
	5:11	Encourage one another
	5:11	Build up one another*
	5:13	Live in peace with one another*
	5:15	Be kind to one another*
Hebrews	10:24	Spur on one another
	10:25	Meet with one another*
	10:25	Encourage one another
	13:1	Love one another*
James	5:16	Confess your sins to one another*
	5:16	Pray for one another*
1 Peter	1:22	Love one another
	3:8	Live in harmony with one another
	4:9	Offer hospitality to one another
	5:14	Greet one another with a kiss of love
1 John	1:7	Have fellowship with one another
	3:11	Love one another
	3:16	Lay down your lives for one another*
	3:23	Love one another
	4:7	Love one another
2 John	5	Love one another

1 Corinthians	4:6	Don't take pride over against one another*
Galatians	5:15	Don't devour one another*
	5:26	Don't envy one another*
	5:26	Don't provoke one another*
Colossians	3:9	Don't lie to one another*
James	5:9	Don't grumble against one another*

*These statements have been changed from "each other" to "one another."

This one-anothering ministry of Christians in small groups finds its identity and purpose through the setting of hearts and minds "on the things above." As the believers looked into their memories of who Jesus was with the Twelve, and as they came to the realization that the Spirit of Jesus was now shared among them in the midst of their meeting together, they developed an awareness—a heart and mind—of the quality of life that God was inviting them to live. This directional beam of light for life together had its source in heaven, from the sustaining relationship of Jesus with Abba God, forever and ever. As a direct projection of heaven's life on earth, the ecclesia were called to be an eschatological reality. They were to be advance glimpses—although dim and obscured—of how heaven was to be. They were small beachheads, platoons of heaven's army scattered over enemy territory, alien groups sent to occupy dark places as enlightened communities. The ecclesia were to reflect the heart of God among a heartless humanity. In each small group the eternal heart of God was to be formed as the heart of the group.

Robert Slocum has said that it is in this intentional development of God's "heart" that Christians are to be able to do real ministry during an extensively and intensively cognitive and intellectual high-tech age. According to Slocum, while high-tech people may be empirical giants, in general they are spiritual and emotional pygmies. They have underdeveloped hearts. Instead, he feels the Christian laity is called to mutual and heartfelt ministry. Slocum believes that small groups are an ideal environment for this ministry to develop. However, even in a Bible-study group, cognitive skills are often more affirmed than affective skills. Slocum argues that the cognitive skills should be servant to the development of the whole person who has a healthy heart, which includes the mind of Christ.[1] The small group is where the heart of God is knowable on earth. The will of God should be done "on earth as it is in heaven." This is the eschatological life of every group gathered "in the name of Jesus."

As the apostle Paul said, "Since, then, you have been raised with Christ, set your hearts . . . [and] your minds on things above. . . . When Christ, who is your life, appears, then you also will appear with him in glory" (Col 3:1-2, 4). The eventual manifestation and demonstration of the people with Christ in glory is already being accomplished on earth and will continue to be completed in heaven. The ecclesia of the apostles were a down payment on God's eternal realm. These small groups were a glimpse of how God desired them to live together in eternity. Their life together now was an anticipation of their life together after death, in the "Day of the Lord." The ecclesia, in their gathering together, in their being a household together and in being a new family, was both a future and a present reality. Small groups who gather in the name of Jesus have eternal purpose and meaning. Heaven is the place where God's people will continue their mutual ministry and the reconciling dynamics of one-anothering they've already begun on earth. Jesus is the *center* and *source* of this eternal ministry of mutuality, for "in everything he has supremacy."

In Colossians 1:15-20 the apostolic call was to see Jesus, the Christ, as the head and source *(kephalē)* of every gathering of Christians and the mind and heart of each ecclesia. The headwaters of Christ were to be poured out in the midst of every group. Every ecclesia was to be a fountain of life, a wellspring in the midst of a dry pagan or legalistic culture. Wherever two or three came together in Christ, they were to adopt his thinking and embrace his love for people. They were to share his grace and love with each other. Their mutual exchanges of love are the freshwater pools beckoning to a thirsty society.

The Continuing Character of One-Anothering in Christ

The kind of one-anothering life together that the house groups modeled was the kind of life Jesus modeled on earth and continues to live in heaven: "compassion, kindness, humility, gentleness and patience," forgiveness and peace. They were to avoid showing lives fragmented by "immorality, impurity, lust, evil desires and greed," "idolatry," "malice" or "slander," which had been modeled in their previous families and cultures of origin (Col 3:5-9). The ecclesia were to put on the relational and conciliatory "clothes" of a new family and destroy the old "clothes" of abusive behaviors sewn in the old family. Positive and productive relational behavior had to replace the negative behavior. Their group character had to reflect the personal character of Jesus if they were to claim the name of Christ.

As Stanley Hauerwas has said, "To be a disciple is to be part of a new community, a new polity, which is formed on Jesus' obedience to the cross. . . . That is, they love their enemies and do good and lend without expecting return . . . a people freed from the threat of death." Jesus is the Story, but more importantly the Person who formed each ecclesia. Each ecclesia formed its group "polity" around Jesus as its center and source. Hauerwas, in describing who Christians should be today, has asserted that small groups in Christ compare with the early ecclesia: "But see how they love one another."[2] The house group had to be the place where Jesus' character was clearly and dramatically displayed, where his love was demonstrated between persons, where they loved one another the way Jesus had loved the Twelve.

The Pervasive Scope of One-Anothering Ministry

The one-anothering character of mutual ministry was to affect all aspects of life together for the ecclesia, even in remembering, teaching and singing. All of these interconnected community disciplines were to be practiced as an affirmation of their mutual ministry. Dwelling in the remembrance of the actions and words of Jesus was their reason for singing and teaching together. The songs and stories of Jesus and of the ancient people of God were community events, shared together out of the memory of God's great ancient acts and the acts of Jesus. As Hauerwas has said,

> Without the Jesus tradition there is no shared memory and therefore, no community. . . . The authority of Scripture derives its intelligibility from the existence of a community that knows its life depends on faithful remembering of God's care of his creation through the calling of Israel and the life of Jesus. . . . The formation of texts as well as the canon required the courage of a community to constantly remember and reinterpret the past.[3]

Their mutual remembering, teaching and singing were group processes in which each committed member had something to share and something to contribute to the whole group. Everything of life was shared so the whole group could benefit, remember, learn and sing together. In the sharing, remembering, learning and singing the story of Jesus became the story of the group. And so Jesus' character formed the group character. And there was nothing of their life together that was not transformed by the story and presence of Christ among them.

The Redemptive Process of Mutual Remembrance

There is a powerful restorative action in the process of remembering (Greek: *anamnesis*). Eric Voegelin, the philosophical theologian, argued that humanity enters into gross distortions and *deformations of existence* when it "listens to tales told by idiots . . . causing the majority of mankind [to live in] subjection under mentally diseased ruling cliques." Therefore, he argues, it is important that humanity be attracted to *larger horizons* and "repelled, if not nauseated, by restrictive deformations." Humanity should "engage in anamnestic exploration" and "go as far back as remembrance of things past would allow in order to reach the strata of reality-consciousness that [is] the least overlaid by later accretions." Humanity should "recapture the childhood experiences that let themselves be recaptured because they were living forces in the present."4

Remembering is a powerful tool and process. It is important that humanity continually goes back to its foundational roots, both corporately and personally, in order to make healthy sense out of a chaotic world. We must be called to remember who we are because we were "created in time by an Eternal Being" who continually calls us back to our origin and creation purpose in relationship. This is why mutual remembering is a necessary, continuing discipline of every group that meets in the name of Jesus. In Jesus' relationship with Abba we are called back to our primitive human purpose: to have intimate community with God and with the people of God. This restoration ultimately directs our relationship with all created things.

Remembering is a relational and dialogical event. Small groups are places where people remember their past, and where Christians remember the stories of God among the people and of Jesus with the Twelve among the crowd. The apostle Paul called the Colossian ecclesia to remember how they had received Christ, how they were rooted in him, and how they were taught to have faith in Christ. They were to remember Christ together and avoid being taken "captive through hollow and deceptive philosophy, which depends on human tradition and the basic principles of this world rather than on Christ" (Col 2:6-8). Their continuing process of helping one another remember Christ was the way to freedom and new community. The small group gathering is where individuals remember their own experience with God. These recited personal and corporate memories have a way of changing our current attitudes and practices. When we remember how Jesus lived with the Twelve, how he confronted the religious and political powers, how he healed the sick, how he forgave sin, how he was willing to die for his group of friends, we cannot continue life as usual. Our life together has then experienced the intervention of a transformational Story and Presence which is dangerous to old values, behaviors and systems. When the remembrances of Jesus were told during the meeting of ecclesia, they were called into new life and new community (koinonia).

As Bernard Lee and Michael Cowan have said,

House churches or intentional Christian communities are small groups of persons sharing a commitment in their own time and place to the ancient practices. . . . It is both an ancient and a new way of being church. . . . We offer it for your consideration, expecting you will sense its danger and trusting that it will likewise reveal to you its liberating hope.

Lee and Cowan call to our remembrance the "Story of the House Church" in order to reform the current ecclesiastical practices of the church as organization and system. "The house church . . . was not a piece or part of the church. *It was* church."[5] This is the same assertion that Robert Banks defends in his book *Paul's Idea of Community*. Reminding us of this primitive definition of "church" is foundational as a critique of the current practices of church.

The Song as an Event of Group Memory

Singing together is a major tool and process of group remembrance, reflection and learning. The ecclesia were able to "teach and admonish [counsel] one another" as they sang "psalms, hymns and spiritual songs" together (Col 3:16). The songs helped them to exercise their memories and functioned as continuing reminders of their new way of life based in the life of Jesus and the lives of the people of God. The poem, litany and song helped the gathering to focus their life together, rehearsing the memories so the past became more active in the present and moved the group into the hope of the future. Singing is simultaneously an act of remembering the past, celebrating the present and anticipating the future.

As Bonhoeffer said,

> On earth it is the song of those who believe, in heaven the song of those who see. . . . Why do Christians sing when they are together? The reason is quite simply, because in singing together it is possible for them to speak and pray the same Word at the same time. . . . All devotion, all attention should be concentrated upon the Word in the hymn. The fact that we do not speak it but sing it only expresses the fact that our spoken words are inadequate to express what we want to say, that the burden of our song goes far beyond all human words . . . the music is completely the servant of the Word. It elucidates the Word in its mystery.

Bonhoeffer, like Calvin, believed that music should support the ministry of the word as an active dialogue in the gathered group. He criticized the practice of music as a self-contained art. He saw music was a discipline to help the group to accomplish the mutual ministry of the word: "The purity of unison singing, unaffected by alien motives of musical techniques, the clarity, unspoiled by the attempt to give musical art an autonomy on its own apart from the words, the simplicity and frugality, the humaneness and warmth of this way of singing is the essence of all congregational singing."[6] Bonhoeffer's view is particularly conducive to the small group ministry setting, and was as much a polemic against the isolation and exaltation of the great German artistic and institutional ego as it was a theology of the value of music and the arts. Extrapolating from these comments, it is not difficult to sense how Bonhoeffer might have felt about the playing of Bach on the great pipe organs in the German Lutheran and Catholic cathedrals. However, through Bonhoeffer's perspective, it is easy to see the potential tension between cathedral music and small group singing. And we must ask the question,

At what point does the art detract from building the community of Jesus and affirm the arrogance of the individual artist? It is important to remember that Bonhoeffer lived in constant tension with Nazi-Aryan tyranny, where the small group could be seen as "counter," "alien" or "hostile" to the fascist state.

From Bonhoeffer's view, the group in song is the group in unison remembrance and in unison thanksgiving for God's gracious actions of the past and present. The group in song is the group anticipating more gracious activity in the future. In singing the group speaks with one voice and one heart, both a symbol and discipline of life together.

The Small Group as a Healing Community

Confess your sins to each other and pray for each other so that you may be healed. (Jas 5:16)

Small groups are potential enlightened places of confession, prayer and healing, or darkened places of hiddenness, superficiality and abuse. When people meet face to face, the opposing movements of approach and avoidance, self-disclosure and self-deception, group openness and *groupthink* are in tension. ("Groupthink" is "a problem solving process in which proposals are accepted without the scrutiny of the pros and cons of the alternatives, and in which considerable suppression of opposing thoughts take place."[7]) The group moves toward either mutual destruction or mutual restoration. Its relationships are serving the law of death (moving apart) or the law of eternal life (moving together). In *The Great Divorce* C. S. Lewis portrays heaven as the *place* where people come closer together and hell as the *space* of persons who move farther and farther apart. He also used a complementary spatial imagery about how there is an amplifying density (solidity) about "real" people and how there is an evacuating ghostliness about unreal people.[8] Small groups either move toward the obscurity of unreality or the concreteness of reality.

Small group members must assert their willingness to take faith risks and make self-disclosures, or they will continue in states of separation, divorce, distance, avoidance, passionlessness and superficiality. The normal state of a group is as separation and divorce until at least one member embraces the grace of God through personal and relational risk. God gives grace by coming to the group, but the group must take the risk of responding to God through opening their interpersonal relationships. As the epistle of James says, "Faith without deeds is dead" (Jas 2:26). In order for the small group to enter into this positive movement of self-disclosure and healing, the members must first recognize their broken state, confess their ambivalence and enter into the risk of vulnerable encounter by the power of God's grace.

The Group Recognition of Sin

All small groups first exist as fragmented communities. Every group is affected deeply and terminally by the reality of sin and full of misdirected relationships. As Bonhoeffer asserted,

> The final breakthrough to fellowship does not occur because, though they have fellowship with one another as believers and as devout people, they do not have fellowship as the undevout, as sinners. The pious fellowship permits no one to be a sinner. So everybody must conceal his sin from himself and the fellowship. . . . The fact is we *are* sinners.[9]

Sin is a relational reality and a constant small group dilemma. It is in this constant disturbance of relationships that sin kills. The lack of human community inevitably leads to murder, either emotionally or physically.

Jesus' teaching in the Sermon on the Mount is about the success or failure of community. Anger becomes murder if it is not handled properly in community. The movement toward reconciliation is a movement away from murder and judgment. Jesus restored the Ten Commandments to their original community-building role in the Sermon on the Mount: "I have not come to abolish [the Law or the Prophets] but to fulfill them. . . . For . . . unless your righteousness surpasses that of the Pharisees . . . you will certainly not enter the kingdom of heaven" (Mt 5:17-20). Righteousness is not just a question of ethics (to which it is often reduced); it is foundationally a question of humanity created and beckoned into community through healthy relationships with God and with one another. Those that block the restoration of community are killers. Small groups can nurture abundant life or become homicidal systems.

Like human organizations and institutions, every small group has its own tendencies toward addictive or codependent behavior. What is true for organizations is also true for every gathering of two or more persons: where two or three are gathered together because they are humanity and sinners, there will be addictive behavior and there will be sin, unless the grace of God intervenes and transforms. As Schaef and Fassel have documented, such addictive behavior and interpersonal dysfunction sin can be observed when tracking a group's patterns of communication. Addictive group behavior is a probable cause if negative communication patterns are visible during group gatherings: indirect communication; avoidance of conflict; vague, confused or ineffective communication; avoidance of face-to-face, eye-to-eye communication; triangulation; gossip; secrets; or intentional miscommunication.[10]

The small group must begin to recognize its own patterns of abuse and addiction. The recognition of any of these negative relational behaviors is to become aware of group sin. The beginning of true koinonia is the recognition and confession of sin. The group's willingness to admit sin, either as dysfunction or mistake, releases the group to deal with its imperfection and poverty of relationships.

The Group Confession of Sin

Self-disclosure and confession are interconnected. Many small group ministry leaders view confession of sin as the riskiest and most threatening level of communication into which one may enter in the small group context. The practice of such personal confession has often been restricted to a mentor, confessor, pastor, spiritual director or therapist. But this privatization of confession may reduce the mutual benefit in struggling groups. If they cannot get to the truth they may miss an opportunity to develop a healthy communication pattern. Such open communication can be an intervention in dysfunctional groups or a regenerative affirmation in healthy groups.[11]

The confession of sin in group contexts must be handled carefully and appropriately. The trust and cohesive levels of the group must be strong enough to handle the stress of the burden of truth. As John Powell has pointed out, self-disclosure and confession is a difficult personal decision: "If I tell you who I am, you may not like who I am, and it is all that I have."[12] If the group's cohesiveness is not well established, the process of confession may overload the group's ability to respond with mercy and grace. For example, there was a group of women who had been together for several months when one of the women confessed she was lesbian. The stress of the knowledge of this self-disclosure was too much for the other members. The group dissolved shortly after her confession. The group had not been prepared to deal with such a confession. They did not have enough mutual grace to receive the news and take the next tough step together.

But threat and potential of failure are not reasons to avoid group confession. Christian small groups must be better prepared for the implications of honesty and transparency, for the cost of bearing one another's burdens, for the cost of the pain of self-examination. When other members of the group realize that they too may fall into the similar hurtful, abusive or addictive behavior, the group is often more receptive to appropriate confessions. A Christian group's inability to deal gracefully with human brokenness, failure or abuse is more a reflection of immaturity in koinonia than it is the inappropriateness of the act of confession. As Bonhoeffer said,

> The Cross of Jesus Christ destroys all pride. . . . It is nothing else but our fellowship with Jesus Christ that leads us to the ignominious dying that comes in confession, in order that we may in truth share in his Cross. . . . We cannot find the Cross of Jesus if we shrink from going to the place where it is to be

found, namely the public death of the sinner. And we refuse to bear the Cross when we are ashamed to take upon ourselves the shameful death of the sinner in confession. In confession we break through to the true fellowship of the Cross of Jesus Christ. In confession we affirm and accept our cross. In the deep mental and physical pain of humiliation before a brother—which means before God—we experience the cross of Jesus as our rescue and salvation.[13]

Small Christian groups must be prepared for confession, but they cannot demand it. Confession of sin must be a voluntary offering of the individual and a voluntary receiving of the group. Confession that is demanded or imposed does not build trust and smothers vulnerability. Drawing out such abrupt admissions of hurt or wrong may be the equivalent of spiritual or psychological rape.

An entire adult Sunday-school class (about sixty men and women) of a large church refused to participate in the development of any small groups within their class structure. When asked about their reticence to participate in small groups, many responded that they had been in Gestalt encounter groups during the 1960s and had been forced by the group leaders to unveil significant hurts, sins and failures. They felt used and felt that they were manipulated to confess. As a result they now wanted nothing to do with building confessional intimacy in groups. Moreover, they wanted nothing to do with small groups at all. Their trauma had inoculated them against the "disease" of small groups.

Confession must grow freely out of the group's maturing intention and skill to embrace one another at deeper and deeper levels of intimacy. Such vulnerability must be gradually and carefully built over extended periods of life together. This process of building confessional human intimacy is greatly supported or reduced through the group's practice of the discipline of prayer.

The Group Ministry of Mutual and Intimate Prayer

Intimacy with God through relationship with Jesus is the foundation for developing intimacy between members of a small group. Just as Jesus was able to enter into intimate communication with God as Abba (Daddy), so those in the ecclesia were empowered to enter into intimacy with Abba alongside of Jesus. The intimate prayer of Jesus became the intimate prayer of the group that met with Jesus. Yet small group prayer, like confession of sin, is risky and threatening. Group members sense the cost of practicing such intimacy and vulnerability in prayer in the presence of one another.

Such intimate, confessional prayer is not superficial or trivial. James Loder of Princeton Seminary has said that "prayer is more intimate than sex."[14] Both prayer and sexuality have to do with intimate community. In this way it is important to talk about a kind of confessional sexuality. This is a haunting fear of many pastors regarding small group ministry. Because of the real intimacy experienced through the deepening spirituality of small group community, men and women in the same group may become sexually attracted to one another. They may even be seduced into a destructive sexual relationship. Prayer and confession are spiritually, emotionally and sexually loaded. The small group that enters into self-disclosure through prayer and confession is entering into a generally unexplored relational abyss. A small group may need a kind of confessional "bathyscaph" to dive into the depths of such deep dark and unexplored waters. Societal norms do not prepare us for these kinds of intimate personal encounters, but intimacy with God does. Discovery of the being and heart of God can move group members to dive into deeper confessional freedom with one another. Prayer is the beginning of confession. Intimacy with God is the way to appropriate and graceful self-disclosure in a small group. In this way confession is explored within the context of spiritual integrity and sensitivity. Intimate prayer prepares the group to release and receive confession. Building trust with God releases trust with people. Group prayer, like group confession, is a deepening movement of trust.

For many American Christians prayer is considered a private discipline: "my relationship with God is no one else's business." This attitude may be connected to a fear of intimacy during a time when rugged individualism continues to be a pervasive American value. In examining this need of Americans to practice individualism, Robert Bellah et al. have said that Americans "are hesitant to articulate our sense that we need one another as much as we need to stand alone, for fear that if we did we would lose our independence altogether."[15] The fear of intimacy may be greatly connected to the fear of losing one's independence. Both prayer and confession are disciplines for building an intentional interdependence, for building mutual community.

To pray together in a healthy group means to give up some independence and to act outside of the bounds of acceptable religious conformity. In an unhealthy group, the opposite may be true. In dysfunctional groups, where prayer is subjected to group pressure and conformity, prayers are often superficial and trivial, full of clichés. Such stereotypical prayers are often repeated by immature and conformist group leaders. Among some current small groups is a practice of what could be called the prayer of the "real" and the "just": "Lord, I *really just* want to praise you." Some healthier people may refuse to enter into group prayer because the patterns of prayer are so superficial and trivial. The prayers lack reality, guts, feeling, honesty, transparency and confession. Too many Christian groups practice *safe* prayer. Prayer by definition is not safe.

Relational prayer is often an unvalued and unpracticed discipline. Small groups that do not have experience and confidence in mutual prayer probably will not be at ease with mutual confession. The freedoms to self-disclose, pray and confess are profoundly interrelated.

Gerald Egan has affirmed the interconnectedness between self-disclosure and love: "A person who cannot love cannot reveal himself. The converse also seems true: the person who cannot reveal himself cannot love. . . . The very sharing of the human condition—in its sublimity, banality, and deformity—pulls people together."[16] The theological implication of Egan's declaration is that the person who is able to receive the love of Abba God gains the self-respect, dignity and courage to self-disclose appropriately before others. The freedom of confession grows out of an awareness and confidence of being loved by God or by another human being. The freedom to share the pain of life together opens a highway into community.

The intentional development of dialogical prayer disciplines are a helpful entrée into the freedom of self-disclosure and confession. Roberta Hestenes has said that

> prayer in a small group can be a wonderful or terrifying experience. People who have never prayed out loud may panic when told they are expected to pray. . . . Prayer can unify a group as nothing else will. To experience unity in Christ through prayer can be a life-changing experience. It is worth the initial awkwardness to learn how to pray together.[17]

It is in the intentional development of group prayer disciplines that members often become more comfortable to express to one another their intimate thoughts and feelings. The discipline and the practice of honest prayer release humanity into community.

Dallas Willard, in *The Spirit of the Disciplines*, distinguishes between the spiritual disciplines of abstinence and of engagement. Small group disciplines are disciplines of engagement, especially prayer, study and sharing.[18] Some small groups have undertaken the intensive and intentional discipline of praying the Psalms together to give them access to the theology of forgiveness and healing reflective of Israel's Wisdom poetry and sayings. In a chapter entitled "Disease and Healing in the Psalms," Conrad L'Heureux has suggested that praying the Psalms "lends itself especially well to group work. It inevitably happens that many participants began to experience healing through the very process of sharing with other persons in a small group."[19] Walter Brueggemann also shares this perspective on the connection between praying the Psalms, inner healing and interpersonal healing.[20] It may be no coincidence that the epistle of James, which contains the call to mutual prayer, confession and healing, has been identified historically as New Testament Wisdom Literature, a set of wise sayings and psalms patterned after the Proverbs and Psalms and written to the ecclesia who were in persecution and diaspora, to "the twelve tribes scattered among the nations" (Jas 1:1). The scattered ecclesia needed to be encouraged to use an Old-Testament-like vehicle such as psalms to help them venture into prayer, confession, forgiveness and healing.

The Forgiving and Healing Presence of a Small Group

Small groups are spaces where mutual prayer and confession can unfold into forgiveness and healing. As group members are allowed space for the consideration and healing of their own inner pain and hurt, they become more open and aware of the inner hurt of others and the hurt between group members.

Flora Slosson Wuellner has said that

> we are small communities within: our bodily and emotional selves, our gifts, our wounds, our memories, our powers, our conscious selves, and our deep sub-conscious. We relate to the people around us the way we relate to our inner selves. As we deepen our consent to the healing of our hurts and powers, recognizing, embracing, reconciling with our inner problems and powers, we become more real and whole to ourselves. Then we begin to be aware of other people as real, as real as ourselves.[21]

Receptivity to the healing presence of Christ in their "inner" community of being releases group members to be empowered healers within the group as well as outside the group. The wounded person who has received healing from Christ can become the wounded healer in the group. As Henri Nouwen has said,

> After so much stress on the necessity of a leader to prevent his own personal feelings and attitudes from interfering in a helping relationship . . . it seems necessary to re-establish the basic principle that no one can help anyone without becoming involved, without entering with his whole person into the painful situation, without taking the risk of becoming hurt, wounded or even destroyed in the process. The beginning and the end of all Christian leadership is to give your life for others.[22]

As group members are freed by Christ's love to love themselves, they are more free to demonstrate love to other members of the group, to treat each member with dignity, respect and honor for their unique personhood and gifts. Flora Slosson Wuellner has also said,

> Along with this growing awareness of the reality and beauty of our own identity comes a growing awareness of the identity of others. We begin to see other people not as just means to our ends, not just as annoying blocks or helping hands, not just as types, cases or categories, but as unique creations. We begin to see the hurts and wounds within them as wounded children. We begin to see their giftedness, their beauty, their loneliness and their longing

to reach out to others. We sense within ourselves, as our own healing grows within us, a desire to reach out in compassion and communication.[23]

The personal healing of prayer in the presence of God becomes the avenue for healing and reconciliation between persons of the group.

Forgiveness and healing are deeply interwoven through the inner community of individual group members and through the interpersonal community between group members. Groups that have been together for long periods of time tend to store up frustration, anger, hurt, guilt and pain with one another. These same feelings and the sense of alienation exist also for members in relationships outside the group. If the members of the small group ecclesia are able to confess their hurt and anger to one another, they will probably have more desire and courage to share pain with significant others outside of the group. The reconciling and healing movement of the small group can become the foundation from which group members can take wider risks to enter other confessional, forgiving and healing processes, both personally and socially. Healthy small groups can contribute to the healing of marriages and families (and vice versa). This is the basic thesis of Scott Peck's book *The Different Drum*. Peck's hope is that as people experience reconciliation and peacemaking behavior in a small group context, they will practice such patterns in the macrosystems of world corporations and governments.[24]

The Small Group as Healing Agent in the World

The experience of the ministry of forgiveness, healing and reconciliation within the small group should lead to practices of compassion and justice in the pain of the world. In reflecting on Martin Luther's theological perspective on real community, Paul Hanson has said,

> The true community of faith, by experiencing in its own life the creative redemptive presence of God, holds before the world an alternative vision, the vision of the whole human family reconciled and living together in peace. . . .
> The people of God is thus a community that, in finding its own needs satisfied by the abundant grace of God, is freed to be present in the world for others in need. It is of the very nature of the community of faith, therefore, that its purpose is not exhausted in its providing for the needs of its members, but extends outward to a self-transcending calling to be present wherever there is loneliness, sickness, hunger or injustice.[25]

As the individual group member receives personal healing and is able to lead the group into healing, the group is then empowered to lead the wider society into healing. The confession, forgiveness and healing of the small group become the model and stimulus for confession, forgiveness and healing in the wider congregation, the wider city and the wider world. Organizations and institutions can be opened to healing through the healing experience of individuals in small groups. As organizational consultants, Schaef and Fassel have confessed that their ability to intervene and bring healing to organizations "came from personal involvement in recovery from our co-dependence." Their participation together in a Twelve-Step group process gave them the needed personal and relational healing experiences to empower them to help other addictive leaders and organizations into recovery.[26]

Mutual small group prayer, confession and healing can transform the world. This is key to being in a community founded on the good news of Jesus Christ. Small groups have an evangelistic calling to take their health in Christ, their personal experience of good news, their mutual recovery, and their confessional and absolutional experience into the world, and make disciples of others who are also freed to practice this healing and reconciling ecclesia.

The Small Group as Community of Love

We should love one another. . . . Anyone who hates his brother [or sister] is a murderer. . . .

This is how we know what love is: Jesus Christ laid down his life for us. And we ought to lay down our lives for our brothers [and sisters]. If anyone has material possessions and sees his brother [or sister] in need but has no pity on him [or her], how can the love of God be in him [or her]? . . . Let us not love with words or tongue but with actions and in truth. This then is how we know that we belong to the truth, and how we set our hearts at rest in his presence. (1 Jn 3:11, 15-19)

"Loving one another" is the essential reality of life together in the ecclesia. In the small group people should be more important than work. In the small group, being and relating are more important than doing. In the loving Christian community, being and relating define and direct the important work to be done. The love of persons is carried out through "actions" that prove their verbal commitments to be the "truth." The truth is love in action. As John's epistle says, "This is how we know what love is: Jesus Christ laid down his life for us." In response and reciprocity the members of the ecclesia are called to lay down their lives for one another. The practice of love is the intentional and sacrificial sharing of persons and possessions with other members of the group. Small group maturity can be measured by observing the freedom of the group to practice agape and koinonia. The group that practices love shares all things and has all things in common.

The New Testament expressions of love (agape) and fellowship (koinonia) are interchangeable expressions of the same movement: God in action; God sharing everything. In the beginning God shared creation with humanity. At the end, God will share all things with humanity through the person of Jesus Christ. Because God shared both Spirit and humanity, love and possessions in Christ, the ecclesia are called to also share their persons and possessions with one another.[27]

Small groups should not just be pleasant meetings of cordial verbal exchange, but Christian small groups should be families in which all things, ideas, feelings, pains and joys are shared, and where the individual with a reasonable need can have that need met by the group.

The Destructive Practices of a Small Group Without Love

In American culture today there is a negative polarity between an individualistic, privatistic ownership and a technical, bureaucratic rationality. The landmark sociological study of American life that was chronicled in *Habits of the Heart* targeted this basic human dialectic and tension. Which is more important, task or relationship, organization or community? A theological perspective on the nature of humanity ultimately guided Robert Bellah et al. to call for a renewed investment in building personal community in America. As they saw it, the human need for relationship and community should define and guide both the task and the organization.[28]

The call to a common sharing of oneself and one's material goods makes it particularly difficult for a small group to be Christian in the American context. In this context, according to Bellah and others, the "empty self" makes sense: "the middle-class individual must leave home and church in order to succeed in an impersonal world of rationality and competition." But if one is to be defined as a "constituted self," one whose identity and purpose comes from a "narrative" and "collective history" of persons in community, then this "dangerous memory" will create a community identity that is deeper than success and more important than productivity and money. If "success" is the overriding value of the individual, ecclesia makes no sense. However, ecclesia becomes a "dangerous" paradigm when juxtaposed to a culture bound in the pursuit of technology, machines, productivity, hierarchy and systems. When systems of human ingenuity take the place of God's original call for humanity to be in personal and intimate community, the human self is lost and the human community is destroyed. The human race is not guided by the overall values of agape and koinonia, but by utilitarianism and materialism.

If a small group moves to define itself primarily through the work it needs to accomplish and not in its building of human community, it misses its foundational theological and christological center. If the completion of the work becomes more important than the concern for persons, in the process of getting the job done the group relationships and members will be destroyed. This is not the way of agape and koinonia. The truth is only visible when the value of persons and community supersedes and navigates the group process through the rocky waters of accomplishment of the task. The group and its purpose can become an idol if its task becomes more important than its concern for persons. Relationship and community must define the nature, direction and extent of the work. The work of ecclesia is agape and koinonia. Christian small groups are called to practice the work of love and demonstrate the truth of community. The ecclesia is called to love God and love one another through the sharing of all good things.

■ SMALL GROUP MINISTRY IMPLICATIONS

1. Based upon an understanding of the process of "complaint" community prayers in the Psalms, Conrad L'Heureux has suggested a disciplined group experience designed to help persons "understand healing by becoming more fully aware of experiences of healing which they themselves have gone through": (1) Have each group member recall an occasion in the past in which they experienced some kind of healing. (2) Have them focus carefully on their experience of healing. (3) Have them identify what the process of healing was for them. Ask them to identify where the healing power came from. (4) Ask them to turn their attention to the part of their body in which they experienced the healing. (5) Have each person put their hand on (or near) that part of their body. (6) Ask them to decide that this part of their body will become a symbol to them that they have experienced healing. (7) After these more personal reflection steps, have each member of the group share with the others what they visualized and how they felt about the exercise.[29]

2. Confession of sin is a delicate group process. Confessional patterns must be carefully modeled and nurtured. The attainment of a nonjudgmental group ethos is an important prerequisite. Condemnation is only released as members of the group are freed by the power of their own confession and forgiveness to receive the confession of another. The confessed person is the only one who can lead a group into healthy confession. Small groups should enter into this dark-side venture only as they have leadership and courage to do so with care. Brash ventures into confessions of sin can do more damage than good.

3. Healing is a function of small group community. Trust is the foundation for healing. If group members trust each other and trust God, there will be healing experienced in the gathered community. God does invite small groups to be partners together in the healing of persons and relationships. But there are no

"group formulas" to make God perform healing. Healing is always a gift and surprise of God. But healing is definitely a group happening. God heals people who are in trusting relationships. Confession, noncondemnation, trust and vulnerability are connected to the freedom to speak the truth in love. Groups do not come by these attitudes and behaviors easily. The freedom to confess, the power to pray, the grace to forgive are all gifts of the Spirit wherever two or more are willing to risk together in the nature of Jesus. Small groups who pray for healing will experience recovery. Healing is more connected to the growing healthiness of a small group community than most Christians ever dare risk or understand. Healing and the development of Christian community are simultaneous actions of the Spirit. One dynamic cannot exist without the other.

4. Many small groups do not like to sing together. Singing, especially without the accompaniment of a support instrument like guitar or piano, is tough for Americans to do. Such a cappella singing is not a regular practice of American culture. Bonhoeffer and Calvin notwithstanding, singing without instrumental support is not the contemporary way. Therefore, a small group who wish to sing together must have a song leader and some musical support. The exception to this is when the group is made up of trained or experienced singers who can enjoy an a cappella song or hymn. Otherwise, the normal group may find the singing experience too embarrassing, and therefore, too threatening. Small group singing is good, but only with the right leadership and support.

5. A helpful exercise would be for a small group to study and reflect upon the "one-anothering" statements in the New Testament. Several small group authors have reinforced this in their books and curricula. For instance a group may want to read and discuss Richard Meyer's book *One-Anothering*. The group could look at one of the key one-anothering passages at each meeting for several weeks. After reading the passage, they could ask themselves the question, "How can we develop this skill of one-anothering in our group?" For example, "How can we practice the skill of encouraging one another?" Such a conversation could last for the entire meeting, ending with prayer, asking for God's help in becoming an encouraging community.

6. Praying in a small group is one of the hardest pursuits for many Westerners. Prayer is an intimate experience. Small groups do not come by the freedom to pray naturally or easily. Teaching a group to pray or helping a group become comfortable with prayer is an intentional discipline. The discipline takes leadership initiative and good modeling. Someone must take the risk to pray and show the group how to pray. Simple prayers are best at first. Written prayers are easier for some than verbal prayers. It is a fatal mistake that Christian leaders make in assuming that relational prayer is an easy thing to do. Good patterns of prayer,

creative group prayer and confessional-healing prayer take months and years to nurture in a group and in a person. Group members should be encouraged to pray in private and bring their private disciplines into the group setting. However, private prayer is a different discipline from communal prayer. Being skilled at private prayer does not make one an expert at communal prayer. The private prayer expert may be embarrassed and tongue-tied in the group context.

21
SMALL GROUP IMAGES AND METAPHORS

When you come together, it is not the Lord's Supper you eat, for as you eat, each of you goes ahead without waiting for anybody else. . . .

Whoever eats the bread or drinks the cup of the Lord in an unworthy manner will be guilty of sinning against the body and blood of the Lord. . . . For anyone who eats and drinks without recognizing the body of the Lord eats and drinks judgment on himself [or herself]. This is why many among you are weak and sick. . . .

So then, my brothers [and sisters], when you come together to eat, wait for each other. If anyone is hungry, he [or she] should eat at home, so that when you meet together it may not result in judgment. (1 Cor 11:20-21, 27, 29-30, 33-34)

The new life together of the new covenant house groups was a mixture of old and new values. Their koinonia—their sharing of all good things—and their enjoyment of the general favor of society moved them to include people who were both changed and unchanged, disciplined and undisciplined. Both the mature and immature lived together in community. The transformation of persons and relationships came through tension and conflict and change between old and new.

Paul's letters, as well as the other epistles, were written to the many ecclesia who continued to struggle in immaturity and conflict. These small house groups were caught between two worlds and two value systems, the realm of God and the realm of human invention (1 Cor 3:1-3). The realm (community) of God that Jesus and the apostles proclaimed "had not come to fulfillment. . . . Members of the community of faith were still afflicted by sickness and the struggle with sin went on."[1] They were not consistently waiting for and sharing with one another. They were not completely able to keep the spirit of "the meal" or the gifts. They were not yet free to give up their old, self-centered behavior for the new, other-centered behavior which Jesus epitomized in his death. They struggled between being members together of one group and being individuals apart who happened to be in the same room. This is a common struggle for every Christian small group. To help these groups form cohesive units, the apostles used several images and metaphors to describe the nature of their lives together.

The Small Group as the Body of Christ

It was in this apostolic understanding of ecclesia, through the breaking of the bread and through the suffering, death and resurrection of Jesus, that the ecclesia became identified as the *body* of Christ.

As the letter to the Ephesian ecclesia says, "It was he [Christ] who gave some to be apostles . . . to prepare God's people for works of service, so that the *body* of Christ may be built up" (Eph 4:11-12). The Spirit who had lived in and through the human body of Jesus became the Spirit who lived in and among those who were called to gather in the name of Jesus. The called gathering of Jesus became the new body of Christ who continued to live in the world. The ecclesia was the local and finite expression of the body of Christ. Wherever two or three gathered in the name of Jesus, he was there to enliven and stimulate the life and action of his ongoing human body, the ecclesia. The actions of the group were seen as the actions of Jesus as they opened themselves to let the Spirit guide and lead their life together.

This movement of the ecclesia becoming the living and continuing body of Jesus in the world was rooted and interpreted in the Last Supper of Jesus with the twelve disciples. Jesus established there the apostolic understanding of the small group gathering as the *body* when he broke the bread and gave it to the Twelve, saying, "This is my body, which is for you" (1 Cor 11:24). In doing so, Jesus demonstrated that his life was to continue as a community life and that his Spirit would be shared among the many. Wherever two or three came together, they together were the body, but their life-giving Spirit was the same Spirit that Jesus had with Abba.

As James Dunn has said, the Holy Spirit is a *shared experience*—the "koinonia of the Spirit."[2] The relationships and life together of the local small group body were sustained by the continuing gracious action of the Spirit. The ecclesia was the demonstration of the Spirit's grace in action. "The body of Christ [was] the charismatic [mutually gifted] community."[3] Just as the bread had been broken and distributed, so the Spirit was dispersed to every member, who then became a living gift to the rest of the group. Every group member participated in the breaking of the bread and the sharing of the Spirit and gifts. Every member was a member of the body. "There are different kinds of gifts, but the same Spirit" (1 Cor 12:4).

There was one Jesus whose body was sacrificed and whose blood was poured out. It was out of the suffering and death of Jesus that the new communities of the Spirit, the new bodies of Christ, were birthed. Jesus shared himself with those who would hear, see and receive him. Each ecclesia was a finite and localized demonstration of this reality of the regathered body of the present Lord. They were the real bodies of real persons who shared the bread and the gifts with one another. The meal and the gifts could be shared only where two or more were present to give to one another. The body can function only where its members are interdependent and there is reciprocity of participation and sharing.

In explaining the nature of the sacraments, Geoffrey Wainwright has referred to the importance of recognizing the regathered body of Christ:

The Christian religion is neither an atomistic affair of isolated individuals nor yet a totalitarian collectivism in which individual identities and responsibilities are submerged. It is rather a case of members integrated into a body. . . . No Christian sacrament is celebrated by an individual acting singly. At least two people are required for them all, and the communal nature of the Church is thereby underlined.[4]

For one of the members of the Christian ecclesia to go hungry while the other members ate was an act in discontinuity with the meaning of a unified body. If food was provided for any part of the body, it was provided for the whole body. If the Lord's Supper was shared with *any* member of the group it was to be shared with *every* member of the group. Whenever a new person was present at a gathering of ecclesia, he or she became instantaneously a member of the body. Such newcomers were immediately invited to share in the nourishment of the body.

This raises questions about serving the Lord's Supper to children or to unbelievers who may visit among a group of Christians. Given this theological foundation of the small group as body, if the meal is shared with some who are present, it should be shared with all who are present, including children and outsiders. For the life of the small group in Christ is immediately available to everyone present at the gathering, whether or not they are aware of the meal's (or sacrament's) theological meaning. Everyone of all ages should participate in the sharing of food. Even the youngest, who may simply want whatever they see others having, are a part of the covenant community. The concrete evidence of food shared is an anticipation of all sharing in the Spirit of Christ. Awareness or maturity is not a prerequisite to the voluntary participation in the sharing of the ecclesia. However, willingness to share in the discipline and patience of sharing is a requirement. As Paul said, if any cannot wait to eat they should eat at home. The symbol of participant sharing was very important.

When Jesus walked the earth he always shared food with everyone who was present. He did not even send a huge crowd away so he could eat alone with the Twelve (Mk 8:1-8). From Jesus' perspective there was always enough to share with everyone present. Even Judas shared the Last Supper with Jesus when Jesus knew he was ready to enter into betrayal (Mk 14:17-18). Any bread (or goods) available for one person in the group should be available to all who are present in the ecclesia.

"Recognizing the body" is the realization that every member of the gathered small group is as important and valued as any other member. The group together learns the discipline of waiting so that no one grabs too much for himself or herself. There is enough for each and every member. Each member of the small group must learn not to steal what belongs to, and should be shared with, all: food, time, energy, attention, leadership, gifts, resources and so on. Attitudes and actions that are not sensitive to the mutual ownership and participation of the group as a whole body are unworthy of Christ and unworthy of this group of persons who have been gathered by Christ.

Every member of the ecclesia needs to become a self-disciplined person with clear "body" thinking to prove, judge and discern the complete life and action of the body (1 Cor 11:28-29). The self-disciplines of judgment, reflection, planning and preparation are individual disciplines to enable the group member to participate more fully in the group experience, so each may pay attention to other group members and relationships that are being formed by Christ's Spirit. It may be appropriate to call this group awareness a "group hermeneutic." American culture in particular lacks this group or community hermeneutic, which leads a small group to a special kind of sensitivity and practice. The group needs to use healthy biblical, theological and relational skills to make decisions and take actions as they participate together in group life. Failure to understand and exercise such self-discipline in group relationships undermines the long-term health of the individual as well as the group.

As the apostle Paul said, "That is why many among you are weak and sick, and a number of you have fallen asleep [died]" (1 Cor 11:30). The continuous practice of such relational insensitivity makes people weak and sick. A lack of "body" awareness in human gatherings will kill people. Bonhoeffer discussed the potential of a killing kind of false human love which can undermine the community of the Spirit: "Here one soul operates directly upon another soul. The weak have been overcome by the strong, the resistance of the weak has broken down under the influence of another person."[5] Bonhoeffer understood that such group neglect or oppression can kill.

In his book *Power and Presence*, Don Kimball has expanded on this idea of a group's temptation to fail to enter into redemptive relationships. He writes about groups having four disabling fears: fear of failure, fear of rejection, fear of pain and fear of death. "Fear can make us hide ourselves inside our relationships, and it can keep us from ever beginning good relationships. Ultimately, it can conceal our free will from us and keep us from making life-giving choices or ruining the few good relationships we have."[6] The lack of relational sensitivity, of discerning the body in the ecclesia, is destructive. Fear moves individual members of a body to take more than their share or to give too little. The whole group must be able to recognize the law of fear at work, confront it, and intervene in love to cast out such fear from controlling the group or an individual.

Once the group recognizes the reality of being the *body* of Christ its members should be willing to enter into the mutual spiritual and relational disciplines which will nurture and sustain them in life together with Christ. Individual hungers and controlling behaviors which are undisciplined or insensitive should be confronted and given corrective attention and care before one is turned loose in the group. A group may have to exercise discerning and assertive group discipline if it is to deal constructively with an undisciplined, immature or dysfunctional member.

However, such constructive correction can be a difficult task. As David Augsburger has said, "Recognizing how unable I am to judge myself brings me to awareness of how unqualified I am to judge a sister or brother." In *Caring Enough to Confront* Augsburger has differentiated between being assertive and passing judgment in order to help group members avoid forming the wrong kind of relational discipline.[7] The apostle Paul described this kind of group discipline as "speaking the truth in love." Careful and loving boundaries must be set around a hurting member so he or she does not unintentionally take the group down with him or her. It shows a lack of love on the part of the group to allow a person to destroy oneself or the group. The group must help the "drowning" person relax and stop struggling out of frantic fear. The calming body has a way of surrounding a sick cell and helping it heal.

Richard John Neuhaus pinpointed a source of society's dysfunctional behavior in the failure of its members to participate in *mediating* dialogue and action.[8] The same is true for every small group: dysfunctional members can create dysfunctional groups if the destructive behavior goes unchecked. A dysfunctional member must be confronted and stopped lest they lead a group to destroy itself over a sustained period of time. Addictive or codependent persons can suck a whole group into addictive or codependent behavior.

This is a point that Anne Wilson Schaef and Diane Fassel have made—addictive persons can create addictive systems if unchallenged.[9] As the addictive person or system continues to live and relate in the group without intervention, the group and its members get weaker and sicker. The apostolic epistles were agents of intervention to help ecclesia who may have allowed addictive personalities to take over or allowed dysfunctional behavior to become a group norm. The apostles like Paul showed profound understanding of the psychology of small groups.

The small group body of Christ as the ecclesia, moves toward health or illness depending on the discipline and health of its individual members and the ability of its members to discern what is healthy or diseased behavior. The development of group skills and spiritual disciplines which empower group members to discern the body of Christ comes with intentionality, practice and mutuality. Such community or body discernment is founded in biblical disciplines and in understanding the hermeneutic of community around which Scripture was formed. Even the apostles were willing to invest in the mutual learning and discerning of their own body to help other ecclesia discover their identity and fulfillment in Christ. This is why every Christian small group needs to invest in a pattern of mutual discovery and mutual sharing.

Roberta Hestenes uses the term *Bible discovery* (just as Oleta Wald does in her book *The Joy of Discovery in Bible Study)* as another name for what is commonly called *inductive* study, the process of allowing the text (or shared subject) to speak for itself.[10] Such inductive learning is mutual learning by the power of the Spirit who calls group members into a shared discovery. Learning as a process of community means learning together and being the discerning mind and body of Christ. The nature of the body is to learn of Christ together. The mind of Christ is only fully discerned when the whole group enters prayerfully into the search.

The Small Group as the New Family of God

To Philemon our dear friend and fellow worker, to Apphia our sister, to Archippus our fellow soldier and to the church that meets in your home . . . Your love has given me great joy and encouragement, because you, brother, have refreshed the hearts of the saints. . . .

I appeal to you for my son Onesimus. . . . Formerly he was useless to you, but now he has become useful. . . .

Perhaps the reason he was separated from you for a little while was that you might have him back for good—no longer as a slave, but better than a slave, as a dear brother. (Philem 1, 7, 10-11, 15-16)

The one-anothering attitude and mutual ministry of the ecclesia were founded in their ethos and identity as families—families of adult brothers and sisters with Jesus the elder brother and God as parent (Abba). As Robert Banks has said, "The meeting of Christians with their God is more analogous to the encounter between adult children and their father."[11] As Paul wrote to the Romans, "Everyone moved by the Spirit is a child of God. The spirit you received is not the spirit of slaves bringing fear into your lives again; it is the spirit of children, and makes us cry out, 'Abba, Father" (Rom 8:14-15 JB). Jesus and the Twelve taught and modeled this metaphor of a new family. The family of Jesus was the gathering of "those who hear God's word and put it into practice" (Lk 8:19-21).

But the practice of the way of Jesus also caused existing families to shatter. When members of a family decided to enter the new family of Jesus, the old family was often divided or driven apart by divergent values and behaviors. The Spirit runs thicker and hotter than blood (Lk 12:47-51).

During the apostolic period, families and heads of families who were converted to Christ quickly practiced this more inclusive and spiritual definition of family, making "their homes available for the assembly (ecclesia) of the community." Gerhard Lohfink has described this practice by pointing to Philemon as an example of those homeowners and heads of households who "conducted vital missionary activity" and "with self-sacrificing hospitality . . . made their houses both the center of community life and a place of support for Christians who were travelling."[12] The building or house itself was not the church, but those who gathered there in the name of Jesus were the ecclesia. Those who shared in the life together were seen and known as family members: brother, sister, beloved, coworker, cosoldier and coprisoner. The emphasis in recognition of the ecclesia as family members was on being *with* one another as a reconstituted household.

The Greek word *sun*, used by Paul here in the Philemon letter, has been called the *"aristocrat* among the prepositions" because it was used sparingly. Its general meaning was "with," "along with" or "in addition to." But its aristocratic meaning had to do with its use as "association (in fellowship) with,"[13] particularly as association with important persons like Jesus and the apostle Paul. We can infer that Paul herein was using *sun* to designate his association with the "royal" Christian family that gathered in the home of Philemon, to whom he was asking Philemon to invite Onesimus to become a full royal family member. It was as though Paul was asking the president to invite a slave to join the exclusive club with full membership benefits.

The Christian family is to be "with" one another in love. Just as Jesus came as Emmanuel (God *with* us; Mt 1:23), so the new family was called to be *with* Jesus and *with* one another. Members of the house group were called alongside one another, to live life together, to walk beside one another and to be full humanity for one another. As Paul described it in his letter to Philemon, they supported one another in "love," "joy," "encouragement" and "refreshment."

The small house group was the transformational environment which redefined people. Instead of seeing them from the perspective of existing social stations, stratas and functions, they viewed every member through the eyes of Jesus as a family member—a brother or sister. Paul himself redefined the role and meaning of Onesimus: his social role was "no longer as a slave, but better than a slave, as a dear brother . . . as a man and as a brother in the Lord" (Philem 16). The value ("usefulness") of Onesimus shifted from his role as a slave to the nature of his being as a man and his new relationship as a brother. He was to be invited to join in the family relationship with Philemon just as Paul. Paul, Philemon and Onesimus were to become family, brothers together, full humanity together, in mutual ministry, shared authority and equal status. Together with Jesus and the other members of the household, they were a small group who were family. As Paul understood, wherever two or three met in Christ there were to be new definitions and roles for persons. The slave became the brother. The wife became the sister. The homeowner became the fellow worker. The Christian small group was space for equity, equality and partnership. They were the adult household and shared the royal inheritance of the God who ruled heaven and earth.

Membership in the group implied full partnership (koinonia) in the ministry of the family business. Ray Anderson and Dennis Guernsey have affirmed this precedence of koinonia, saying that "the filial bond, formed as a biological or natural order, gives way to the higher demand of covenant partnership."[14] Paul attempted to persuade Philemon to invite Onesimus into a partnership in the family business: "So if you consider me a partner, welcome him as you would welcome me" (Philem 17). Their common humanity in Christ became more important than societal definition and expectation. Onesimus' "usefulness" was transformed from a slave owned by Philemon to brother and partner who worked alongside Philemon. Paul's textual play on the Greek words *useless* and *useful* were interactive with the meaning of the name *Onesimus*, which meant "useful" (see NIV footnote on v. 11). Onesimus' value was no longer determined by the roles he was given to play in the culture, but by his new membership in a family of men and women, young and old, who worked together alongside their elder brother Jesus, who had shown them how to be a family. His *usefulness* was reoriented through being in community with Jesus and with the "saints."

For Onesimus, to be "useful" was to be free to be a full human being, to be a "prisoner" of Christ, not a prisoner of the system of slavery. Paul reoriented the temporal human view of imprisonment from the perspective of Jesus. Even though one may be sitting in a Roman jail, one was free to be a full human being. Freedom was not to be defined as the state of a person's outer world, but the state of their inner world, their intimacy with God and the freedom to enter into intimacy with human beings nearby. So Paul and Onesimus were in prison together, but they were free to be family together, as men who were open and vulnerable, face to face in mutual confession, forgiveness, help and ministry. Onesimus and Paul were an ecclesia in a Roman jail (Philem 1, 13). But in Christ they were free from all other forms of human imprisonment, free to enter into the full equity of human relationships, free to be full human family together.

The freedom for the ecclesia to become redeemed and renewed family came about through the letting go of previous family systems abuse and addictions. The ecclesia provided a healing environment for the slave to let go of the abuse and codependency of slavery and for the master (who was also a slave to the system) of the house to let go of abusive and addictive behaviors of control and intimidation over wife, children, slave or employee. In the new family the head of the house and the servant of the house learned to share in all things as brothers and sisters in Abba God's house. The ownership of the household was deeded to God. All discovered that the family and its goods belonged to their heavenly Father.

In *Addiction and Grace* Gerald May has articulated a theological perspective of the new family being a place of restoration and healing from addictions. As May has suggested, in this new family the members practice discernment, honesty, dignity, community, responsibility, discipline, simplicity, loving and longing for God. Our thirst for community is only quenchable through intimacy with God and with one another. Only in community do we find the loving power to be released from our addictive behavior. Grace, according to May, is the working of healing relationships between God and human beings.[15]

Even the influential and powerful apostle Paul refused to pull rank or dictate policy when addressing his family of brothers and sisters. Paul's appeal to Philemon assumed no rank or positional demand—it was the appeal of one brother to one another (Philem 14). Because they had been family together, they were able to address one another as members of Christ's family (even as mutual prisoners" of Christ). Obedience was not to be attained by a demand of the apostle but by a voluntary response to God in Christ. The apostle did not "command" the family but "appealed" to them to hear the commands of Christ. This modeling of apostolic mutuality with other adult members of the new family sent a clear message to all who would join the group. They were invited to come and be men and women together where no one person or no one ruling subgroup has chief authority, but where all, even apostles, share the Spirit and the authority of

Christ together as they meet. Whoever gathers in the group and commits allegiance to Jesus Christ receives the responsibility and freedom to become a full partner and brother or sister, a joint heir of God with Christ.

Gerhard Lohfink has noted that Paul's concern in Philemon was not with the human institution of slavery, but with the transformational inner culture of the ecclesia:

> Paul never sought to oppose the ancient institution of slavery on a general social level. Not only would he have had no possibility of success but a struggle of this sort also could not have stood within his intentions. What he was decisively concerned with was the community: where it assembled as community, where the eschatological people of God was present, the distinction between slaves and free could no longer be permitted.[16]

This transformed inner culture of community also affected the way Christians treated one another in the outer culture. As their humanity and relationships were redefined so were their personal and social interactions. Because they had become family together in ecclesia, they began to see the reality and hope of being family with humanity beyond the ecclesia. Such a drastic attitudinal reorientation about power had powerful implications in the world. The disenfranchised were often too quick to grab it and the enfranchised were often too resistant to accept it.

In addition to being a small group of brothers and sisters who shared all humanity and possessions, the new family was to be a community of persons who constantly reinforced for one another that their life together was to be sustained in mutual forgiveness and refreshment. They were not to hold on to emotional debts and vendettas. These debts were to be paid together by the shared humanity and goods equity of the group. Since Jesus had paid their debt of sin, they were free to pay one another's debts of hurt, anger, vengeance, adultery, greed, etc.

Paul made himself an example of this joint ownership of the debt of a brother or sister. As he said to Philemon concerning Onesimus, "If he has done you any wrong or owes you anything, charge it to me" (v. 18). The possible debt of Onesimus became the potential debt of Paul. A majority of biblical theologians, including Lohfink, have seen Paul's strong advocacy for Onesimus as a payment for forgiveness because "he had run away from Philemon." Even though this is a commonly inferred understanding of Onesimus's state and Philemon's call, there is no textual or historical evidence to support his runaway status. Nowhere does Paul directly state that Onesimus is guilty of any offense toward Philemon. Rather, Paul only makes the conditional statement, "if he has done you any wrong." This is not the request of one who is seeking forgiveness for a slave who has sinned, but that of a brother who is adopting a new brother and is willing to share all.

For Paul any debt of Onesimus became a family debt, because Christ had paid all their debts. The ecclesia was to function as a debt-free, forgiveness-bound subculture within the greater society so the gospel could be seen in action as a debt-canceling community (koinonia) when they came together and when they went out. Their partnering, refreshing, sharing, family-ing, fellow-ing, welcoming and loving were all demonstrations of a new way of life. This life with Jesus on earth was also life in the Spirit with Christ in heaven.

This new life and new community are demonstrated today in and through small groups that meet in homes, schools, businesses and church buildings. This new pattern of life can be a source and sign of *hope* in an otherwise indebted and imprisoned society of abusive and addictive family systems and organizations. In quoting a *New York Times* article, "Remaking the American CEO," Schaef and Fassel have said that

> many [CEOs] are adopting a new creed that puts corporate survival above all else. The result: a generation of ruthless management. . . . The new order eschews loyalty to workers, products, corporate structure, business, factories, communities and even the nation. All such allegiances are viewed as expendable under the new rules. With survival at stake, only market leadership, strong profits and a high stock price can be allowed to matter. . . . [Corporate leaders are] going through a massive rethinking process, and their response to the imperative to change has been to become more ruthless, more manipulative, more dishonest, more rigid, less creative and less willing to take risks.[17]

This is the agonized state of a culture where humanity and human relationships are undervalued and expendable. In this kind of dehumanized culture a pervasive state of hopelessness and despair grows rampant. While a few may take hope in quick gain, the general population becomes more indebted, loses power and lags in energy. Schaef and Fassel call for intervention into these imprisoning corporate climates and these relationally impoverished family systems. This is the kind of humane intervention that the ecclesia accomplished in the era of Jesus and the apostles. And the kind of new human family values which can be established wherever two or three meet together in the name of Jesus Christ.

The Small Group as Royal Priesthood

> You also, like living stones, are being built into a spiritual house to be a holy priesthood, offering spiritual sacrifices acceptable to God through Jesus Christ. . . .

> "a chosen and precious cornerstone,
> and the one who trusts in him
>   will never be put to shame.". . .

You are a chosen people, a royal priesthood, a holy nation, a people belonging to God, that you may declare the praises of him who called you out of darkness into his wonderful light. Once you were not a people, but now you are the people of God; once you had not received mercy, but now you have received mercy. (1 Pet 2:5-6, 9-10)

The Christian small group is a spiritual house of priests who offer themselves individually and as a group to be living sacrifices for the healing and reconciling of persons and society. Their priesthood is essentially their redeemed humanity and their restored community together. To be in pursuit of the wholeness of persons and relationships is to be a participant in ministry and to be a priest with Jesus, who is the great high priest of the ecclesia, the household of priests. The ecclesia were scattered communities of God's priests in a pagan world full of idols and false gods.

The priesthood of Jesus defines the priesthood of each person in the small group. Hebrews 4:14—5:3 describes the great high priest as one who is able to sympathize with weakness, has undergone and overcome temptation, is able to give access to God, is able to offer sacrificial intervention for sin, is able to deal gently with the ignorant and straying, is able to admit weakness, does not take personal glory, offers up prayers and petitions with passion and emotion, and has learned obedience through suffering. These priestly characteristics were to be as true of the small group as of the individual. They are character traits of people who have been rebuilt in community with Christ.

Such a priesthood is discovered and nurtured amid the community (kingdom) of priests. From the beginning, the people of God were gathered to become a community of priests (Ex 19:6). So the apostles understood that the ecclesia were to be small priestly communities. Today Christian small groups are called by their high priest Jesus to be courts of "royal priests." Living together in the presence of the King, who is also the high priest, empowers a small group to enter into the nobility and royalty of a shared priestly ministry.

In Acts 17 Luke implied that the royalty of the Berean community was manifest as they practiced a priestly mediation of the Scriptures with the apostle Paul. A small group that practices mutual priesthood enables each member to be restored to her or his full human dignity and reigning magnificence of earth, sharing dominion of creation in community together with Jesus. Through their life together as a group, they share in the wealth of becoming a full human community in the presence and glory of God.

In the *Great Divorce*, C. S. Lewis pictured the inhabitants of heaven as royal persons, surrounded in procession by the many who were helped and served by them on earth.[18] Lewis understood that a life of priestly community on earth has a reward of royal honor in the eternal realm of heaven.

The Small Group as "Stone Building"

While the small group may be a taste of heaven on earth and a court experience in the presence of Christ, the group does have to exercise their priestly vocation in a hostile world. The small group has to minister together between a rock and a hard place. With the rock of Christ in their midst, the vulnerable small group can become a tough "stone building" in a hardened world.

This is the general message of 1 Peter: "though now for a little while you may have had to suffer grief in all kinds of trials. These have come so that your faith—of greater worth than gold . . . may be proved genuine and may result in praise, glory and honor when Jesus Christ is revealed" (1 Pet 1:6-7). The ecclesia were "like living stones . . . being built into a spiritual house to be a holy priesthood" (1 Pet 2:5). They were being built together as a sturdy community to weather a stormy world.

The passionate, intense and solid small Christian group can be a bright and intense light in a very dark culture. In a society where human relationships and persons are bent, broken and dying the group practicing mutual priesthood is called to intervene and transform hardened institutional systems. The bright light of the healthy small group will draw blinded persons out of their ignorance and misunderstanding about the value of persons to share in the newness of a healing human community. The Christian small group is the ecclesia built up together by the chief cornerstone, Jesus Christ, to minister together as living stones between the rock of God and the hard place of sterile political, social, religious, familial and corporate systems.

It has already been noted that an important agenda of liberation theology is to advocate for the formation of intentional Christian communities with specific political agendas. But such an agenda is not only advocated by the liberationist perspective. It is a foundational biblical principle of ecclesia to be a community guided by spiritual and human values which are *not* of this world. In this sense, every time two or three come together in the name of Jesus, they form a countercultural presence and prohuman conclave which can transcend all other human systems, even the institutional church. As Bernard Lee and Michael Cowan have said, "Because the Christian Great Story is not identical with the American great story in certain very important respects, the ethos called for on the part of the members of intentional Christian communities within the U.S. culture will be complex and often counter-cultural."[19] A caring small group may be the only intervening reality supporting a person who is being ignored or attacked by a huge corporate or governmental system. If the group is not rock-solid in Christ, it may not withstand the overwhelming complexity and resistance of the encroaching "principality and power."

Where inhumane systems demand productivity and performance without mercy or compassion, the small group of persons who meet together in Christ are given the privilege and priesthood of mediating the same mercy they have received and experienced together in Christ. These life-changing clusters of priests gather as counterparadigms to the resistant walls of hardened institutional oppression.

In his book *Maximize Your Ministry* Robert Slocum has argued for a universal ministry strategy of scattering clusters of Christian laity and clergy throughout world systems, just as small groups of Christians were scattered throughout the catacombs of a "hostile and difficult" Rome.[20] They are to be groups of "strangers in the world, scattered throughout" organizational systems as sprinklings of the blood ties of Jesus (1 Pet 1:1-2). If a group hermeneutic is used in interpreting this christological statement of 1 Peter, then the word *sprinkling* is parallel to the word *scattered.* Thus the scattered groups are the lifeblood of Jesus being sprinkled throughout the greater world. Their loving and assertive presence is not meant to destroy the fabric of institutional life but to transform and reform old structures with the new lifeblood of Jesus Christ. This is not done by revolution but by "spiritual sacrifice," humility, love, forgiveness and eternal vision. It is founded upon the gentle but solid rock of Christ, who is the cornerstone of all new and renewed human organization. The small group is the spiritual sub-contracting team called in by Christ as the architect and construction manager to renovate a broken-down humanity.

These small group clusters of priests become *rock*-hard in their spiritual conditioning and exercise of discipline as they achieve an ability to persevere through abuse and pain. But they must also become *heart*-soft[21] in their warmth, affection and affirmation for human life and nurturing healthy community together. Their raw-cut shalom in Christ brings peace, health, wholeness and completeness to the broken world in which they prosper in spite of all hostility, destitution, fragmentation, isolation and rejection.

■ SMALL GROUP MINISTRY IMPLICATIONS

1. To return to a deeper connection with the New Testament community of ecclesia, there must be ways found to help small groups celebrate the sacraments of baptism and the Lord's Supper. This is a source of ecclesiastical concern for

most mainline denominations because of the historical assumption that the presence of clergy brings theological integrity to the sacramental moment. This question cuts at the very nature and heart of Christian community. If indeed, wherever two or three are gathered together is the place to experience sacramental life, then how we do sacraments in the institutional church often misses the fabric of relational life which is to be nurtured through the sacraments. To only serve Communion or celebrate baptism when the larger body is lined up in rows of pews all facing the clergy is to dramatically miss the power of the face-to-face family gathering. The sacraments should be celebrated in small group situations as well as large group situations. This is an issue today for the institutional church to study and decide. But if we are to return to our biblical small group foundations, the sacraments must be experienced in the circles of intimacy as well as the formal institutional orders.

2. Small groups should be assisted to do biblical studies of the four biblical metaphors which describe their nature and function: the body, the family and the building. Groups should have time to think through how these metaphors help form their life together. They also need constructive ways to help them connect with other small groups so they see themselves as interconnected with the larger body network of groups. As a group studies these metaphors, they should be encouraged to ask questions such as: How does this image inform how we should be and act as a group? How do we feel about seeing our group as a body, a family or a building? How do we see the role of Jesus with us in each of these metaphors? If these metaphors are glimpses of what heaven is like, what can we say about heaven? How do you feel our group lives up to any one of these images? When you think of our group, what other images or metaphors come to mind to describe who we are?

3. Clergy and lay leaders need to carefully think through the implications of this chapter which may demand a fairly radical reforming of ecclesiology for some. Some may simply disagree with the premise of a small group being the complete ecclesia. In any case leaders must help groups discover the profound meaning of their life together through New Testament images. This process of discovery will help small groups develop a stronger sense of purpose and dignity. If institutional church leaders are not yet comfortable with such a radical reframing of their ecclesiology, there is still a powerful place for small group ministry in the church. The metachurch model, for example, sees the small group as the "cell" of the large church body, and so it is. This chapter suggests the small group is the body, as well. Whether a macro or micro view of body is assumed, there is still much the institutional church must do to affirm intentional small group ministry wherever possible. Our institutional church future depends upon our

ability to make some ecclesiastical adjustments regarding the role and power of small group communities as the ongoing ministries of Jesus Christ.

4. Every small group should think about how it uses food as a discipline and symbol of its life together. Groups should plan to eat together. Groups should plan to use this meal time in some special way to signal the specialness of their life together. Even if there is not permission in the denominational framework to celebrate an official Lord's Supper, in most denominations there are similar kinds of celebrations called "agape feasts" or "disciple meals." Key small group network leaders may want to suggest ways for groups to celebrate special meals which resonate as reenactments of the Last Supper.

5. Leaders should create ways for small groups to celebrate children coming into their family life. Some small group ministries are "adults only" gatherings. Special group events where the children are invited and intentionally included are a truer reflection of our biblical small group roots. For example, even if it is not possible for a small group to host an official baptism or dedication for a newborn, it may be possible for a small group of parents, relatives and friends to gather with their children to have a baptismal party following the larger worship service. Every child needs to be nurtured and raised by more than just their two parents. This is a very important dimension of covenant community which is lost in the bent toward individualism and the nuclear family. Small groups should be a responsible space to nurture mutual family values. This is especially true in congregations where extended family live in other parts of the country. The small group should become the extended family.

22

THE SMALL GROUP
IN MINISTRY
AND MISSION

They devoted themselves to the apostles' teaching and to the fellowship, to the breaking of bread and to prayer. Everyone was filled with awe, and many wonders and miraculous signs were done by the apostles. All the believers were together and had everything in common. Selling their possessions and goods, they gave to anyone as he had need. Every day they continued to meet together in the temple courts. They broke bread in their homes and ate together with glad and sincere hearts, praising God and enjoying the favor of all the people. And the Lord added to their number daily those who were being saved. (Acts 2:42-47)

The practice of small group disciplines provided a strong identity and base from which the ecclesia could do ministry and venture into mission. In fact, the extended practice of the disciplines *became* the ministry. Luke's description of the ministry of these early Christian small groups included selling their possessions and goods and giving to anyone who had need, meeting daily, breaking bread and eating together, and praising God (Acts 2:45-47). They met together as a base for ministry as well as to provide a supportive environment for the apostles to do "many wonders and miraculous signs" (Acts 2:43). James Dunn has described this early community "as living in an atmosphere of the miraculous."[1] Did the ecclesia live within this "atmosphere" of signs and wonders or did the signs and wonders live within the atmosphere of the ecclesia? Were the apostles empowered directly by the Holy Spirit as individuals or through the communities of prayer and faith? In either case, there was an intimate and symbiotic relationship between the disciplines of the ecclesia and the apostolic ministry with signs and wonders.

The apostles not only initiated the new small communities, they also received the discernment, affirmation and commissioning of these local ecclesia. Luke describes several occasions in which the ecclesia practiced discernment, prayer, laying on of hands and sending of apostles to do specific ministry (Acts 13:3). It seemed to be the action of the whole group that gave the apostles direction and intention in their mission and ministry.

The apostles intentionally tried to guide these communities into early ownership and mutuality of Christ's ministry. As Robert Banks has pointed out, the apostles participated in the ministry of the community and the community participated in the ministry of the apostles. "Apostle and community are indissolubly tied together from beginning to end . . . a parent-*adult* child rather than parent-*infant* child relationship . . . recognizing their self-sufficiency in the Spirit . . . seeking their voluntary decisions." The apostles and the ecclesia worked together as partners in ministry.[2]

Banks has further argued that apostolic authority was not exercised through formal structures but through personal and familial relationships, "not . . . in an authoritarian manner." The apostle was part of a family for whom Jesus was friend and brother and God was Abba (loving and caring Father). Apostolic authority flowed out of personal relationships with God, with Jesus and with those gathered in their Spirit. The apostles ministered *out of* community as well as *for* and *to* community.[3]

The apostolic delegation of authority for ministry to the whole ecclesia was rather rapid. In the leadership paradigm of Paul Hersey and John Blanchard, the apostolic leadership style, like Jesus' leadership style, was definitively and intentionally situational: as the ecclesia matured the apostles' delegated ministry.[4] The house groups quickly took responsibility for themselves as the apostles had to move on to other cities to plant other ecclesia. In reading the apostolic epistles, however, It is apparent that the spiritual maturity of the communities did not necessarily coincide with their technical maturity. Their knowledge and experience in how to function as a group often was more advanced than their emotional or volitional discipline for healthy relationships.

Their real authority for ministry was the authority of the Spirit at work in and through the community, through the mutual ministry of persons who gathered together in the name of Jesus. As Robert Banks has said, "Christians are to submit to one another in the community: each is the bearer to the other, in some degree, of the word and life of Christ . . . 'to be a sort of Christ to one another' . . . to 'be subject to one another out of reverence for Christ.' "[5] The full authority for ministry came from the power of the Spirit at work in the group, not from the presence of the apostle or any other human authority.

All practices and activities of the group consistent with the life and ministry of Jesus with the Twelve became ministries of the ecclesia. Their ministry emerged out of their gathering to share their common life—their persons, their relationships, their possessions, their food, their meetings and their worship—with whomever had need for them. Their life together became their ministry.[6]

The Small Group Ministry of Selling and Giving

Since their lives were now intimately connected to one another in Christ, the ecclesia had everything in common: people, relationships, goods, lands, houses and problems. They saw themselves as the new family of Jesus. As Banks has said, the bonding, intimacy and love of the gatherings was "more analogous to the encounter between adult children and their father, where they were able to relate to Him not only in the most intimate, but increasingly in the most mature fashion."[7] What they had owned individually was now seen as owned by the family, by the household of God, for which they were stewards together with Christ as Lord and brother.[8] The common goods were shared to provide for the needs of the whole. And God was seen as the Provider for all the members together in the household.

This common sharing of life and goods extended to any nearby who had need. As the members of the ecclesia shared their common life with each other, they drew others into the small group circle to share the common life of Christ. The sharing of money and goods was the concrete expression of the real experience of the group with Christ and with one another. As Christ had shared his life and his Spirit with them, they were free to share their life, money and goods with anyone who had need for them. "All the believers were one in heart and mind. No one claimed that any of [their] possessions was [their] own, but they shared everything they had" (Acts 4:32; see vv. 33-35). This movement of commonness was intimately connected to the apostles' presence and teaching, which had its roots in their life together as the Twelve and others with Jesus. The common life of Jesus with the Twelve became the common life of the apostles among the ecclesia, which became the common life of the ecclesia as household for any who had need, so "there were no needy persons among them."

This sharing among the ecclesia of their physical lives and possessions provided the arena in which "the apostles performed many miraculous signs and wonders among the people" (Acts 5:12-16). The inward ministry of the ecclesia was a ministry of sharing physical life together. The outward ministry was the ministry of the apostles, based in ecclesia, who healed the sick and exorcised evil spirits.

God's provision for meeting real physical human need was demonstrated through both the sharing of goods in ecclesia and the sharing of healing through the apostles. The ministry life of the ecclesia was the foundation from which the apostles had the power and freedom to fulfill their mission of proclamation and healing. The healing presence and power of Christ was intimately connected to the sharing of life as ecclesia and household. The small group community provided the context and support for the apostolic ministry, all of which was a direct reflection of the continuing ministry of Jesus among the Twelve. Through the small group koinonia the real human needs of people were met. This attitude of shared life is foundational for all small group ministry.

The Small Group Ministry of Daily Meetings
Just as a household or family would gather daily, so the ecclesia gathered daily in the home, synagogues and marketplace. The discipline of meeting together set the context for the consistent meeting of one another's needs. The frequency of meeting together created an intensity and synergy of life together that moved individuals, families and social structures to change. Change always happens in the midst of great resistance. Transformational ministry carries a cost.

Such vital, intimate and personal sharing of life together in Christ has continued to be a threat to power structures throughout salvation history. Where two or three have gathered, their life together has been a counterlife to other systems and structures that would seek to define, control or orient life in a manipulative or oppressive way. Societal systems are confronted by this new pattern of communal freedom in Christ and the battle lines are drawn.

The more frequent and diligent their meeting together in Christ, the more fear other systems had that their dominions would be destroyed by this koinonia. There is a proportional and reciprocal relationship between the intensity of life together in Christ and the intensity of the social system's attempt to rid itself of this alien presence. The two ways and systems cannot coexist.

As we read in Acts, the proclamation and demonstration of the "full message of this new life" caused the religious and social leaders to be "filled with jealousy" (Acts 5:17-20). The daily intensity and pervasiveness of this new pattern of living was taking over the city of Jerusalem and breaking down ancient and traditional structures. Reaction from the leaders of threatened power structures was inevitable. The impact of hundreds of small groups meeting daily around the city was great, and the response on the part of other political and religious systems was fear. Lee and Cowen have noted this ongoing threat of the ecclesia to existing structures:

The house church communities . . . are made up of Christian persons who have deliberately chosen to cast their lots with other Christian people. This deliberate choice makes them intentional communities rather than random gatherings . . . agents of social reconstruction. Their memories are dangerous because they spawn hopes that require that present social arrangements be put under prophetic critique.

The liberationist view of the house church or base community is that intentional life together through small Christian communities will effect social change and induce social resistance. While the traditional Catholic and Protestant churches are heavily invested in making existing social structures work, generic small group community, almost by definition, seems to become a countercultural movement in any existing structure. This sets up a fundamental tension and concern for the ministry of small groups within any religious structure. Wherever two or three come together in Christ, the Spirit may not move them to fall in line with the prevailing social structure, religious or political. Herein is the inherent *danger* of small group ministry.[9] However, the apostle Paul was assertive in his recommendation to the ecclesia that "every person be subject to the governing authorities. . . . Whoever resists authority resists what God has appointed" (Rom 13:1-2 NRSV). While groups may, by the very nature of Christ, call institutions to accountability, they are to be vigilant not to act as terrorists or espionage teams to intentionally destroy an organization.

The ministry of meeting together frequently was focused on personal and social transformation. Small group research has shown there is a direct relationship between the frequency of meeting and group cohesiveness. The more frequently the group meets together, the more the individuals in the group begin to adopt the life of the group and begin to use the group life to affect change in those parts of their life outside of the group. This is one of the principles behind the formation of Twelve-Step groups. Meeting consistently and frequently provides a base from which habits and patterns can be changed and persons can be held accountable to continue in that change.[10]

In the process of meeting together, people and their values are transformed and systems and structures are reformed. The ministry of daily meeting was the discipline of dramatizing a new way of living in Christ. Just as the Twelve were transformed through daily life together with Jesus, the apostles now called the new followers of Jesus to be transformed as they met daily with one another in the presence of Jesus by the power of the Spirit. As already asserted, these small group gatherings became new family systems formed to break the power, habits and values of the "principalities and powers" (Eph 6:12) that controlled people's lives and relationships.

Walter Wink has suggested that "the powers are the inner aspect of material reality." The spirit of an institution takes on its own life and affects human lives. On the dark side, instead of the institution or system serving the redemption of humanity, humanity is subjugated to serve and sustain the institution. Institutions develop a suprahuman life of their own. The early church *gatherings* understood this. They refused to worship the imperial rule and bowed to a higher power. This intervention of Christ and confrontation with the power of Rome was made possible through their new experience of the presence of God and the Lordship of Jesus Christ as they gathered in small groups and practiced prayer and mutual ministry.[11] Part of the process of being saved "from this corrupt generation" (Acts 2:40) was the intentional daily meeting together to act out new behaviors of relationship, ownership and stewardship.

These daily meetings of the Christian groups reinforced the reality that the kingdom and will of God had come into being on earth as it was in heaven. As Dunn has suggested, in the early home communities "the Lord's Prayer was obviously used frequently."[12] The use of the prayer of Jesus called attention to Jesus' life with the Twelve and his continuing life with the ecclesia. God's invisible rule was now visible daily on earth, in the homes and courts of Jerusalem, for individuals, families, men and women, young and old together.

In the daily meeting self-discipline and group discipline constantly reinforced, encouraged and supported changed attitudes. The ecclesia were called to a life of repentance, forgiveness and baptism, a life in the name of Jesus, to live out the "gift of the Spirit." These new values led to more healthy behaviors. In *Covenant to Care* Louis Evans Jr. has explained that the life of repentance, of living out one's baptism, is possible only in a community of self-discipline, that is, a covenant community. Evans has named eight basic covenants which help keep the small group discipline tuned toward ministry: affirmation, availability, prayer, openness, honesty, sensitivity, confidentiality and accountability.[13] The daily cycle of shared experience helped to develop mutual trust that nurtured mature groups and individuals as they met together over extended periods of time. Bruce Powers has suggested that this intense cycle of shared experience and mutual trust is koinonia, and that those who live in this cycle of koinonia become mature through the process and in time.[14]

The mutual ministry that took place in the daily meeting of the ecclesia was the foundation from which the ecclesia launched its mission and outward ministry. As Lee and Cowan have so clearly said, both koinonia and diakonia, shared life and service, community and mission, are part of the Christian base group. Their inner ministry opens out into mission. The primary relational group becomes a secondary task group.

A primary group is one in which the bonding is very effective in character.

It is a natural grouping, based upon family or friendship bonds. The quality of their interpersonal life is a primary concern. The other kind of group is a secondary group, with characteristics more like those of a formal organization. The secondary group exists for some purpose other than their personal relationships . . . they have a shared task and that is their real reason for being a group.

Lee and Cowan define the ecclesia as a hybrid group because "it has some characteristics of both the primary group and the secondary group."[15]

The stronger their life together, the more potent their mission apart. Like the Twelve and the seventy, their mission was accomplished through subgroups—teams of persons in twos, threes and fours—sent out by the parent group (Acts 13:1-3). It was while the ecclesia in Antioch were "worshiping the Lord and fasting" that the Holy Spirit spoke to them to send Barnabas and Saul. Their mission emerged out of their worship and life together. Likewise, the other subgroups consisted of "friends," "fellow workers" and "fellow soldiers" together in ministry (Philem 1-2). Paul's letter to Philemon was also addressed "to the church that meets in your home." The team ministry and mission of the "joint worker" and "joint soldier" was evidently experienced, even for Paul, from the base of meeting together in Philemon's home. These mission teams cared for one another while venturing into the tough and hostile environments of the villages and cities to share the good news of Christ. The daily meetings provided daily support for their ventures into the marketplace and courts as well as to distant cities. The daily meetings also provided space for theological reflection and feedback, visioning and strategic planning to risk the greater mission and ministry. The daily meeting of the ecclesia was both the arena of ministry and the center for mission.

The Ministry of Breaking Bread and Eating Together

As earlier affirmed, the sharing of life and goods with all those who had need was focused in the sharing of meals, and ultimately enacted in the sharing of the Lord's Supper. Eating the common loaf and drinking the common wine was both the symbolic and real center of the community's understanding of life in Christ. When the Lord's Supper was shared, the message was clear: this ecclesia is the body of Christ. And whoever ate with the ecclesia was being invited to share life and ministry together. The sharing of the Lord's Supper was an act of covenant and commitment to the common life of the ecclesia. The shared meal was a common discipline to launch the group into the ministry and mission reflected out of the very nature of the shared meal. And the invitation to share the meal was a key evangelistic strategy as well as key ministry training event.

Sharing the Lord's Supper set up a style and character of community that was to be worked into other meals and influence outside group situations as potential ministry. As Robert Banks has affirmed, the Lord's meal was not a token or a part of a meal, but the whole meal, the main meal of the gathering, "the one to which guests were generally invited"[16] (1 Cor 11:17-34). In his first letter to the Corinthians Paul discusses the way the ecclesia was to share the meal (1 Cor 11:17-24). His admonishment "when you come together to eat, wait for each other" is a profound call to merge the Lord's Supper with the attitude that should permeate all general meals. The meals were to be the center place of mutual ministry, and the Lord's Supper was the ultimate expression of this sacred center and of this attitude and display of mutual ministry. The meal was a ministry and a base for mission. The meal was the mission when guests were invited. The mission of the group was to demonstrate to visitors what life together in Christ was all about. For around the table, the members of the ecclesia told their stories of transformation in Christ so the novice could be touched and invited to join the group.

The discipline of mutual ministry was very important to maintain. All aspects of the group's life were interconnected for mutual ministry. In Ephesians there is a clear apostolic emphasis on individual gifts being for ministry to and through the body, "to prepare God's people for works of service, so that the body of Christ may be built up" (see Eph 4:1-16). The common meal implied a common ministry where each member had a unique contribution to make to the group, in the group, through the group and from the group to the world.

The sharing of the meal set the character and meaning of all other group ministry. As Robert Banks has said, "it is primarily by *assembling* that the responsibilities of members to one another are fulfilled."[17] Patience, discernment, sensitivity and self-discipline had to be the distinguishing marks of the ecclesia's mutuality. How the Lord's Supper was shared was the preeminent demonstration of how all things would be shared, of how all things would be administered, of how the group would venture into mission.

The ministry implications of the meal are numerous. Both men and women should wait for and wait on each other in meal and ministry. The meal and ministry were always to be mutually accomplished. There was no hint that the apostles had special or privileged status in either the meal or the ministry. There were no clergy-laity distinctions for service or mutuality. The meals, like the ministries, were visible demonstrations that heaven had come to earth, that life now was eternal through the resurrected Christ, and that God was calling humanity to live in reconciled community forever and ever. The meal was the center of ministry and the fuel for mission.

The Small Group in Worship and Praise of God

The ecclesia's glad sharing of food and goods was a demonstration of their worship of God. Their worship and praise of God was interwoven with their mutual ministry. The nature of their community (koinonia) and their way of worship were intimately interconnected. The warmth and affirmation of gathering together led to their "glad" and "sincere" expressions of what God was doing for them and with them. Worship and fellowship were simultaneous and symbiotic.[18] As they shared their meals, their goods and their money, they were constantly announcing their worship (work) of God, the one Jesus called Abba. The Greek term translated "praise" here in Acts 2 emphasizes the verbal announcement and affirmation of God's work among them and through them. This reflects the telling of personal experiences in the group meetings and attributing them to God's work with amens from the hearers. Their horizontal expressions of love for one another were pivotally connected through the present Christ to their vertical exclamations of love for God. What was enjoyed in their life together became a basis for praise of God. What was important in their praise of God became a source of affirmation for their life together. Both worship and community were converging axes of the cross of Jesus. The worship and the ministry of the ecclesia exuded from and to the spontaneous and reconciling joy of God's movement toward them through a resurrected Christ. Their embracing movement toward one another was an anticipation of an eternal communal realm with God.

The gatherings of ecclesia were guided by spontaneity and excitement, unencumbered with formal structuring. As has been previously stated, the groups had some basic disciplines and patterns, but their order of community ministry was immediately adjustable to the needs and offerings of everyone present. The simplicity of their life together affirmed living in the here and now as a way of showing the there and then. They were an immediate "eschatological" reality.[19] The character of the ministry of the community was a direct reflection of the character of their life together and their life with God in Christ. Their mission flowed out of their joy in worship. The fulfillment of their worship was the action of their mission.

The Social Impact of Early Christian Small Groups

There was a strong and sustained social impact as the many small groups gathered in the courts and homes: "everyone was filled with awe" (Acts 2:43; "fear came to every soul"); they were "enjoying the favor of all the people. And the Lord added to their number daily those who were being saved" (Acts 2:47). The continuous meetings of many small groups who exemplified new values and new character could not go unnoticed in the close urban context. These groups attracted much attention and the general feeling was favorable. Outsiders liked what they saw happening in and through these ecclesia. Their life together was an attractive life. Their ministry struck feelings of amazement and awe in those who were healed as well as in those who watched. But most important, their new life together began to affect how more and more other people lived and worked.

These ecclesia, as microcosms of a new world view, began to transform the dynamics of the city's macroculture, its power structures and its political balance, at the grassroots level. Through the small and local gatherings of real people who experienced transformed character and relationships, larger societies and structures were redirected, reformed and restructured.

A contemporary case in point could be that of the Presbyterian Church (USA), which is committed to the historical Reformation concept of "reformed and always being reformed." The denomination's recent series of "reformation" moves have been a restructuring of the bureaucratic organization of the institution. The biblical and theological imperative of Jesus, as well as the apostolic teaching and modeling, is that true reform will come through the gathering renewal and ministry of small groups of people at the grassroots, which will put pressure on the institution to change. This change must include new personal and relational dynamics which will redefine the meaning of the larger organizational dynamics from the inside out. Foundational and radical reform works from the bottom up, not from the top down; out of transformed hearts, not out of organizational legislation. This is not to say that persons in higher places of organizational life cannot effect substantial change, but the key is not the change of the structure but the transformation of the people in the structure (which will lead to important structural changes). The Presbyterian Church (USA), like other mainline denominations, will be reformed by the radical renewal of small group networks in local congregations.

In *Small Is Beautiful* E. F. Schumacher has said that

we need the freedom of lots and lots of small autonomous units, and at the same time, the orderliness of large-scale . . . unity and coordination. When it comes to action we obviously need small units, because action is a highly personal affair, and one cannot be in touch with more than a very limited number of persons at one time. . . . The church in an area will be stunted to the extent that any believers are not committed to one another in a home church. . . . "It is with these that we are going to set about the work of spreading the gospel."[20]

David Prior has pointed out that organizational officials have a need to control. This is as endemic to the institutional church as it is to any secular government:

The human need to control situations for which we are held responsible becomes very urgent. . . . It is very tempting to keep tight control even while decentralizing and delegating . . . "The grassroots communities . . . are not the fruit of a scientific design or formula, but rather the dynamic action of the Spirit who forms the family of God despite so many human limitations and shortcomings."[21]

One of the results of the apostolic ecclesiastic ministry was political tension with power structures. This was the result of their fear of losing control over the people who fed their organizational power. The ecclesia were symbols to the principalities and powers that they were no longer the primary influence in the people's thinking and practice. The transforming social impact of the ecclesia was the result of people seeing a new way to live life and a new way of being in relationship to one another.

The miracles (the signs and wonders) caused fear among the people, but the sharing of life together in the courts and homes induced the favor of all the people. The social impact of ecclesia was both fear and favor, avoidance and approach. The society had a love-hate relationship with these ecclesia. While their good attitudes and loving actions were appreciated, their radical ideas and assertions were upsetting. While there was some social benefit of having them around, they upset the existing balance of power. Their presence was a growing reminder that all was not well with the rest of the world, and that "this world in its present form is passing away" (1 Cor 7:31). In *The Cost of Discipleship* Bonhoeffer quotes this verse to reinforce his point that the visible community of Christ is an alien community. "In the world the Christians are a colony of the true home, they are strangers and aliens in a foreign land. . . . They seek those things that are above and not those things that are on the earth." He also suggested that the *favor* of the people may have been the result of spiritual naiveté, that "they could not see that the secret of this common life was the cross of Christ."[22]

The adding each day to the number who participated in the ecclesia was a subtracting from those who had been pawns and slaves to existing religious, political and military systems. The more who joined the small communities of those "being saved" (Acts 2:47), the fewer who were willing to remain imprisoned by the manipulation, isolation, fragmentation and oppression of the structures being abandoned. The evangelism of the apostolic ecclesia was not good news to existing powers. Bonhoeffer pointed out an irony in the hostile reaction of the social powers to the ecclesia's ministry: "Above all they pray for all in authority, for that is their greatest service."[23]

The salvation of humanity through ecclesia was interpreted by world leaders as a potential threat to existing power structures.[24] The loving life together on the inside of the small Christian groups impacted the less human and disjointed life of the culture on the outside. The developing togetherness and bonding of their inner circles released these men and women to assist in unraveling the bondages of institutional principalities and powers. As Walter Wink has said, "The social demonic is the spirit exuded by a corporate structure that has turned its back on its divine vocation as a creature of God and has made its own goals the highest good."[24] The role of the ecclesia was to be a new community driven at its heart by the love of persons and the value of healthy human relationships as modeled and empowered by the Spirit of Christ. Therefore, there was immediate and constant tension with the *spirits* of the opposing *gathering* forces. Those gathered to Jesus were continually frustrating the *powers* of those gathered to Rome, to Judaism, to paternalism, to mammon, and so forth. Their small group experience of the power of love gave the ecclesia the courage to venture into the larger world of power where strength, size and intimidation were the predominant values. Their life together valued human beingness for each unique person in a world that mostly valued human productivity and success for a few at the top. But as renewing as their inner circles of love and koinonia were, there were continuing struggles and conflicts among the members of the groups as they lived together week after week trying to become new families and heavenly communities on earth.

■ SMALL GROUP MINISTRY IMPLICATIONS

1. Small groups need to see themselves as places for mutual ministry. Members should be encouraged to minister to each other during group meetings and in between group meetings. This suggests there needs to be training to help members learn the basic disciplines of mutual ministry. Groups should think of themselves as ministry situations. Group members should be helped to practice healthy ministry skills and disciplines such as listening, asking good questions, feedback, prayer, leading discussions, using "I" language rather than "you" language, developing noncondemning responses, doing inductive Bible study, etc. Such key small group skills are the core of developing good Christian community. The group needs to be a place where people can practice their skills and get feedback for improvement of skills. Some groups are not able to handle such a developmental approach to their life together. This may mean that special mutual training experiences are created so small group members may set aside special time and energy to work on the skills of mutual ministry.

2. Groups should also see themselves as ministry bases. As Robert Slocum has said in *Maximize Your Ministry*, the small group is the base from which individual members should be sent out into the world in the name of Christ. There should be space in the group for all members to reflect upon their everyday life as

situations for ministry. Whether they find themselves at home, at work, at church, at play or alone, they need to be able to talk with the group about their lives as ministers of Christ scattered out into the world. Small groups need to recognize and support the ministry of the laity as base camps for climbing up secular mountains and climbing over religious walls. If the laity has no such base ministry group, they will continue to venture out into hostile worlds with no sense of community support. At minimum, we all need to know there is a group who loves us and prays for us in the midst of a world which seems to be getting crazier. Sometimes these base groups are better developed if they are more homogeneous: men's groups, women's groups, professional groups, labor groups, management groups, labor-management groups, CEO groups, middle-management groups, single-parent groups, etc. Every Christian needs to know they are anchored to Christ through a small group which is a safe harbor next to the stormy secular seas of life. Small groups are not just bases to support the ministry of individuals scattered but also for the ministry gathered of the institutional church. Every member of the congregation should have an opportunity of service and a group to support them in their individual places of service within the church as organization.

3. And groups should view themselves as ministry teams. Children's ministry, youth ministry, music ministry, evangelism ministry, etc., can all be done through small group ministry teams or committees who also function as communities. This is especially true of mission teams (short-term or long-term) who prepare together, work together, rest together and reflect together about what God is calling them to accomplish as a faith task community. Short-term mission communities are the fastest growing form of small group ministry in the church. Such teams need special ministry training and preparation with a focus in dealing with the crosscultural situations in which they will find themselves.

4. Small groups need to be given the authority and power to do what they need to do in ministry and mission. Small group empowerment for ministry and mission means that the clergy needs to give away the responsibility and privilege of ministry to groups, train them to do the ministry, support them to do the ministry, and expect them to do the ministry. This means that professional staff needs to learn to work well with today's volunteer who has less time to work, wants more freedom to act, wants carefully defined ministry job descriptions, and wants the support systems to be successful at the jobs. If groups are going to take responsibility for ministry and mission, they need to be trained, encouraged, supported and affirmed for their ministry ventures. Such a development of the ministry of the laity demands a new role for clergy which is typically not taught or modeled in the seminary context. Clergy may need to go back to school for

continuing education which helps them support small group ministry and mission.

5. The frequency and intensity of small group meeting schedules impacts their ability to enter into the depth of ministry demands. Groups which meet once a month will not have the same team energy needed for ministry and mission as a group who meets once a week or more for intense periods of prayer and preparation. Long-term mission groups may do well with the once a month sustenance and support meeting, but groups just beginning their ministry or mission venture need more frequent and more intense meetings to get off the ground. Such groups are like launching a mission rocket. Huge amounts of group energy are needed at the beginning to get the mission going, but once it's launched, the ongoing power needed to keep it going is not as great. Give ministry and mission teams a lot of up-front attention, training, support, encouragement and affirmation.

23
SMALL GROUP INTEGRITY AND DESTINY

Let us draw near to God. . . . Let us hold unswervingly to the hope we profess, for he who promised is faithful. And let us consider how we may spur one another on toward love and good deeds. Let us not give up meeting together, as some as in the habit of doing, but let us encourage one another—and all the more as you see the Day approaching. (Heb 10:22-25)

The gathering together of a small group in the name of Christ focuses on a target point into an eternal future. This awareness of a destiny of an eternal life together empowers the group to a current lifestyle of "love and good deeds."

Hope Becomes a Reality in Meeting Together
Where there is no intimacy with God among humanity there is no eternal hope. Temporal hope flourishes in the presence of other persons who love and care for one another. Temporal hope is transcended by eternal hope amidst a group who experiences the love of God alongside the mutual love of members.

James Loder of Princeton Seminary has explored the experience of the "void" as preparatory to the experience of the "Holy." He has interpreted Sartre's experience of the "absence" and observed the human determination to "self-fulfill" this "void" through "self achievement." As Loder has said, this "third dimension" of human life can only be met by "another reality," the "Holy." A small group's sense of the "Holy" in the midst of the "void" can be an experience of the *com-*

munity of a small group as well as an experience of the community of the Spirit in *solitude*. In both contexts, human loneliness hungers to venture out of the void and into the Holy. It is in the midst of this *void* that the *Holy One* meets us as community and gives us real *hope*. As Loder has said, "the Holy *in* us cries out for the manifestation of the Holy *beyond* us."[1] When we encounter another beyond us, we find validation, meaning and completion for who we are as human beings. We experience this validation or hope as we participate in the gift of community with God and with others.

This reality of loving action and hope is made possible in a context where people give and receive love from the Holy One and one another. The mutual divine and human exchange of love and encouragement brings hope. In the absence of intimacy and community, there is a sense of abandonment and alienation, or as Loder has said, "the presence of the absence."[2] This confrontation with absence and void can drive the isolated individual or group into a state of despair and hopelessness. In such despair the hunger for a community of like beings grows ravenous. Hope is the experience that another has come to free us and give us meaning.

Jacques Ellul has argued that the church shows signs of feeling abandoned in its manifestation of mediocrity, institutionalism, dryness or conformity. When the vitality of vibrant and passionate relationships are drained from the institution because there is no real face-to-face meeting together, when the people of God are more focused on the *doing* of the work rather than their *being* in relationship, human beings, both individually and corporately will tend to feel abandoned by one another and by God. Ellul has argued this is the result of living in an increasingly "closed" world where the church is imprisoned by the confining or empty relationships of the culture. The contemporary question is whether the church has the courage to practice the alternative real worldview of apostolic community in such circumstances. There seems to be a connection between the world-wide restoration of small Christian communities and hopeful signs of the church regaining its passion, life, intimacy and community with God. Hope and community are interrelated. There is no hope where there is no sense and experience of the *presence* and *love* of the *Holy Other*.[3]

Hope Is Experienced in Small Group Suffering and Pain

Hope and community are deeply interrelated through the travail of suffering. Douglas John Hall has declared it is in the community's participation in the sufferings of Christ that real hope blossoms.[4] In the midst of anxiety and dissonance they are able to see the world as it really is and see Christ's forgiveness and healing with more clarity. The clearer view of the meaning of the cross releases the small group community to experience a more complete hope. The way to new life together is through accepting suffering and death as a reality of community. This is the nature of hope. Hope is the courage to face death as an act of service in intimacy with another. Hope is the realization that God's love is greater than death. And the community is the space where we come to know God as the loving Other who exists beyond the darkness and is there to receive us. Hope is that God will include us in an eternally loving community where we have a purpose and a place.

The practice and experience of love in the midst of pain releases hope. Small groups are places where Christians can practice the disciplines of relationship through hard times. It is as two or more Christians gather together and open themselves to participate in one another's joy and pain that they can experience the healing and hope of Christ. The small group which opens itself to listening and responding to the pain of its members discovers, in brief glimpses, what heaven is like. The small group who learns to suffer in grace and joy may be one of the brightest lights and hopes for human culture which tends to live in the dark side.

As Douglas Hall has said, "the presence in (the world) of a community which, without having to, enters into solidarity with its suffering may be a better sign of hope than are the schemes of those who promise paradise." Even a small Christian community can bring light to great places of darkness. In pain and in sharing the suffering of Jesus, the small group brings hope to itself and to many who watch and are enlightened from a distance.[5]

The Hopelessness of Not Meeting Together

Consistent with the concern of the letter to the Hebrew ecclesia, Christians who give up meeting together give up their ability and opportunity to "encourage" and "spur one another on toward love and good deeds." This mutual *encouragement* and *spurring* only happens in face-to-face encounters of living spirits. This "encouraging" (exhorting) and "spurring" (inciting) process is only possible in the continuation of "meeting together" and "drawing near to God" (Heb 10:24-25). It can only happen when the ecclesia meets together in spite of difficult and painful times.

In Hebrews 10 the call to continued "meeting together" is immediately followed by an exhortation:

Remember those earlier days after you had received the light, when you stood your ground in a great contest in the face of suffering. Sometimes you were publicly exposed to insult and persecution; at other times you stood side by side with those who were so treated. You sympathized with those in prison and joyfully accepted the confiscation of your property because you knew that you yourselves had better and lasting possessions.

You need to persevere. (Heb 10:32-34, 36)

The ceasing of meeting together in small house groups would undermine the ability of the saints to help one another through the terrors of persecution and pain. Those who do not meet together have no group of friends and family in Christ to spur, to encourage, and to help them keep going when there are no other visible signs hope. The meeting together in the group may be the only visible hope during the darkest moments. This is what was said of Bonhoeffer in the face of death:

Bonhoeffer always seemed to me to spread an atmosphere of happiness and joy over the least incident and profound gratitude for the mere fact he was alive. . . . He was one of the very few persons I have ever met for whom God was real and always near. . . . He found just the right words to express the spirit of our imprisonment, the thoughts and resolutions it had brought us.[6]

Bonhoeffer had found the presence of the Holy in the midst of the void and the joy of living in the community of the Spirit even in prison and the face of eminent death. He simply found joy in being with another human being.

Hope can be felt in an exchange of persons in trouble. It is in the transaction of reflections, conversations and feelings of persons together who look to an eternal community even in the predicament of life. One person alone is unable to hear the verbal affirmation or feel the physical warmth of another. Hope emerges as the small group practices the one-anothering disciplines of Christian faith. For in the practice of the community disciplines space is created to remember God's gracious past and affirm God's promised future.

In *Covenant to Care* Louis Evans presented five points of mutual accountability to be practiced in a small covenant group which can bring hope to a person in the predicament of life: identification of the bondage, recognition of the causes, alternatives for a solution, choice of the best solution, and development and implementation of a plan to deal with the bondage. The small group can act as participant alongside the hurting person to work this process and hold them accountable for change.[7] These transactions can only happen when the group is gathered, when persons are in face-to-face speaking and hearing with one another. The group's faith substitutes for the troubled individual's lack of faith and provides them a way of hope in their mess.

As Ernst Becker has argued in *The Denial of Death*, death is "the worm at the core" of everyone's existence and relationships. It is ultimately how the reality of death is faced that sustains real hope (eternal) or pseudo (short-lived) hope. Absence also is a kind of death. For instance, Becker pointed out that children are terrorized when they come to recognize the reality of the absence of parents. The loss of an important or significant other contributes to hopelessness. Dealing with such a loss in the presence of other significant family and friends enables one to share the burden of the emotional pain and terror of the loss.[8] If there is no coming together, there is no possible human exchange for hope. There is only murky confrontation with the absence or loss. One is left alone in the darkness.

However, this is not to say there is absolutely no hope if there is no human meeting. Persons in isolation or solitary confinement have access to the living God through their Great High Priest Jesus. But the Spirit of Jesus is most often mediated through the ecclesia, through the gathering together. Hope is the fruit of real relationships with God and God's people. It is only a very mature, unusual and empowered faith which can be sustained without the regular presence of human encounter, dialogue and affirmation (Heb 10:21-22). In such cases God has usually given the individual an extraordinary sense of divine presence and comfort. Even in such an ecstatic moment, it is the sense of grace in divine community which sustains the lonely one.

God's faithfulness to the small groups of the past is a real basis for hope. Hope is foundationally formed in personal relationship to God, through Jesus' resurrected and eternal humanity. As Hebrews urges, the ecclesia are called to "fix [their] thoughts on Jesus" (Heb 3:1), to "encourage one another" (Heb 3:13), to "hold firmly to the faith we profess. For we do not have a high priest who is unable to sympathize with our weaknesses . . . but . . . one who has been tempted in every way, just as we are—yet was without sin. Let us then approach the throne of grace so that we may receive mercy and find grace in our time of need" (Heb 4:14-16).

It is in the context of this intimacy with God, through the life and eternal being of Jesus, which ultimately enables small groups to have hope. It is in the mutual experience of the group that God keeps promises and demonstrates love which sustains them with hope in the present. It is their mutual "remembering (anamnesis) of those earlier days" that gives them hope in their predicament of "today" (Heb 10:32). If God has helped them in the past, they need to remind one another that God will help them again in the present and again in the future.

Hope Is Demonstrated Through the Group's Mutual Encouragement

The fact that there are others gathered with me in the group is a statement of hope. The initial sense of a present God has called the group together to celebrate. In the celebration of God's presence, there is also a celebration of one another's presence. As Genesis 1-2 states, it is *not good* to be alone, but it is *very good* to be together (Gen 1:31 and 2:18). In being together we receive the hope of one another's presence and the haunting sense there is "Another" who is also there.

Donald Joy has suggested hope has a sexual dimension as we desire human community. Joy suggests that for a man to be in the presence of a woman is somehow more completing and hopeful than for a man to be in the presence of another man. At the same time, this does not negate the hope in the gathering of men with men and women with women. Jesus did not say where there are "two or three men and women gathered," at least one man with one woman, there he is present. However, there is a continuing mystery of the desirability for male and female to be in ecclesia together.[9] For in the gathering of men and women together there is a reflection of the full nature of God and a fulfillment of the reconciling work of Jesus Christ. If men and women can dwell together in equity, reciprocity and responsibility, there is an intrinsic hope made visible on earth that diversity can live in community and that God's very nature says "Amen" to this. Small groups who nurture the koinonia of men and women together are signs of hope in an alienated world.

If men and women are together, it is an affirmation that God has created and empowered us to be together. We are filled with hope because we feel and experience the betterment of being together. In such an affirmation of hopeful gathering, there is a hint that *despair* may be the result of persons who sense they should be *together* but realize how *separated* they really are. Despairing persons have usually lost their sense of being loved or valued by another. We may become forlorn when we see how painful it is to be together. Or we may grow hopeless when we see alienated persons trying to get together without success. We can only become hopeful when we see how God's grace can reconcile divorced persons.

The experience of being together in face-to-face relationships is intensified and clarified in the invisible presence of God. Quoting Kierkegaard, John MacQuarrie has elaborated that human love is always an interconnection between God and humanity: "The love relationship is a triangular relationship of the lover, the beloved and love—but love is God."[10] The visible demonstration of love is the visible statement of hope, but both reflect the invisible presence of God who loves and gives hope to the small group. The visible hope is in seeing the physical presence of two or more persons meeting and sharing life together. The visible gathering is a reflection of the invisible divine community of the Son and the Father in the Spirit. The Father's affirmation of Jesus, "This is my Son, whom I love; with him I am well pleased" (Mt 17:5), was declared in the presence of three disciples. The small group can sense the encouraging words of God toward them as they look to Jesus with Abba as the center of their hope.

The Small Group Is Enactment and Expectation of the "Day"
Hope is the response of a small group coming to the realization that their life together now is an enactment and anticipation of eternal life with Jesus Christ. If the group discovers how good life together can be, here and now, in the penultimate realm, then they can glimpse how much more glorious will life be, then and there in the heavenly realm. As the apostle Paul said to the Roman ecclesia in troubled times, "We rejoice in the hope of the glory of God. Not only so, but we also rejoice in our sufferings, because we know that suffering produces perseverance, perseverance [produces] character, and character [produces] hope. And hope does not disappoint us" (Rom 5:2-5). Hope is the product of a community of persons who have lived together with God through difficult times and have experienced firsthand that God is faithful to get them through the pain to a more wonderful time. For some, the more wonderful time is briefly given on earth, but for all, the more wonderful place is community in heaven.

"Hope . . . implies trust in the future," MacQuarrie asserted. Hope is the result of a trust relationship with people and God. Because we find God has been faithful in the past, we are more apt to believe God will be faithful in the future.[11] The same is true of human community. If the small group has been trustworthy in the past, the group is more inclined to have hope together in their mutual trust for the future. If the gathered group develops mutual trust in Christ, that same trust is projected into the future of their mutuality in Christ. Their hope is founded on the realization that if they have the gift of divine community now, how much more probable it is they will have even better community in the future. Such trust (faith) can only be attained through the sharing of the truth: feelings, values, pain, joy, anger or anxiety through conflict, confrontation, confession, forgiveness and perseverance.

In his bestselling book *Why Am I Afraid to Tell You Who I Am?* John Powell has listed five levels of communication and has suggested that interpersonal trust is only developed when a group is willing to share the whole spectrum of their values, hopes and fears. The way for a small group to build hope is through the freedom of its members to share honestly about their most painful concerns.[12] Hope is a birthing process of a small group's experience of working through conflict, frustration and separation until restoration and redemption are gained. Continuing to persevere to meet together when group relationships are rocky establishes among the group a toughness to persevere into the higher ground of trust and hope. This toughening sustains the group through another cycle of hard times and opens them to more growth in the future.

Scott Peck has articulated four stages of building community: *pseudocommunity, chaos, emptiness* and *community.* He has argued that unless a group can work through the superficialities of clichéd relationships, deal with real pain and conflict and go through a period of feeling loss, they will not come to a place of real community and of real hope. Similar descriptions of stages of small group life can be found in many books about group process. The most frequently used terms to define these trust-building stages are *forming, storming, norming, performing* and *reforming* (they may appear in different order according to the bias of the theory being communicated).[13] In any case, the sustaining of hope to help the small group go through the painful times together is a cyclical process that can spiral a group to reach new levels of relational and spiritual maturity. As the group experiences more and greater glimpses of the glories of heaven on earth, they build together an anticipation of what life will finally be in the final "Day" of Christ's completed rule.

The positive growth of the group and the increasing experience of hope blossoms as the group perseveres and continues to grow over long periods of life together. Like a long-term healthy marriage, the small group will go through cyclical periods of *conflict* and *differentiation*. If the group has the desire, skill and perseverance to work through these times of recognizing differences (Peck's *emptiness* phase), they will break through into a new level of trust and community, and a new level of hope. As the long-term group continues to work through these periods of conflict and change over the months and years, their personal and corporate maturity will grow with each new cycle of conflict, loss, reclamation, trust and hope.

However, these periods of difference, pain, conflict and change are threatening to the life of the small group. Marriages, friendships, small groups, congregations and organizations all go through cycles of community and sometimes divide or fragment in the midst of such dissonance and transition. In order to work through the stress and arrive at resolution, healing and hope on the other side (as suggested in James 5:16), there are basic Christian disciplines for the group to practice: confession, forgiveness, prayer and repentance.

Integrity of the Group's Balance Between Task and Relationship

To the angel of the church in Ephesus . . . I know your deeds, your hard work and your perseverance. . . . You have persevered and have endured hardships for my name, and have not grown weary.

Yet I hold this against you: You have forsaken your first love. (Rev 2:1-4)

The hard work, good deeds and endured hardships of an ecclesia are not sufficient to keep its integrity of life together. Suffering and hard work are not the essential bonding ingredients for a balanced Christian group. The Christian small group is essentially defined by the Spirit who is God's loving relationship with

humanity through the person of Jesus Christ. The group is only Christian ecclesia if it meets in the presence and nature of Jesus who looked to God as Abba.
Their relationship to God through Jesus defines the life and work of every Christian small group. All its work and endurance is of value only as it has been
immersed in the love of a communal life with Christ. The ministry of the group
is the continuing ministry of Jesus, who loved the world to the extent of death
on a cross.

It was Bonhoeffer's strong belief that the gathering of God's people was "held
together solely in Jesus Christ. . . . Between the death of Christ and the 'Last
Day' it is only by a gracious anticipation of the last things that Christians are
privileged to live in visible fellowship with other Christians. It is by the grace
of God that [an ecclesia] is permitted to gather visibly in this world and share
God's Word and Sacrament."[14] God is both the source and gatherer of the
community. The community is only made visible through the death and resurrection of Jesus.

Therefore, the small group must be continually recalled and re-beckoned to
embrace its "first love." The *first love* is the love of the Spirit who is the love of
Jesus for the Father (Abba), and the love of Abba for humanity. Any other
substitute relationship, value system, focused interest or person which draws
away the group's primary attention is idolatry. Groups who work, decide, manage, act or risk without the balancing center of love in Christ miss the nature
of life together. Integrity is only maintained when the group's work flows out
of its intimacy with Christ. As Paul said, "If I give away all my possessions . . .
but do not have love, I gain nothing" (1 Cor 13:3 NRSV).

The Small Group Is a Potential Idol
When the group becomes too self-contained, too self-reliant, too self-possessed
or too self-determining, it has become its own *idol*. The life of a small group is
not an end to itself. Its life is immersed in the life of Jesus who loves and empowers the group to love and give. Meeting and giving for other reasons is
idolatry, a forsaking of the first love. The group can become an *idol* when a leader
takes the place of Jesus, when the study of the Bible takes the place of Jesus, when
the security of being together takes the place of Jesus, when the social ministry
takes the place of Jesus, or when evangelism takes the place of Jesus. Instead, all
things and actions of the group need to find their center, source, meaning and
being in Christ.

The body of Christ was given so the ecclesia could become his body. If the
group belongs to anyone or anything else, it is not Christ's body, it is a secondary
love and an idol. The passion and intimacy of the group's first love with God in

Christ is maintained and intensified as the group practices receiving the love of Abba and, as the body of Christ, returns the love of Jesus to Abba.

The small group lives in the community of groups. Christian small groups should not stand alone, disconnected from other small or larger groups. The self-secure, self-standing, self-contained or exclusive small group is an idol. Ecclesia were called to be in relationship with one another even as they were in relationship with Abba God. Every Christian small group should be a participant in a network of groups which are interdependent with Abba God and one another through the power of Christ's Spirit. The one-anothering of members within the group is a parallel paradigm to the one-anothering that should exist between groups. In the same way that God is the gatherer of persons into ecclesia, God is also the gatherer of ecclesia into families and networks. If a group avoids the interdependent disciplines of community with other groups, it is likely to become its own idol.

Robert Banks has said that Paul's practices of ecclesia provide an ongoing critique of historical ecclesiologies which trace their roots and practices back to Peter, Paul and the apostles. Banks says:

[Paul's] understanding of what constitutes community raises serious questions both for established ecclesiastical structures which claim a historical link with Paul and the counter culture groups which ardently promise 'community' to those who join them. The former have excluded many of Paul's basic insights into the nature of community and frozen others into a rigid form that prevents their constructive exercise.

Isolated small groups which live outside of mutuality, interdependence and accountability with other groups have little to help them keep their first love. No one small group can stand alone before God, just as no one person can stand alone before God. The community of groups, the macro ecclesia, is a necessary continuity and support for the growing body of Christ. Mutual accountability of groups for one another helps individual groups from becoming idols unto themselves.

The Small Group Ministry Structure as Potential Idol

Just as the individual *micro* group life can take upon itself an idolatrous character, so the network or *macro* system of small groups together can become an *idol* of ministry. This is one reason that ecclesia in both micro and macro forms must continually look to their first love for transformation and reformation. If that first love is lost from sight, the ecclesia, in both micro and macro forms, tend to develop a kind of structural inflexibility and slide into a narcissistic idolatry. They can fall in love with their own polity and lust after their own bureaucracy.[15] Small group network systems are only temporary earthly frameworks to allow the community of God to form on earth.

Edward Schillebeeckx has pointed out, "Adaptations of a religion to its cultural environment which are often unavoidable in cultural terms are often given a subsequent religious legitimation. Contingent legacies are then given an ideological substructure."[16] The church tends to take on the form of the popular cultural structures of its day. In doing so it is often left trying to preserve the structure after the death of its heart and community. The skeleton continues, but the flesh and blood of the koinonia and agape are deteriorated. The body may continue to function on artificial support systems, but it's brain dead. Through an increasing formality, rigidity and hardening structure, the ecclesia in both micro and macro forms may still be able to continue the practice of their "deeds, hard work, perseverance and endured hardship" (Rev 2:2), but the heart of their community, their intimacy with God and one another, has evaporated. The church invests less and less into spirituality and community with God and more and more into orders, laws, and processes of political governance. The growing loss of mutual trust creates a vacuum for organizational security.

Structures, organizations and institutions have an amazing self-sustaining power. Like the institution of marriage, the functionality of the outward actions and liturgy of daily living in organizations can go on indefinitely after the intimacy is long dead. The group's or network's relationships and persons become emotionally and spiritually dead. This is the frightening cyclical reality for the institutional church. It can wonderfully function as an independent organization even though God is not present. The unknowing and undiscerning observer will not know the difference. It is not just the good work, perseverance or endurance that keeps the ecclesia alive, but the passion, intimacy and community with Jesus and Abba in their midst. Every individual small group is as susceptible to this hollow form as is any larger religious organization. Idolatry haunts every community as soon as it's organized.

So also the small group ministry program can continue to function structurally long after its intimate relation with and purpose in Christ has been lost. The institutional church structure, like the political and corporate structures of society can lose its inner identity, character, community and purpose, becoming a "form of godliness, but denying [the personal] power" (2 Tim 3:5).

A seduction for the ecclesia in these last days has always been the temptation to take upon itself the style and character of evil cultural systems and leave the real power of Christ's love behind. Such cultural submission is death for a network or group. They are to "have nothing to do with" such values (2 Tim 3:5). The micro and macro ecclesia do not have to be imprisoned by limited cultural norms and forms. Christ died to rescue the ecclesia from the values of the present evil systems (Gal 1:4). The micro and macro structures of ecclesia do not have to be conformed to the mechanical and idolatrous structures of the culture, but can be transformed through a new way of thinking (Rom 12:2) about the nature of humanity, a way of thinking formed through Jesus' vulnerable relationship with Abba and modeled among the Twelve. The Spirit must create and enliven the form and structure of micro ecclesia and the networks and programs of macro ecclesia to be the body of Christ scattered wherever two or three or more gather together. And the Spirit is always re-creating and reforming.

In reflecting on the meaning of Galatians 1:4 and Romans 12:2, Gerhard Loh-fink has said:

> The baptized person is rescued from the world to the realm of Christ's rule (ecclesia). The world . . . is more than just the summation of many individuals who do evil. It is simultaneously the potency of evil which has been deposited in social structures by the sins of many and which has perverted the world into the realm of the power of evil. The church (ecclesia) . . . needs no longer live in the bondage of evil according to the false structures of pagan society. . . . This new creation grasps not only the spirit of the church (ecclesia), but also its body, its form . . . its structures. . . . The form and the spirit of the churches (ecclesia) must not be adapted to the form and spirit of the rest of society.[17]

The nature and community of Jesus with Abba God is the Spirit which calls and forms (structures) the ecclesia. When the structure of ecclesia is more a determination of the culture than the Spirit, it is idolatrous and deadly. The key principle of formation of ecclesia is first love (agape): living in the agape of God, the agape of self, and the agape of one another.

The Primary Character and Purpose of Small Group Ministry

Today, Jesus continues to call the ecclesia together to participate with him in the power of the Spirit who is the power for building community. The greatest commandment and the greatest parameter of covenant for ecclesia is "Love the Lord your God with all your heart and with all your soul and with all your mind. . . . Love your neighbor as yourself" (Mt 22:37-39). Louis Evans Jr. has said, "God's love is the basis of (small) covenant groups."[18]

It is no biblical accident that Jesus' affirmation of Leviticus 19:18 was articulated in the presence of the religious structuralists and sacred systems engineers, the Sadducees and Pharisees. They were for Jesus the fundamentalists of polity and religious structure. It was these religious and political formalists and structuralists who crucified Jesus and persecuted the ecclesia (Mt 22:37-40).

Preoccupation with agendas, skills, techniques, strategies, structures, curricula, evaluations or observations of small group dynamics, not centered in the covenant of Jesus' love, is futile. As the Revelation of John says, God stands in judgment, over against the group, "holding this against the group," not that these good works are bad, but that these important deeds and values are meaningless unless Christ's relationship with Abba is at the core of the community, forming their life together in the small group or small group ministry. It is this common and shared life of Christ with Abba God in ecclesia that is the foundation of all small group life and brings meaning and fulfillment to all the groups' activity and ministry. Love is both the integrity and destiny of each small group. But it must be the love (agape) of Abba and Son.

As Mary Wolff-Solin has stressed, "In an apostolic community (ecclesia), the primary relationship of the religious is considered to be with God . . . however crucially important community and ministry may be."[19] Catholic communities have continually affirmed their center and identity in Christ even though they practice the rules of different saints, whether it be Benedict, Francis or Dominique. It is this balancing tension on the side of the person of Christ as presence in the midst of the group, over against the practices of other personal and group disciplines, that keeps communities vibrant and transforming. The common presence of Christ and the common meal (mass) are still the center and source of the community discipline.

The First and Last Love of the Small Group

As the final words of Scripture affirm from the mouth of Jesus Christ, "I am the Alpha and the Omega, the First and the Last, the Beginning and the End" (Rev 22:12-21). For every gathered group, Jesus is both their ongoing integrity and their final destiny. Jesus Christ is the preeminent person and presence in the midst of his ecclesia, his bride. He is the bright Morning Star that beckons the ecclesia to participate in an eternal new day. He invites small groups to join in his holy city, the eternal community, of which the ecclesia is a penultimate expression of the ultimate heavenly community sharing in the intimacy and glory of Jesus' love of Abba God. The thirsty small group can "come and take the free gift of the water of life" out of the source (headwaters) of Christ, and share in the "tree of life" which is a partaking of the fruit of life together. To the awaiting ecclesia and the greater networks of ecclesia, the Lord Jesus says, "I am coming soon." Stay centered in the presence, person and relationship of Jesus Christ. Do not give up the passion of first love.

And in response to God's beckoning of the small group to share in the life of Jesus Christ, the ecclesia in response, offers its one great confessional hymn and prayer of affirmation, "Amen. Come Lord Jesus!" It is in the small group gatherings that "the grace of the Lord Jesus [will] be with all the saints" (Rev 22:21 NRSV).

■ SMALL GROUP MINISTRY IMPLICATIONS

1. If Jesus is both the integrity and destiny of the small group, then each small group must work at learning the identity and way of Jesus, personally and biblically. Small groups should look at the Gospels through the special lenses of small group life. They should also commit to asking what the original disciples asked of Jesus, "Lord, teach us to pray." Learning the pattern of Jesus' group life and the pattern of Jesus' prayer life in the Gospels is an excellent foundation and consistent discipline for small groups to practice to maintain their integrity and destiny.

2. Small groups need to measure their life together by degrees of hopefulness. They should be asking themselves the question, "How does this group provide us a sense of hopefulness, both in the short-term sense and the eternal sense?" Such a pattern of growing hopefulness develops over a longer period of life together. Sustained and growing hope emerges from a deep sense of connectedness to Christ and to one another. Groups need to take time to share with one another about how hopeful they are about life and about how their group has helped them develop more hope. If group members get in touch with a sense of losing hope while being in the group, the group has failed to provide an adequate access to Christ and may need to make some changes as to how they relate to one another. Groups may approach this discussion by responding to the question, "What gives me a sense of hope?" or "What things, persons or events in my life have given me a sense of hope?"

3. Small groups are the key places to help people face their pain and fear. Everyone suffers, but many Americans have no place to speak of their sense of hurt or pain. Small groups need to be places where it is safe to share about suffering. Not that suffering is the only thing small groups should discuss. Sharing of pain should always lead into prayer and the group's intentional seeking of God for meaning in the midst of the pain. The group's responsibility is not so much to find solutions to eliminate the pain, but to find reasons and meaning for the pain. Groups need to develop a theology of community pain which validates the trauma each member feels and sustains, but also calls each person to seek God in the midst of their pain to discover what God is saying to them as a group and as individuals. No matter what, pain is not something to be denied, avoided or trivialized. The group can only get to the starry space of hope by going through the black hole of pain. However, some groups have members who love

to stew in their pain. When an individual uses a group to keep talking about his or her pain without finding meaning or changing, then the group is being used as a whipping post for the individual's hurt. The group must hold that person accountable "to move on" and find healing in Christ. Some groups do not want to hold such individuals accountable or confront them with their stuckness. If the group does not confront the advocating person, the group will tire of the broken record and fall apart. Groups must find the balance between hearing the pain and being numbed by the pain. Anesthetized groups have little sense of hope.

4. Groups who know how to help members find meaning and healing through pain become good evangelists in a world full of pain. The world is hungry to find a community of caring persons who can pronounce the forgiveness and healing of Christ to their pain. The group who carries such wounded persons to Christ and sees them made whole becomes a very attractive family to the outside world. Healthy and hopeful groups are naturally evangelistic. Such groups need to sense how much pain they can bear in Christ before it is an overload. Every group has its limit to how much pain it can bear in the name of Christ. The group must have touch with an abundance of hope in order to deal with limited pain. If the pain overcomes the hope, the group has taken on too much or they have forgotten their source of healing is in Christ and not in them.

5. There are some small groups who think they can preserve their vitality of life even though they do not meet together. A life together without being together is simply not possible. Small groups must have a regular and disciplined schedule of meeting together. Groups who do not meet become hopeless. People with busy schedules must find time and space to meet together. This is the powerful admonition of Hebrews: "do not neglect meeting together." Hope comes through the meeting with Christ in the faces of people who know Christ. American Christians who do not set aside time to meet with other Christians will never experience the fullness of hope life in Christ can provide. To be in Christ is to be in an active community of face-to-face relationships. This must be preached, taught and modeled by key leadership. Sometimes leaders are the most "cut-off" from the community because they don't take the time to be in a small group, or they feel being in such a group makes them too vulnerable to be esteemed as a strong leader. Such an attitude is still taught in some seminaries and by significant pastoral mentors. This is not good. We who are in leadership must embrace the value of being "in Christ" as being in a small group with a few other Christians. Lord help us if we fail at this foundational understanding of and commitment to faith in Christ.

6. It may be helpful for a small group to think of themselves as an outpost or beachhead or glimpse of heaven. Some groups have so little sense of their eternal

purpose and potential in Christ that they never associate themselves as a fore-taste of heaven on earth. Such a view may give groups a clearer sense of purpose. It may also wake up a few groups who are more like hell on earth. If small groups become little hells for their members, but they never stop to think or talk about it, small groups become the reverse of what Christ intended. Instead of persons looking forward to being in groups which bring them close to heaven, they avoid groups like the plague, fearing they will be caught in hells on earth. We must have the freedom to confront such hells and see them transformed into families of heaven. Sometimes if members of the group have grown up in hellish families, they fear being in groups which are also hellish. Sometimes such persons bring their hellish family systems along with them and try to recreate their little hells in the new group. The group must have the courage to see this and say no to such perpetration. The group must have the freedom and power to discern the difference between a hellish group and heavenly group.

24

THE CHURCH
AS SMALL GROUP
NETWORK

Those who accepted his [Peter's] message were baptized, and about three thousand were added to their number that day. They devoted themselves to the apostles' teaching and to the [koinonia], to the breaking of bread and to prayer. . . . Every day they continued to meet together in the temple courts. They broke bread in their homes and ate together with glad and sincere hearts, praising God and enjoying the favor of all the people. And the Lord added to their number daily those who were being saved. (Acts 2:41-47)

According to James Dunn, the preferred translation of *koinōnia* is "community." The definition of *koinōnia* embodies themes of commonness, sharing, togetherness and unity in diversity. The first mention of koinonia in the New Testament is immediately after the event of Pentecost. Dunn has argued that the disciples of Jesus became "self-conscious" about their communal identity at the event of Pentecost. They "emerged" into their understanding of being the new "eschatological community of Israel," a continuity with the Twelve, who were a "symbol" of that eschatological community with Jesus. The experiences and lessons learned by the Twelve (and the one hundred twenty) as a small group became the key lessons in community for a whole network of ecclesia, and the prime model of ecclesia who have gathered throughout the ages.[1] They had full human community experiences with Jesus parallel to the experiences individual ecclesia and networks of ecclesia continued to have after Pentecost with the risen Lord. The experience of the Twelve as a real community has become the experience of every small group or network of small groups who come together "in the name of Jesus."

Building the Network

The group of twelve, among the other small groups gathered around Jesus, including the women and the family of Jesus (Acts 1:14), were the genesis of multiple groups who met in homes throughout the city of Jerusalem. Many other groups also met together in the temple courts. These diverse circles of disciples were an interconnected network through the Twelve and one hundred twenty. The ecclesia in Jerusalem after the day of Pentecost became a community of communities, interconnected and interdependent. This network of small group communities continued to expand to other villages, cities, nations and continents.

Their network spiritual center, while the apostles were alive, was the circle of those who had walked with the earthly Jesus and had lived in close relationship to him. They had visual memories and concrete feelings which could be traced back to their personal and historical relationships with Jesus. They could validate their experience of the Spirit with their personal experience of the earthly Jesus. They could provide hands-on direction to the growing network of ecclesia because they had personal and intimate images of the earthly Lord who had become the risen Lord. As the apostle John said to the networks of small ecclesia:

> That which was from the beginning, which we have heard, which we have seen with our eyes, which we have looked at and our hands have touched—this we proclaim concerning the Word of life. The life appeared; we have seen it and testify to it, and we proclaim to you the eternal life, which was with the Father and has appeared to us. We proclaim to you what we have seen and heard, so that you also may have fellowship [koinonia] with us. And our fellowship [koinonia] is with the Father and his Son, Jesus Christ. (1 Jn 1:1-3)

Jesus brought individuals together who had not been together. Jesus brought groups of people together who had not been together. Jesus brought households together who had no previous common life. This unique character of life in the Spirit of Jesus has continued to be demonstrable through the microcosms of small group gatherings and the macrocosm of small group networks.

As Robert Banks has described, these home gatherings "could have exceeded forty to forty-five people," "as few as ten," or "as many as one hundred. . . . The moderately well-to-do household could hold around thirty people comfortably. . . . The meetings of the 'whole church' were small enough for a relatively intimate fellowship to develop between members."[2] But it was how these ecclesia households were interconnected and interdependent with one another from village to village, street to street, city to city, section to section, that provided a connectional vehicle for the unlimited and spontaneous growth of the larger body of Christ. The foundation of small group ecclesia "wherever two or three are gathered" was the first miracle of the postresurrection establishment of the realm of God on earth. And the phenomenal expanded growth of the realm was miraculously powered through the interlocking and mutual support of interpersonal ecclesia who provided hospitality via the koinonia grapevine through persons by word-of-mouth communications wherever disciples of Jesus traveled. These scattered households provided living stepping stones of support along a precipitous way of exodus life in the midst of a universally hostile world.

The early development of ecclesia was not just one group at a time, but a sudden development of networks of small house groups gathered all over the city of Jerusalem. And it was not long before these networks of groups spread into greater Judea, Samaria and the rest of the known world. The early ecclesia were quickly guided into a city-wide networks of interconnected leadership, purpose, ministry and mission. Their central leadership was the twelve apostles and their decentralized leadership network may have been many teams of two or three from the one hundred twenty in the upper room. Their common source of life was the present Spirit and their personal memories of the resurrected Christ.

The urban context which gave the ecclesia birth was culturally diverse, especially during the celebration of Pentecost "when God-fearing Jews from every nation under heaven" heard the good news in their own language. The Holy Spirit of the divine community had come into the midst of a fairly homogeneous (they had a common language and geography) group of Galileans. It was the recognition of the miracle—that humble Galileans were speaking the sophisticated languages of peoples from diverse and far away places—"Parthians, Medes and Elamites; residents of Mesopotamia, Judea and Cappadocia, Pontus and Asia, Phrygia and Pamphylia, Egypt and the parts of Lybia near Cyrene; visitors from Rome (both Jews and converts to Judaism); Cretans and Arabs" (Acts 2:9-11)—that attracted so much attention.

The first powerful ministry of the Spirit among the ecclesia was to scatter the Word of God among all existing networks of peoples and languages and establish small base communities around common cultures and languages. The Spirit had established a core leadership community (the Galilean Twelve and the one hundred twenty) from which increasing networks of diverse cultures and languages could meet together. The individual ecclesia were the common language groups. The network of ecclesia based in the one hundred twenty was the unifying, bridging, reconciling and peacemaking interconnection of multiple homogeneous groups crossing dramatic boundaries of diversity. The gifts of diverse tongues were given by the Spirit to build diverse languaged groups and interconnect them together with a common leadership network and language—most of all, a common Lord.

This early tension between the network of different culture and language ecclesia and the common bond of the apostolic community is illustrated in Acts 6 in a disagreement between the Grecian Jews and those of the Aramaic-speaking community because the Grecian widows were being overlooked in the daily distribution of food. The choice of the "seven" to serve the household tables from "among" the individual ecclesia was an empowering move by the core apostolic ecclesia to provide fair representation for the diverse ecclesia. This "fair distribution" small group of seven Grecians was created to provide a common connection and mutual service to both Aramaic and Grecian ecclesia. They were the first small group network-based para-ecclesia ministry established to bring equity and common life between the growing multiplicity of diverse ecclesia. The networking of the common apostles' "ministry of the word and prayer" alongside the common diaconate ministry of food distribution gave the various ecclesia a visible common connection to mediate their increasing diversity of culture and economics. The new ecclesia network had real connections because of their shared spiritual resources and shared physical resources. This interwoven core ecclesia of Galilean apostles and Grecian deacons affirmed daily the common life of individual ecclesia in spite of their uncommon languages and cultures. This somewhat chaotic but carefully woven fabric of interdependent life through interlocking circles of apostles, deacons and disciples was founded in the basic affirmation of Jesus, "where two or three come together in my name, there am I with them" (Mt 18:20).

The ecclesia were tied together through interlocking networks of leadership circles who also shared their lives together. Every small group was interdependent with every other small group. No group was isolated from the larger network within the city. No city network was isolated from the larger network of cities and villages, and no national network was isolated from other national networks of ecclesia. The tremendous power of the interwoven gatherings, wherever two or more came together around Christ, empowered the rapidly expanding numbers of disciples to be in personal and intimate connection with wider and more complex networks of ecclesia all over the known world. All disciples were members of individual ecclesia and networks of ecclesia. All disciples were nurtured in body and spirit through the intimate and personal face-to-face care of interlocking groups.

A Caring Small Group Network

The international body of Christ was a complex mutuality of caring ecclesia in all cultures and places. And as the apostle Paul was to affirm, all the networks of ecclesia needed one another even across great physical and cultural barriers. In 2 Corinthians, Paul describes how the Macedonian ecclesia even in "their extreme poverty welled up in rich generosity" (2 Cor 8:2). "They [the ecclesia] urgently pleaded with us for the privilege of sharing [koinonia] in this service to the saints" (2 Cor 8:4). Paul's desire was that there might be "equality" among the ecclesia. While some were in poverty, others lived in abundance. The hunger in the face of some was met by compassion in the face of others. This long-distance network and mutuality of ecclesia was made possible by real persons (usually small group teams of twos and threes) who traveled between ecclesia to share the stories and life together of one small group with another. Paul's words to the Corinthian ecclesia clarify this mutual trust, confidence and interpersonal community:

> I thank God, who put into the heart of Titus the same concern I have for you. For Titus not only welcomed our appeal, but he is coming to you with much enthusiasm and on his own initiative. And we are sending along with him the brother who is praised by all the churches [ecclesia] for his service to the gospel. What is more, he was chosen by the [ecclesia] to accompany us as we carry the offering. . . . In addition, we are sending with them our brother who has often proved to us in many ways that he is zealous, and now even more so because of his great confidence in you. As for Titus, he is my partner [koinonos] and fellow worker among you; as for our brothers, they are representatives [apostles] of the churches [ecclesia] and an honor to Christ. (2 Cor 8:16-23)

While the earliest ecclesia networks were primarily Jews and Gentiles who had converted to Judaism, it was not long before unconverted Gentiles were also invited by the Spirit into the network. These "uncircumcised" ecclesia existed across a greater faith chasm and a greater gulf of cultural diversity than many Jewish ecclesia could understand or accept. Yet, they, also, gathered together to affirm "Jesus is Lord." These postpagan Gentile gatherings were also in households where persons were given open hospitality and invited into mutual face-to-face community as if they were family. As the ecclesia spread to less Jewish populations, their common bond was still the risen Jesus Christ and those who had walked on earth with Christ in personal community.

In Acts 10, the dramatic movement of the Spirit bringing Cornelius and Peter together was accomplished through home visits and hospitality, that is, through small group encounters. Cornelius "and all his family were devout and God-fearing" (Acts 10:2). His vision was of Peter "staying with Simon the tanner, whose house is by the sea" (Acts 10:6). Peter's vision was of a home meal prepared as an act of Gentile hospitality including "all kinds of four-footed animals, as well as reptiles of the earth and birds of the air" (Acts 10:12). Cornelius' servants met Peter at Simon's house. A small group of "three men" met him to take him to Cornelius' home, and Peter "invited the men into the house to be his guests" (Acts 10:23). Peter entered Cornelius's home. And Cornelius affirmed, "We are all here in the presence of God to listen to everything the Lord has commanded you to tell us" (Acts 10:33). So Peter affirmed his intimate connection to Jesus before all Cornelius' household by saying the resurrected Jesus "was not seen by all the people, but . . . by us who ate and drank with him after he rose from the dead" (Acts 10:41). This entire historical scene of dramatic reconciliation between Jew and Gentile is played out as an affirmation of permission for them to visit and dwell in each other's household gatherings. The entire dramatic movement was a series of small group encounters.

The implication of this Gentile mission was dramatically clear for all ecclesia: the call of the Spirit was for small groups of both circumcised and uncircumcised to be able to gather together as ecclesia in the same family household. The networks of the more homogeneous Jewish ecclesia were to become networks of heterogeneous Jewish and Gentile ecclesia. People from diverse cultures, religions, languages and politics were to be brought together by the Spirit to be in the same family of Christ, even in the same household ecclesia, even in the same small group.

The roots of the ministry of the apostle Paul were deeply planted in the lifeblood and growth of this expanding network of ecclesia. At Stephen's execution by stoning, "Saul began to destroy the church [ecclesia]. Going from house to house, he dragged off men and women and put them in prison. Those who had been scattered preached the word wherever they went" (Acts 8:3-4).

Just as Saul's persecution of the ecclesia "house to house" scattered the people to other cities and nations, so the Spirit called Paul to proclaim Christ both "publicly and from house to house" (Acts 20:20). Paul's ministry was to gather wherever there were two or more who were willing to listen and reason together, share their life, help them build their community and invite them to live with one another in the presence of the living Christ. He was able to nurture such strong and intimate community in the ecclesia that when he had to depart from Ephesus, "he knelt down with all of them and prayed. They all wept as they embraced him and kissed him. What grieved them most was his statement they would never see his face again" (Acts 20:36-37).

Paul had been so transformed by the community of the Spirit that he moved from being one who caused the ecclesia tears in persecution, to being the one for whom they shed tears in grief of his departure. For both the unconverted Saul and the transformed Paul, it was in his personal encounters with household ecclesia that the koinonia of Christ was shared and lives were transformed, both in death and in life. So it was this intimate apostolic friend of the scattered ecclesia who was able to say,

I thank my God every time I remember you. In all my prayers for all of you, I always pray with joy because of your partnership [koinonia] in the gospel from the first day until now. . . .

I want to know Christ and the power of his resurrection and the fellowship [koinonia] of sharing in his sufferings. (Phil 1:3-5; 3:10)

Paul discovered it was in the face of his Christian friends, gathered in face-to-face community, that he came to more fully see the face of the Lord Jesus Christ. And so he became the great apostolic midwife of small groups throughout the Roman world, interweaving these varied ecclesia into a great interdependent network of life together, of a transcendent and transnational partnership in Christ.

The Historical Eclipse of Small Group Community

It was not more than three hundred years after this dramatic appearance of the apostolic small group movement in salvation history that the form and character of the "church" suddenly changed. The ecclesia as small group community disappeared and the church as formal institutional structure appeared. This transition was a major paradigm shift of the very nature of God's presence on earth. In many ways this change eclipsed the full light of ecclesia as the presence of Christ among culture. The more formal structures which emerged in Christendom hid the ongoing reality of the value and importance of face-to-face community after the nature of God in Christ. The value of faces and persons and relationships were obscured by the higher valuing ascribed to structure, positional authority, lines of communication, layers of power, books of order and laws of the church. The light of community renewal still broke through the organizational darkness as sporadic inoculations against a deadly disease, but over the centuries it became more obvious that the church as formal institution was terminally ill and would someday die a painful death. As Leonard Sweet has so well articulated, "the church's understanding of connectionalism has changed from a 'connectional people' to a 'connectional structure.' "[3]

It is generally affirmed today by theologians, historians and ecclesiologists, that the church is at a dramatic "paradigm shift" in history. For the past 1,700 years, the realm of God has been strongly guided by this organizational and institutional mooring precipitated by the conversion of Constantine in A.D. 313. "Instead of the congregation being a small group that constituted the church in that place, the understanding of the congregation had been enlarged to include everything in the Empire. The congregation was the church; the church was the Empire."[4]

As mainline denominational church consultant Loren Mead has declared, this "paradigm of the age of Christendom" seems to be collapsing and a "third paradigm" for the realm of God has yet to appear.[5] Mead has suggested these "relics of the Christendom model" have "largely ceased to work."[6] But he can only hint at what the new paradigm of the realm of God on earth might look like. Could it be that the third paradigm of the church in God's plan of salvation history will resemble that which was established by Jesus with the apostles, except in a new time and pattern? Many signs point to such a rising from the dead of the church as small group networks. Manufacturer and educator Hallock B. Hoffman has said, "In a world of big aggregations of people and strong pressures to aggregate, the only hope is in finding small communities."[7] Leonard Sweet goes on to say,

> The future of the post-modern church lies chiefly in its small intimate bed and breakfast communities. . . . For humans to feel secure there must be an intimate and supportive small group. . . . Metanoized selves interact into small groups; metanoized groups interact into larger honeycombed communities; and the possibilities multiply exponentially.[8]

Venerable institutional systems around the world are dying or changing. Denominations, governments and corporations are among these "dinosaurs" threatened by extinction. The World Council of Churches has become a kind of denominational "Jurassic Park." The end of the industrial age and the launching of the information age seems to be exacerbating this "third wave"[9] structural change and "powershift."[10]

In John Naisbitt's articulation of these "megatrends," there may be significant implications for the church to reenter a more apostolic-looking period of community (koinonia)-focused formation. The movement from an "industrial society" to an "informational society" may mean that hard institutional structures may give way to soft and flexible connections of persons (small groups). The movement into "higher technology" may demand a parallel movement into "higher touch" contexts (small groups). The movement from "centralized" control systems to "decentralized" empowerment systems implies hands-on responsibility and training in small groups. The movement from "institutional help" to "self-help" suggests persons need to be able to help one another in small groups. The movement from "representative democracy" to "participative democracy" suggests republican governmental systems (like the Presbyterian Church USA) may collapse in the face of members' hunger for hands-on decision-making (small groups). The disintegration of "hierarchies" and the emergence of "networks" sounds like a historic turn from Christendom and a return to the interconnections of apostolic ecclesia (small groups). The restrictive boundaries of "either/or" opening into the more chaotic and freeing opportunities of "multiple options" suggests the need for many diverse forms and contexts of ministry (small groups).[11]

The common values of the church's international "global village" may only come together into ecumenical reality through the flexibility and adjustability of small group networks. As Sweet has also said,

> Networking is the real nature of Nature as God made it. Hierarchical or centralized control structures are not how things will get done in the future. Networking is indispensable to disseminating information in a post-modern world. Post-modern religious communities will be constructed, less as independent separate parts, and more as networking centers and social organisms constituting an indivisible whole in which relations to other people and things are constitutive of actual entities. . . . Part and whole, individual and community, are relationally constituted by each other through dramatic feedback systems and connected units, part dependent upon part, such as mass gatherings, face-to-face communities and small groups.[12]

For many years mainline denominations have tried to force this unity as an international institutional treaty through formed institutional covenants. However, this more formal, structural and institutional approach to fitting diverse organizational structures together is not organic unity. It is not based upon the foundation of God's nature and the hunger for human community. No matter what we try to do, ecumenical systems are not community in the face-to-face sense. In a postmodern and post-Christendom context institutional merging systems will fail because they are not a person-to-person covenantal network of real people in real places. Much of this is an attempt to unify and reorganize the dying systems of Christendom. Too often, "small groups today are committees through which the maintenance demands of the denomination sap much of the church's energy and vitality."[13] Only real communities of loving people in face-to-face relationships and mutual trust can be sustained as the true and eternal ecclesia of Jesus Christ.

Worldwide Networks

As it was in the age of the apostles, worldwide ecumenical unity may come about through loose-knit networks of small groups in various and diverse cultures and religious bases. This international fabric of small group networks is already greatly connected. Out of the ashes and decomposition of fallen and crumbling communism, and up from the fertile ground of participatory democratic soil are springing the grass roots of mutually empowered people in all places around the globe. With the growth of incredible telecommunications and accessibility of millions to immediate international travel, small groups in distant and diverse places can be in verbal touch with one another in a matter of seconds and personal touch with one another in a matter of hours. With these powerful shifts in communication and travel, the need for heavy industrial age institutional religious structures is all but eliminated. As Sweet has said, the "protrusion of the fundament" is the "inescapable power of small groups," that is, "the hardest and most chemically stable" social order of humanity where twelve atoms "can be packed around a central atom to touch it."[14] Jesus' life with the Twelve can be reimaged and reproduced wherever two or three gather around Jesus as Lord at the center.

The international small group leader Roberta Hestenes has told the story of visiting Nepal and China and discovering that hundreds, if not thousands, of Christian small groups have been meeting under cover of the oppressive Chinese government. From her home in Philadelphia, Pennsylvania, it was only a matter of hours for her to be in face-to-face conversations with such underground Christians in remote parts of the world.[15] Similar experiences have been related by other Christian leaders who travel into Muslim countries and other oppressive contexts. Many who visit from the Western church into the Eastern world context are finding that ecclesia are expanding in spite of little outside or professional support. Here is a missionary's observation about this "house church" phenomenon: "Is it not humbling to see what God has been doing in China these 30 years without a single foreign missionary? . . . Yet what an ironic spectacle to see so many foreign organizations jockeying for position and eager to go galloping in to tell mainline Christians how to do things."[16]

The current estimates are of 50 million Chinese in home ecclesia, "an indigenous movement that began around 1911."[17] Birkey also lists similar kinds of small group gatherings of Christians in India, North Korea, North Africa, Vietnam, Cambodia, Indonesia, South Korea, Japan and South America. John De Vries of the World Home Bible League has said there are thousands of small home Bible studies being started in India and Mexico using a very simple inductive method while teaching the illiterate to read.[18] A rural pastor of South Korean villages told a story that he ventured into the illiterate countryside of South Korea to teach the people how to read and study the Bible with an inductive method. The result after several years was the establishment of seven Christian villages where the people cared for one another, helped one another learn to read, studied and taught the Scripture, made ethical decisions based upon their mutual discussions as groups and helped surrounding villages get through hard times when weather, illness or famine rocked their land.[19]

Robert and Julia Banks in their book *The Home Church* have noted in reflection of Stanley Hauerwas that "the democratic society in which [Americans and English] live did not begin primarily from abstract doctrines, but from the living experience of the Puritan congregations as a fellowship of equals. . . . The most lasting contribution the church can make is . . . to be itself, a genuine community."[20] The Bankses go on to quote Art Gish, who said,

The creation of Christian community is the most radical political action one can ever experience, especially if it involves breaking down social barriers, proclaiming liberty to the captives and establishing justice. It is coming to the concrete reality of a new life that will not only show what is wrong with the old, but point so clearly to the new which is possible that the old can no longer command our loyalty and devotion. . . . Our responsibility to the world is always first to be the church: to embody what God wants to say to the whole world, to live and demonstrate what salvation means.[21]

The Roman Catholic Church with the Second Vatican Council has certainly moved to embrace small group renewal networks in various dioceses, opened themselves to charismatic renewal through small groups throughout America, and committed themselves to rediscover the meaning of church as ecclesia through the establishment of base communities in diverse sections of the Latin world. Many Catholics have returned to the radical definition and purpose of the church as ecclesia. As Edward Schillebeeckx has said,

In everyday Greek of this time *ekklesia* denoted the assembly of free citizens of a polis or city to hold elections . . . the first Christians only used the term of themselves. . . . To translate *ekklesia* "church" is therefore in one sense an anachronism . . . the New Testament word *ekklesia* does not just mean the actual assembly of Christians, but above all the Christian group itself, whether local or dispersed as many house communities all over the then world . . . the Christian groups were integrated into an already existing network of face-to-face relationships both internally . . . and externally.[22]

Popular Models of Small Group Ministry

The common threads of life together between each of these small group movements in the Roman Church are mutual personal support (koinonia), Bible study and prayer. Add to these three the frequently found components of worship and mission and these five common characteristics are simultaneous with most Protestant small group formats. There is more common ground in life together as lived through small home groups of Catholics and Protestants than there could ever be in the formal theology and structure of so many diverse ecclesiologies and denominations. As the Brazilian Franciscan priest Leonardo Boff has said in *Ecclesiogenesis: Base Communities Reinvent the Church*, basic church communities "signify a new ecclesiological experience, a renaissance of the very church." They are a "lay movement" engaged in rebirthing the church.

We are not dealing with an expansion of an existing ecclesiastical system, rotating on a sacramental, clerical axis, but with the emergence of another form of being church, rotating on the axis of the word and the laity. We may well anticipate from this movement, of which the universal church is becoming aware, a new type of institutional presence of Christianity in the world may now be coming into being.[23]

On the Protestant front, these new models of ecclesia are finding expression through the widely expanding "meta-church model" which found its genesis in the Full Gospel Church of Seoul, Korea and the leadership of Paul (David) Yonggi Cho. This 700,000 member church is composed of a well-connected and intricate network of 50,000 cell groups which meet in homes for worship, teaching, prayer, mutual care and evangelism. The New Hope Community Church of Portland, Oregon, has developed a similar cell-group model based upon the ministry philosophy of Robert Schuller: "find a need and fill it, find a hurt and heal it." The pastor, Dale Galloway, has said, "Cells are not another ministry of our church, they *are* the church."[24] The church strategist and consultant Carl George has declared this meta-church model to be a key structure for the future church. The term *meta* simply means "change." George is calling for the church, both nationally and internationally, to enter into a massive change of thinking about the nature and structure of the church, to create systems and networks of small group ecclesia which can adjust quickly to the needs of diverse people and fast-changing cultures. This "metropolis-wide convention of mice-sized groups . . . furry balls of life . . . home based clusters of believers . . . can become structured so that its most fundamental spiritual and emotional support centers never become obsolete, no matter how large it becomes overall."[25] When the structure is seen as an adjustable, flexible and adaptable network, the numbers of connections, points of connection, ways of connection, and kinds of groups connected are constantly free to change.

Roadblocks to Community

This reaffirmation of the small group as ecclesia and the redevelopment of the ecclesia as a network of interdependent cells of international connectivity is a clear return to our biblical roots: reflecting the very nature of God in community, that image of God reflected as humanity in community, the ministry of Jesus with small groups of men and women, and the intercultural and intergenerational house churches of the apostolic age. However, as Carl George has cautioned, this "model (new way of thinking) fundamentally conflicts with how most North American Christian leaders have been taught to think!"[26] Tex Sample has called for the mainline churches to get in touch with the diversity of U.S. lifestyles, saying, "A church effective in reaching diverse lifestyles will be a congregation of congregations."[27] This is another way of saying the church of the future must be a network of small and medium group communities who meet various cultures of people in their own languages and cultures of life.

The creation, empowerment and support of such heterogeneous and flexible face-to-face communities is not a significant part of most clergy education and preparation. Such preparation of church leadership for the development of small group networks is usually outside the educational parameters of seminaries. Leaders must experience the apprenticeships of real face-to-face communities in order to lead the more traditional church into such neo-apostolic ministry of diverse networks of ecclesia. Local churches which pursue various models of small group networking should invest in helping seminaries prepare men and women to experience such community-based ministry. Seminaries also need to teach foundational courses in the radical nature of biblical ecclesiology as to call future church leaders to think and plan for a church in a pluralistic world.

Lesslie Newbigin has asked the crucial question, "How is a Christian message to be credible if its meaning is not being illustrated in patterns of action which correspond to it?"[28] How is a postmodern, postindustrial and post-Christendom world to be able to embrace the gospel of Jesus Christ unless they can see the visible body of Christ in action, unless they can see Jesus wherever two or more Christians come together in face-to-face community? How can they embrace the full community life of God in Christ unless they can see, taste, touch, hear, feel and experience the loving and reconciling presence of Christ with Abba God in the midst of conflict, dissonance and alienation? There must be a personal connection between word and deed, proclamation and presence, orthodoxy and orthopraxy. As Newbigin has said,

> It was not the superiority of the Church's preaching which finally disarmed the Roman imperial power, but the faithfulness of its martyrs. . . . The central reality is neither word or act, but the total life of a community enabled by the Spirit to live in Christ. . . . The words explain the deeds, and the deeds validate the words. . . . Jesus . . . did not write a book but formed a community. This community has at its heart the remembering and rehearsing of his words and deeds. . . . It exists in him and for him. He is the center of its life.[29]

Newbigin has suggested there is only one way the people of God can make the gospel credible: "the only answer, the only hermeneutic of the gospel, is a congregation of men and women who believe it and live it . . . they have power to accomplish their purpose only as they are rooted in and lead back to a believing community."[30] These ecclesia of real people, in real places, dealing with real issues, and in touch with human reality, as Calvin said, are the "real" expression of Christ on earth as the community of God is in heaven. These ecclesia come in diverse form and style, through various cultural expressions and languages, meeting wherever people live and work and play, facing one another and the hardness of life. These ecclesia are the church. They are the personal and relational expression of God on earth where Jesus is their model leader. These small group congregations are where members "are trained, supported and nourished in . . . their priestly ministry in the world." They are the "frontier-groups" working in all human arenas of government, business, education and leisure. They are the "community of mutual responsibility."[31]

Western individualism and privatism are roadblocks to such real expressions of Christian community. As Newbigin has said,

> The deepest root of contemporary malaise of Western culture is an individualism which denies the fundamental reality of our human nature as given by God—namely that we grow into true humanity only in relationships of faithfulness and responsibility toward one another. The local congregation is called to be, and by the grace of God often is, such a community of mutual responsibility.[32]

The face-to-face community of small group gatherings brings persons close enough together to make space for such life together. The church must regain its original apostolic identity and become a network of primary groups. "A primary group is a group small enough to be characterized by intimate face-to-face association." Too often the small groups of the institutional church are secondary groups: "larger, more formal . . . more coldly impersonal" where the members "know each other only as adherents of the same organization . . . they do not know each other personally or intimately. The christendom model of the church rooted from the third century is a secondary group model."[33] The structural church of the future must become an intentional network of small and intimate primary groups interwoven with functional secondary groups who work at "turning committees into communities."[34]

The generic life together with Jesus Christ is in small group networks and is indeed common (koinonia) life no matter what corner of the world, no matter what diverse culture or language, no matter what religious structure or theological bias it is found amidst. This is not to say that theology and belief are not important. But it is to say that the real orthodox life of Christ is found in the meeting of persons who invite Jesus to be in their midst. The religious Babels of earth cannot reach up into heaven and demand the community of God come to earth, but the gracious love of Abba with Jesus has descended like a dove and come into the midst of the secular and sacred principalities and powers through small face-to-face gatherings of caring people in every nook and cranny of the world. As the Benedictine biblical scholar Demetrius R. Dunn has reflected, "the ultimate hospitality is, then, an entertainment of divine mystery in human life."[35]

The salvation life of God is visible among humanity wherever two are three are gathered and Jesus is invited to become the divine host of the group. The hundreds and thousands and millions of small groups who gather in Jesus' name around the world are the "salt" and the "light" and the "cities on the hill" (Mt 5:13-16), visible, enlightening and seasoning for all humanity lost in valleys, darkness and tastelessness, chaos, ambivalence and ambiguity. This is the church. This is the Christian small group.

May God give us the courage to become and live as the ecclesia of Jesus Christ. May the Spirit pray through all the small group gatherings around the world, "Lord, come quickly."

■ SMALL GROUP MINISTRY IMPLICATIONS

1. There are myriads of models and combinations of models for a church to embrace in the development of a full-scale small group ministry. Buying the predeveloped, complete and unchanged package of another church, a consultant or denominational agency is usually fatal. All ministry models must be carefully and prayerfully contextualized. Each ministry situation is unique. Each set of ministry gifts in a particular church is unique. Each leadership community vision in a church is unique. We are past the industrial age of Western life when programs can be transplanted into various places as if they were in common soils and climates. The planting environments are very different today. The seed of ecclesia is planted in diverse places to grow up looking like native vegetation but empowered by life in Christ.

2. Planting a new small group organism is much different than transplanting a new shoot onto an existing organizational tree. Such grafting is precarious, especially as a new branch hybrid of fast-growing meta-church may try to be grafted onto an old and craggy no-growth, slow-growth or dying traditional mainline oak. Such major shifts of paradigm may kill both the old tree and the new graft. It's not impossible, but it is very difficult.

3. Shifting ministry paradigms takes time, lots of planning, prayer, attention and constant evaluation. If it is a new ministry being developed from the ground up, it must have much careful attention particularly at the beginning. It must have a well-gifted entrepreneurial leadership team who can think on their feet and adjust quickly to surprises. It must have a well-prepared planting place that is ripe for sudden and sustained growth. It must have enough protection from "the slings and arrows of outrageous fortune" to survive the stormy blasts of hard storms, fickle members, young and naive leaders and oppressive outside institutional systems.

4. If a new ministry paradigm is being started alongside an old ministry par-

adigm, the old must be nourished while caring for and growing the young new model. These two ministry systems must run side by side for an extended period of time, long enough for the new to become viable and stand on its own. There must be enough leadership and money to maintain the old and launch the new. This is why the change agency of old organizational systems often takes twice the amount of time and leadership as starting from scratch. Change agency of old institutions is a unique and hard calling in the mainline church today. This is a much different kind of gift than the entrepreneurship of beginning a new church. Most existing churches will need to consider this entrepreneurial approach to small group ministry. Start small. Build slowly. Train leaders for the new model. And don't force the old onto the new. Allow persons absorbed in the old model to voluntarily shift at their own time and of their own choice. Allow the old and new to coexist as long as both are viable. Most churches will eventually form a style of small group ministry which is a merger or hybrid of the old and new simultaneously. This is why each ministry context is so important. The newly changed institution which incorporates small groups must be grounded in the reality of ministry that has worked in that place before and the reality of ministry that will work in the future. It is the art of preserving old wine in old wineskins and making new wine in new wineskins. This takes a new vineyard steward who knows the old ways, but risks developing new ways.

5. Small group networks should be able to handle all different kinds of groups: covenant, study, evangelism, new members, discipleship, support, recovery, ministry, mission, accountability, and so on. The ingredient combination of each group may differ but there are common life disciplines which group leaders must know, affirm and model: personal sharing and caring, study and learning, worship and prayer, ministry and mission, evaluating and decision-making. All small groups will have these ingredients in varying amounts. Each kind of group may also need specialized leadership development. The connections between all groups need to be personal and communal more than functional and formal. The networking connectivity is like the group life—primary community before secondary task. Networking leadership must be able to provide various small groups with personal support, advice on relational technology, guidance on problems, crisis intervention and visional connection to the whole ministry of the organization or larger community. Networks must have their common values and life in Christ continually confirmed and affirmed.

6. Most significant small group ministry start-ups or transitional changes need the help and support of outside consultants, organizational mentors or parallel models. The leaders of small group ministry networks need a face-to-face mentoring community for discussion, reflection, feedback, support and problem-solv-

ing. Most churches or organizations cannot afford to hire new full-time special-ists in small groups (and there are few to be found). It is better to seek out among the small group ministry networks those persons who have been most helpful to others who are going in a parallel direction. As in the very nature of human community, it is not good for the small group leader or the small group church "to be alone."

Conclusion
A SUMMARY OF BIBLICAL
& THEOLOGICAL FOUNDATIONS
FOR SMALL GROUP
MINISTRY

1. From the beginning, God has existed as a community of Being. In human history God has revealed this community of Being as Father, Son and Spirit, an eternal small group, a Trinity of Being and relationship, around whom the greater community of eternal beings is gathered, both angelic and resurrected.

2. From the beginning of human history, the eternal God in Community created humanity as community. Humanity reflects the eternal community of God as man and woman together with God. These three form the primeval small group of human history. The minimum group of two, together with the Community of God, is called to live in intimate, reciprocal, dialogical and growing relationship. Around this prototype small group of the first divine-human community, God has gathered the greater human community of history.

3. From the beginning the human community has struggled with maintaining its integrity of community with God. As the human community continually chooses to develop itself outside of intimate community with God, its relationships and individuals break and die. Except for the continuing intervention of the beckoning and gracious community of God, human community would be self-possessed, broken and lost permanently. The microcosm small group of divine-human community continues in a state of brokenness. But there is hope. From the beginning of the fragmentation of divine-human community, God has worked to restore and complete this to be a community of intimacy, mutual knowing and mutual working.

4. Cut off from God, the human community can choose to receive or reject God's gracious offering to restore divine-human community. In rejecting intimacy with God, the human community continues in a state of sin, broken relationships and dying persons. Thus the fragmented human small group will reflect a shallow form of community, immersed in addictive and abusive behavior and continuing in a struggle for control, identity, intimacy and meaning. Humanity tries to approach one another, but the approach is stifled in avoidance because God is not present to define, empower and complete the face-to-face meeting.

5. If the broken human community chooses to accept God's gracious and personal embrace of restored divine-human community, God works at the redemptive process of restoring and completing the human community by re-interjecting divine community in the midst of human community. The return intervention of divine community into the human dilemma is covenantal. God calls humanity to return to its ontological moorings and prosper through intimate relationship with divine community. As humanity is willing to respond to this gracious invitation to reinvest in the presence of God, humanity takes on a redemptive form of family with God in their midst. The microcosm of this covenantal redeemed family is a small group around whom the larger covenantal community is called into existence.

6. The ultimate and focused demonstration of God's reconciling movement toward humanity comes in the person of the Son, Jesus Christ, who, in his own being as both God and human, enters the human arena as a man who does the work of restoring community between God and humanity. The man Jesus, himself, is the divine act of intervention and restoration between God and humanity. Jesus surrounded himself with small groups of men and women who looked to him as the Lord and model of One who builds divine-human community. The small group who lives and walks with Jesus discovers how humanity can live with God and live with one another in shalom and sabbath. Jesus reconciles, restores and completes the purpose of the primeval small group. Jesus restores the larger community of children and adults, male and female, Jew and Gentile. Even though the human political and religious systems—built in the sin of broken relationships, addiction and abuse—killed Jesus, he demonstrated, in resurrection, that divine-human community will not be destroyed, even in death. In his resurrection, Jesus, the incarnate God, has continuing and growing community with humanity in the presence of Abba God.

7. The small groups of men and women who responded to, lived with and loved the historical Jesus came together as a new community with the resurrected Christ. They shared in his ongoing intimacy with Abba and learned the freedom of intimacy with one another. The gathered men and women came to understand and experience the community of the Spirit, in whom the relationship of Jesus and Abba becomes the relationship of human community sharing with Jesus and Abba. The Spirit of the man Jesus in intimate community with Abba God becomes the Spirit of the human community in intimate community with Jesus and Abba God. In this ongoing experience of sharing in the Spirit the new community comes to realize that wherever two or three or more human beings meet with Jesus, they are a microcosm of divine-human community, an ecclesia.

8. Wherever the person of Jesus calls together two or more other persons, male or female, young or old, Jew or Gentile, there is the divine-human community in microcosm, the ecclesia, a Christian small group. The Spirit of God as the community of God in Christ is shared wherever two or more are gathered together. The Spirit shares the ministry of Jesus with the ecclesia, those called together by Jesus. The ongoing ministry of Jesus through the Spirit is the ministry of building divine-human community, of reconciling men and women to God and to one another. Small groups who meet in the nature and name of Jesus are communities of reconciliation. Small groups are communities where persons can experience forgiveness, healing and maturity. They are spaces where human relationships can take on the character of Jesus with Abba God, like Jesus with the Twelve. It is in this small group community of love and trust that broken persons and relationships experience the freedom to share failure, pain, hurt and addiction. They have the freedom to self-disclose, to confess and to listen and respond with truth and love.

9. The ecclesia are small groups of Christians who are scattered around the world, bound together by a common Spirit. Meeting in all arenas of human systems and organizations, these ecclesia are networked together in multiple groupings of various numbers and configurations. These small group networks form institutional bonds. The network systems and institutional bonds are structures of flexibility to enable and enact the service of the Spirit. When the system or institutional bond becomes more important than life in the Spirit, and when the group becomes too inflexible to move with the wind of the Spirit, the group organization stands in the judgment of the Spirit as idol in need of reformation. Persons who sustain and support inflexible small group formats and systems are in need of personal renewal and of returning to their first love who is Jesus in relationship with Abba God. The Spirit reforms human systems and organizations. The small group is the microcosm of human community and organization. The Christian small group is the microcosm and agent of God's continuing transformation and reformation of human community, organization, institution and system.

10. All small groups, and groups of groups, who come together in the name and nature of Jesus, all ecclesia and networks of ecclesia, are being beckoned to participate in the eternal community of Jesus with Abba God. Every Christian small group is being drawn into eternal community with Father, Son and Spirit. The Christian small group is a penultimate expression of an ultimate eschatological reality. The ultimate expression of human community is the eternal community between God and humanity, focused in Jesus Christ. The life together of Jesus and the Twelve, of the Spirit and ecclesia, is an anticipation of the permanent and complete divine-humanity community forever and ever. Wherever two or three gather on earth in the nature and Spirit of Jesus, they anticipate in the age to come, in the eternal realm of God, the reality of small groups participating in the ontological and teleological reality of God. God desires to be with humanity in community forever and ever.

Notes

Chapter 1: Small Group Origins

[1]Leonard Sweet, *Quantum Spirituality: A Postmodern Apologetic* (Dayton, Ohio: Whaleprints, 1991), pp. 106, 109.
[2]T. S. Eliot, "Choruses from 'The Rock,' " *Complete Poems and Plays* (New York: Harcourt and Brace, 1952), p. 101.
[3]Hans Walter Wolff, *Anthropology of the Old Testament* (Philadelphia: Fortress, 1981), pp. 161-62.
[4]Ray Anderson, *On Being Human: Essays in Theological Anthropology* (Grand Rapids, Mich.: Eerdmans, 1982), p. 73.
[5]Sweet, *Quantum Spirituality*, pp. 124-25. Sweet's discussion of spiritual "pathos" includes a piercing analysis of the nature, spectrum and direction of Christian community in a postmodern world.
[6]Charles Olsen, *The Base Church: Creating Community Through Multiple Forms* (Atlanta: Forum House, 1973), p. 9. Olsen argues that the small group is the base community or base church that provides a way for the constant "self-renewing" of the church in a rapidly changing world.
[7]Paul Hanson, *The People Called: The Growth of Community in the Bible* (San Francisco: Harper & Row, 1986), p. 129. Hanson suggests that the garden theme of Genesis has the overtone of homestead.
[8]Ibid.
[9]Karl Barth, *Church Dogmatics* 3/1, *Doctrine of Creation* (Edinburgh: T. & T. Clark, 1958), p. 98.
[10]Hanson, *People Called*, pp. 130-31.
[11]Wolff, *Anthropology of the Old Testament*, pp. 160-65.
[12]Barth, *Church Dogmatics* 3/4, *Doctrine of Creation* (Edinburgh: T. & T. Clark, 1961), pp. 116-17.
[13]Wolff, *Anthropology of the Old Testament*, p. 162. Whereas Wolff affirms, like Barth, the image and likeness of God in man and woman together, Wolff tends to see this more

as an affirmation of marriage rather than the general mutual dominion of men and women together. Wolff will affirm the need for plural dominion, but he does not explicitly advocate their ruling plurality over creation as male and female together.

[14]Wolff, *Anthropology of the Old Testament*, p. 164. Hanson, *People Called*, p. 132.

[15]David Johnson and Frank Johnson, *Joining Together: Group Theory and Group Skills*, 4th ed. (Englewood Cliffs, N.J.: Prentice Hall, 1991), pp. 172-73.

[16]Sweet, *Quantum Spirituality*, pp. 118-20, 124-30.

[17]Ibid., p. 111.

Chapter 2: Small Group Paradox

[1]Kenwyn K. Smith and David N. Berg, *Paradoxes of Group Life: Understanding Conflict, Paralysis and Movement in Group Dynamics* (San Francisco: Jossey-Bass, 1987), p. 9.

[2]Hans Walter Wolff, *Anthropology of the Old Testament* (Philadelphia: Fortress, 1981), p. 171.

[3]Paul Hanson, *The People Called: The Growth of Community in the Bible* (San Francisco: Harper & Row, 1986), pp. 130-31.

[4]Lillian B. Rubin, *Intimate Strangers: Men and Women Together* (New York: Harper & Row, 1983), pp. 65-67. What Rubin says about male-female relationships is true for all human relationships.

[5]Wolff, *Anthropology of the Old Testament*, p. 172.

[6]John Bradshaw, *Healing the Shame That Binds You* (Deerfield Beach, Fla.: Health Communications, 1988), p. 3.

[7]Hanson, *People Called*, p. 131.

[8]Keith Miller, *Sin: The Ultimate Addiction* (Waco, Tex.: Word, 1987).

[9]C. S. Lewis, *The Great Divorce* (New York: Macmillan, 1946), pp. 16-25.

[10]William Pannell, conversations in the Doctor of Ministry Faculty Committee, Fuller Theological Seminary, 1989.

[11]Calvin Hernton, *Sex and Racism in America* (New York: Grove Press, 1988), p. xviii.

Chapter 3: Small Group Covenants

[1]Ray Anderson and Dennis Guernsey, *On Being Family: A Social Theology of the Family* (Grand Rapids, Mich.: Eerdmans, 1985), p. 33.

[2]Karl Barth, *Church Dogmatics 4/1, Doctrine of Reconciliation* (Edinburgh: T. & T. Clark, 1956), p. 22.

[3]Anderson and Guernsey, *On Being Family*, p. 40.

[4]Ibid., p. vii.

[5]Hans Walter Wolff, *Anthropology of the Old Testament* (Philadelphia: Fortress, 1981), pp. 220-21.

[6]Paul Hanson, *The People Called: The Growth of Community in the Bible* (San Francisco: Harper & Row, 1986), p. 56.

[7]Ibid., p. 58.

[8]Ibid., p. 57.

[9]Ibid., p. 60.

[10]Ibid., p. 61.

Chapter 4: The Ten Commandments for Small Groups

[1]Paul Hanson, *The People Called: The Growth of Community in the Bible* (San Francisco: Harper & Row, 1986), p. 56.

[2]Ibid., p. 53. Hanson would affirm the desirability of contemporizing the Decalogue in more positive terms as he himself works to do in this extended section, pp. 53-63.

[3]Louis Evans, *Covenant to Care* (Wheaton, Ill.: Victor Books, 1977), pp. 13, 17-21.

[4]Hanson, *People Called*, p. 56. While he hints at this perspective, Hanson does not develop this concept of leadership. This is my extrapolation from the biblical text and from Hanson's implied direction.

[5]Ibid., p. 57.

[6]Anne Wilson Schaef and Diane Fassel, *The Addictive Organization* (San Francisco: Harper & Row, 1988), p. 79.

[7]Ibid., p. 7.

[8]John Powell, *Why Am I Afraid to Tell You Who I Am?* (Allen, Tex.: Argus, 1969), p. 54.

[9]Ernst Becker, *The Denial of Death* (New York: Free Press, 1973), p. 284.

[10]Keith Miller, *Hunger for Healing* (San Francisco: Harper & Row, 1992).

[11]Hanson, *People Called*, p. 61.

[12]Ibid., p. 60. Hanson ascribes to Luther the suggestion that the fourth commandment is the pragmatic development of the first two commandments.

[13]Keith Brown, "Definition of Koinonia" (Bethlehem, Penn.: First Presbyterian Church, 1990). Brown is copastor of this congregation which has affirmed the serious pursuit of small group ministry for over 30 years.

[14]Hanson, *People Called*, p. 61.

[15]Ibid.

[16]Ibid.

[17]James Loder, Seminar on Prayer, Edmond, Oklahoma, 1984. In a lecture statement Loder suggested that prayer is "more intimate than sex."

[18]Hans Walter Wolff, *Anthropology of the Old Testament* (Philadelphia: Fortress, 1981), pp. 166-76.

[19]Hanson, *People Called*, p. 62.

[20]Sherod Miller, Elam Nunnally and Daniel Wackman, *Talking Together* (Minneapolis: Interpersonal Communication Programs, 1984), p. 20. These consultants affirm four stages of learning disciplines: initial learning, awkward use, conscious application and natural use.

[21]Hanson, *People Called*, p. 64.

[22]Ibid., p. 65.

[23]Roberta Hestenes, *Using the Bible in Groups* (Philadelphia: Westminster, 1983), pp. 28-29.

[24]David Johnson and Frank Johnson, *Joining Together: Group Theory and Group Skills*, 2nd ed. (Englewood Cliffs, N.J.: Prentice Hall, 1982), pp. 388-90. Groups go through a process of establishing trust. This predictable cycle of establishing trust in stages is outlined by Johnson and Johnson as well as by many other small group theorists.

[25]Hestenes, *Using the Bible*, pp. 31-34.

[26]Dietrich Bonhoeffer, *Life Together* (New York: Harper & Row, 1976), pp. 36-38.

[27]Hanson, *People Called*, pp. 70-78.

[28]Ibid., p. 72.

Chapter 5: Small Group Relationships

[1]Paul Hanson, *The People Called: The Growth of Community in the Bible* (San Francisco: Harper & Row, 1986), p. 56.

[2]Roberta Hestenes, "Building Christian Community Through Small Groups," Doctor of Ministry Syllabus (Pasadena, Calif.: Fuller Theological Seminary, 1983).

[3]Gerald Egan, *Face To Face: The Small-Group Experience and Interpersonal Growth* (Monterey, Calif.: Brooks-Cole, 1973), pp. v-vi.

[4]Hanson, *People Called*, pp. 212-13.

[5]David Johnson and Frank Johnson, *Joining Together: Group Theory and Group Skills*, 4th ed. (Englewood Cliffs, N.J.: Prentice Hall, 1991), pp. 234-36.

6Hanson, *People Called*, pp. 212-13.

7Dietrich Bonhoeffer, *The Communion of Saints: A Dogmatic Inquiry into the Sociology of the Church* (New York: Harper & Row, 1963), p. 60.

8Hanson, *People Called*, p. 213.

9Peter Block, *The Empowered Manager* (San Francisco: Jossey-Bass, 1987), p. 24.

10Ibid., p. 180.

11Ibid., pp. 181-88.

12Bonhoeffer, *Communion of Saints*, p. 55.

13Ibid., p. 71.

14Block, *Empowered Manager*, pp. 178-88.

15Dietrich Bonhoeffer, *Life Together* (New York: Harper & Row, 1976), pp. 110-22.

16John Powell, *Why Am I Afraid to Tell You Who I Am?* (Allen, Tex.: Argus, 1969), pp. 50-62.

Chapter 6: Small Group Leadership

1James Strong, *The Exhaustive Concordance of the Bible and Dictionary of the Hebrew* (New York: Abingdon, 1890), p. 46.

2Paul Hanson, *The People Called: The Growth of Community in the Bible* (San Francisco: Harper & Row, 1986), p. 91.

3Ibid., pp. 175-76.

4Kenwyn K. Smith and David N. Berg, *The Paradoxes of Group Life* (San Francisco: Jossey-Bass, 1990), p. 134.

5Paul Hersey and Ken Blanchard, *Management of Organizational Behavior: Utilizing Human Resources* (Englewood Cliffs, N.J.: Prentice Hall, 1982), pp. 149-69.

6Robert Bellah et al., *Habits of the Heart: Individualism and Commitment in American Life* (Berkeley: University of California Press, 1985), p. 34.

7Dan Williams, *Seven Myths About Small Groups* (Downers Grove, Ill.: InterVarsity Press, 1991), pp. 56-81.

8Hersey and Blanchard, *Management of Organizational Behavior*, pp. 150-70.

Chapter 7: Small Group Structures

1Jim and Carol Plueddemann, *Pilgrims in Progress: Growth Through Groups* (Wheaton, Ill.: Harold Shaw, 1990), pp. 1-2.

2Werner G. Jeanrond, "Community and Authority," in *On Being the Church: Essays on the Christian Community*, ed. Colin E. Gaston and Daniel P. Hardy (Edinburgh: T. & T. Clark, 1989), p. 96.

3Alvin Toffler, *Power Shift* (New York: Bantam Books, 1990), p. i.

4Ibid., p. 177.

5Peter Drucker, *Managing for the Future* (New York: Truman Talley Books, 1992), pp. 328-51.

6John Naisbitt, *Megatrends: Ten New Directions Transforming Our Lives* (New York: Warner Books, 1984).

7Rosabeth Moss Kanter, *The Change Master: Innovation and Entrepreneurship in the American Corporation* (New York: Simon and Schuster, 1983), p. 241.

8Loren Mead, *The Once and Future Church: Reinventing the Congregation for a New Mission Frontier* (New York: Alban Institute, 1991), pp. 22-27.

9Carl George, *Prepare Your Church for the Future* (Old Tappan, N.J.: Revell, 1991), pp. 15-19.

10Paul Yonggi Cho, *Successful Home Cell Groups* (Plainfield, N.J.: Logos International, 1981), p. 19. The term *cell* has been used in church-growth literature and may have originated with the thinking of Paul Cho. The image is that of the body made up of thousands of cells.

[11]George, *Prepare Your Church*, p. 57.

[12]The name Mizraim (NIV) is translated as "Egypt" in the New Revised Standard version.

[13]*The New Encyclopaedia Britannica*, 15th ed. (Chicago: Encyclopaedia Britannica, 1987), vol. 18, p. 151.

Chapter 8: Small Group Ministry

[1]Bernard Lee and Michael Cowan, *Dangerous Memories* (Kansas City, Mo.: Sheed and Ward, 1986), p. 12.

[2]Gordon Dalbey, *The Healing of the Masculine Soul* (Waco, Tex.: Word, 1988), pp. 188-201.

[3]Martin Luther, "A Mighty Fortress Is Our God" (German hymn, "Ein' feste Burg," 1529).

Chapter 9: The Small Group of Twelve

[1]Because it is commonly recognized that "kingdom" tends to carry sexually exclusive images and implications for the maleness of God and the maleness of the apostolic community, it has often been used to enforce an exclusivity of male leadership in the faith community. Therefore, for the purposes of this book, whenever possible such terms as *realm* or *divine community* will be used in place of *kingdom* with full understanding of their exegetical limitations.

[2]John Mallison, *Growing Christians in Small Groups* (Sydney, Australia: Scripture Union, 1989), pp. 3-4.

[3]Gerhard Lohfink, *Jesus and Community* (Philadelphia: Westminster Press, 1989), pp. 33-35.

[4]*Webster's New World Dictionary* (New York: World Publishing, 1970), p. 401.

[5]C. Norman Kraus, *The Authentic Witness* (Grand Rapids, Mich.: Eerdmans, 1979), p. 17.

[6]Lohfink, *Jesus and Community*, p. 32.

[7]Ibid., p. 65.

[8]Robert Coleman, *The Master Plan of Evangelism* (Old Tappan, N.J.: Revell, 1987).

[9]Ibid., p. 24

[10]Paul Hanson, *The People Called: The Growth of Community in the Bible* (San Francisco: Harper & Row, 1986), p. 397.

[11]Stanley Hauerwas, *A Community of Character* (Notre Dame: University of Notre Dame Press, 1981), p. 41.

[12]Ibid.

[13]Ibid., pp. 36-52.

[14]Ibid., p. 45.

[15]Ibid., p. 49.

[16]Kraus, *Authentic Witness*, pp. 13-26, 27-50.

[17]Ibid., p. 19.

[18]Ibid., pp. 27-50.

[19]Ibid., p. 19.

[20]Ibid., pp. 31-35.

[21]Lohfink, *Jesus and Community*, pp. 32-33.

[22]Janet Hagberg, *Real Power: Stages of Personal Power in Organizations* (San Francisco: Harper & Row, 1984).

[23]William C. Byham and Jeff Cox, *Zapp! The Lightning of Empowerment* (New York: Harmony Books, 1988).

Chapter 10: Gathering the Small Group

[1]Richard Peace, "Jesus and the Twelve," a lecture to the National Conference on Small Groups, Fuller Seminary, Pasadena, Calif., 1987.
[2]*Webster's New World Dictionary* (New York: World Publishing, 1970), p. 929.
[3]John Mallison, *Growing Christians in Small Groups* (Sydney, Australia: Scripture Union, 1989), p. 3.
[4]Ibid.
[5]David Johnson and Frank Johnson, *Joining Together: Group Theory and Group Skills*, 2nd ed. (Englewood Cliffs, N.J.: Prentice Hall, 1982), pp. 372-74.

Chapter 11: Modeling Group Life

[1]David Prior, *Jesus and Power* (Downers Grove, Ill.: InterVarsity Press, 1987), p. 75.
[2]James Dunn, *Jesus and the Spirit* (Philadelphia: Westminster Press, 1975), pp. 68-92.
[3]George R. Beasley-Murray, *John*, Word Biblical Commentary 36 (Waco, Tex.: Word, 1987), p. 62.
[4]George Ladd, *A Theology of the New Testament* (Grand Rapids, Mich.: Eerdmans, 1974), p. 107.
[5]Robert Guelich, *The Sermon on the Mount: A Foundation for Understanding* (Waco, Tex.: Word, 1982), pp. 52-53.
[6]David Prior, *Parish Renewal at the Grassroots* (Grand Rapids, Mich.: Asbury Press, 1983), pp. 28-35.
[7]A. B. Bruce, *The Training of the Twelve* (1894; reprint, Grand Rapids, Mich.: Kregel, 1988), pp. 1-10.
[8]Richard Foster, *Money, Sex and Power: The Challenge of the Disciplined Life* (San Francisco: Harper & Row, 1985), pp. 1-15.
[9]David Johnson and Frank Johnson, *Joining Together: Group Theory and Group Skills*, 4th ed. (Englewood Cliffs, N.J.: Prentice Hall, 1991), p. 374.

Chapter 12: Leading the Small Group

[1]John Mallison, *Growing Christians in Small Groups* (Sydney, Australia: Scripture Union, 1989), p. 4.
[2]Ibid.
[3]David Johnson and Frank Johnson, *Joining Together: Group Theory and Group Skills*, 4th ed. (Englewood Cliffs, N.J.: Prentice Hall, 1991), pp. 372-74.
[4]Paul Hersey and Ken Blanchard, *Management of Organizational Behavior: Utilizing Human Resources*, 4th ed. (Englewood Cliffs, N.J.: Prentice Hall, 1982), pp. 150-55.
[5]Mallison, *Growing Christians*, p. 4. It is somewhat evident in the use of the words *association* and *delegation* that Mallison has interacted with the stages of discipleship articulated by Robert Coleman in *The Master Plan of Evangelism* (Old Tappan, N.J.: Revell, 1964).
[6]Coleman, *Master Plan*, pp. 82-93. "Delegation" is one of the stages Coleman articulates as the small group mission plan of Jesus.
[7]David Prior, *Jesus and Power* (Downers Grove, Ill.: InterVarsity Press, 1987), pp. 75-87.
[8]James Fowler, *Stages of Faith: The Psychology of Human Development and the Quest for Meaning* (San Francisco: Harper & Row, 1981), p. 202.
[9]Henri Nouwen, *In the Name of Jesus: Reflections on Christian Leadership* (New York: Crossroad, 1989), pp. 11-12.
[10]Ibid., pp. ix-x.
[11]Dietrich Bonhoeffer, *Life Together* (New York: Harper & Row, 1976), p. 20.
[12]Nouwen, *Name of Jesus*, p. 17.
[13]Ibid., p. 18, quoting Matthew 4:4.

14Henri Nouwen, *Making All Things New* (San Francisco: Harper & Row, 1981), p. 47.
15Ibid, p. 67.
16Nouwen, *Name of Jesus*, pp. 20-21.
17Ibid., pp. 30-31.
18Roberta Hestenes, *Using the Bible in Groups* (Philadelphia: Westminster Press, 1983), p. 32.
19Nouwen, *Name of Jesus*, pp. 56-57.
20Ibid., p. 59.
21Johnson and Johnson, *Joining Together*, pp. 56-57.
22Richard Halverson, chaplain of the U.S. Senate (from a consultation with him and several PCUSA pastors, Wellspring Conference Center, Washington, D.C., February 1990).
23Gordon Dalbey, *The Healing of the Masculine Soul* (Waco, Tex.: Word, 1989), p. 197.
24"The Career, the Husband, the Kids and Everything," *Working Woman*, December 1990, pp. 94-98.
25Nouwen, *Name of Jesus*, p. 60.
26Malcolm Knowles, *The Modern Practice of Adult Education: Andragogy Versus Pedagogy* (New York: Association, 1970), pp. 22-29.
27Hersey and Blanchard, *Management of Organizational Behavior*, p. 308.
28Nouwen, *Name of Jesus*, p. 62.
29Ibid., p. 63.
30Ibid., p. 65.
31Ibid., pp. 38-40.
32Ibid., pp. 41-42.
33Ibid., pp. 43-44.
34Ibid., p. 45.
35James Dunn, *Jesus and the Spirit* (Philadelphia: Westminster Press, 1975), p. 21.
36Max DePree, *Leadership Is an Art* (New York: Doubleday, 1989).

Chapter 13: Observing Small Group Dynamics
1Dallas Willard, *The Spirit of the Disciplines* (San Francisco: Harper & Row, 1988), p. 176.
2M. Scott Peck, *The Different Drum: Community Making and Peace* (New York: Simon and Schuster, 1987), pp. 257-58.
3Dietrich Bonhoeffer, *Life Together* (San Francisco: Harper & Row, 1976), pp. 21-26.
4George Barna, "Small Groups—A Key To Growth," *Christian Marketing Perspective*, Winter 1988 (a publication of the Barna Research Group, Glendale, California).
5Richard Peace, "Jesus and the Twelve: A Case Study in Small Group Process," a lecture delivered at the National Conference on Small Groups, Fuller Seminary, Pasadena, Calif., 1987.

Chapter 14: Training Small Group Leaders
1John Mallison, *Growing Christians in Small Groups* (Sydney, Australia: Scripture Union, 1989), p. 4. Here Mallison refers to J. S. Stewart, *The Life and Teachings of Jesus Christ* (Saint Andrew Press), to accent the importance of the disciples' daily living with Jesus, to be with him and watch him in all situations, "learning by association."
2Ibid.
3Ibid.
4Richard Peace, "Jesus and the Twelve," a lecture delivered at the National Conference on Small Groups, Fuller Seminary, Pasadena, Calif., 1987.
5David Prior, *Jesus and Power* (Downers Grove, Ill.: InterVarsity Press, 1987), p. 75.

[6]Ibid., pp. 76-77.
[7]Gordon Dalbey, *The Healing of the Masculine Soul* (Waco, Tex.: Word, 1988), pp. 180-82.
[8]Anne Wilson Schaef and Diane Fassel, *The Addictive Organization* (San Francisco: Harper & Row, 1988), pp. 57-76.
[9]*Webster's New World Dictionary* (New York: World Publishing, 1970), p. 1171.
[10]Gerhard Lohfink, *Jesus and Community* (Philadelphia: Westminster Press, 1989), p. 72.
[11]Schaef and Fassel, *Addictive Organization*, pp. 224-28.
[12]Karl Barth, *Church Dogmatics 3/1, Doctrine of Reconciliation* (Edinburgh: T. & T. Clark, 1956), pp. 330-31.
[13]James Dunn, *Jesus and the Spirit* (Philadelphia: Westminster Press, 1975), pp. 80-82.
[14]Dietrich Bonhoeffer, *Life Together* (New York: Harper & Row, 1976), pp. 21-26.
[15]George Ladd, *A Theology of the New Testament* (Grand Rapids, Mich.: Eerdmans, 1974), pp. 64-69.
[16]Dunn, *Jesus and the Spirit*, p. 81.
[17]Edwin H. Friedman, *Generation to Generation: Family Process in Church and Synagogue* (New York: Guilford Press, 1985).
[18]Dunn, *Jesus and the Spirit*, pp. 21-26.

Chapter 15: Empowering Small Group Members
[1]Peter Block, *The Empowered Manager* (San Francisco: Jossey-Bass, 1987), pp. 10-11.
[2]C. S. Mann, *Mark: A Commentary* (New York: Doubleday, 1986), p. 223.
[3]Ibid., p. 225. The very rare biblical word literally means "unroof."
[4]Ibid., p. 226.
[5]Robert Slocum, *Maximize Your Ministry* (Colorado Springs: NavPress, 1991).

Chapter 16: Mobilizing the Small Group for Ministry
[1]James Dunn, *Jesus and the Spirit* (Philadelphia: Westminster Press, 1975), p. 81.
[2]Ibid., p. 79.
[3]Ibid., p. 70.
[4]Gerhard Lohfink, *Jesus and Community* (Philadelphia: Westminster Press, 1989), pp. 47-49.
[5]Karl Barth, *Church Dogmatics 4/2, Doctrine of Reconciliation* (Edinburgh: T. & T. Clark, 1958), pp. 667-71.

Chapter 17: The Ecclesia as an Extension of the Twelve
[1]Stanley Hauerwas, *A Community of Character: Toward a Constructive Christian Social Ethic* (Notre Dame, Ind.: University of Notre Dame Press, 1981), p. 18.
[2]Ibid., pp. 12-35.
[3]C. Norman Kraus, *The Authentic Witness* (Grand Rapids, Mich.: Eerdmans, 1979), p. 90.
[4]Geoffrey Wainwright, *Doxology: The Praise of God in Worship, Doctrine and Life* (New York: Oxford University Press, 1980), p. 273.
[5]Ray Anderson, *Historical Transcendence and the Reality of God* (Grand Rapids, Mich.: Eerdmans, 1974), pp. 227-38.
[6]Carl George, *Prepare Your Church for the Future* (Old Tappan, N.J.: Revell, 1991), p. 57.
[7]Hauerwas, *A Community*, p. 131.
[8]Kraus, *Authentic*, p. 89.
[9]Hauerwas, *A Community*, pp. 132-33.
[10]Bernard Lee and Michael Cowan, *Dangerous Memories* (Kansas City, Mo.: Sheed and Ward, 1986), p. 159.

Chapter 18: Small Group Direction and Disciplines

[1]James Dunn, *Jesus and the Spirit* (London: SCM Press Ltd., 1975), pp. 272-75.
[2]Robert Banks, *Paul's Idea of Community* (Grand Rapids, Mich.: Eerdmans, 1980), pp. 34-35.
[3]Bernard Lee and Michael Cowan, *Dangerous Memories* (Kansas City, Mo.: Sheed and Ward, 1986), p. 190.
[4]Banks, *Paul's Idea of Community*, p. 45.
[5]Donald Postema, *Space for God* (Grand Rapids, Mich.: CRC Publications, 1983).
[6]*Webster's New World Dictionary* (New York: World Publishing, 1970), p. 1252.
[7]Ibid., p. 995.
[8]Eric Voegelin, *Anamnesis* (Notre Dame, Ind.: University of Notre Dame Press, 1978), p. 10.
[9]Dunn, *Jesus and the Spirit*, pp. 184-85.
[10]Ibid., p. 187.
[11]*Webster's New World Dictionary*, pp. 368, 718.
[12]Dunn, *Jesus and the Spirit*, pp. 260-65.
[13]Banks, *Paul's Idea of Community*, pp. 180-87.
[14]Dietrich Bonhoeffer, *Life Together* (New York: Harper & Row, 1976), p. 31.

Chapter 19: Small Group as Formational and Transformational Community

[1]Edwin H. Friedman, *Generation to Generation: Family Process in Church and Synagogue* (New York: Guilford Press, 1985), pp. 14-15.
[2]Ibid., pp. 308-9.
[3]Dietrich Bonhoeffer, *Life Together* (New York: Harper & Row, 1976), p. 116.
[4]Robert Bellah et al., *Habits of the Heart: Individualism and Commitment in American Life* (Berkeley: University of California Press, 1985), p. 37.
[5]Karl Barth, "The Growth of the Community," in *Theological Foundations for Ministry*, ed. Ray Anderson (Grand Rapids, Mich.: Eerdmans, 1979), p. 275.
[6]Ibid., p. 258.
[7]Paul Hanson, *The People Called: The Growth of Community in the Bible* (San Francisco: Harper & Row, 1986), p. 509.
[8]Lillian Rubin, *Intimate Strangers: Men and Women Together* (New York: Harper & Row, 1983), pp. 65-80.
[9]Em Griffin, *Getting Together* (Downers Grove, Ill.: InterVarsity Press, 1982), pp. 113-33.
[10]Gordon Dalbey, *The Healing of the Masculine Soul* (Waco, Tex.: Word, 1989), p. 195.
[11]Anne Wilson Schaef, *Escape from Intimacy* (San Francisco: Harper & Row, 1989), pp. 136-37.
[12]Griffin, *Getting Together*, p. 118.
[13]Hanson, *People Called*, p. 510.
[14]Bonhoeffer, *Life Together*, pp. 7-13.
[15]Hanson, *People Called*, p. 515.
[16]Anne Wilson Schaef and Diane Fassel, *The Addictive Organization* (San Francisco: Harper & Row, 1988), p. 47.
[17]*Growing in the Life of Christian Faith*, a report approved by the 201st General Assembly, Presbyterian Church (USA), 1989, pp. 24-25.

Chapter 20: Mutual Ministry in the Small Group

[1]Robert Slocum, *Ordinary Christians in a High-Tech World* (Waco, Tex.: Word, 1986), pp. 55-63.
[2]Stanley Hauerwas, *A Community of Character* (Notre Dame, Ind.: University of Notre Dame Press, 1981), pp. 49-50.

[3]Ibid., p. 53.

[4]Eric Voegelin, *Anamnesis* (Notre Dame, Ind.: University of Notre Dame Press, 1978), pp. 6-13.

[5]Bernard Lee and Michael Cowan, *Dangerous Memories* (Kansas City, Mo.: Sheed and Ward, 1986), pp. vi, 23.

[6]Dietrich Bonhoeffer, *Life Together* (New York: Harper & Row, 1976), pp. 57-61.

[7]David Johnson and Frank Johnson, *Joining Together: Group Theory and Group Skills*, 2nd ed. (Englewood Cliffs, N.J.: Prentice Hall, 1982), pp. 415-17.

[8]C. S. Lewis, *The Great Divorce* (New York: Macmillan, 1946), pp. 16-25.

[9]Bonhoeffer, *Life Together*, p. 110.

[10]Anne Wilson Schaef and Diane Fassel, *The Addictive Organization* (San Francisco: Harper & Row, 1988), pp. 137-45.

[11]Roberta Hestenes, *Using the Bible in Groups* (Philadelphia: Westminster Press, 1983), p. 97, and Em Griffin, *Getting Together* (Downers Grove, Ill.: InterVarsity Press, 1982), p. 114.

[12]John Powell, *Why Am I Afraid to Tell You Who I Am?* (Allen, Tex.: Argus, 1969), p. 20.

[13]Bonhoeffer, *Life Together*, p. 114.

[14]James Loder, lecture delivered at First Presbyterian Church, Edmond, Oklahoma, 1984.

[15]Robert Bellah et al., *Habits of the Heart: Individualism and Commitment in American Life* (Berkeley: University of California Press, 1985), pp. 142-63; quote is p. 151.

[16]Gerard Egan, *Face-to-Face: The Small Group Experience and Interpersonal Growth* (Monterey, Calif.: Brooks/Cole, 1973), p. 41.

[17]Hestenes, *Using the Bible*, pp. 107-8.

[18]Dallas Willard, *The Spirit of the Disciplines: Understanding How God Changes Lives* (San Francisco: Harper & Row, 1988), pp. 175-91.

[19]Conrad L'Heureux, *Life Journey and the Old Testament: An Experiential Approach to the Bible and Personal Transformation* (New York: Paulist Press, 1986), pp. 107-44.

[20]Walter Brueggemann, *Praying the Psalms* (Winona, Ind.: St. Mary's Press, 1986).

[21]Flora Slosson Wuellner, *Prayer, Fear and Our Powers: Finding Our Healing, Release and Growth in Christ* (Nashville: Upper Room Books, 1989), p. 110.

[22]Henri Nouwen, *The Wounded Healer* (New York: Image Books, 1972), p. 72.

[23]Flora Slosson Wuellner, *Prayer, Stress and Our Inner Wounds* (Nashville: Upper Room Books, 1985), p. 76.

[24]M. Scott Peck, *The Different Drum: Community Making and Peace* (New York: Simon and Schuster, 1987).

[25]Paul Hanson, *The People Called: The Growth of Community in the Bible* (San Francisco: Harper & Row, 1986), p. 503.

[26]Schaef and Fassel, *Addictive Organization*, pp. 47-48.

[27]See Raymond E. Brown, *The Community of the Beloved Disciple: The Life, Loves and Hates of an Individual Church in New Testament Times* (New York: Paulist Press, 1979).

[28]Bellah et al., *Habits of the Heart*, pp. 152-53.

[29]L'Heureux, *Life Journey*.

Chapter 21: Small Group Images and Metaphors

[1]Paul Hanson, *The People Called: The Growth of Community in the Bible* (San Francisco: Harper & Row, 1986), p. 443.

[2]James Dunn, *Jesus and the Spirit* (Philadelphia: Westminster Press, 1975), pp. 259-60.

[3]Ibid., p. 262.

[4]Geoffrey Wainwright, *Doxology: The Praise of God in Worship, Doctrine and Life* (New York: Oxford University Press, 1980), pp. 142-43.

5Dietrich Bonhoeffer, *Life Together* (San Francisco: Harper & Row, 1976), pp. 31-39.

6Don Kimball, *Power and Presence: A Theology of Relationships* (San Francisco: Harper & Row, 1987), pp. 69-102.

7David Augsburger, *Caring Enough to Confront* (Scottdale, Pa.: Herald Press, 1973), p. 82.

8Richard John Neuhaus, ed., *Confession, Conflict and Community* (Grand Rapids, Mich.: Eerdmans, 1986).

9Anne Wilson Schaef and Diane Fassel, *The Addictive Organization* (San Francisco: Harper & Row, 1988), pp. 57-76.

10Roberta Hestenes, *Using the Bible in Groups* (Philadelphia: Westminster Press, 1983), p. 57.

11Robert Banks, *Paul's Idea of Community* (Grand Rapids, Mich.: Eerdmans, 1980), p. 54.

12Gerhard Lohfink, *Jesus and Community* (Philadelphia: Westminster Press, 1989), pp. 106-15.

13James Moulton and George Milligan, *The Vocabulary of the New Testament* (London: Hodder and Stoughton, 1963), pp. 599-600.

14Ray Anderson and Dennis Guernsey, *On Being Family: A Social Theology of the Family* (Grand Rapids, Mich.: Eerdmans, 1985), pp. 144-54.

15Gerald May, *Addiction and Grace* (San Francisco: Harper & Row, 1988), pp. 162-81.

16Lohfink, *Jesus and Community*, pp. 94-95.

17Schaef and Fassel, *Addictive Organization*, p. 3.

18C. S. Lewis, *The Great Divorce* (New York: Macmillan, 1946), pp. 106-14.

19Bernard Lee and Michael Cowan, *Dangerous Memories* (Kansas City, Mo.: Sheed and Ward, 1986), p. 68.

20Robert Slocum, *Maximize Your Ministry* (Colorado Springs: NavPress, 1991), pp. 213-23.

21Ibid., pp. 53-123.

Chapter 22: The Small Group in Ministry and Mission

1James Dunn, *Jesus and the Spirit* (Philadelphia: Westminster Press, 1975), p. 163.

2Robert Banks, *Paul's Idea of Community* (Grand Rapids, Mich.: Eerdmans, 1980), pp. 175-79.

3Ibid., pp. 171-73.

4Paul Hersey and Ken Blanchard, *Management of Organizational Behavior: Utilizing Human Resources*, 4th ed. (Englewood Cliffs, N.J.: Prentice Hall, 1982), p. 157.

5Banks, *Paul's Idea of Community*, pp. 180-87.

6Dietrich Bonhoeffer, *Life Together* (New York: Harper & Row, 1976), pp. 90-109. Bonhoeffer lists seven mutual ministries of the Christian community.

7Banks, *Paul's Idea of Community*, p. 54.

8Ibid., pp. 52-54. These two words, *household* and *steward*, have the same root, *oiko*, meaning "common home."

9Bernard Lee and Michael Cowan, *Dangerous Memories* (Kansas City, Mo.: Sheed and Ward, 1986), pp. 90-91.

10Dorwin Cartwright and Alvin Zander, *Group Dynamics: Research and Theory*, 3rd ed. (New York: Harper & Row, 1968), p. 104.

11Walter Wink, *Naming the Powers: The Language of Power in the New Testament* (Philadelphia: Fortress Press, 1989), pp. 104-13.

12Dunn, *Jesus and the Spirit*, p. 187.

13Louis Evans Jr., *Covenant to Care* (Wheaton, Ill.: Victor Books, 1982), pp. 17-21.

14Bruce P. Powers, *Christian Leadership* (Nashville: Broadman Press, 1979), pp. 116-18.

15Lee and Cowan, *Dangerous Memories*, pp. 34-35.

16Banks, *Paul's Idea of Community*, p. 84.

[17]Ibid., p. 63.
[18]Dunn, *Jesus and the Spirit*, pp. 182-88.
[19]Paul Hanson, *The People Called: The Growth of Community in the Bible* (San Francisco: Harper & Row, 1986), pp. 435-38.
[20]E. F. Schumacher, *Small Is Beautiful* (London: Abacus, 1973), pp. 53-54.
[21]David Prior, *Parish Renewal at the Grassroots* (Grand Rapids, Mich.: Francis Asbury Press, 1983), p. 25.
[22]Dietrich Bonhoeffer, *The Cost of Discipleship* (New York: Macmillan, 1963), pp. 302-4, 285-86.
[23]Ibid., p. 303.
[24]Hanson, *People Called*, p. 435.
[25]Walter Wink, *Unmasking the Powers: The Invisible Forces That Determine Human Existence* (Philadelphia: Fortress Press, 1988), pp. 41-43.

Chapter 23: Small Group Integrity and Destiny
[1]James Loder, *The Transforming Moment* (San Francisco: Harper & Row, 1981), pp. 79-91; quote is p. 85.
[2]James Loder in a lecture delivered at First Presbyterian Church, Edmond, Oklahoma, 1984.
[3]Jacques Ellul, *Hope in Time of Abandonment* (New York: Seabury Press, 1977), pp. 131-56.
[4]Douglas John Hall, *God and Human Suffering: An Exercise in the Theology of the Cross* (Minneapolis: Augsburg, 1986), pp. 123-47.
[5]Ibid., pp. 146-47.
[6]John Doberstein, introduction to Bonhoeffer's *Life Together*, p. 13.
[7]Louis Evans Jr., *Covenant to Care* (Wheaton, Ill.: Victor Books, 1982), pp. 96-97.
[8]Ernest Becker, *The Denial of Death* (New York: Free Press, 1973), pp. 11-24.
[9]Donald Joy, *Bonding: Relationships in the Image of God* (Waco, Tex.: Word, 1985), pp. 14-21.
[10]John MacQuarrie, *In Search of Humanity: A Theological and Philosophical Approach* (New York: Crossroad, 1983), p. 186.
[11]Ibid., p. 245.
[12]John Powell, *Why Am I Afraid To Tell You Who I Am?* (Allen, Tex.: Argus, 1969), pp. 43-85.
[13]M. Scott Peck, *The Different Drum: Community Making and Peace* (New York: Simon and Schuster, 1987), pp. 86-106.
[14]Bonhoeffer, *Life Together*, pp. 18-19.
[15]Robert Banks, *Paul's Idea of Community* (Grand Rapids, Mich.: Eerdmans, 1980), pp. 190-91.
[16]Edward Schillebeeckx, *The Church with a Human Face: A New and Expanded Theology of Ministry* (New York: Crossroad, 1987), pp. 69-73.
[17]Gerhard Lohfink, *Jesus and Community* (Philadelphia: Westminster Press, 1989), pp. 127-28.
[18]Evans, *Covenant to Care*, p. 33.
[19]Mary Wolff-Salin, *The Shadow Side of Community and the Growth of Self* (New York: Crossroad, 1988), p. 35.

Chapter 24: The Church as a Small Group Network
[1]James Dunn, *Jesus and the Spirit* (Philadelphia: Westminster Press, 1975), p. 183.
[2]Robert Banks, *Paul's Idea of Community* (Grand Rapids, Mich.: Eerdmans, 1980), pp. 40-42.
[3]Leonard Sweet, *Quantum Spirituality* (Dayton, Ohio: Whaleprints, 1991), p. 145.

4Loren B. Mead, *The Once and Future Church: Reinventing the Congregation for a New Mission Frontier* (New York: Alban Institute, 1991), p. 15.

5Ibid., p. 8.

6Ibid., p. 18.

7Sweet, *Quantum*, p. 144.

8Ibid., p. 144-45.

9Alvin Toffler, *The Third Wave* (New York: Bantam, 1980).

10Alvin Toffler, *Power Shift* (New York: Bantam, 1990).

11John Naisbitt, *Megatrends* (New York: Warner Books, 1982). See contents page.

12Sweet, *Quantum*, p. 143.

13Ibid., p. 145.

14Ibid.

15Roberta Hestenes, plenary lecture at the East Coast Conference on Small Groups, Philadelphia, June 2, 1993.

16Del Birkey, *House Church* (Scottdale, Penn.: Herald Press, 1988), p. 71. This quote is taken from James H. Taylor III, in "Brief Case," *Eternity* (June 1983): 14.

17Ibid.

18Conversation with John De Vries at Fuller Seminary, D.Min. course on Small Groups, May 1987.

19"Building Christian Community Through Small Groups," Fuller Theological Seminary Doctor of Ministry Course at the Asian Center for Theological Studies in Seoul, Korea, July 1989.

20Robert and Julia Banks, *The Home Church* (Sydney, Australia: Albatross, 1986), p. 231. This is reflection from Stanley Hauerwas, "Politics, Vision and the Common Good," *Vision and Virtue: Essays in Christian Ethical Reflection* (Notre Dame, Ind.: University of Notre Dame Press, 1981), pp. 239-40.

21Banks, *Home Church*, p. 233. Quoting Art Gish, *Living in Christian Community* (Sydney, Australia: Albatross, 1979), p. 293.

22Edward Schillebeeckx, *The Church with a Human Face* (New York: Crossroad, 1987), pp. 42-46.

23Leonardo Boff, *Ecclesiogenesis: The Base Communities Reinvent the Church* (New York: Orbis Books, 1986), pp. 1-2.

24Elmer Towns, *Ten of Today's Most Innovative Churches* (Ventura, Calif.: Regal, 1990), pp. 73-88.

25Carl George, *Prepare Your Church for the Future* (Old Tappan, N.J.: Fleming H. Revell, 1991), pp. 50-52.

26Ibid., p. 53.

27Tex Sample, *U.S. Lifestyles and Mainline Churches* (Louisville, Ky.: Westminister/John Knox, 1990), p. 141.

28Lesslie Newbigin, *The Gospel in a Pluralist Society* (Grand Rapids, Mich.: Eerdmans, 1989), p. 131.

29Ibid., pp. 137, 227.

30Ibid., p. 227.

31Ibid., pp. 230-31.

32Ibid., p. 231.

33Birkey, *House Church*, p. 64.

34Roberta Hestenes, *Turning Committees into Communities* (Colorado Springs: NavPress, 1991).

35Sweet, *Quantum*, p. 1.

Bibliography

Christian Small Groups

Arnold, Jeffrey. *The Big Book on Small Groups*. Downers Grove, Ill.: InterVarsity Press, 1992.

Bangham, William. *The Journey into Small Groups*. Memphis: Southern Baptist Lay Renewal, 1974.

Banks, Robert. *Paul's Idea of Community: The Early House Churches in Their Historical Setting*. Grand Rapids, Mich.: Eerdmans, 1988.

Banks, Robert and Julia. *The Home Church: Regrouping the People of God for Community and Mission*. Sydney, Australia: Albatross Books, 1986.

Birkey, Del. *The House Church: A Model for Renewing the Church*. Scottdale, Penn.: Herald Press, 1988.

Bonhoeffer, Dietrich. *Life Together*. San Francisco: Harper & Row, 1954.

Branick, Vincent. *The House Church in the Writings of Paul*. Wilmington, Del.: Glazier, 1989.

Building a Small Groups Program from the Bottom Up. Menlo Park, Calif.: Menlo Park Presbyterian Church, 1990.

Cho, Paul Yonggi. *Successful Home Cell Groups*. Plainfield, N.J.: Logos International, 1981.

Clarke, Jean Illsley. *Who, Me Lead a Group?* Minneapolis: Winston Press, 1984.

Coleman, Lyman. *Small Group Training Manual*. Littleton, Colo.: Serendipity House, 1992.

Corey, Marianne Schneider, and Gerald Corey. *Groups: Process and Practice*. 4th ed. Pacific Grove, Calif.: Brooks-Cole, 1992.

Cosby, Gordon. *Handbook for Mission Groups*. Washington, D.C.: Church of the Savior, 1975.

Dibbert, Michael T., and Frank B. Wichern. *Growth Groups: A Key to Christian Fellowship and Spiritual Maturity in the Church*. Grand Rapids, Mich.: Zondervan, 1985.

Douglass, Paul F. *The Group Workshop Way in the Church*. New York: Association Press, 1956.

Ellas, John W. *Church Growth Through Groups*. Searcy, Ariz.: Resource Publications, 1990.

Eller, Vernard. *The Outward Bound: Caravaning as the Style of the Church*. Grand Rapids, Mich.: Eerdmans, 1988.

Evans, Louis H., Jr. *Covenant to Care*. Wheaton, Ill.: Victor Books, 1977.

Finney, John. *Groups: Asking the Right Questions*. Nottingham, U.K.: Grove Books, 1985.

Gaede, S. D. *Belonging: Our Need for Community in Church and Family*. Grand Rapids, Mich.: Zondervan, 1985.

Galloway, Dale. *20/20 Vision: How to Create a Successful Church with Lay Leaders and Cell Groups.* Portland: Scott, 1986.

George, Carl. *Prepare Your Church for the Future.* Old Tappan, N.J.: Fleming H. Revell, 1991.

Gorman, Julie. *A Training Manual for Small Group Leaders.* Wheaton, Ill.: Victor Books, 1991.

Griffin, Em. *Getting Together: A Guide for Good Groups.* Downers Grove, Ill.: InterVarsity Press, 1982.

Hadaway, C. Kirk et al. *Home Cell Groups and House Churches.* Nashville: Broadman, 1987.

Hamlin, Judy. *The Small Group Leaders Training Course: Trainer's Manual and Participant's Manual.* Colorado Springs: NavPress, 1990.

Hestenes, Roberta. *Turning Committees into Communities.* Colorado Springs: NavPress, 1991.

———. *Using the Bible in Groups.* Philadelphia: Westminster Press, 1983.

Icenogle, Gareth Weldon. *Growth Groups Handbook I.* Dallas: Highland Park Presbyterian Church, 1985.

———. *Growth Groups Handbook II.* Dallas: Highland Park Presbyterian Church, 1989.

Johnson, David W., and Frank P. Johnson. *Joining Together: Group Theory and Group Skills.* 4th ed. Englewood Cliffs, N.J.: Prentice Hall, 1991.

Korth, Russ, and Ron Wormser. *Lively Discussions.* San Bernardino, Calif.: Churches Alive, 1988.

Kunz, Marilyn, and Catherine Schell. *How to Start a Neighborhood Bible Study.* New York: Neighborhood Bible Studies, 1966.

Lee, Bernard J., and Michael A. Cowan. *Dangerous Memories: House Churches and Our American Story.* Kansas City, Mo.: Sheed and Ward, 1986.

Leslie, Robert C. *Sharing Groups in the Church.* Nashville: Abingdon, 1979.

McBride, Neal F. *How to Lead Small Groups.* Colorado Springs: NavPress, 1990.

Mallison, John. *Building Small Groups in the Christian Community.* West Ryde, Australia: Renewal Publications, 1978.

———. *Christian Lifestyle: Discovery Through Small Groups.* West Ryde, Australia: Renewal Publications, 1977.

———. *Creative Ideas for Small Groups in the Christian Community.* West Ryde, Australia: Renewal Publications, 1978.

———. *Growing Christians in Small Groups.* Sydney, Australia: Scripture Union, 1989.

Meier, Paul, et al. *Filling the Holes in Our Souls: Caring Groups That Build Lasting Relationships.* Chicago: Moody Press, 1992.

Meyer, Richard C. *One-Anothering: Biblical Building Blocks for Small Groups.* San Diego: LuraMedia, 1990.

Miller, Keith. *The Hunger for Healing.* Colorado Springs: Pinon Books. 1992.

Miller, Sherod, et al. *Connecting with Self and Others (Textbook and Workbook).* Littleton, Colo.: Interpersonal Communication Programs, 1988.

Napier, Rodney W., and Matti K. Gershenfeld. *Groups: Theory and Experience.* 4th ed. Boston: Houghton Mifflin, 1989.

Nichols, Ron, et al. *Good Things Come in Small Groups.* Downers Grove, Ill.: InterVarsity Press, 1985.

———. *Small Group Leaders' Handbook.* Downers Grove, Ill.: InterVarsity Press, 1982.

Nyquist, James, and Jack Kuhatschek. *Leading Bible Discussions.* Downers Grove, Ill.: InterVarsity Press, 1985.

Oden, Thomas C. *The Intensive Group Experience.* Philadelphia: Westminster Press, 1975.

O'Halloran, James. *Living Cells: Developing Small Christian Communities.* New York: Orbis Books, 1984.

———. *Signs of Hope: Developing Small Christian Communities.* Maryknoll, N.Y.: Orbis Books, 1991.

Olsen, Charles M. *Cultivating Religious Growth Groups*. Philadelphia: Westminster Press, 1984.

Ott, E. Stanley. *The Vibrant Church: A People-Building Plan for Congregational Health*. Ventura, Calif.: Regal Books, 1989.

Peace, Richard. *Small Group Evangelism: A Training Program for Reaching Out with the Gospel*. Downers Grove, Ill.: InterVarsity Press, 1985.

Peck, M. Scott. *The Different Drum: Community Making and Peace*. New York: Simon and Schuster, 1987.

Plueddemann, Jim and Carol. *Pilgrims in Progress: Growing Through Groups*. Wheaton, Ill.: Harold Shaw, 1990.

Prior, David. *Parish Renewal at the Grassroots*. Grand Rapids, Mich.: Zondervan, 1987.

Richards, Lawrence O. *Sixty-nine Ways to Start a Study Group*. Grand Rapids, Mich.: Zondervan, 1973.

Rinker, Rosalind. *Prayer: Conversing with God*. Grand Rapids, Mich.: Zondervan, 1959.

Rothwell, J. Dan. *In Mixed Company: Small Group Communication*. Philadelphia: Harcourt Brace, 1992.

St. Romain, Philip. *How to Form a Christian Growth Support Group*. Liguori, Mo.: Liguori Publications, 1985.

Scheidel, Tom, and Laura Crowell. *Discussing and Deciding: A Desk Book for Group Leaders and Members*. Chicago: Macmillan, 1979.

Seemuth, David P. *How Dynamic Is Your Small Group? Seven Keys to Improving Your Small Group Dynamics*. Wheaton, Ill.: Victor Books, 1991.

Slocum, Robert. *Maximize Your Ministry* (with small group study guide). Colorado Springs: NavPress, 1990.

Smith, Kenwyn, and David Berg. *Paradoxes of Group Life: Understanding Conflict, Paralysis and Movement in Group Dynamics*. San Francisco: Jossey-Bass, 1990.

Springle, Pat, and Richard Price. *Rapha's Handbook for Group Leaders*. Houston: Rapha Publishing, 1993.

Stewart, Ed, and Nina Fishwick. *Group Talk: A Complete Plan for Leading Adult Bible Discussion Groups*. Ventura, Calif.: Regal Books, 1986.

The Twelve Steps for Christians. San Diego: Recovery Publications, 1990.

Wald, Oletta. *The Joy of Discovery in Bible Study*. Minneapolis: Augsburg, 1975.

Watson, David Lowes. *Covenant Discipleship: Christian Formation Through Mutual Accountability*. Nashville: Discipleship Resources, 1991.

————. *The Early Methodist Class Meeting*. Nashville: Discipleship Resources, 1987.

Williams, Dan. *Seven Myths About Small Groups*. Downers Grove, Ill.: InterVarsity Press, 1991.

Williamson, David. *Group Power: How to Develop, Lead and Help Groups Achieve Goals*. Englewood Cliffs, N.J.: Prentice Hall, 1982.

Wink, Walter. *Transforming Bible Study*. 2d ed. Nashville: Abingdon Press, 1989.

Small Group Ministry Strategies

Adler, Ron, and Neil Towne. *Looking Out/Looking In: Interpersonal Communication*. 6th ed. Fort Worth, Tex.: Holt, Rinehart and Winston, 1990.

Augsburger, David. *Caring Enough to Confront*. Ventura, Calif.: Regal Books, 1981.

Building a Small Groups Program from the Bottom Up. Menlo Park, Calif.: Menlo Park Presbyterian Church, 1990.

Castillo, Metasalem Q. *The Church in Thy House*. Manila: Alliance Publishers, 1982.

Clemmons, William, and Harvey Hester. *Growth Through Groups: Innovative Approaches to Renewal*. Nashville: Broadman Press, 1974.

Clinebell, Howard. *Growth Groups*. Nashville: Abingdon, 1977.

Coleman, Lyman. *Serendipity Training Manual for Groups*. Littleton, Colo.: Serendipity House, 1992.

Cosby, Gordon. *Handbook for Mission Groups*. Washington, D.C.: Church of the Savior, 1973.

Ellas, John W. *Church Growth Through Groups: Strategies for Varying Levels of Christian Community*. Searcy, Ariz.: Resource Publications, 1990.

Galloway, Dale E. *20/20 Vision: How to Create a Successful Church with Lay Pastors and Cell Groups*. Portland: Scott, 1986.

Hadaway, C. Kirk, Stuart A. Wright and Francis M. DuBose. *Home Cell Groups and House Churches*. Nashville: Broadman Press, 1987.

Hagberg, Janet, and Robert Guelich. *The Critical Journey: Stages in the Life of Faith*. Dallas: Word, 1989.

Hersey, Paul, and Ken Blanchard. *Management of Organizational Behavior: Utilizing Human Resources*. Englewood Cliffs, N.J.: Prentice Hall, 1988.

Leypoldt, Martha M. *Forty Ways to Teach in Groups*. Valley Forge, Penn.: Judson Press, 1967.

Logan, Robert E. *Beyond Church Growth: Action Plans for Developing a Dynamic Church*. Old Tappan, N.J.: Revell, 1989.

Olsen, Charles M. *The Base Church: Creating Community Through Multiple Forms*. Atlanta: Forum House, 1973.

Prior, David. *Parish Renewal at the Grassroots*. Grand Rapids, Mich.: Zondervan, 1987.

Interpersonal Skills

Adler, Ronald B., and Neil Towne. *Looking Out—Looking In*. 2d ed. New York: Holt, Rinehart and Winston, 1978.

Augsburger, David. *Caring Enough to Confront: How to Understand and Express Your Deepest Feelings Toward Others*. Scottdale, Penn.: Herald Press, 1980.

Carnes, Patrick J. *Understanding Us*. Littleton, Colo.: Interpersonal Communications, 1987.

Drakeford, John. *The Awesome Power of the Listening Ear*. Waco, Tex.: Word, 1972.

Fisher, Roger, and Scott Brown. *Getting Together: Building a Relationship That Gets to Yes*. Boston: Houghton Mifflin, 1988.

Fisher, Roger, and William Ury. *Getting to Yes: Negotiating Agreement Without Giving In*. New York: Penguin Books, 1981.

Johnson, David. *Reaching Out*. Englewood Cliffs, N.J.: Prentice Hall, 1981.

Jones, Jerry. *201 Great Questions*. Colorado Springs: NavPress, 1988.

Miller, Sherod, Elam Nunnally and Daniel Wackman. *Talking Together*. Minneapolis: Interpersonal Communication Programs, 1984.

Miller, Sherod, et al. *Connecting Skills Workbook*. Littleton, Colo.: Interpersonal Communication Programs, 1989.

―――― . *Connecting with Self and Others*. Littleton, Colo.: Interpersonal Communication Programs, 1988.

Tanner, Ira J. *Trust: The Key to Lasting Relationships*. Minneapolis: Augsburg, 1989.

The Psychology of Group Dynamics

Baird, John E., and Sanford B. Weinberg. *Communication: The Essence of Group Synergy*. Dubuque, Iowa: William C. Brown Publishers, 1977.

Beebe, Steven A., and John T. Masterson. *Communicating in Small Groups: Principles and Practices*. 4th ed. New York: HarperCollins, 1993.

Berne, Eric. *The Structure and Dynamics of Organizations and Groups*. New York: Grove Press,

1963.

Brilhart, John K. *Effective Group Discussion*. 2d ed. Dubuque, Iowa: William C. Brown Publishers, 1974.

Burgoon, Michael, Judee K. Heston and James McKroskey. *Small Group Communication: A Functional Approach*. New York: Holt, Rinehart and Winston, 1974.

Cartwright, Dorwin, and Alvin Zander, eds. *Group Dynamics: Research and Theory*. 3d ed. New York: Harper & Row, 1968.

Cathcart, Robert, and Larry A. Samovar. *Small Group Communication*. Dubuque, Iowa: William C. Brown, 1979.

——. *Small Group Communication: A Reader*. 3d ed. Dubuque, Iowa: William C. Brown Publishers, 1981.

Clinebell, Howard. *Growth Groups*. Nashville: Abingdon, 1977.

Corey, Gerald and Marianne. *Groups: Process and Practice*. Monterey, Calif.: Brooks-Cole, 1977.

Coynyne, Robert K. *How Personal Growth and Task Groups Work*. Newbury Park, Calif.: Sage Publications, 1989.

Cragan, John F., and David W. Wright. *Communication in Small Group Discussions: A Case Study Approach*. St. Paul, Minn.: West, 1980.

Egan, Gerard. *Face to Face: The Small Group Experience and Interpersonal Growth*. Monterey, Calif.: Brooks-Cole, 1973.

Gitterman, Alex, and Lawrence Shulman, eds. *Mutual Aid Groups and the Life Cycle*. Itasca, Ill.: F. E. Peacock Publishers, 1986.

Goldberg, Alvin A., and Carl E. Larson. *Group Communication: Discussion Processes and Applications*. Englewood Cliffs, N.J.: Prentice Hall, 1975.

Gulley, Halbert E., and Dale G. Leathers. *Communication and Group Process: Techniques for Improving the Quality of Small Group Communication*. 3d ed. New York: Holt, Rinehart and Winston, 1977.

James, John W., and Frank Cherry. *The Grief Recovery Handbook: A Step-by-Step Program for Moving Beyond Loss*. New York: Harper & Row, 1988.

Johnson, David W., and Frank P. Johnson. *Joining Together*. 3d ed. Englewood Cliffs, N.J.: Prentice Hall, 1982.

Kemp, C. Gratton. *Small Groups and Self-Renewal*. New York: Seabury Press, 1971.

Kiesler, Sara. *Interpersonal Processes in Groups and Organizations*. Arlington Heights, Ill.: Harlan Davidson, 1978.

Leth, Pamela C., and JoAnn F. Vandemark. *Small Group Communication*. Menlo Park, Calif.: Cummings, 1977.

Mabry, Edward A., and Richard E. Barnes. *The Dynamics of Small Group Communication*. Englewood Cliffs, N.J.: Prentice Hall, 1980.

Scheidel, Thomas M., and Laura Crowell. *Discussing and Deciding: A Desk Book for Group Leaders and Members*. New York: Macmillan, 1979.

Shulman, Lawrence. *The Skills of Helping Individuals and Groups*. 2d ed. Itasca, Ill.: F. E. Peacock Publishers, 1984.

Smith, William S. *Group Problem-Solving Through Discussion: A Process Essential to Democracy*. Indianapolis: Bobbs Merrill, 1965.

Tiger, Lionel. *Men in Groups*. New York: Marion Boyars, 1984.

Williamson, David. *Group Power: How to Develop, Lead and Help Groups Achieve Goals*. Englewood Cliffs, N.J.: Prentice Hall, 1982.

Sociological and Cultural Foundations

Bellah, Robert, et al. *Habits of the Heart: Individualism and Commitment in American Life*. Berkeley:

University of California Press, 1985.

Bormann, Ernest G. and Nancy C. *Effective Small Group Communication.* 2d ed. Minneapolis: Burgess, 1976.

Gaede, S. D. *Belonging: Our Need for Community in Church and Family.* Grand Rapids, Mich.: Zondervan, 1985.

Neuhaus, John Richard, ed. *The Believable Future of American Protestantism.* Grand Rapids, Mich.: Eerdmans, 1988.

Shepherd, Clovis R. *Small Groups: Some Sociological Perspective.* San Francisco: Chandler, 1964.

Wuthnow, Robert. *The Struggle for America's Soul.* Grand Rapids, Mich.: Eerdmans, 1989.

History and Theology of Christian Community

Anderson, Ray S., and Dennis B. Guernsey. *On Being Family: A Social Theology of the Family.* Grand Rapids, Mich.: Eerdmans, 1985.

Banks, Robert. *Paul's Idea of Community: The Early House Churches in Their Historical Setting.* Grand Rapids, Mich.: Eerdmans, 1989.

Bonhoeffer, Dietrich. *The Communion of Saints: A Dogmatic Inquiry into the Sociology of the Church.* New York: Harper & Row, 1963.

————. *Life Together.* New York: Harper & Row, 1954.

Bridges, Jerry. *True Fellowship: The Biblical Practice of Koinonia.* Colorado Springs: NavPress, 1985.

Dunn, James D. G. *Jesus and the Spirit.* Philadelphia: Westminster Press, 1975.

Hanson, Paul D. *The People Called: The Growth of Community in the Bible.* San Francisco: Harper & Row, 1986.

Hauerwas, Stanley. *A Community of Character: Toward a Constructive Christian Social Ethic.* Notre Dame, Ind.: University of Notre Dame Press, 1981.

Joy, Donald M. *Bonding: Relationships in the Image of God.* Waco, Tex.: Word Books, 1985.

Kimball, Don. *Power and Presence: A Theology of Relationships.* San Francisco: Harper & Row, 1987.

Kinnamon, Michael. *Truth and Community: Diversity and Its Limits in the Ecumenical Movement.* Grand Rapids, Mich.: Eerdmans, 1988.

Kraus, C. Norman. *The Authentic Witness: Credibility and Authority.* Grand Rapids, Mich.: Eerdmans, 1979.

Lee, Bernard J., and Michael A. Cowan. *Dangerous Memories: House Churches and Our American Story.* Kansas City, Mo.: Sheed and Ward, 1986.

L'Heureux, Conrad E. *Life Journey and the Old Testament: An Experiential Approach to the Bible and Personal Transformation.* New York: Paulist Press, 1986.

Lohfink, Gerhard. *Jesus and Community.* Philadelphia: Fortress Press, 1989.

MacQuarrie, John. *In Search of Humanity: A Theological and a Philosophical Approach.* New York: Crossroad, 1983.

Neuhaus, John Richard, ed. *Confession, Conflict and Community.* Grand Rapids, Mich.: Eerdmans, 1986.

Pannenberg, Wolfhart. *Ethics.* Trans. Keith Crim. Philadelphia: Westminster Press, 1981.

————. *Human Nature, Election and History.* Philadelphia: Westminster Press, 1977.

Schillebeeckx, Edward. *The Church with a Human Face: A New and Expanded Theology of Ministry.* New York: Crossroad, 1987.

Smedes, Lewis B. *Love Within Limits: A Realist's View of I Corinthians 13.* Grand Rapids, Mich.: Eerdmans, 1978.

Snyder, Howard A. *The Community of the King.* Downers Grove, Ill.: InterVarsity Press, 1977.

————. *Liberating the Church: The Ecology of Church and Kingdom.* Downers Grove, Ill.: Inter-

Varsity Press, 1983.
———. *The Problem of Wineskins: Church Structure in a Technological Age.* Downers Grove, Ill.: InterVarsity Press, 1975.
Watson, David Lowes. *The Early Methodist Class Meeting.* Nashville: Discipleship Resources, 1987.

Social Psychology
Brown, Charles T., and Paul T. Keller. *Monologue to Dialogue.* Englewood Cliffs, N.J.: Prentice Hall, 1979.
Dalbey, Gordon. *The Healing of the Masculine Soul.* Waco, Tex.: Word, 1988.
Lerner, Harriet Goldhor. *The Dance of Anger.* New York: Harper & Row, 1985.
May, Gerald G. *Addiction and Grace.* San Francisco: Harper & Row, 1988.
Peck, M. Scott. *The Different Drum: Community Making and Peace.* New York: Simon and Schuster, 1987.
Powell, John. *The Secret of Staying in Love.* Allen, Tex.: Argus, 1974.
———. *Why Am I Afraid to Love?* Allen, Tex.: Tabor Publishing, 1982.
———. *Why Am I Afraid to Tell You Who I Am?* Allen, Tex.: Argus, 1969.
Rubin, Lillian B. *Intimate Strangers: Men and Women Together.* New York: Harper & Row, 1983.
Schaef, Anne Wilson. *Escape from Intimacy: The Pseudo-Relationship Addictions.* San Francisco: Harper & Row, 1989.

Conflict Resolution
Fenton, Horace L., Jr. *When Christians Clash: How to Prevent and Resolve the Pain of Conflict.* Downers Grove, Ill.: InterVarsity, 1987.
Haugk, Kenneth C. *Antagonists in the Church: How to Identify and Deal with Destructive Conflict.* Minneapolis: Augsburg, 1988.
Huggett, Joyce. *Creative Conflict: How to Confront and Stay Friends.* Downers Grove, Ill.: InterVarsity Press, 1984.
Joy, Donald M. *Re-bonding: Preventing and Restoring Damaged Relationships.* Waco, Tex.: Word, 1986.
Lewis, G. Douglass. *Resolving Church Conflicts: A Case Study Approach for Local Congregations.* San Francisco: Harper & Row, 1981.
Malony, H. Newton. *When Getting Along Seems Impossible.* Old Tappan, N.J.: Revell, 1989.

Organizational and Systems Psychology
Block, Peter. *The Empowered Manager: Positive Political Skills at Work.* San Francisco: Jossey-Bass Publishers, 1987.
Friedman, Edwin H. *Generation to Generation: Family Process in Church and Synagogue.* New York: Guilford Press, 1985.
Hagberg, Janet O. *Real Power: Stages of Personal Power in Organizations.* San Francisco: Harper & Row, 1984.
Hersey, Paul, and Ken Blanchard. *Management of Organizational Behavior: Utilizing Human Resources.* Englewood Cliffs, N.J.: Prentice Hall, 1982.
Schaef, Anne Wilson, and Diane Fassel. *The Addictive Organization.* San Francisco: Harper & Row, 1988.

Spirituality and Community
Brueggemann, Walter. *Praying the Psalms.* Winona, Minn.: St. Mary's Press, 1986.
Jones, Alan. *Exploring Spiritual Direction: An Essay on Christian Friendship.* San Francisco: Harper & Row, 1982.

Leckey, Dolores R. *The Ordinary Way.* New York: Crossroad, 1982.

Nouwen, Henri. *Lifesigns.* New York: Doubleday, 1986.

————. *Making All Things New: An Invitation to the Spiritual Life.* San Francisco: Harper & Row, 1981.

Nouwen, Henri, Donald P. McNeill and Douglas A. Morrison. *Compassion: A Reflection on the Christian Life.* Garden City, N.Y.: Image, 1983.

Winter, Gibson. *Community and Spiritual Transformation: Religion and Politics in a Communal Age.* New York: Crossroad, 1989.

Wolff-Salin, Mary. *The Shadow Side of Community and the Growth of Self.* New York: Crossroad, 1988.

Wuellner, Flora Slosson. *Prayer, Fear and Our Powers: Finding Our Healing, Release and Growth in Christ.* Nashville: Upper Room Books, 1989.

————. *Prayer, Stress, and Our Inner Wounds.* Nashville: Upper Room Books, 1985.

Inductive Bible Study

Hunt, Gladys. *How-to Handbook for Inductive Bible Study Leaders.* Wheaton, Ill.: Harold Shaw, 1971.

Navigators. *How to Lead Small Group Bible Studies.* Colorado Springs: NavPress, 1982.

Nyquist, James F., and Jack Kuhatschek. *Leading Bible Discussions.* Downers Grove, Ill.: InterVarsity Press, 1985.

Wald, Oletta. *The Joy of Discovery in Bible Study.* Minneapolis: Augsburg, 1975.

Wink, Walter. *Transforming Bible Study.* 2d ed. Nashville: Abingdon, 1989.

Family Groups and Clusters

Nutting, R. Ted. *Family Cluster Programs: Resources for Intergenerational Bible Study.* Valley Forge, Penn.: Judson Press, 1977.

Sawin, Margaret M. *Family Enrichment with Family Clusters.* Valley Forge, Penn.: Judson Press, 1979.